The Halakhic Process: A Systemic Analysis

Volume XIII in the **Moreshet Series,**
Studies in Jewish History, Literature, and Thought

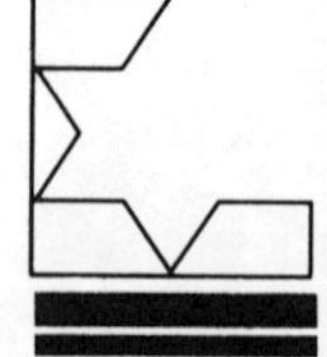

A CENTURY OF ACHIEVEMENT

The Halakhic Process: A Systemic Analysis

JOEL ROTH

A Centennial Publication of
The Jewish Theological Seminary of America
New York 1986

Library of Congress Cataloging-in-Publication Data

Roth, Joel.
The halakhic process.

(Moreshet series ; v. 13)
Includes index.
1. Jewish law—Interpretation and construction.
2. Jewish law—Methodology. I. Title. II. Series.
LAW 296.1'8 86-7460
ISBN 0-87334-035-3

Manufactured in the United States of America

To
my wife Barbara
and my children
Akiva Doron, Ariel Ilan and Tamar Shlomit

Contents

Acknowledgments

I gratefully acknowledge the support tendered to me by the leadership of the Jewish Theological Seminary of America in every phase of the preparation of this volume. I express my thanks, as well, to the friends and colleagues who read part or all of this book and offered me their insights and comments. Most of all, I am deeply indebted to Mrs. Shari Friedman for her thorough and helpful editorial assistance.

Introduction

The term *halakhah* is used in two different ways. It is generally used to signify the normative prescription or proscription that is the end result of the legal reasoning of a recognized *posek,* or legalist. When used thus, the term ignores the process that led the *posek* to his conclusion, and its meaning is limited to the resultant norm. When norms are severed from the decision-making process, they appear simple, clear, and definitive. "The *halakhah* forbids eating poultry with milk" sounds the same as "The *halakhah* forbids bowing to an idol." The statements themselves do not reflect that the former may be disputed by other *posekim* (legalists), while the latter is universally affirmed by all *posekim;* or that the former was not always considered universally normative, while the latter was; or that the former is grounded in a rabbinic decision, while the latter is grounded in the dictates of the Torah itself. Both norms appear simple, clear, and definitive.

The term *halakhah,* however, is also used to signify the process by which legal conclusions are reached. In this sense the term refers to all of the factors that must or that might be considered by a *posek* before rendering his *pesak* (decision). When all of these factors are expounded together with the resultant norm, it rarely appears simple, clear, or definitive. It is, rather, complex, ambiguous, and replete with grounds for disagreement among *posekim.*

As indicated by its title, the primary focus of this volume is on the halakhic process, and not upon the actual norms. I have concentrated upon an analysis of the phenomenon of halakhic decision-making—the phenomenon of *pesak*—and not upon the phenomenon of obedience to the law.

As a legal process, *halakhah* is governed by systemic principles, that is, principles that *govern the way in which the process works,* as opposed to those that govern the determination of the law in any given case within the system. The latter are legal principles. Certain legal principles are also systemic principles, but many systemic principles are not legal in nature at all. The principle that the Supreme Court of the United States is the final arbiter of constitutionality is a systemic principle, but not a legal one. There is no specific case in which the knowledge of this principle will determine the final decision.

Systemic principles fall into two categories: explicit and implicit. Explicit principles are those that have been stated in the legal literature, while implicit principles are those that can be deduced from the legal literature, even though they have not been explicitly stated.

Among the explicit systemic principles of the halakhic system would be included:

1. In a dispute between earlier and later sages, the law follows the position of the later sages: *Hilkheta ke-vatraei.*
2. In a doubtful case the source of which is biblical, the stricter opinion prevails, whereas in a doubtful case the source of which is rabbinic, the more lenient position prevails: *Safek de-oraita le-ḥumera ve-safek de-rabbanan le-hakel.*
3. Rabbi X is sufficiently worthy to be relied upon in time of great need: *Kedai hu R. Peloni lismokh alav bi-she'at ha-deḥak.*
4. It is better that people should disobey the law inadvertently than that they should do so willfully: *Mutav she-yehu shogegin ve-al yehu mezidin.*

All four of the above are explicit principles because they have been stated in the legal literature. They are all also systemic because they embody principles that *govern the process by which the system works.* In addition, the former two are legal principles as well, insofar as each is sufficient in and of itself to determine the law in a given case.[1]

The principle that the halakhic system *requires,* not merely allows, the distinction between biblical and rabbinic injunctions, and the principle that the system affirms the possibility of co-opting sociological material in halakhic contexts, are examples of implicit systemic principles, since neither has been stated in the primary legal literature.

Clearly, implicit systemic principles are more problematic than explicit principles, since their "implicitness" makes it possible to deny that they actually exist. As a case in point, it is clear that many deny the existence of one or the other of the principles posited above, even if to others their existence is "irrefutably" implied by the legal literature.

---

1. Principles such as the annulment of forbidden substances mixed with permissible substances in proportion of 1:60 (*bittul be-shishim*) or the right of an agent to serve also as a witness (*shali'aḥ na'aseh ed*), for example, are legal principles alone, having to do only with the determination of the law in any given case, but not with the way in which the halakhic system functions *qua* process.

The halakhic process, from the talmudic era through modern times, has been oriented more to the pragmatic than to the theoretical. The Talmud and the responsa are more directly comparable to case law than to treatises on legal theory. Even explicit principles—and surely implicit principles—generally lack thorough theoretical treatment in the primary sources. Analysis of most explicit systemic principles (and surely the discovery of implicit principles) must be based upon hypotheses gleaned from the primary sources inductively.

Analysis should reveal, first, whether and to what degree old systemic principles have remained stable, the degree to which they have been modified or abrogated, and whether new systemic principles have evolved. Second, it should test whether, under what circumstances, and to what degree data generally considered nonhalakhic (e.g., scientific, sociological, psychological) have been utilized in the decision-making process and are governed by systemic principles which validate their use *within the system*. And finally, it should demonstrate whether, how, and under what conditions new findings in rabbinic and biblical scholarship have been and can continue to be authentically incorporated into the existent halakhic process through the employment of systemic principles that legitimately govern their use.

The volume begins by distinguishing and examining the sources of all legal systems, including the halakhic. This leads, in Chapter 2, to an analysis of the concepts of *de-oraita* and *de-rabbanan*, the existence of which concepts is postulated as a fundamental systemic principle of the halakhic system. This analysis examines the difficulties inherent in the attempt to assign specific norms to either the category of *de-oraita* or the category of *de-rabbanan*, and deals also with the systemic principles that govern the relationship between the two categories. Chapter 3 introduces and defines the various kinds of legal questions that *posekim* deal with and explains the legal significance of the various types in relationship to one another. An appendix is added to Chapter 3 that analyzes several halakhic sources in the terms introduced in the chapter itself. By the beginning of Chapter 4 it will have become clear that the halakhic system allows an extremely broad discretionary latitude to its *posekim*. Therefore, the chapter itself is devoted primarily to an examination of the systemic principles that govern the use of precedent in halakhic decision-making.

In Chapter 5 we discuss the systemic principles that govern the source and scope of rabbinic authority, and by the end of the chapter we shall have discovered that the entire halakhic system is dependent upon its recognized authorities. Chapter 6, consequently, is devoted to discussion of the systemic principles that govern the qualifications of these authorities, both the academic and the characterological requirements for authority. Chapter 7 is devoted to an analysis of the systemic principles that govern the crucial question of rabbinic authority regarding matters that are *de-oraita*.

In Chapter 8 we shall deal with the systemic principles that govern the use of custom within *halakhah,* and in Chapter 9 I shall demonstrate that data generally considered nonhalakhic, have, in fact, always been legitimate factors in halakhic decision-making. I shall call these factors "extralegal sources," and, in addition, I shall analyze the systemic principles that have governed their legitimate use and prevented their illegitimate use. Since, however, discussion of many of the concepts involved in these extralegal sources is couched, in the modern world, in the specific terminologies of the physical and social sciences, while halakhic literature is generally prescientific, Chapter 10 is an editorial digression in which it is asserted that there is no special type of language that qualifies a decision as religious or nonreligious: The use of scientific language in halakhic decisions can be as religious, perhaps even more so, than disguising such factors in prescientific, but religious-sounding, circumlocution. And, finally, Chapter 11 is devoted to an analysis of the systemic principles that govern the legitimate use of the findings of modern rabbinic and biblical scholarship in halakhic decision-making.

Chapter One

Sources of the Legal System

The norms of all legal systems derive from two kinds of sources: historical and legal. Comprehending the difference between them is crucial to understanding the legal process *qua* process.

Legal sources are "those sources which are recognised as such by the law itself."[1] Historical sources are "those sources lacking formal recognition by the law itself."[2] Legal sources are norms the authority of which is accepted by and integral to the legal system; they serve as the sole *legal* justification of any new legislation and as the ultimate *legal* ground of judicial decisions. The myriad tomes of law, the *corpora* of judicial decisions, the various state and local constitutions or charters are all legal sources of the American legal system.[3] As these sources function within the system of American law, the philosophical, political, sociological, or economic factors that may have been instrumental in their becoming legal norms are considered to be irrelevant; these factors constitute historical sources, and are not accounted *legally* significant by the system. One reads occasionally of some judge who was forced to render a certain decision on the basis of valid statute, the origin of which had been clearly predicated on a reality different from that of the present. However, since the norm had never been amended or abrogated by the system, it remained authoritative and legal, and the judge

1. P. J. Fitzgerald, ed., *Salmond on Jurisprudence*, 12th ed. (London: Sweet and Maxwell, 1966), p. 109. See also Menachem Elon, *Jewish Law: History, Sources, Principles* (Hebrew) (Jerusalem: Magnes Press, 1977), 1:211–13.

2. Fitzgerald, *Salmond*, p. 109.

3. Some of these are literary sources as well. For a definition of this term, see Fitzgerald, *Salmond*, p. 112, footnote (c), and Elon, *Jewish law*, 1:211.

was compelled to render his decision in accordance with it. His knowledge of the historical antecedents that gave rise to the norm in the first place was irrelevant. He could not decide *legally* in a manner contrary to its dictates.

The Jewish legal system is no different from any other in this regard. Its recognized legal norms operate independently of the historical sources that may have given rise to them. So long as a norm has not been amended or abrogated by the halakhic system, its origin as a reaction to Roman practice, as an emulation of Roman practice, or as a concession to the economic realities of Christian Europe, to suggest only several possibilities, is irrelevant to its validity as a norm of the halakhic system.

For this reason, historical sources are of a unique nature. At that point in time when they influence the introduction of new ideas into the legal system they are extremely important; yet their importance rests solely on the fact that their persuasive powers are sufficient to convince the authoritative *legal* body (or bodies) to incorporate them into the system as *legal* sources. Barring such incorporation, their influence on the legal system is merely potential, not actual, and regardless of their original importance, they fade into *legal* irrelevance once norms based on them are incorporated into the system as legal sources. So singularly unimportant to the functioning of the system are they, then, that inability to reconstruct the historical sources of any legal norm has no bearing whatsoever on the binding and authoritative nature of the norm.

Sir John Salmond summarized the difference between legal and historical sources as follows:

> The legal sources of law are authoritative, the historical are unauthoritative. The former are allowed by the law courts as of right; the latter have no such claim; they influence more or less extensively the course of legal development, but they speak with no authority. . . . The legal sources are the only gates through which new principles can find entrance into the law. Historical sources operate only mediately and indirectly. They are merely the various precedent links in that chain of which the ultimate link must be some legal source to which the rule of law is directly attached.[4]

From the fact that historical sources are legally insignificant, it follows that the demonstration by scholars that the true historical sources of a given norm are different from what had generally been assumed is an

4. Fitzgerald, *Salmond*, pp. 109–10.

interesting revelation, but *legally* insignificant. We shall return in due course to the implications of this statement for the halakhic system in particular.

Salmond also wrote:

> All rules of law have historical sources. As a matter of fact and history they have their origin somewhere, though we may not know what it is. But not all of them have legal sources. Were this so, it would be necessary for the law to proceed *ad infinitum* in tracing the descent of its principles. There must be found in every legal system certain ultimate principles, from which all others are derived, but which are themselves self-existent. Before there can be any talk of legal sources, there must be already in existence some law which establishes them and gives them authority. . . . These ultimate principles are the grundnorms or basic rules of recognition of the legal system.[5]

This statement of Salmond's reflects the Kelsenian theory according to which the nature of a legal system is such that all of its norms are derived from one basic norm, which is itself *presupposed* by the system. Kelsen writes:

> If we ask why the constitution is valid, perhaps we come upon an older constitution. Ultimately we reach some constitution that is the first historically and that was laid down by an individual usurper or by some kind of assembly. The validity of this first constitution is the last presupposition, the final postulate, upon which the validity of all the norms of our legal order depends. It is postulated that one ought to behave as the individual, or the individuals, who laid down the constitution have ordained. This is the basic norm of the legal order under consideration. . . . That the first constitution is a binding legal norm is presupposed, and the formulation of the presupposition is the basic norm of this legal order.[6]

The concept of the basic norm is complex, yet indispensable. Its complexity derives mainly from the fact that this *grundnorm* is at once

---

5. Ibid., pp. 111–12, quoted by Elon, *Jewish Law,* 1:213.

6. H. Kelsen, *General Theory of Law and State,* trans. Anders Wedberg (Cambridge, Mass.: Harvard University Press, 1945), p. 115, quoted by Lord Lloyd of Hampstead, in *Introduction to Jurisprudence,* 3d ed. (New York: Praeger, 1972), p. 302. Cf. H. Kelsen, *Pure Theory of Law,* trans. May Knight (Berkeley and Los Angeles: University of California Press, 1967), pp. 194 f.

"metalegal" and "legal," that is, while its validity is presupposed by the system, it functions *legally* as a norm of the system.[7] Any attempt to prove the validity of the basic norm must belong to a realm other than the legal. To the extent that its validity can be proved at all, the proof must be theological, philosophical, or metaphysical. Yet it is this norm that serves as the ultimate basis of the legal system and has definite legal functions. Put succinctly, the orderly functioning of any legal order requires of its adherents a "leap of faith" concerning the validity of the basic norm of the system. Although leaps of faith do not fall within the realm of law, such a leap of faith is the ultimate validation of the legal system.[8]

Furthermore, it is important to grasp that presupposing the existence of a *grundnorm* is an amoral and nonvaluative act. The fact that a tyrant may have promulgated a constitution, obedience to which is the basic norm of a particular legal system, does not affect its status as a *grundnorm.* A postulated *grundnorm* is the *sine qua non* of a legal system, not a statement of the desirability, morality, or positive nature of the system. In many instances, such considerations will vary with the perspective of the viewer. The *grundnorm* of the American legal system was created as the result of an act of rebellion against a legal sovereign. To some, it was a necessary and ethical rebellion; to others, it was an immoral act of rebellion against the British crown. But even to this latter group, the *grundnorm* is the basic norm of the American system. Presupposing the basic norm of the American system is necessary in order to comprehend the functioning of the system, but carries no valuational implications whatsoever concerning the rectitude of the framers of the Constitution in postulating it. Thus, every legal system—democracy, monarchy, dictatorship, benevolent despotism—presupposes a basic norm; that fact, however, is independent of any consideration of the desirability of the system itself.

---

7. Lloyd, *Introduction to Jurisprudence,* p. 279.

8. The question of the relationship between "validity" and "efficacy" is not relevant here. The present discussion is restricted to theoretical validation alone. A *grundnorm* and all of its derivative legal norms can be valid even if nobody abides by them. That this is the case can be demonstrated, at least on one level, by the fact that analysis of defunct legal systems is possible, culminating in the definitions of their *grundnorms,* which are their ultimate validations.

Similarly, the present context of discussion permits ignoring the matter of sanctions and enforcement of the legal system. While it may be that one refrains from speeding in order to avoid the payment of a fine, the imposition of the fine is not what validates the law against speeding (although it surely enhances its efficacy). Rather, the imposition of the fine is itself the manner in which the courts demonstrate the validity of the law prohibiting speeding. Theoretically, the fine is legitimate only because the law for which it is a sanction is a valid legal norm—not vice versa.

How, then, shall the *grundnorm* of the halakhic system be formulated so as to express the presupposed axiom that validates the system *legally?* The following seems reasonable and correct: The document called the Torah embodies the word and will of God, which it behooves man to obey, and is, therefore, authoritative.[9] Remembering that the basic norm is both "metalegal" and "legal," certain points follow. The first is that the individual legal statements of the Torah are legal sources of the system, i.e., they are norms the authority of which is accepted by and integral to the system. The second is that the concept conveyed by the rabbinic term *de-oraita* (norms having the authority of the *grundnorm* itself) is postulated by the system itself as a *sine qua non* of its functioning,[10] and implies, as well, a distinction (as yet undefined) between itself and the concept *de-rabbanan* (norms that are not *de-oraita*).

The third point is that any quest to establish the "truth" of the historical claims of the Torah is irrelevant to the halakhic process, since that quest seeks only clarification of the historical sources of the legal system, not its legal sources. Since in the halakhic system, as in all others, presupposing the existence of a *grundnorm* requires a "leap of faith," the truth or falsity of the historical claims of the *grundnorm* is legally irrelevant. Once norms are incorporated into the system as legal sources, the persuasive influence of the historical sources, originally so important, fades into legal insignificance.

Thus, it follows on one important level that the halakhic system *qua* system is independent of any considerations of the accuracy of the historical claims of its basic norm. Whether or not it is "true" that the Torah embodies the word and will of God is of great historical and theological significance, but of no legal significance. Even if one has traced the origins of the Torah to documents called J, E, P, and D, he may have uncovered the historical sources of the legal norms, but he has in no way abrogated the *grundnorm* of the halakhic system, which is *presupposed* by the system. As any number of observant scholars can attest, the system continues to function on the basis of its presupposed

---

9. Cf. Elon's formulation in *Jewish Law,* 1:215–16, and also his quotations from rabbinic sources, ibid., 1:216–17.

10. Since the *grundnorm* of the halakhic system mentions God, and implies the concept *de-oraita,* it ought to be stressed that every legal system has its *de-oraita* equivalent, whether or not the *grundnorm* mentions God. Since the *grundnorm* is presupposed by the system irrespective of historical sources, the United States Constitution is no more *de-rabbanan* within the American system, because God is not part of the *grundnorm,* than the Torah is *de-rabbanan* in the halakhic system. In any system in which the *grundnorm* is embodied in a written document, that document is *de-oraita* in that system. Postulating God in the *grundnorm* becomes a much more relevant factor only when the amendment of the *grundnorm* is at issue.

grundnorm regardless of the contention that the historical claims of the *grundnorm* may be inaccurate.

If one is so inclined, one may reformulate the *grundnorm* in the light of modern scholarship as follows: The document called the Torah embodies the word and the will of God, which it behooves man to obey, as mediated through the agency of J, E, P, and D, and is, therefore, authoritative. An alternative possible formulation might be: The document called the Torah embodies the constitution promulgated by J, E, P, and D, which it behooves man to obey, and is, therefore, authoritative. The first formulation has the advantage of incorporating God into the *grundnorm*. It is theologically self-evident that it behooves man to obey His will; thus, the "leap of faith" is simply in affirming that His word and will are mediated through J, E, P, and D. The second formulation obviates this "leap of faith" but replaces it with the presupposition that it behooves man to obey the will of J, E, P, and D. In either case, the halakhic system is ultimately predicated on a presupposition that it behooves man to obey the document called the Torah, regardless of the historical realities of its promulgation. Any discussion of the validity of the *grundnorm* must be nonlegal, i.e., philosophical, theological, or metaphysical. Legally, the *grundnorm* is posited and presupposed by the system to be true, and is therefore beyond discussion in a legal context.

The primary systemic assumption of the halakhic system, therefore, is the existence of an undeniable legal category that is called *de-oraita*. Any legal sources so categorized are, by definition, authoritative, since they are included in that document which, by presupposition, it behooves man to obey.

While the distinction drawn heretofore between legal and historical sources seems very precise, it has been justly criticized as too neat.[11] Surely it is the case that the line between the persuasive powers of historical sources, on the one hand, and their lack of legal recognition, on the other hand, is narrow indeed. Is there not a time at which the opinion of a great philosopher is incorporated into law not solely because he is persuasive, but because he is also authoritative? Does not the Congress of the United States often consider the historical sources of laws in determining whether or not the laws should be abrogated at present? Indeed, the same state of affairs obtains within the sphere of *halakhah*, too. Is the widespread acceptance of the *takkanot* (edicts) of

---

11. See, for example, C. K. Allen, *Law in the Making*, 7th ed. (Oxford: Oxford University Press, 1964), pp. 268 ff. Elon takes note of the objections in *Jewish Law*, 1:213, n. 3, but opts for Salmond's distinction without further clarification.

Rabbenu Gershom or Rabbenu Tam, and their incorporation into the legal sources of so many communities, solely a factor of their persuasiveness, or also a factor of their authority?

Salmond himself was not oblivious to the problem. He wrote: "But the line between legal and historical sources is not crystal clear. . . . The distinction between legal and historical sources, while useful as a starting point, must not be pressed with too Procrustean zeal."[12] The implication seems to be that there might be, and often is, a nexus between legal and historical sources; while the distinction is real and extremely relevant, the two types of sources do not *always* function independently of each other. Thus, because modern scholarly invesgitation of Jewish sources concerns itself primarily with historical sources, we must, at some point, raise the issue of a nexus between the halakhic process and the findings of modern scholarship, a nexus governed by systemic principles.[13]

Since systemic principles, including those that are not legal principles and those that are only implicit, function as legal norms, that is to say, since the nature of systemic principles is such that any legislation or any judicial decision consonant and consistent with their requirements and stipulations is recognized as valid by the system, it follows that if one were able to articulate what the systemic principles were, it would be possible to determine with relative precision the validity and admissibility of any new legislation or judicial decision. (In practice, however, this is more likely to be true when one is dealing with explicit systemic principles than with implicit principles.[14] This is not because the premise is false, but because of the problematic nature of implicit systemic principles.)[15]

Furthermore, it follows that if we are able to determine those systemic principles that govern the nexus between modern scholarship and the

12. Fitzgerald, *Salmond,* pp. 110–11.

13. Should it be the case that no nexus is possible, it would not follow that the system is not viable. The statement that the halakhic system operates independently of modern scholarship in no way implies its inability to confront new problems in general. It implies only that in confronting those situations, it does not permit the use of critical scholarship as considerations.

14. The phrases "more likely to be true" and "relative precision" are employed in order to imply recognition of the problems involved even with explicit systemic principles when they are not also legal principles. Examples (3) and (4) found on p. 2 are paradigms. In (3), for example, the validity of the legislation or of the judicial decision can be determined only with relative precision because there may be a dispute concerning the applicability of the systemic principle to any given Rabbi X, or concerning the definition of the time in question as one "of great need." In this regard, then, explicit systemic principles that are not also legal principles share some common ground with implicit systemic principles.

15. See above, p. 2.

halakhic process, it will be possible to determine with relative precision whether or not any new legislation or judicial decision is consonant and consistent with the requirements and stipulations of those systemic principles and, consequently, acceptable as valid by the system.

In anticipation of future detailed analysis, it should be pointed out even at this point how varied the grounds of dispute over such a determination might be. Disputants might disagree about whether the new legislation is consonant and consistent with the requirements of the systemic principle, while agreeing that if it were, it would be recognized as valid. They might disagree about the precise definition of the systemic principle, but agree that some such principle is, in fact, implicit in the system. They might disagree about the existence of such a systemic principle, yet agree that there are systemic principles that are operative and that address themselves to the nexus between modern scholarship and the halakhic process. Ultimately, the disputants may trace their disagreement to the question of the existence within the halakhic system of any systemic principle governing such a nexus.

Chapter Two

The Concepts of *De-oraita* and *De-rabbanan:* Meanings and Implications

Having established the centrality of the concepts *de-oraita* and *de-rabbanan* within the halakhic system, it is necessary to define them more precisely, to pursue the implications of these definitions, and to analyze the way these concepts work within the system.

On the surface, the definition of *de-oraita* seems to be straightforward; as will become clear, however, this is not the case. As a first attempt, let us define *de-oraita* as meaning any legal statement that can be shown to be directly from the Torah.[1] The corollary would be that any legal statement that cannot be shown to be directly from the Torah is to be considered *de-rabbanan*.

It is a well-known fact of rabbinic literature, however, that the talmudic sages regularly employ recognized exegetical principles to interpret the words of the Torah.[2] Shall norms based upon the use of these principles be considered *de-oraita*, or are they *de-rabbanan?* Several examples will suffice to demonstrate the complexity of the issue. The

1. The terms *mi-shel Torah, divrei Torah,* and *devar Torah* are synonymous with *de-oraita,* and are so treated in this discussion. Similarly, the terms *mi-divreihem* and *mi-divrei soferim* are synonymous with *de-rabbanan*. Regarding *mi-divrei soferim,* however, see Elon, *Jewish Law,* 1:194, n. 88.

2. See ibid., chaps. 12 and 13, for a comprehensive analysis of the use of exegesis in post-talmudic literature.

biblical verse from which the law dictating the use of phylacteries is derived (Deut. 6:8) neither mentions them explicitly nor describes them. Are phylacteries, therefore, to be considered *de-oraita* or *de-rabbanan?* Exodus 21:23–25 seems clearly to imply *lex talionis,* but was interpreted by the sages to refer, instead, to financial restitution.[3] Shall the legal implications of this interpretation be considered *de-oraita* or not? The verse in Deuteronomy 25:3 states that a man may receive forty lashes. On the basis of exegesis, however, the majority of the rabbis deduced that thirty-nine was the maximum number of lashes permissible.[4] What shall we claim is the law *de-oraita?*[5]

The question of the proper categorization of legal norms is important for two reasons. First of all, and soon to be discussed at length, is the matter of the differences between the two categories with regard to enforcement and amendment. Secondly, the tradition seems to posit a specific number of *mizvot de-oraita,* and even subdivides them between positive and negative. Thus, in essence, we are restricted to only 613 *mizvot* that can be called *de-oraita,*[6] of which 248 must be positive and 365 negative.[7] Consequently, it is not possible to proliferate the number of

---

3. Bava Kama 83b.

4. Makkot 22a.

5. The final two examples indicate, in addition, a further complexity, with which we shall deal later. Namely: if we consider rabbinic interpretations to be *de-oraita,* and those interpretations clearly contradict the *peshat* of the verse, what is the halakhic status of the *peshat* itself? And if we consider the exegesis to be *de-rabbanan,* by what right do the sages allow themselves to abrogate the clear statement of the *grundnorm?* Rava himself called attention to the latter problem when he said: "How foolish are those who stand before the Torah, but do not stand before a great sage. For the Torah says 'forty' and the sages reduced it" (Makkot 22b).

6. On the 613 commandments see Solomon Schechter, *Studies in Judaism,* First Series (Philadelphia: Jewish Publication Society, 1920), p. 112; E. Urbach, *The Sages* (Hebrew) (Jerusalem: Magnes Press, 1969), pp. 301–20; Max Kadushin, *Worship and Ethics* (Chicago: Northwestern University Press, 1964), p. 200; and Simon Greenberg, "The Multiplication of the Mitzvot," in *Mordecai M. Kaplan Jubilee Volume* (New York: Jewish Theological Seminary, 1953), pp. 381–97. Particularly interesting is Greenberg's quotation from a personal communication to him from Prof. Louis Ginzberg (p. 388, n. 37). Ginzberg says: "The number of 613 *mizvot* in the Torah is an outgrowth of the aggada concerning the number of letters in the Ten Commandments. In its ancient form the aggada read: "The 613 letters in the Ten Commandments correspond to the value of the Torah, to indicate that the entire Torah is contained within them. . . . With the passage of time, the letters 'grew into' *mizvot,* and they said: 'There are 613 *mizvot* in the Torah.' "

7. The specificity of the tradition gave rise, naturally enough, to an entire corpus of literature which was specifically designed to enumerate the 613 *mizvot*. The earliest such enumeration is that of the *Halakhot Gedolot* of Rabbi Shimon Kayyara (photo-offset of Venice ed., Tel Aviv, 1962 [5722]), in the ninth century. The best known is *Sefer ha-Mitzvot* of Maimonides, ed. Rabbi Joseph Kafih (Jerusalem: Mossad Harav Kook, 1971), which contains, in essence, a rebuttal of Rabbi Shimon's enumeration, followed by Maimonides' own enumeration. The offshoots of this genre are described by Elon, *Jewish Law,* 3:1042 ff.

mizvot de-oraita freely.[8]

The source for the number 613 can be found on page 23b of Makkot.

> Rabbi Simlai[9] expounded: "613 commandments were stated to Moses:[10] 365 negative commandments corresponding to the days of the solar year, and 248 positive commandments corresponding to the number of a man's limbs." Rav Hamnuna[11] asked: "What scriptural verse supports this view?: Moses commanded us the Torah, an inheritance [Deut. 33:4]. The word 'Torah' in *gematria* equals 611, plus 'I am the Lord your God' and 'You shall have no other gods before Me' [i.e., the first two of the Ten Commandments], which we heard directly from God."

The number 613 appears in the Midrash regularly as the number of *mizvot;*[12] in the Babylonian Talmud it appears five times.[13] In none of these occurrences, except one,[14] is there any indication that there is any disagreement about the number.

---

8. It is interesting to note, however, that while there are many talmudic sections that deal with the proper categorization of specific *mizvot,* there is none in which any sage either justifies or is asked to justify his position through recourse to the possible number of such *mizvot.*

9. Second half of the third century C.E.

10. *Ne'emru lo le-Mosheh,* in the printed editions of the Talmud. The Munich manuscript reads *ne'emar lo le-Mosheh be-Sinai* (unrecorded by Raphael Rabbinovicz in *Dikdukei Soferim* [Brooklyn, N.Y.: Jerusalem Press, 1960]) and thus also in *She'iltot,* Deut. 166.

11. Fourth century C.E.

12. See *Genesis Rabbah* 24:5, Theodor-Albeck ed. (Jerusalem: Wahrman Books, 1965), p. 234; *Exodus Rabbah* 33:7 (62b); *Tanḥuma, Koraḥ* 13, *Va-yelekh* 2; *Numbers Rabbah* 18:21 (76d); *Pirkei de-Rabbi Eli'ezer,* Warsaw ed. (1852), end of chap. 41, p. 98a; *Yalkut Shimoni,* par. 952; *Midrash Tehillim* 17 (missing in the Buber ed.); *Song of Songs Rabbah* 1:2 (4c). See also *Mekhilta, Yitro, parashah* 5, ed. Meir Ish Shalom, p. 67a (Horovitz Rabin ed., [Jerusalem: Bamberger and Wahrman, 1960] p. 222, variants to line 1).

13. Shabbat 27a, Yevamot 47b and 62a, Nedarim 25a, and Shevu'ot 29a.

14. In *Song of Songs Rabbah* 1:2, we read the following: R. Yehoshu'a b. Levi said: "The Jews heard two commandments directly from God, 'I am the Lord' and 'You shall have no other gods before Me,' as it says 'He kissed me with some of the kisses [*mi-neshikot*] of His mouth', [Song of Songs 1:1]: not all the kisses." But the sages claim that Israel heard all of the commandments directly from God. Rabbi Yehoshu'a of Sikhnin explained the view of the sages in the name of R. Levi, based on the fact that the verse "You [Moses] speak with us and we will listen, but let not the Lord speak with us, lest we die" (Exodus 20:16) appears in the Torah after all of the Ten Commandments. Rabbi Yehoshu'a b. Levi disagrees, on the basis of the principle that there is no chronological order in the Torah . . . Scripture says, "Moses commanded us the Torah." The entire Torah contains 613 commandments, the word *Torah* totals 611 in *gematria,* which is the number Moses spoke to us, for "I am the Lord" and "You shall have no other gods before Me" we heard not from Moses, but directly from God—as it says: "He kissed me with some of the kisses of His mouth."

It clearly follows from this *midrash* that Rabbi Yehoshu'a b. Levi's position is not

However, regarding the question of the classification of norms derived by means of recognized exegetical principles, there is a very broad dispute between Maimonides and Naḥmanides. As a foreword to his *Sefer ha-Mizvot,* Maimonides devotes fourteen chapters to a description of the bases upon which he decides whether any given norm is to be included among the 613. In the second of these chapters he addresses himself to the question of the classification of norms derived by means of exegesis.

Maimonides begins this chapter by affirming that the majority of all halakhic norms are derived by means of the common exegetical principles. Nonetheless, these norms fall into two classes, and the class of each norm determines its classification as either *de-oraita* or *de-rabbanan.* Norms derived by means of common exegesis may be either disputed or undisputed, that is, if there are sages who disagree with a norm, it could not possibly be designated as *de-oraita,* since no sage could possibly disagree with a norm that was given to Moses at Sinai. An absence of dispute, on the other hand, is evidence that a norm is a long-standing tradition, dating back to Moses, and that it is to be counted as *de-oraita.* Furthermore, should one wonder why an undisputed norm, given directly to Moses at Sinai, might be *proved* by later sages by means of exegesis, one should not wonder overly much. The fact that an undisputed norm *can* be derived by means of exegesis reflects the nature of Torah. That it *can* be so derived does not mean that it *needs* to be so derived. Undisputed norms *can* often be derived by means of exegesis, they never *need* to be so derived.

Since it is the case that norms deduced by means of exegetical principles may be both disputed and undisputed, it follows that exegetical derivation is not sufficient, in and of itself, to determine their proper categorization as either *de-oraita* or *de-rabbanan.*

> We cannot say of everything that we find that the sages deduced by means of any of the common exegetical principles that it was stated to Moses at Sinai. Nor can we say of everything that we find in the Talmud deduced by means of the common exegetical principles that

universal. The question is whether the disagreement is restricted to the *derivation* of the number 613 (i.e., to the verse quoted as proof), or to the number of 613 itself. Surely, if the sages used the same verse, they would have to conclude that there are 621 commandments (Torah = 611, plus Ten Commandments heard directly from God). Since there is no other statement in rabbinic literature that alludes to a number of *mizvot* other than 613, and since even here there is no indication of disagreement with that number, but rather over the issue of how many of the Ten Commandments were heard directly by the people, it would seem unlikely that this source indicates a disagreement over the number of commandments *in toto.*

it is *de-rabbanan,* since it is possible that it is an undisputed opinion *(perush mekubbal).*[15]

If the manner of their derivation is not sufficient, there must be another criterion by which the determination is made. Maimonides proceeds to define it as follows:

> Concerning any norm that is not stated explicitly *(meforash)* in the Torah, yet one finds that it is deduced in the Talmud by means of the common exegetical principles: If [the talmudic sages] themselves clearly state that [the norm] is a pillar of the Torah *(guf Torah)* or that it is *de-oraita,* it should be counted among the 613, since the transmitters of the tradition *(ma'atikei Torah she-be-al peh)* have said that it is *de-oraita;* but if they have neither made that clear nor stipulated it, the norm is *de-rabbanan,* since there is no place in the Torah that indicates it.[16]

Thus, according to Maimonides one can categorize a *miẓvah* as *de-oraita* (1) if it is explicitly stated in the Torah,[17] or (2) if it is derived by means of an exegetical principle, and is described by the sages themselves, transmitters of the tradition, as being *de-oraita.*[18] Barring such a statement by the sages, any legal norm deduced by means of exegetical principles is to be considered *de-rabbanan.*

After listing some of the errors of those who have not followed his criteria for categorizing matters *de-oraita,* both because they count among the 613 *miẓvot* certain norms which are clearly *de-rabbanan*—since those norms are deduced by means of rabbinic exegesis and are in no way implied by the explicit meanings *(peshat)* of the verses upon which

---

15. Maimonides, *Sefer ha-Mitzvot,* ed. Rabbi Joseph Kafih (Jerusalem: Mossad Harav Kook, 1971), p. 13.

16. Ibid.

17. This criterion is stated more explicitly in one of Maimonides' responsa: *Ve-ein shem min ha-Torah ella davar she-hu meforash ba-Torah ke-gon sha'atnez ve-khilayim ve-shabbat ve-arayot o davar she-ameru ḥakhamim she-hu min ha-Torah ve-hen kemo sheloshah arba'ah devarim bilvad* (*Teshuvot ha-Rambam,* ed. Jehoshua Blau [Jerusalem: Mekiẓe Nirdamim, 1960], vol. II, responsum 355, p. 632 = Alfred Freiman, ed., *Teshuvot ha-Rambam* [Jerusalem: Mekiẓe Nirdamim, 1934], responsum 166, p. 162).

18. Maimonides repeats this contention in the responsum quoted above. Yet the end of the responsum clearly indicates that the rabbinic statement of the *de-oraita* nature of the *mizvah* need not be explicit, for there he deduces that betrothal by document is *de-oraita,* although that conclusion is based on his deduction from rabbinic statements, not on any *explicit* statement. See, also, Chaim Tchernovitz (Rav Tzair), *Toledot ha-Halakhah,* 2d ed. (New York: Jubilee Committee, 1945), 1:49, n. 1.

they are based[19]—or because they omit *mizvot* which, even according to their own systems, should have been counted,[20] Maimonides states that if, in fact, one were to count as *de-oraita* all those legal norms derived by means of exegetical principles, the *mizvot de-oraita* would be in the thousands.[21] Maimonides concludes that his refusal to count most norms deduced by means of exegesis among the *mizvot de-oraita* has nothing to do with their "truth," but, rather, that any offshoots of the roots which are those things clearly stated to Moses on Sinai (i.e., the 613 commandments),

> even if the one who deduced them was Moses himself, are not to be counted. Proof for all of which is found in the claim of the Gemara [Temurah 16a]: "Seventeen hundred arguments from minor to major, and from deductions based on the appearance of the same word in two contexts, and from rabbinic deductions *(dikdukei soferim)* were forgotten during the period of mourning for Moses . . ."

---

19. For example, counting the obligation to respect sages (*yirat ḥakhamim)* as one of the positive commandments, based on Rabbi Akiva's exegesis of the verse in Deuteronomy 10:20, *Et ha-shem elohekha tira,* to include the veneration of the sages (Pesaḥim 22b). Or, similarly, including visiting the sick *(gemilut ḥasadim)* and comforting mourners, based on the exegesis of verse 18:20 in Exodus: *ve-hodata la-hem ha-derekh yelekhu vah* (Bava Kama 99b–100a).

20. For example, not counting the obligation to honor one's stepparents and older brother, based upon the exegesis of verse 20:12 in Exodus: *Kabbed et avikha ve-et immekha* (Ketubbot 103a).

21. It is highly unlikely that Maimonides' refusal to count derived laws among the 613 follows from his version of Rabbi Simlai's statement (*ne'emru le-Mosheh be-Sinai;* see chap. 1 of his foreword to *Sefer ha-Mitzvot*), in contradistinction to the apparent reading of Rabbi Shimon Kayyara in *Halakhot Gedolot (niẓtavvu Yisra'el)*—see photo-offset of Venice edition (Tel-Aviv: Leon Litho-offset, 1962 [5722], p. 2b). Aside from Naḥmanides' contention that, even if Kayyara had read as Maimonides does, he would, nonetheless, have counted derivative norms, Maimonides' own examples buttress the claim that the difference in readings is probably not crucial. Thus, for example, Maimonides questions on historical-chronological grounds Kayyara's counting of the Ḥanukkah lights and the reading of Esther as positive commandments, discounting the possibility that anyone (even Kayyara) could imagine that Moses was commanded to tell the people that when the historical events occurred, they would become obligated to perform those *miẓvot.* This possibility is unthinkable whether the reading is *ne'emru le-Mosheh be-Sinai* or *niẓtavvu Yisra'el.* Furthermore, Maimonides contends that if Kayyara counted these among the 613 on the basis of the verse "Thou shall not deviate" (Deuteronomy 17:11), he should have counted myriad other norms on the same basis. Since Maimonides himself does not count them, even though *lo tasur* is *de-oraita,* it follows that even if his reading were *niẓtavvu Yisra'el,* he would have to establish some criterion for restricting the number to 613. That criterion would most likely have been the same as the one he establishes on the basis of his own reading. It is true, nonetheless, that Maimonides' reading simplifies the defense of his criterion.

In any event, even if one could demonstrate that Maimonides' position is totally dependent upon his reading, that proof would constitute no more than a historical source for a systemic principle.

> And if these were forgotten, how great must have been the total number from among which these seventeen hundred were forgotten, for it is not likely that everything had been forgotten! If so, there is no doubt that the laws deduced by *kal va-ḥomer* and other exegetical principles numbered many thousands. And these had all been deduced in the lifetime of Moses, for seventeen hundred were forgotten during the mourning after his death. Thus it is perfectly clear that rabbinic deductions come even from Moses' day, for everything that was not heard explicitly by him at Sinai is called *mi-divrei soferim* ("from the words of the scribes" = *de-rabbanan*).[22]

This quotation from Temurah proves, therefore, that for Maimonides the sages understood that norms not explicit in the Torah but derived only by means of exegetical principles are to be considered *de-rabbanan,* even if their origin is extremely ancient. For Maimonides, the only exception would be norms that fit into the two categories described above.

In his *Hassagot* to Maimonides' work, Naḥmanides takes strong exception to the criteria Maimonides established for the categorization of the *miẓvot.*[23] He argues that Maimonides' distinction between undisputed norms derived by means of exegetical principles that are *perushim mekubbalim,* qualifying them to be counted among the 613, and those not so qualified because they are not *perushim mekubbalim,* though they, too, have been deduced by means of exegesis, does not bear careful scrutiny.[24] If real "truth" is embodied in the explicit meaning of a verse, and not in its exegesis as derived by means of recognized principles, the basic foundation of the Talmud is undermined. And if it is the case, as Maimonides claims, that the "truth" of matters derived by means of recognized exegetical principles is not gainsaid by their being classified as *de-rabbanan,* it is impossible, claims Naḥmanides, to justify calling some *de-oraita* and others *de-rabbanan.* The fact that the sages specifically called some *de-oraita,* and not others, in no way justifies the Maimonidean distinction, for even those specifically called *de-oraita* by the sages were derived through utilization of the same principles as those not so

---

22. Maimonides, *Sefer ha-Mitzvot,* Kafih ed., p. 15.

23. Fascinating to read as demonstrations of Naḥmanides' exemplary erudition are his numerous examples indicating inconsistency on the part of Maimonides himself with regard to his own criteria, and his quotation of talmudic statements that appear to disprove Maimonides' conclusion. Equally interesting are the defenses of Maimonides by other commentators (printed in the traditional editions of the *Sefer ha-Miẓvot*).

24. *Hassagot to Sefer ha-Miẓvot* (Jerusalem: Makhon Ḥatam Sofer, 1968 [5728]), p. 37, s.v. *ve-akhshav.*

called. Furthermore, Maimonides' claim that a *perush mekubbal* qualifies as a *mizvah de-oraita* on the grounds that its status is derived more from the rabbis' statement that it is *de-oraita* than from its derivation according to exegetical principles, also does not bear analysis. For, writes Naḥmanides, if the exegetical principles are "true," then all norms derived by means of their employment are equally "traditional." Maimonides himself would have to admit, claims Naḥmanides, that since he accounts norms that, although transmitted since the days of Moses, were *not* derived by means of exegesis *(halakhot le-Mosheh mi-Sinai)* as *de-rabbanan* rather than *de-oraita*[25]—and whose "truth," therefore, is surely dependent upon their being "traditional"—it follows that being "traditional" is not a sufficient condition for being considered *de-oraita*.

Having thus dealt with Maimonides' theoretical analysis, Naḥmanides proceeds to deal with Maimonides' claim that the derivative laws are *de-rabbanan* because they are offshoots of the basic 613 roots. This rationale, also, is fallacious on the grounds that if it were true it would follow that certain things stated explicitly in the Torah should also be considered *de-rabbanan*, because they, too, are offshoots of other roots that are also clearly stated in the Torah.[26] Rather, claims Naḥmanides, Maimonides should have categorized all laws derived by

---

25. Stated explicitly by Maimonides in his *Commentary on the Mishnah*, Tractate Kelim, chap. 17, *mishnah* 12, Kafih ed. (Jerusalem: Mossad Harav Kook, 1968), p. 161: *Shi'uro mi-divrei soferim . . . ki kol mah she-lo nitba'er bi-leshon ha-Torah, mi-divrei soferim kore'in oto, va-afillu devarim she-hem halakhah le-Mosheh mi-Sinai*. See also his responsum (above, n. 17). For a more detailed discussion of *halakhah le-Mosheh mi-Sinai*, see his *Introduction to the Commentary on the Mishnah*, ed. Joseph Kafih (Jerusalem: Mossad Harav Kook, 1963), Seder Zera'im, pp. 16 ff.

26. Naḥmanides does not give specific examples of this category. The primary thrust of his argument is that legitimately derived "offshoots" should be no less authoritative (i.e., *de-oraita*) than the "roots" themselves. He blurs the thrust, however, by stating that certain statements *in the Torah itself* should be considered *de-rabbanan* by Maimonides, because they are "offshoots" of "roots." For Maimonides, however, the distinction between being derived and being explicitly stated is a crucial difference, even if both may be "offshoots" of "roots." In chaps. 7 and 11 of his foreword to the *Sefer ha-Mizvot*, Maimonides states clearly that not all legal statements of the Torah are to be counted. Neither the details (*dikdukim*, chap. 7) nor the parts (*ḥalakim*, chap. 11) of a *mizvah* are to be counted separately from the "root" of the *mizvah* itself. Yet, of course, Maimonides cannot claim that these are *de-rabbanan*, since they are not *derived*. Maimonides distinguishes, therefore, between explicitly stated "offshoots" (*de-oraita*, though not counted) and derived "offshoots" (*de-rabbanan*). Naḥmanides, on the other hand, stresses the "rootness" or "offshootness," ignoring the distinction between explicitly stated and derived "offshoots." Essentially, however, the dispute between Maimonides and Naḥmanides concerns the status of derived "offshoots," not the status of explicitly stated "offshoots." (See Abraham Alegre's comment to chap. 7 in his commentary, *Lev Same'aḥ* [Jerusalem: Makhon Hatam Sofer, 1968 (5728)], regarding the reason for Maimonides' division of *dikdukim* and *ḥalakim* into separate chapters.)

means of exegetical principles as *de-oraita*. These matters would then be subdivisible into two categories: (1) those that are offshoots of particular *mizvot*, in which case they would not be counted among the 613 basic *mizvot*, although they would have *de-oraita* status, and (2) those that are not offshoots of *mizvot*, in which case they would be considered not only *de-oraita* but also included within the 613.[27]

In the same way that one gets the feeling that Maimonides would have liked to call only the explicit meaning of a verse *de-oraita*, but could not because of clear rabbinic statements calling some exegetical derivations *de-oraita*, one gets a similar feeling that Naḥmanides would have liked to call all exegetical derivations *de-oraita*, but could not because of clear rabbinic statements that certain purported exegetical proofs are *de-rabbanan*, only in the realm of "hints" *(asmakhta)*—which surely cannot be designated *de-oraita*.[28]

Consequently, it seemed most appropriate to Naḥmanides to claim the opposite of Maimonides,[29] namely, that every norm which is deduced in the Talmud by means of the common exegetical principles is *de-oraita*, except if the sages say of it that it is *asmakhta*.[30] The term *de-oraita*

---

27. While Naḥmanides does not say so explicitly, it is clear that these are, in fact, the criteria which he himself uses for determining which of the *mizvot* shall be included in the 613 total.

28. Naḥmanides, *Hassagot*, p. 40.

29. As with Maimonides (see above, n. 18), Naḥmanides does not actually require specific mention of the *asmakhta* nature of the exegesis. See, for example, his commentary to Deuteronomy 14:22: *ve-ein ḥayyavim min ha-Torah kelal . . . ve-yesh baraitot shenuyot be-Torat kohanim u-ve-sifrei le-asmakhtot, ve-hem mutot*.

30. At least it is so from a legal-theoretical perspective, even if not from a practical point of view. Those who seek to demonstrate that the distance between them is not as great as it appears stress the practical perspective, i.e., that there are instances in which Maimonides postulates certain matters as *de-oraita* even in the absence of clear statements to that effect by the sages (see above, n. 18), or that Naḥmanides postulates certain matters as *de-rabbanan* even though they are apparently deduced by exegesis (see above, n. 29). See especially, Isaak Halevy, *Doroth Harischonim* (Berlin: Benjamin Harz, 1918), pt. 1, vol. 5, pp. 503–4. Those who emphasize the distance between them stress the theoretical perspective, i.e., these general postulates of Maimonides and Naḥmanides, which are, in truth, diametrically opposed. See Zacharia Frankel, *Darkei ha-Mishnah* (Tel Aviv: Sinai, 1959) p. 17, and Tchernovitz, *Toledot ha-Halakha*, pp. 49 ff.

Even assuming that Frankel and Tchernovitz are correct in claiming that the Maimonidean position reflects the view that the laws precede their exegesis and that the Naḥmanidean position reflects the view that the laws are derived from their exegesis, their claim would constitute no more than a historical source of a systemic principle. As such, it is irrelevant to the halakhic process, except insofar as we may later define and stipulate the ramifications of the nexus between historical and legal sources. (For a summary and analysis of the prevalent modern views on the subject, see Elon, *Jewish Law*, 2:243–49, 254–63.)

Similarly, the attempts of Tchernovitz (op. cit., pp. 11–15) and Benjamin DeVries (*Toledot Hahalachah Hatalmudit* [Tel Aviv: Abraham Zioni Publishers, 1962 (5722)], pp. 69–95) to

is, therefore, not restricted to 613 *mizvot,* but encompasses many more, while the number 613 delimits only the basic *mizvot,* of which all others, both *de-oraita* and *de-rabbanan,* are subcategories.

The very existence of a dispute between Maimonides and Naḥmanides concerning the proper categorization of *mizvot,* coupled with the fact that other sages and scholars at various times have sided with one or the other (the majority leaning toward the Naḥmanidean view), is sufficient to demonstrate that universal agreement on the category of any given *mizvah* is not a *sine qua non* of the orderly functioning of the system. This is the case even though there can be far-reaching ramifications resulting from the assignment of the *mizvah* to one or the other category. Whatever the reason for their disagreement, however, both Maimonides and Naḥmanides clearly affirm the existence of the distinction between *de-oraita* and *de-rabbanan.* Unstated though it may be, the ultimate justification for the retention of that distinction lies not in the fact that the sources refer to both categories and distinguish between them, but in the fact that the *grundnorm* of the system, as understood by the sages, demands such a distinction.

One wonders whether a dispute between Maimonides and Naḥmanides regarding the authority of Rabbi Simlai's statement may not be at the core of their disagreement about the categorization of *mizvot.* If one allows oneself to hypothesize for a moment that the number of *mizvot de-oraita* (either derived or explicit) might not be predetermined but subject, rather, to the varying perceptions of scholars and of generations, the dispute between Maimonides and Naḥmanides would dwarf considerably. First, the issue would be raised only in those cases in which the distinction is relevant; i.e., in those cases in which one of the systemic principles applicable to one or the other of the categories becomes an issue.

Second, even in such a case, the disputants would be free to disagree over the proper categorization of the *mizvah* in question on the basis of their own reading and understanding of the sources involved, without any concern about an absolute number of *mizvot de-oraita.* Such an analysis would allow them to categorize a given *mizvah* as *de-rabbanan* even if the sources seem to reflect that it is a *perush mekubbal* (i.e.,

---

analyze the concepts *de-oraita* and *de-rabbanan* on the sole basis of talmudic references are also irrelevant. Even if their analyses are correct, these possibilities, too, would constitute only historical sources. To the extent that these analyses may buttress or refute either the Maimonidean or the Naḥmanidean position, they may persuade one to favor one or the other position, both of which, though conflicting, have been incorporated into the halakhic process as systemic principles. But these analyses are incapable of eliminating one or the other position from systemic legitimacy.

undisputed), on the grounds that the exegetical deduction upon which it is based is merely a hint (i.e., that it is an *asmakhta*). Conversely, it would allow them to categorize a given *mizvah* as *de-oraita* even if the sources reflect that it is not a *perush mekubbal*.

Those involved in the study of rabbinic literature will recognize that the hypothetical situation just outlined is, in fact, the reality. Except in those works dealing specifically with the enumeration of the 613 commandments, the question of whether a norm is *de-oraita* or *de-rabbanan* is raised only when that question is relevant. Moreover, the *rishonim* do not hesitate to categorize them as either *de-oraita* or *de-rabbanan* on the basis of their own reading of the sources involved.[31] Only when one hypothesizes a predetermined number of *mizvot de-oraita* does it become necessary to seek definitive criteria for their categorization.

There is not one talmudic section in which the number of *mizvot de-oraita* is an important factor. In most, even when the discussion does revolve around the proper categorization of a *mizvah*, there is no mention of any specific number of permissible *mizvot de-oraita*. And in those passages where the number of 613 appears, its context is always aggadic or quasi-aggadic.

Naḥmanides himself raises serious questions about the authority of Rabbi Simlai's statement. In his comments on the first chapter of Maimonides' *Sefer ha-Mizvot*, he questions whether Rabbi Simlai's statement is universally accepted, or whether it is a matter of dispute.[32] *Inter alia*, he raises the problem of those instances in which one sage claims a *mizvah* to be obligatory, and another claims it to be nonobligatory *(reshut)*.[33] In those cases it must follow that for the former the *mizvah* is counted among the 613, while the latter, for whom it is not counted, must replace it with another *mizvah* (either positive or negative, depending on the nature of the nonobligatory *mizvah*) in order to complete the required number of *mizvot*. In addition, the replacement must be of such a nature that the sage who counted the original *mizvah* as obligatory cannot count its replacement at all. Yet we find no such discussions or analyses anywhere in the Talmud. Indeed, Naḥmanides wonders whether Rabbi Simlai's statement is itself *halakhah le-Mosheh mi-Sinai* (i.e., whether God told Moses specifically that He was giving him 613 commandments to transmit to the people), or whether his statement simply reflects an *asmakhta* based upon his *gematria*. It is possible, claims Naḥmanides, that Rabbi Simlai's statement is not universally accepted,

31. See the entire discussion in Halevy, *Doroth Harischonim*, referred to in n. 30.
32. See above n. 14.
33. E.g., Sotah 3a, Zevaḥim 65b, Kiddushin 21a, and Makkot 12a.

but just his enumeration of the *mizvot* as he saw them, and that, consequently, no one else is obligated to accept it as authoritative. Finally, asserts Naḥmanides, Rabbi Simlai's scriptural proof for the number 613 is, indeed, only an *asmakhta*. The Talmud, therefore, never raises the number of *mizvot* as an objection to any sage, because it assumes that the sage is simply disagreeing with the *asmakhta* posited by Rabbi Simlai.

Naḥmanides concludes, however, that "though we may posit [the number of *mizvot*] as a matter of dispute, we admit that it is definitive *(halakhah)* because the Talmud does."

Naḥmanides' analysis clearly indicates his recognition and acceptance of the fact that the number of *mizvot* is irrelevant to the system. And while great caution must be exercised before accepting an argument from silence, it does not seem unreasonable to anticipate that at least one talmudic section would deal with the enumeration of the *mizvot* if that enumeration were, in fact, a datum of the system.

It should be noted that Naḥmanides' own system for categorizing the *mizvot* is a brilliant synthesis of his doubt that the number 613 is definitive and his acceptance of it as such. Granting *de-oraita* status to derivations from recognized exegetical principles, while refusing to count them among the 613 if they can be considered as offshoots of other *mizvot*, preserves the sacrosanct number 613, while making it functionally irrelevant.

One further point. The proposition that there are 613 *mizvot* cannot be construed in any way to be a legal source of the halakhic system. First of all, there is nothing inherently legal about a number. Furthermore, the number 613 does not serve as the legal justification of any legislation whatsoever, or as the legal grounds for any judicial decision.

Thus, it is possible to conclude the following regarding the concept *de-oraita:* (1) it is a postulate of the system; (2) the system itself does not give any precise definition of it or any criterion on the basis of which to categorize *mizvot* as *de-oraita* or *de-rabbanan;* (3) there is no definite number of *mizvot* that must systemically be defined as *de-oraita* (whether one accepts either the Maimonidean or the Naḥmanidean hypothesis, that acceptance is a theological datum, not a legal one); and (4) a legitimate difference of opinion concerning the status of any given *mizvah* can have possible ramifications of consequence.

The legal ramifications that can result from the assignment of a norm to one of the two categories in question are determined by a variety of systemic principles, both explicit and implicit. But since, as we shall see, some of these systemic principles are in conflict with each other, we shall have to continue to search in order to discover whether there are yet other systemic principles that, in truth, govern the ultimate choice of the appropriate principle.

To begin with, there is a general tendency to treat matters *de-rabbanan* more leniently than matters *de-oraita*. This tendency is reflected in at least the following seven different ways, some more prevalent and more widely invoked than others, but all clearly demonstrable from talmudic sources.

1. In cases of doubt arising from an unsolved matter that is a necessary factor in determining the law in a specific case, apply the systemic principle *Kol sefeka de-oraita le-ḥumera, kol sefeka de-rabbanan le-kula* ("any matter of doubt which arises concerning an issue that is *de-oraita* is resolved according to its stringent implications; a matter of doubt which arises concerning an issue that is *de-rabbanan* is resolved according to its lenient implications").[34] The following example from Shabbat 34a will clarify the application of the principle: Two men commission an agent to place the necessary accouterments for an *eruv teḥumin* for each of them at different places.[35] For one, the agent places the accouterments at the required location while it is still daytime, but they are eaten (by a passerby or a dog) at twilight *(bein ha-shemashot)*. For the other, the agent places the accouterments at the required location at twilight, but they are eaten by nightfall. The legal status of twilight is the matter in doubt, it being unclear whether twilight is legally considered as daytime or nighttime. Thus, it follows that only one of the two *eruvin* placed by the agent would be valid, i.e., if the legal status of twilight is as daytime, the *eruv* of the first individual would be invalid, since it was not in its place (but, rather, had been eaten) at the onset of the Sabbath. If, however, the legal status of twilight is as nighttime, the *eruv* of the second individual would be invalid, since it was placed in its required location after the onset of the Sabbath. Yet Rava affirms that both *eruvin* are valid because the legal status of twilight is in doubt, and, since the institution of *eruv teḥumin* is *de-rabbanan*, we apply the principle *Kol sefeka de-rabbanan le-kula*.[36] If, however, the institution of *eruv teḥumin* were *de-*

34. Beiẓa 3b. Another wording of the same principle is *Ki gazeru rabbanan be-vada'an, bi-sefekan lo gazeru* (Berakhot 25a, Shabbat 34a, Yevamot 24a).

35. An *eruv teḥumin* is a rabbinic institution whereby the placing of foodstuffs sufficient for two meals at a location distant from one's home, but within the distance which it is permitted to traverse on the Sabbath without violating it, creates the legal fiction that one's domicile extends to the point at which the footstuffs have been placed, and allows the person for whom they were placed to walk an additional 2000 cubits from that spot. In order to be considered valid, the *eruv* must be in place at the onset of the Sabbath.

36. I.e., for the former we resolve that twilight is legally nighttime, so that his *eruv* was in place at least for an instant at the onset of the Sabbath; and for the latter we resolve that twilight is legally daytime, so that his *eruv* was placed in the required location prior to the onset of the Sabbath.

oraita, and the legal status of twilight in doubt, neither *eruv* would be considered valid, because of the application of the principle *Kol sefeka de-oraita le-ḥumera*.[37]

2. In cases of doubt about the proper adjudication of a matter, not because of any doubt about whether the matter is *de-oraita* or *de-rabbanan*, but because of a dispute among the sages about whether the facts of the case fit the applicable norm, apply the systemic principle *Be-shel Torah halokh aḥar ha-maḥmir, be-shel soferim halokh aḥar ha-mekel* ("follow the more stringent view when the issue of dispute is *de-oraita*, and the more lenient view when it is *de-rabbanan*").[38] The following example from Avodah Zarah 7a will clarify the application of the principle. A man suspects that an object of his may have become ritually impure.[39] He explains the specifics of the case to two sages, one of whom declares the object to be impure, and the other, pure. If the legal status of the impurity in question is *de-oraita* (i.e., *be-shel Torah*), the object should be considered impure *(halokh aḥar ha-maḥmir)*; if, on the other hand, the legal status of the impurity in question is *de-rabbanan* (i.e., *be-shel soferim*), the object should be considered pure *(halokh aḥar ha-mekel)*.

Thus, the tendency toward leniency in matters *de-rabbanan* is reflected in two types of doubtful cases: one in which the law itself (in this case the legal status of twilight) is in doubt, and the other in which the proper adjudication with regard to the facts is a matter of dispute among the sages. The two principles governing these two kinds of cases have been widely employed by Jewish legalists throughout the ages.

3. Significant financial loss is often considered grounds for leniency in matters *de-rabbanan*, but not in matters *de-oraita*. The Talmud gives the following example:[40] A drainpipe that is clogged by twigs, and that is therefore overflowing and causing damage to one's roof, can be unclogged on the Shabbat by treading on the blockage with one's foot (*ki-le-aḥar yad*;[41] to push the impediments through the pipe and relieve the

---

37. I.e., for the former we would resolve that twilight is legally daytime, so that his *eruv* would be invalid because it was not in place (but, rather, eaten) at the onset of the Sabbath; and for the latter we would resolve that twilight is legally nighttime, so that his *eruv* would be invalid because it had not even been placed by the onset of the Sabbath.

38. Avodah Zarah 7a.

39. There are many different kinds and degrees of ritual impurity. For the comprehension of this systemic principle, however, it is sufficient to be aware that certain ritual impurities are *de-oraita*, and others *de-rabbanan*. A concise summary of the kinds and degrees of ritual impurity can be found in English in *The Mishnah*, ed. H. Danby (Oxford: Oxford University Press, 1933), Appendix 4.

40. Ketubbot 60a.

41. I.e., differently from the manner in which that activity is generally carried out. In this case it would be common to remove the blockage either with a shovel or with one's hands.

blockage), without any concern about violating the Sabbath. For, since the prohibition of work *ki-le-aḥar yad* is *de-rabbanan* and not *de-oraita*,[42] the prohibition may be superseded in instances of significant financial loss. The corollary is stated most succinctly by Rav Papa: *Issura de-oraita ve-at amrat ha-Torah ḥasah al mamonan shel Yisrael* ("the matter is forbidden *de-oraita*, and you claim that the Torah is concerned for the financial welfare of Jews as an argument for leniency?!").[43]

4. Concern for a man's honor *(kevod ha-beriyyot)* can also, at times, become a valid reason for leniency in matters *de-rabbanan*, but not in matters *de-oraita*. Thus, for example, the Talmud dictates,[44] concerning the biblical injunction against *kilayim*,[45] that if one discovers that his garment contains a forbidden mixture, he must remove it forthwith, even if he is in a public place, such as the marketplace. In responding to a question about the source of the statement, the verse from Proverbs is quoted: *Ein ḥokhmah ve-ein tevunah ve-ein eẓah le-neged ha-shem* ("there is neither wisdom nor understanding nor counsel against God").[46] If, on the other hand, one of the fringes on the corner of one's garment becomes torn on the Sabbath (in which case, since they are no longer valid fringes, wearing them while walking constitutes "carrying," and is forbidden on the Sabbath), he may continue to wear them on his garment and walk from a *karmelit* to his home.[47] Since the prohibition against carrying in a *karmelit* or from a *karmelit* to a private domain is *de-rabbanan*, the man's honor takes precedence over the violation of a prohibition *de-rabbanan*.[48]

5. It is well known that the *halakhah* demands that students behave toward their teachers with the utmost respect and deference, yet the distinction between *de-oraita* and *de-rabbanan* can become relevant in this area as well. If a student hears a sage permit an act which he knows to be forbidden, and can so demonstrate, he should, nonetheless, allow the act to be completed before questioning the propriety of the decision if the nature of the prohibition is *de-rabbanan*. If, however, the nature of

---

42. I.e., it is a *shevut*, an activity forbidden by the sages as inconsistent with the spirit of the day, though not forbidden *de-oraita*. See Mishnah Beiẓa 5:2.

43. Ḥulin 49b.

44. Berakhot 19b.

45. Deuteronomy 22:11.

46. 21:30.

47. A *karmelit* is a type of domain which, though not technically a public domain *de-oraita*, has been ordained *de-rabbanan* to bear the same restrictions as a public domain regarding the norms of carrying on the Sabbath.

48. Menaḥot 37b–38a.

the prohibition is *de-oraita*, he should question the decision before the act is carried out.[49]

6. While the matter is legally complex, and many subdivisions are possible, it is clear that the prohibition against purposely mixing a forbidden substance with a sufficient quantity of permissible substances in order to "annul" the forbidden substance *(ein mavattelin issur le-khatteḥilah)* is more leniently applied to substances which are forbidden *de-rabbanan* than to substances forbidden *de-oraita*.[50]

7. In general, a man cannot be held responsible for the violation of an oath in which he swears to refrain from an action already forbidden to him *de-oraita*. For example, if he swears that he will not eat carrion or improperly slaughtered meat, and proceeds to eat them, he is not in violation of his own oath, which is considered null and void, because he is already forbidden to eat those meats *de-oraita*.[51] If, however, he swore to refrain from a beahvior already forbidden to him *de-rabbanan*, and proceeded to engage in that behavior, he is in violation both of the rabbinic injunction and his own oath.[52]

There is, as well, a subcategory of the tendency toward leniency in norms *de-rabbanan* that is not only illustrative of the tendency itself, but that even allows for the possibility of abrogating or amending norms *de-rabbanan* in certain circumstances. This subcategory is reflected in the systemic principle *Hem ameru ve-hem ameru* (lit. "They said, and they said"). The principle means that the sages can decide to abrogate a requirement of a norm in certain cases in which that requirement was imposed as a result of a rabbinic enactment and is not a requirement *de-oraita*.

---

49. Eruvin 67b. This category could also be classified as a subcategory of the preceding, for it reflects the extreme concern for *kevod ha-beriyyot*, in this instance, one's teacher. It is "extreme" because it allows the willful and *preventable* violation of an *issur de-rabbanan* to take place because of *kevod ha-beriyyot* of a special type. The fact that the student questions the decision afterwards does not negate the principle, because the wording of the question by the student will not indicate that the student knows the sage to be mistaken, but rather his desire to be taught by the teacher wherein he, the student, is mistaken. (Cf. Kiddushin 32a.) Indeed, this case demonstrates how seriously the sages entertained the possibility that the student might, in fact, be mistaken. For had they not considered that to be plausible, they would probably have allowed the student to question before the violation actually took place. Only when the *issur* is *de-oraita* did they refuse to take the chance that the student may be wrong.

50. See *Talmudic Encyclopedia* (Hebrew) (Jerusalem: Talmudic Encyclopedia Publishers, 1947) 1:297, s.v. *ein mevattelin issur le-khatteḥilah*.

51. Shevu'ot 23b.

52. While, at first blush, it may appear that this category reflects a stringency of norms *de-rabbanan* over norms *de-oraita*, rather than a leniency, insofar as liability for the violation of the oath is concerned, the leniency lies in the *theoretical* applicability of an oath to an *issur de-rabbanan*, which does not apply to an *issur de-oraita*.

The principle is explicitly stated in the Palestinian Talmud. And although it is not stated explicitly in the Babylonian Talumd,[53] its implications are reflected there, and the commentators and legalists refer to the principle explicitly in their comments on those sections in which its implications are reflected. Two examples will demonstrate how the principle is applied in the Palestinian Talmud.

The following two legal assertions underlie the first example: (1) any Jew is considered a valid witness unless he is shown to be disqualified for some reason, and (2) the determination of the beginning of the month is made on the basis of the testimony of witnesses.

The *mishnah* in Rosh ha-Shanah stipulates that the High Court in Jerusalem must know the man who comes to testify concerning the new moon.[54] If it does not know him, it is the obligation of the court from the city of the witness's residence to send a second witness with him to Jerusalem, so that the second witness can testify concerning the acceptability of the witness about the new moon. The requirement of the second witness is a rabbinic enactment, imposed after an incident in which a witness deliberately deceived the court about a new moon. The court, of course, had accepted his testimony on the basis of the principle that any Jew is a valid witness unless he can be shown to be otherwise. The important point, however, is that the *mishnah* clearly implies that only one witness is necessary to testify as to character, a fact contrary to the norm stated in Deuteronomy 19:15, according to which two witnesses are required for all matters.

The Yerushalmi raises this problem and answers it as follows: *Be-din haya she-lo ye-hu ẓerikhin edim, ve-hem ameru she-yehu ẓerikhim edim, ve-hem ameru ed eḥad ne'eman* ("by right, they needed no witness; *they said* that witnesses are needed, and *they said* that one witness is acceptable").[55] That is, the sages were lenient in a matter in which they themselves had imposed the stringency.[56] According to the law, no character witness was required at all. However, *they* (the sages) *said* that character witnesses were required, and *they said* that in this case one witness was acceptable. Since the requirement of two witnesses applied to this case only as a result of a rabbinic enactment necessitating the appearance of character witnesses, the rabbis themselves modified that requirement in this case.

---

53. Its appearance in Eruvin 67b is excepted, because its meaning there is not the same as in the general usage.

54. Rosh ha-Shanah 2:1.

55. Rosh ha-Shanah 2:1, 57b.

56. See David Fraenkel, *Korban ha-Edah* (a traditional commentary on the Palestinian Talmud), s.v. *mi-she-lekha*.

The second instance in which the principle is explicitly stated in the Yerushalmi deals with *terumah,* a percentage of their produce given by Jews to the priests.[57] *Terumah* could be eaten only by members of the priestly class. According to this *mishnah* a bound bundle of *terumah*-spices that had been dipped into a pot, thereby rendering the contents of the pot *terumah,* and was then removed from the first pot and dipped into a second pot, also rendered the contents of the second pot *terumah* if the act of the first dipping had not nullified the seasoning potential of the bundle completely. If the first dipping had nullified the seasoning potential of the bundle completely, the contents of the second pot were not rendered *terumah* and could be eaten by nonpriests. The Yerushalmi asks what distinguishes the bundle of *terumah*-spices from dill, concerning which the *mishnah* states that if *terumah*-dill was dipped into a pot and flavored it and was then removed, it no longer had the status of *terumah* (whether or not its flavor was completely nullified), nor could it become impure.[58] The answer is: *Be-din haya she-lo tittame tumat okhelin, ve-hu ha-din terumah. Ve-hem ameru she-tittame tumat okhelin, ve-hem ameru, mi-keivan she-natenah ta'am ba-kederah, betelah* ("According to the law, dill is not susceptible to ritual impurity [since it is not legally called food *de-oraita*], and, for the same reason, it cannot become *terumah.* However, *they said* that it was susceptible to ritual impurity, [thereby giving it the status of food and the potential to become *terumah,*] and *they said* that it loses its food status if it has flavored a pot, even if all of its flavoring potential has not been dissipated").

This example demonstrates clearly the distinction between *de-rabbanan* and *de-oraita.* The sages could abrogate the legal requirement demanding that the food status of a substance be considered unchanged unless and until all of its flavoring potential is dissipated only in the case where the attribution of food status was itself *de-rabbanan.* Where it is *de-oraita* they could not abrogate the norm.

While, as we have noted, the Babylonian Talmud does not articulate the principle of *Hem ameru, ve-hem ameru* explicitly, it clearly employs it. In Ketubbot, for example, the Talmud says: "The sages ordained a marriage contract of 200 *zuz* for a virgin and 100 *zuz* for a widow, and they believed a husband who claimed that he found his wife to be a nonvirgin."[59] Rashi explains this case as an example of the employment of the principle *Hem ameru, ve-hem ameru.*[60] Why is it such a case?

---

57. Terumot 11:1, 47c.
58. Ukẓin 3:4.
59. Ketubbot 10a.
60. Ketubbot 10a, s.v. *ḥakhamim.*

Because the effect of believing the claim of the husband is that on the sole basis of the husband's claim, the woman loses all rights to collect her marriage contract. Under ordinary circumstances, the testimony of two witnesses would be required, and the husband would not even be entitled to testify about his wife. However, it was the *sages* who *said* that a man must write a marriage contract for his wife's protection, and it was *they* who *said* that he is to be believed if he claims that he married her on the assumption that she was a virgin and found that she was not.

In other cases in which the rabbis allowed the tesitmony of a witness who would, under normal circumstances, have been considered invalid, their acceptance of such a witness is justified by the Talmud on the grounds that *Heimenuhu rabbanan bi-de-rabbanan* ("the sages accepted the testimony because the very requirement of testimony in these cases was itself rabbinically ordained").[61] And in each of these cases, Rashi explains the leniency as following from the principle *Hem ameru, ve-hem ameru*.[62]

What distinguishes this systemic principle as a subcategory of the general tendency toward leniency in matters *de-rabbanan* is the fact that the kinds of circumstances in which this principle is invoked cannot be neatly categorized as concerning any specific realms of affairs. Indeed, the willingness of the sages to invoke the principle in some cases and not in others is inexplicable, except, perhaps, *ad hoc*.

Thus, the halakhic system clearly includes certain systemic principles that can, depending on the categorization of the relevant norm, lead to significant ramifications. Before drawing any specific conclusions from this fact, however, it is necessary to examine the systemic principles that are in apparent conflict with those we have been discussing.

The general tendency toward greater leniency in the application of *de-rabbanan* norms than in the application of *de-oraita* norms reflects the fact that rabbinic norms are secondary legislation, while *de-oraita* norms are primary legislation. Yet the halakhic system also reflects systemic principles whose aim is, curiously, to enhance and protect the authority of this secondary legislation.

---

61. Ketubbot 28a and Pesaḥim 4b.

62. Ketubbot 28a, s.v. *heimenuhu;* Pesaḥim 4b, *bi-de-rabbanan.* Other examples of the Bavli's employment of the systemic principle can be found in Kiddushin 17b, regarding the rabbinically ordained right of a convert to inherit from his gentile father. See Tosafot, s.v. *ella.* Also, Bava Batra 48b, concerning betrothal by means of the payment of money, which may be *de-rabbanan.* See Rashbam on Bava Batra. R. Yom Tov Lippman Heller refers to the principle *Hem ameru ve-hem ameru* in his commentary on the Mishnah in Berakhot 3:5, Kilayim 2:1, Yoma 8:1, and Ḥagigah 3:4.

On the most abstract level, cognizance of the need for such enhancement and protection of the authority of rabbinic legislation is reflected in the dictum *Divrei Torah einam ẓerikhim ḥizzuk, divrei ḥakhamim ẓerikhim ḥizzuk* ("the words of the Torah, [i.e., matters *de-oraita*] need no strengthening, while the words of the sages [i.e., matters *de-rabbanan*] require reinforcement"). This abstract stipulation does not define the degree of "strengthening" that matters *de-rabbanan* require, only that they do need *ḥizzuk*. And while there are systemic principles that do define the degree of *ḥizzuk* it is possible to apply (to which we shall turn shortly), the abstract principle is often invoked alone. Several examples will clarify the application of the principle.

1. In parallel cases involving a *sukkah* and a *mavoi*,[63] in one of which a part of the covering of the *sukkah*, and in the other of which a part of the crossbeam of the *mavoi*, is higher than 20 cubits from the ground, the Talmud, according to one explanation, declares the *sukkah* to be valid and the crossbeam of the *mavoi* to be invalid (thereby forbidding carrying within the *mavoi* on the Sabbath).[64] In seeking to clarify why such similar cases result in opposite rulings, the Talmud explains: *Hallalu divrei Torah, ve-ein divrei Torah ẓerikhim ḥizzuk; hallalu divrei soferim ve-divrei soferim ẓerikhim ḥizzuk* (the *sukkah*, being *de-oraita*, requires no strengthening; the *mavoi*, being *de-rabbanan*, does require strengthening).

2. Fasting is forbidden not only on the actual day of rabbinically ordained days of celebration,[65] but also on the day prior and the day following. Regarding Sabbaths or biblical holidays, however, the restriction is limited to the actual day. The reason: *Hallalu divrei Torah ve-ein divrei Torah ẓerikhin ḥizzuk; hallalu divrei soferim ve-divrei soferim ẓerikhin*

---

63. A *mavoi* is a relatively narrow street or alleyway which runs off a public thoroughfare. Generally, several courtyards containing homes, or individual homes themselves, open into the *mavoi*, which is generally closed from three directions. The *mavoi* itself is not considered to be a public domain *de-oraita*, and carrying, therefore, is permitted within it. Since it was used by so many people (the inhabitants of all of the courtyards and/or houses which opened onto it), however, to gain access to the public domain, and might, therefore be misconstrued to be legally equal to the public domain, the sages ordained that carrying on the Sabbath was forbidden therein, unless certain measures were taken. Among the measures was the requirement that a crossbeam be placed from one wall of the *mavoi* to the other, at its open end. The beam was to serve as a clear distinction of the *mavoi* from the public domain. Therefore, it had to be clearly recognizable to anyone entering the *mavoi*. According to rabbinic calculations, the maximum height between the ground and the crossbeam at which it would be clearly recognizable is 20 cubits. Similarly, the most distinguishing factor of a *sukkah* was its obviously temporary covering. Thus, it, too, had to be recognizable to people entering the *sukkah*, and could be no higher, generally, than 20 cubits from the ground. The case described in this example involves a *sukkah* covering and a *mavoi* crossbeam which meet the requirement *partially*, but not entirely.

64. Eruvin 3a.

65. For example, those enumerated in Megillat Ta'anit.

ḥizzuk (Sabbaths and biblical holidays, being *de-oraita,* require no strengthening; rabbinically ordained days of celebration, being *de-rabbanan,* do require strengthening).[66]

3. The Talmud distinguishes between marriages forbidden *de-oraita,*[67] in which, although the woman must be divorced, she may yet collect her marriage contract; and marriages forbidden *de-rabbanan,* in which she may not collect.[68] In explanation of the apparent discrepancy Rabbi Judah the Prince affirms: *Hallalu divrei Torah ve-ein divrei Torah ẓerikhin ḥizzuk; hallalu divrei soferim ve-divrei soferim ẓerikhin ḥizzuk* (marriages forbidden *de-oraita* require no strengthening, those forbidden *de-rabbanan* do require strengthening).

These examples indicate not only that the principle is operative within the halakhic system, but also that its application is not restricted to any specific type of norm (i.e., ritual, ethical, etc.).[69] Thus, on the one hand we have systemic principles that affirm the generally more lenient nature of the law in matters *de-rabbanan* than in matters *de-oraita,* and on the other hand, a systemic principle that affirms that as a result of a deliberate act of strengthening on the part of the sages themselves, the law in matters *de-rabbanan* can be made to be of a more stringent nature than in matters *de-oraita.*[70]

66. Ta'anit 17b, Rosh ha-Shanah 19a.

67. E.g., the marriage of a widow to the High Priest (Leviticus 21:14) or of any priest to a divorcee (Leviticus 21:7). These marriages are forbidden *de-oraita,* but are not punishable by execution either by the court or by God (*karet*). While these marriages are forbidden before the fact, they are binding after the fact, and can be dissolved only through death of the husband or by divorce. There are parallel cases of rabbinically forbidden marriages, called *sheniyyot la-arayot* (see Yevamot 21a). In both categories the rabbis insisted that the husband divorce his wife. In any legal marriage, the wife is entitled, upon divorce, to collect the sum stipulated in her marriage contract.

68. Yevamot 85b.

69. Admittedly, one does not find this principle applied to purely monetary matters. The reason for this fact, however, lies in a different systemic principle, viz., that in monetary matters even if one is *Matneh al mah she-katuv ba-Torah tena'o kayyam* ("makes a stipulation contrary to the Torah, it is valid"). Even if one adopts the contrary position (i.e., that *tena'o batel,* "his stipulation is invalid"), the implication of the principle is that it applies only to *mah she-katuv ba-Torah,* but not to monetary matters *de-rabbanan.* It is true, however, that if one adopts this position, it would be theoretically conceivable to apply the principle *Ḥakhamim asu ḥizzuk le-divreihem ke-shel Torah* (see below, p. 34), thereby invalidating a *tenai* in a monetary case *de-rabbanan.* It is further true that even if one adopts the former position, it would be theoretically possible to apply the principle *Ḥakhamim asu ḥizzuk le-divreihem yoter mi-shel Torah,* and invalidate the *tenai* in a monetary case *de-rabbanan,* even though it would be valid in a monetary case *de-oraita.* One strongly suspects, therefore, that there is some internal logic to the principle *Matneh al mah she-katuv ba-Torah* that restricts the application of principles of *ḥizzuk* to it. On such logic, see Elon, *Jewish Law,* 1:159–63.

70. It should be pointed out that the principle *Divrei ḥakhamim ẓerikhin ḥizzuk* ("positions of the sages require strengthening") is so pervasive that even its exceptions have been

Futhermore, with regard to the principle that permits strengthening the law in certain matters *de-rabbanan* there are still other conflicting systemic principles that govern the degree to which rabbinic enactments may be strengthened (assuming that the norm *de-rabbanan* in question is one to which the sources apply the principle of strengthening rather than the tendency toward leniency).

One wording of the first principle that deals with the question of degree of strengthening is: *Ḥakhamim asu ḥizzuk le-divreihem ke-shel Torah* ("the sages strengthened their words to equate them with matters *de-oraita"*). This wording appears only once in the Talmud, and the implication of the words, clearly, is that rabbinic legislation is to be the equal, in terms of severity, enforcement, and legal implications, of legislation *de-oraita*. The Mishnah in this particular case[71] offers a list of the consecrated foods for which one must add an extra one-fifth of the total value[72] to his restitution if he has eaten of them inadvertently. The restitution, including the one-fifth, was paid *in specie* and itself became consecrated. Included in the list is the category *terumat ma'aser shel demai*.[73] The problem lies in the application of the biblical requirement of

---

defined by systemic principle. To wit: *Milleta de-la shekhiḥa la avadu bah rabbanan ḥizzuk, milleta di-shekhiḥa avadu bah rabbanan ḥizzuk* ("the sages did not strengthen their own position in unusual or infrequent matters, but only in common or frequent matters" [Ketubbot 56b]. Another, more common, wording of the same principle is: *Milleta de-la shekhiḥa la gezaru bah rabbanan* ("the sages make no enactments regarding infrequent matters"). Example: A vessel which had become impure on *erev yom tov* may not be immersed for purification on *yom tov*, by rabbinic decree. The logic behind the decree is as follows: The rabbis forbade the immersion of vessels on the Sabbath, since they are likely to be carried to the *mikveh* (bath for ritual immersion), thereby involving the owner in a violation of the Sabbath. That fear does not apply to *yom tov*, on which carrying is permissible. Yet the sages forbade immersion of vessels on *yom tov* because of the possibility of confusion between the Sabbath and *yom tov*. If, however, the vessel became impure on *yom tov* itself, it could be immersed on that very day (and used for nonsacred foods). The grounds for this leniency are that it is unusual for vessels to become impure on *yom tov* itself. Thus, the likelihood of vessels becoming impure on *yom tov* through contact with impure handlers is minimal (i.e., *la shekhiḥa*). Therefore, the systemic principle *Milleta de-la shekhiḥa la gezaru bah rabbanan* applies, and the vessel may be immersed without concern for the possible confusion with the Sabbath (Beiẓa 18a). Other instances of the application of this principle may be found in Eruvin 63b, Beiẓa 2a, Kiddushin 28b, Gittin 5a and 44b, Nazir 55a, Bava Meẓi'a 46b and 47a, Bekhorot 3a, and Niddah 34a.

71. Bava Meẓi'a 4:8, 55b.

72. Leviticus 22:14.

73. *Demai* is defined as produce which one acquires from a person who is not reliable enough to be trusted to have separated all of the necessary consecrated portions required by the law (i.e., an *am ha-areẓ*). The rabbis ordained that one who acquires such produce should separate the consecrated portions (except for *terumah*, for which the *am ha-areẓ* could be trusted). Among these portions is the *terumat ma'aser*, the tithe of the tithe (i.e., 10 percent of the levitical tithe which the Levites themselves were required to give to the priests [Numbers 18:26]), which, in the case of *demai*, the purchaser himself was to separate. The separation of the consecrated portions from *demai* is obligatory only *de-rabbanan*, not *de-oraita*.

the addition of one-fifth of the value of consecrated foods in the case of inadvertent eating of *terumat ma'aser shel demai*, when this particular prohibition is only *de-rabbanan*. In its solution, the Talmud explains: *Ḥakhamim asu ḥizzuk le-divreihem ke-shel Torah* ("the sages strengthened their words to equate them with matters *de-oraita*"). Thus, even the inadvertent eating of *terumat ma'aser shel demai* requires the additional one-fifth.[74]

The more frequent form in which the principle appears is: *Kol de-takkun rabbanan ke-ein de-oraita takkun* ("whatever the sages ordained, they ordained as equal to *de-oraita*"). While this wording appears eight times in the Babylonian Talmud, one of the eight passages appears in two different locations, leaving us with seven independent occurrences of this formula in the Babylonian Talmud. It is sufficient for the clarification of the principle merely to indicate the context of six of these, and to dwell only on the seventh.

The first use of the principle is in a case dealing with the rabbinic prohibition against the use of wine from which a libation had been poured to idolatry *(yayin nesekh)*.[75] The second[76] is a case concerned with the possibility of using bitter herbs from one's second tithe[77] in fulfillment of the Passover obligation to eat bitter herbs, if one is celebrating the *seder* in Jerusalem. The third[78] deals with the exemption of a blind person from the recitation of the *Haggadah* on Passover.[79] The fourth use

74. This passage is the only one in which the principle, in any version, is attributed specifically to one man, Rabbi Me'ir. The Tosafot (s.v. *ve-khi*) point out, correctly, that the principle in fact reflects a widespread opinion, not only that of Rabbi Me'ir. They justify its attribution to him on the grounds that this specific case, as well as the case from which it is deduced that Rabbi Me'ir holds the view that *Ḥakhamim asu ḥizzuk le-divreihem ke-shel Torah*, is such that one would not logically assume that the principle should be invoked concerning it. Thus, it is not the principle itself which is being noted as Rabbi Me'ir's view, but its applicability to the case of *terumat ma'aser shel demai;* the principle itself is well-nigh universal. While the explanation of the Tosafot is weak, its implication is correct. It follows from what they say that Rabbi Me'ir himself never applied the principle explicitly to the case of *terumat ma'aser shel demai*, rather, that the Talmud itself deduced that its application in this case is consonant with the view of Rabbi Me'ir. Since the case from which *terumat ma'aser shel demai* is deduced as consonant with his view does not itself invoke the principle explicitly, it follows that its application to *terumat ma'aser shel demai* does not really imply either original or exclusive authorship of the principle to Rabbi Me'ir.

75. Pesaḥim 30b and Avodah Zarah 34a.

76. Pesaḥim 39b.

77. The "second tithe" refers to that produce which was separated for consumption in Jerusalem (Deuteronomy 14:23) or for redemption for monies which were to be used in Jerusalem (Deuteronomy 14:24–26). The requirement of the second tithe for vegetables (which includes, or course, bitter herbs) is *de-rabbanan*, not *de-oraita*.

78. Pesaḥim 116b.

79. The exemption is based on a *gezerah shavah* (a hermeneutic principle that allows for the derivation of identical norms to different contexts on the basis of an identical word that appears in them) between *ba'avur zeh* (Exodus 13:8), regarding Passover, and *benenu zeh*

applies to the case of the cowife *(zarah)* of a woman who is considered as an unfaithful wife *(sotah) de-rabbanan.*[80] The fifth deals with a rabbinic requirement for the immersion of a leper.[81] The sixth concerns the right to give tithes from one species in fulfillment of the tithing requirement of another, when both of the species in question require tithing *de-rabbanan,* but not *de-oraita.*[82] In each of these instances the systemic principle *Kol de-takkun rabbanan ke-ein de-oraita takkun* is applied, as appropriate. Since it will soon become relevant to the analysis, it should be pointed out that none of these talmudic sections posits any restriction concerning the type of rabbinic enactments to which this systemic principle might theoretically apply. Yet it should also be noted that the cases in which the Talmud itself applies the principle are such that the basic subject matter (e.g., bitter herbs, recitation of the *Haggadah,* tithes, etc.) underlying the rabbinic enactment can be traced to the Torah itself.

The last talmudic passage in which the systemic principle is stated explicitly is concerned with the right of a minor (i.e., one who has not yet attained puberty) to obtain something for the sake or benefit of others *(lizkot la-aherim).*[83] With reference to a *shittuf mavoi,*[84] the Mishnah

---

("this son of ours") (Deuteronomy 21:20), regarding a rebellious son. As in the latter the sages deduced (Sanhedrin 8:4, 71a) that the demonstrative pronoun could apply only in a case where the parents could identify the boy visually (thus exempting the offspring of blind parents from culpability), so, too, in the former they deduced that the obligation to recite the *Haggadah* could apply only when the reciter could identify the paschal lamb visually. The sages affirmed the exemption even after the destruction of the Temple (when the paschal lamb was no longer eaten), when the eating of *mazah* was itself *de-rabbanan,* on the grounds that *Kol de-takkun rabbanan ke-ein de-oraita takkun.* Thus, just as a blind person was exempt during Temple days when eating *mazah* was *de-oraita* (and, therefore, could not be the agent through whom others fulfilled their obligation), so, too, is he exempt now, even though *mazah* is *de-rabbanan.* Of particular interest, however, is the talmudic evidence that the application of the principle was not accepted by all. Rav Joseph and Rav Sheshet (both of whom were blind) recited the *Haggadah* in their own academies, based on the premise that since the eating of *mazah* in their time was only *de-rabbanan,* they were permitted to recite the *Haggadah,* even as agents for others. Thus, while there is no evidence that either of these sages denied the validity of the systemic principle *Kol de-takkun rabbanan ke-ein de-oraita takkun,* they did not apply it in this specific instance.

80. Yevamot 11a.

81. Yoma 31a.

82. Bekhorot 54a.

83. Gittin 64b–65a.

84. This is a rabbinic institution which permits the inhabitants of the homes and courtyards whose access to the public domain required traversing a common *mavoi* (see above, n. 63) to carry on the Sabbath both within the alleyway and from one courtyard to another via the alleyway. The *shittuf* (lit. "partnership") is accomplished by placing a jug containing any food, except salt or water, someplace within the alleyway. Most of the time the jug's contents belonged to only one of the inhabitants. The "partnership" was created by that person's granting possession of the contents of the jug to all of the people whose access to their property was from the *mavoi,* with, usually, one person "accepting" the contents of the jug for all. Obviously, that agent had to be legally entitled to acquire *(zokheh)* for others in order for the *shittuf* to be valid.

states that a man may place his own jug in the *mavoi* for the benefit of all of the inhabitants who use the *mavoi* for access to their own dwellings.[85] He is also empowered to grant possession of the contents of the jug to those inhabitants by means of a variety of agents, including a Jewish maidservant. Since, by law, a Jewish maidservant goes free upon attaining puberty, it follows that her inclusion in the list of agents who may acquire for the sake of others should prove that a minor may be *zokheh la-aḥerim* ("obtain for the sake of others"). To this point the Talmud responds that this case is exceptional in allowing a minor to be *zokheh la-aḥerim,* because the institution of *shittuf mavoi* is only *de-rabbanan,* but that in a matter *de-oraita* a minor would not be so permitted. In rebuttal, the Talmud claims that this distinction is invalid because of the systemic principle *Kol de-takkun rabbanan ke-ein de-oraita takkun.* Then the Talmud adds a qualification to the application of this principle, namely: *Ki amrinan kol de-takkun rabbanan ke-ein de-oraita takkun be-milleta de-it lah ikkar min ha-Torah, aval milleta de-let lah ikkar min ha-Torah, lo* ("the principle under discussion is applicable only when the subject matter to which it is being applied can be traced to the Torah, but if it cannot, the principle is inapplicable"). Thus, since the concept of a *shittuf mavoi* cannot be traced to the Torah in any way, the principle does not apply, and the inclusion of a Jewish maidservant in the list of agents does not prove the general right of a minor to be *zokheh la-aḥerim.*

If, in fact, this proviso can be found to be widely accepted as a qualification of the systemic principle *Kol de-takkun rabbanan ke-ein de-oraita takkun* we may have a first indication of conditions under which one of the two conflicting systemic principles concerning strengthening and leniency is to be preferred over the other.

No less an authority than Joseph Caro (1488–1575), in his *Kelalei ha-Gemara,* accepts the qualification that the subject matter must be traceable to the Torah as an integral part of the systemic principle.[86] Yet it is not clear that it is so recognized by most other authorities. There are several responsa of well-known authorities that indicate that the assumption of a necessary connection between the proviso and the systemic principle is, at best, a matter of dispute.

According to rabbinic enactment, a nursing mother may not remarry within twenty-four months of the birth of her child. If she does, she must separate from her husband for the remainder of that time, though she need not be divorced. Rabbi Isaac ben Sheshet Perfet (Ribash, 1326–

85. Eruvin 7:6.

86. *Kelalei ha-Gemara,* appended to *Halikhot Olam* by Rabbi Jeshu'a b. Joseph ha-Levi (Venice, 1639), p. 114b.

1408) was asked whether such a woman might live in the same *mavoi*[87] as her husband during the period of separation.[88] He responded that she should not be allowed to do so. He compared the case of the unmarried nursing mother to a case of a previously divorced woman who married a priest. The latter had to be divorced by her priest-husband,[89] and was not allowed to live in the same *mavoi* as he did. One might claim, said Perfet, that the law concerning the priest and his wife should be stringent (forbidding them to live in the same *mavoi*) because the marriage had taken place in violation of a norm *de-oraita,* while the law concerning the unmarried nursing mother should be lenient (allowing her and her husband to live in the *mavoi* during their separation) because the marriage had taken place in violation merely of a norm *de-rabbanan.* Yet, asserts Perfet, that distinction does not obtain because *Kol de-takkun rabbanan ke-ein de-oraita takkun.* Since the prohibition against a nursing mother's remarriage within twenty-four months of the birth of the child cannot be traced to the Torah in any way, it follows that the Ribash did not accept the proviso as integral to the application of the systemic principle.

In response to a query concerning the obligation of women to hear the reading of the Scroll of Esther, which is a time-bound rabbinic *miẓvah (miẓvah de-rabbanan she ha-zeman geramah),* Rabbi Solomon ben Simon Duran (Rashbash, 1400–1467) answered that they are exempt.[90] He supported his view with the contention that the sages made no distinction between *miẓvot de-rabbanan* and *miẓvot de-oraita* in terms of obligation or exemption of women. Thus, since women are exempt from time-bound *miẓvot de-oraita,* they are also exempt from time-bound *miẓvot de-rabbanan.* And since the obligation to hear the reading of the Scroll of Esther is a time-bound *miẓvah de-rabbanan,* women are exempt from that obligation.[91] The grounds for his position: *Kol de-takkun rabbanan ke-ein de-oraita takkun.* Since the rabbinic obligation to hear the reading of Esther cannot be traced to the Torah in any way, it follows that in this instance, too, the qualification was not considered (this time by the Rashbash) to be a necessary part of the systemic principle.

Similarly, the Tosafot affirm that women are exempt from the recita-

87. See above, n. 63.

88. *Responsa of Ribash* (Jerusalem, 1968 [5728]), no. 360, p. 99c.

89. See above, n. 67.

90. *Responsa of Rashbash* (Jerusalem: Sh. Monzon Offset, 1968 [5728]), no. 452, p. 87d. See below, n. 91.

91. In fact, the Rashbash affirms that women are obligated to hear the Book of Esther, but not because the principle does not apply. Rather, their obligation stems from the fact that they were participants in and affected by miracle (*af hen hayu be-oto ha-nes*). See also Tosafot Pesaḥim, 108b, s.v. *she-af.*

tion of *Hallel*, although its recitation is *de-rabbanan*, on the basis that they are exempt from positive time-bound commandments, both *de-oraita* and *de-rabbanan*.[92] Since the obligation to recite the *Hallel* cannot be traced to the Torah either, this constitutes another instance in which the proviso was not considered to be an integral part of the systemic principle.

Clearly, if the proviso is applied, it restricts the scope of the principle significantly, and lends greater weight to the principle that affirms that, as a general rule, matters *de-rabbanan* are less weighty than matters *de-oraita*. If the proviso is not taken as integral to the systemic principle, the right of the sages to strengthen their own enactments to the point where they are equal to those of the Torah is greatly enhanced. In no place, however, do the sources reveal the criteria according to which one should decide which of the two conflicting systemic principles applies in any given case. There seems to be no inherent reason why greater leniency was shown in the matters *de-rabbanan* discussed above[93] than was shown in these last three examples.[94]

Several factors lead one to conclude, finally, that the proviso is not integral to the systemic principle. First is the failure of the Talmud itself to mention it in any but one case,[95] and second is the fact that the responsa literature does not list it as a guiding principle to follow in rendering legal opinions. Even its inclusion in the *Kelalei ha-Gemara* of Caro does not constitute overwhelming evidence of its importance. Since the Talmud is not basically a work of legal theory, it is only to be expected that *any* purely theoretical statements that do exist would be included in a genre of literature (to which *Kelalei ha-Gemara* belongs) designed to abstract talmudic theory. Moreover, there is evidence from other of Caro's writings that he himself did not apply the proviso assiduously.[96]

---

92. Berakhot 20b, s.v. *bi-tefillah*. See also Tosafot Pesaḥim, 108b, s.v. *she-af*.

93. Pp. 25–28.

94. There is, in addition, one source which adds a further restriction to the application of the principle *Kol de-takkun rabbanan ke-ein de-oraita takkun*. Elijah Mavorakh Galipapa (Rhodes, d. 1749) claims, in his work *Yedei Eliyahu* (Constantinople, 1728), enactment 92, that it is his opinion that the principle could be applied only to enactments of *tanna'im*, but not to enactments of *amora'im*. This restriction is adopted by Malachi b. Jacob ha-Cohen (Italy, d. 1785–90) in his book *Yad Malakhi* (Berlin, 1852), letter *kaf*, no. 331. No earlier authority adopts this position.

95. It should be remembered, however, that all other explicit occurrences of the principle are, indeed, instances in which the subject matter can be traced somehow to the Torah itself. See above, p. 36.

96. See below, p. 45. If the principle *Kol de-takkun rabbanan ke-ein de-oraita takkun* applies only to matters *de-it le-hu ikkar min ha-Torah*, surely the same could be claimed about the systemic principle *Ḥakhamim asu ḥizzuk le-divreihem yoter mi-shel Torah*. Yet Caro applies this latter principle to a subject about which he states explicitly *ve-ein lah semakh ba-Torah*.

An interesting subcategory of the principle *Kol de-takkun rabbanan ke-ein de-oraita takkun* is reflected in the question of the legitimacy of coercion for positive *miẓvot de-rabbanan.* According to the Talmud,[97] it is permissible for the court to compel compliance with positive commandments.[98] According to Rashi, the principle applies only to positive *miẓvot de-oraita,*[99] but the Tosafot affirm the application of the principle to positive *miẓvot de-rabbanan* as well.[100] Thus, according to Rashi, the matter of compulsion with regard to positive commandments accords with the general tendency of matters *de-rabbanan* to be disposed of less strictly than matters *de-oraita.* According to the Tosafot, however, the systemic principle *Kol de-takken rabbanan ke-ein de-oraita takkun* applies, as well, to coercion.[101]

If one operative systemic principle indicates that rabbinic matters may be decided less stringently than matters *de-oraita,* and another principle indicates that they may be decided equally as stringently as matters *de-oraita,* there exists only one other logically possible principle that can govern the relationship between the two categories of *miẓvot:* the principle that rabbinic matters should be dealt with *more* stringently than matters *de-oraita.* This principle, too, is widely reflected in rabbinic literature, and is worded: *Ḥakhamim asu ḥizzuk le-divreihem yoter mi-shel Torah* ("the sages strengthened their words more than the Torah"). Nevertheless, while the existence of the principle is theoretically logical, pragmatically it is problematic. Even if the need for strengthening rabbinic legislation is granted, it does not seem reasonable to maintain that the sages should be empowered to reinforce their own enactments through the imposition of stringencies unknown in the Torah. This apparently led the Tosafot to maintain that the principle really means that, in certain cases, the sages strengthened their own words more than the Torah strengthened its own words.[102] That is, they did not arrogate to themselves the right to impose limitations and restrictions foreign to the Torah, but in certain cases, they allowed themselves to impose legitimate and Torah-like restrictions on their enactments which,

97. Ketubbot 86a, Zevaḥim 132b.

98. The principle does not apply to negative commandments, since the appropriate time for coercion would be after the transgression had already taken place, when it is already too late.

99. Rashi, Ketubbot 91b, s.v. *miẓvah.*

100. Tosafot, Ketubbot 86a, s.v. *peri'at* (end).

101. As is generally the case, later legalists are also divided on the issue. In this case, most side with the Tosafot. For a full treatment of the issue, see *Sedei Ḥemed* (New York: Kehot Publishers, 1949), letter *kaf,* principle no. 39, 3:110–112.

102. Tosafot Zevaḥim 101a, s.v. *ḥakhamim.* See also R. Jonah on the *Alfasi,* Berakhot, p. 10a.

in similar cases, the Torah itself did not impose on *its* own enactments. Thus, the Tosafot understood the wording of the principle to be shorthand for *Ḥakhamim asu ḥizzuk le-divreihem yoter mi-mah she-asetah Torah li-devarehah* ("the sages strengthened their words more than the Torah strengthened its words"). Moreover, although the Tosafot do not do so, the problematic wording of the principle *Ḥakhamim asu ḥizzuk le-divreihem yoter mi-shel Torah* could have been explained both as a literary parallel and as a literary contrast to the formulation of the principle *Ḥakhamim asu ḥizzuk le-divreihem ke-shel* ("equal to") *Torah*. Whatever the reason for the problematic *wording* of the principle, the *explanation* of the Tosafot is not only reasonable but, as examples of the application of the principle will demonstrate, undoubtedly correct. Therefore, it is this meaning that is implied throughout this discussion.

The principle is explicitly applied only five times in the Babylonian Talmud. Of these five, two are indicative not only of the meaning and use of the principle itself, but also of the total absence of criteria that can determine where and when the conflicting principles we have been discussing should be applied.

1. The Talmud records that Rav forbade carrying in or across a domain which, were it between two domains defined *de-oraita*, would have been permitted.[103] Being, however, between two domains defined only *de-rabbanan*, he forbade carrying therein. The Talmud explains the stringency as: *Ḥakhamim asu ḥizzuk le-divreihem yoter mi-shel Torah*.

2. The Mishnah stipulates that a priest who is an *onen*[104] should not receive any portion of consecrated foods, even if the food is to be eaten at night.[105] Since the idea that the status of *onen* is operative at night is only *de-rabbanan*, but *de-oraita* the status of *onen* is not operative at night, we may ask why he cannot receive consecrated portions for use at night. The answer given is: *Ḥakhamim asu ḥizzuk le-divreihem yoter mi-shel Torah*.

3. Rabbi Yehuda maintains that *Matneh al mah she-katuv ba-Torah be-davar she-be-mamon tena'o kayyam* ("one may validly stipulate something contrary to the Torah in monetary matters"), and also that the institution of the *ketubbah* (marriage contract) is *de-rabbanan*. Nonetheless, he invalidates[106] a husband-imposed condition that his wife affirm that she has received partial payment of her marriage contract, even though she has,

103. Eruvin 77a and 85b.

104. I.e., one of whose relatives has died that day. The status of *onen* applies *de-oraita* only on the day of death. However, it applies *de-rabbanan* for that night as well, even if the burial had already taken place; also, it applies *de-rabbanan* until the time of the burial, if that takes place after the day of the death. Cf. the case of an *onen* and the offering of the paschal lamb, Mishnah Pesaḥim 8:6.

105. Zevaḥim 12:1, 100b.

106. Ketubbot 56a.

in fact, received none.[107] If this condition were to be considered valid, it would create a legal fiction that would enable the husband to pay less for a marriage contract than the allowable minimum. This view of Rabbi Yehuda's is puzzling, indeed, since he permits stipulations concerning monetary matters contrary even to the Torah itself, and therefore it would seem logical that a stipulation in monetary matters contrary to rabbinic dictates (in this case, the institution of the *ketubbah)* would be judged valid. His grounds for disallowing a *tenai be-davar she-be-mamon* here, however, is that since the *ketubbah* is *de-rabbanan,* the systemic principle *Ḥakhamim asu ḥizzuk le-divreihem yoter mi-shel Torah* applies.[108] It follows logically that had Rabbi Yehuda held the position that the *ketubbah* is *de-oraita,* he would have affirmed his position that a stipulation concerning monetary matters is valid, and would have allowed the document to be written for a sum less than the allowable minimum, since the requirement for *ḥizzuk* would be absent.

The preceding three examples have demonstrated the use of the principle *Ḥakhamim asu ḥizzuk le-divreihem yoter mi-shel Torah.* The following two examples will also be examples of the use of this principle. One of them will, however, also utilize the principle indicating the general tendency toward leniency in matters *de-rabbanan;* the other will also utilize the principle *Ḥakhamim asu ḥizzuk le-divreihem ke-shel Torah.* Indeed, these examples will invoke these two principles in such a way as to buttress our contention that there are no criteria that can determine where and when the conflicting principles should be applied.

The Talmud[109] presents several possible distinctions between two cases that are comparable, except for the fact that one is *de-oraita* and the other is *de-rabbanan.* The first case (a) is that of a man who contracts a Levirate marriage with his sister-in-law in apparent compliance with the law (Deuteronomy 25:5–10). In reality, however, the woman was preg-

107. I.e., if the marriage contract is *written* for an amount less than the allowable minimum. See Me'iri's *Beit ha-Beḥirah,* ed. Abraham Schreiber (Jerusalem: Mercaz, 1947), and the commentary of Ritba and others *ad loc.*

108. It should be noted that Rabbi Yehuda's objection is not to the right of the woman to forgo a portion of the marriage contract to which she is entitled. Rather, it is to the fact that in the case described, the rabbinic requirement of a certain minimum sum would apparently be overridden, *and so indicated in writing* in the *ketubbah,* which would stipulate a sum lower than the minimum. He does permit the legal fiction to be created if the marriage contract stipulates the allowable minimum and the woman writes a receipt for a part thereof or affirms orally that she has received a part thereof. Since, in that case, the rabbinically ordained minimum has not been overridden *in theory,* as indicated by its stipulation in the marriage contract, he allows the application of his position that *be-davar she-be-mamon tena'o kayyam.*

109. Yevamot 36b.

nant by her first husband at the time the levirate marriage was consummated. If the child is not viable, the *mishnah* allows them to remain married, but Rabbi Eli'ezer insists that *yoẓi be-get* (he send her away by writing her a bill of divorce). This view of Rabbi Eli'ezer is a penalty imposed upon the brother of the first husband because he contracted a relationship that could have turned out to be forbidden *de-oraita (paga be-eshet aḥ).*

The second case (b) is that of a man who married a woman who was pregnant by her previous husband at the time of the new marriage. According to a rabbinic enactment, a man may not marry a pregnant or nursing woman within twenty-four months of the birth of the child. In case (b), Rabbi Me'ir maintains *Yoẓi ve-lo yaḥazir olamit* (i.e., he must divorce her with a bill of divorce, and in addition, relinquish any right to remarry her even after the twenty-four month period has elapsed).

The two cases are exactly parallel, except that the prohibition in (a) is *de-oraita,* and in (b), *de-rabbanan. Prima facie,* therefore, it would seem plausible that Rabbi Eli'ezer and Rabbi Me'ir would agree with each other in these cases. Yet the Talmud offers two hypotheses indicating a possible disagreement. According to one hypothesis, Rabbi Me'ir would affirm his own position in (b) on the grounds that *Ḥakhamim asu ḥizzuk le-divreihem yoter mi-shel Torah.* In (a), however, he would agree with the view of the *mishnah* and allow them to remain married. Since the prohibition involved would have been *de-oraita* and would not require *ḥizzuk,* the imposition of a penalty on the man is unnecessary. According to the second hypothesis, Rabbi Eli'ezer would affirm his own position in (a), while disagreeing with Rabbi Me'ir in (b). His disagreement would be based on the premise that since the prohibition in (b) is only *de-rabbanan,* which matters are generally treated more leniently than matters *de-oraita,* it is necessary to separate temporarily (i.e., until the end of the twenty-four months), but not to be divorced. In fact, this is exactly the position of the sages who disagree with Rabbi Me'ir.

Since the Talmud voices no objection to the application either of the principle dictating the leniency of matters *de-rabbanan* or of the principle *Ḥakhamim asu ḥizzuk le-divreihem yoter mi-shel Torah,* it follows, clearly, that the application of either principle to either of these two cases would have been theoretically legitimate. It is also clear that there are no objective criteria on the basis of which to decide which of the conflicting systemic principles to apply in a particular case.

The final explicit reference to the systemic principle *Ḥakhamim asu ḥizzuk le-divreihem yoter mi-shel Torah* deals with a husband's right to inherit from his wife. Rabban Simon b. Gamli'el affirms that a man inherits from his wife, regardless of any stipulation he may have made, at any time, in which he disclaimed his rights, present and future, to her possessions and usufruct thereof.[110] The grounds for Rabban Simon's view are that such a stipulation is invalid because it is contrary to the Torah. Rav claims that the law is, indeed, according to Rabban Simon b. Gamli'el, but not for the reason that he claims. In attempting to determine the precise difference between Rabban Simon and Rav, the Talmud offers two hypotheses that bear on the systemic principles under discussion. According to the first hypothesis, the difference between them lies in the following: Rabban Simon holds the position that a husband's right to inherit from his wife is *de-oraita,* and since he affirms that *Matneh al mah she-katuv ba-Torah tena'o batel* ("any stipulation that one makes that is contrary to the Torah is invalid"), his stipulation was invalid; whereas Rav holds that *Matneh al mah she-katuv ba-Torah tena'o kayyam* ("one can make a valid stipulation contrary to the Torah"), and also that a husband's right to inherit is *de-rabbanan.* If so, why is the husband's stipulation invalid according to Rav? Because *Ḥakhamim asu ḥizzuk le-divreihem yoter mi-shel Torah.* This hypothesis is rejected by the Talmud, which proposes an alternative theory, to wit: Rabban Simon holds as described above, and Rav agrees that *Matneh al mah she-katuv ba-Torah tena'o batel* ("any stipulation that one makes that is contrary to the Torah is invalid"), implying, however, that *bi-de-rabbanan tena'o kayyam* ("in a matter *de-rabbanan* the stipulation is valid"). Since Rav maintains that the husband's right to inherit from his wife is *de-rabbanan,* the question again arises as to why he affirms that the husband's stipulation is invalid. This time, in answer, the Talmud explains: *Ḥakhamim asu ḥizzuk le-divreihem ke-shel Torah.*

It is essential to note again that each time the Talmud rejects a hypothesis, it never implies that the systemic principle upon which the hypothesis is based is not applicable, but, rather, it implies that its choice is based upon other factors. One cannot say, therefore, that there is something inherent in the nature of the last case that permits only one of the two systemic principles to apply to it. In fact, the opposite seems to be true, namely, that there are no objective criteria that dictate the use of any of the applicable systemic principles in any given case.

This lack compelled later scholars to seek various explanations for the various choices made by their predecessors. Thus, for example, the Tosafot explain that in matters of penalty *(kenasa)* the sages applied the principle *Ḥakhamim asu ḥizzuk le-divreihem yoter mi-shel Torah;* in matters of prohibition *(issura)* they applied the principle *Ḥakhamim asu ḥizzuk le-divreihem ke-shel Torah,* and in monetary matters *(mamona),* the sages did

110. Ketubbot 83b–84a.

not strengthen their position at all.[111] Interestingly, however, Rabbi Yom Tov ben Abraham Ishbili (Ritba, ca. 1250–1330) attributes the same degree of strengthening on the part of the sages with regard to the category of *issura* ("prohibition") as did the Tosafot to the category of *kenasa* ("penalty").[112] It seems clear that explanations of this sort must be considered *ad hoc* attempts to objectify the nonobjectifiable. At most they can be credited with making reasonable sense of some of the applications of a given systemic principle, but in no way do they explain all the applications of the given principle. No further proof of this situation is required other than examination of those cases to which the Talmud itself applies the principle *Ḥakhamim asu ḥizzuk le-divreihem yoter mi-shel Torah,* in order to ascertain whether the category of *kenasa* applies to them.

A more logical way to proceed would be that, in the absence of objective criteria, there should be great hesitancy in applying the systemic principle except in those cases where the Talmud itself applies it. This, in fact, is the position of Malakhi-ha-Cohen in *Yad Malakhi,*[113] Ja'ir Ḥayyim Bacharach (author of *Ḥavot Ya'ir,* 1638–1702) in *Sefer Ḥut ha-Shani,*[114] and Ḥayyim Joseph David Azulai (Ḥidah, 1724–1806) in *Ya'ir Ozen.*[115] Azulai, however, adds that to the best of his recollection, not all the legalists agree to this restriction. One example will suffice to demonstrate that Azulai is correct. Joseph Caro, in dealing with the matter of rowing on Yom Kippur, writes: "The prohibition is *mi-de-rabbanan* and has no basis in the Torah, yet they did not allow it because *Ḥakhamim asu ḥizzuk le-divreihem yoter mi-shel Torah.*"[116] He clearly applies the principle to this case even though it is not explicitly mentioned as applicable anywhere in the Talmud.

At this point it is possible to state a few preliminary conclusions about the halakhic process. The first is that the firm and undisputable *grundnorm* of the system posits the existence of a category of norms called *de-oraita,* the inevitable corollary of which is the existence of a category of norms not *de-oraita,* that is, a category of norms *de-rabbanan.* Yet we must also conclude that the only thing about these two categories that is not subject to dispute is the fact that they exist. To which of the two categories any given norm should be assigned can be a matter of

111. Ketubbot 55b, s.v. *ha.*
112. Ritba to Yevamot 36b, s.v. *ad kan.* Cf. Rashba, Yevamot 36b.
113. No. 287.
114. No. 18, p. 21a.
115. Letter ḥet, no. 15.
116. *Beit Yosef* to *Tur, Oraḥ Ḥayyim* 613.

considerable dispute, as indicated by the widely different positions held by Maimonides and Naḥmanides on this issue. Moreover, we have learned that it is not necessary to the functioning of the halakhic system that there be a definite number of legal norms that must be classified as *de-oraita*. The traditional number for such norms, 613, is at best either a historical source (and therefore legally insignificant) or a non-normative aggadic statement.

We have seen, in addition, that the proper categorization of a given norm may have far-reaching consequences, depending upon which of the systemic principles that govern the two categories is applied in a given case. The categorization of a norm as *de-rabbanan* might result (a) in a more lenient application of that norm than if it were classified as *de-oraita;* or (b) in applying the norm in exactly the same way that it would be if it were classified as *de-oraita;* or (c) in a stricter application of the norm than if it were classified as *de-oraita*. But although we have been unable, thus far, to discover any objective criteria on the basis of which to determine which of the available systemic principles should be invoked with regard to any given norm, it is nevertheless clear that the halakhic process has built-in directives aimed at strengthening the authority of secondary (rabbinic) legislation as needed, and that clearly indicate that secondary legislation cannot be blithely ignored or abrogated.

Up to this point, the systemic principles that have been discussed pertain directly only to the category *de-rabbanan*, and to the category *de-oraita* only by implication. Concerning the category *de-oraita* in its own right, it seems possible to say (with some hesitancy, to be explained shortly) that clear and unambiguous statements of the Torah itself should be so categorized. This is not to say that other norms may not also be categorized as *de-oraita*, but only that their categorization as such might not be undisputed.

Since the terms *clear* and *unambiguous* are themselves undefined abstractions, further discussion is in order. That *melakhah* ("labor") is forbidden on the Sabbath seems undisputably *de-oraita*.[117] That the thirty-nine basic categories of *melakhah*[118] are also *de-oraita* is not undisputable, since the Torah itself does not define the term *melakhah*. That a written document is required to effect a divorce seems undisputably *de-oraita*.[119] That only a husband may divorce his wife, but not a wife her husband, is not undisputably *de-oraita*, since one can point out cases

117. Exodus 19:10.
118. Mishnah Shabbat 7:2.
119. Deuteronomy 24:1. Note the masculine forms of the verbs *ve-natan* and *ve-khatav*.

within the Torah in which the masculine is not interpreted to apply to men alone.[120] That animals that have a cloven hoof and chew their cud are *kasher* seems undisputably *de-oraita.*[121] That the specific characteristics that render such an animal *terefah* are *de-oraita* is not undisputable.[122] In each of these examples, the only claim being made is that these matters are disputable, not that they are not, in fact, considered *de-oraita* by many legalists.

The hesitancy to which I alluded earlier about the terms *clear* and *unambiguous* arises from the fact, for example, that while the right of the court to impose a punishment of forty lashes seems undisputably *de-oraita,*[123] the sages, as a matter of fact, restricted the right to thirty-nine lashes.[124] The implication is either that forty lashes is not *de-oraita* or that the sages are empowered somehow to amend or abrogate matters that are *de-oraita.*[125] The issue will be discussed at length later, but it should be noted now that since the *peshat* of a biblical verse (i.e., its meaning within the socioeconomic-historical milieu in which it was written) must be considered a historical source of the system rather than a legal source, it follows that the *peshat* of a verse is also not necessarily *de-oraita.*

It should be stressed again, however, that in many, if not the vast majority of cases, the category to which any given norm is assigned may be an irrelevant legal consideration. In the absence of any consideration that would call for leniency (e.g., great financial loss, or a man's honor), indeed, in the absence of any specific motivation, either for leniency or for severity, to apply any of the systemic principles we have examined to a given norm, it is not at all essential that the actual category of the norm be determined. All that remains essential in such a case is the recognition that, theoretically, if its proper category became an important consideration, the norm could be categorized. Thus, for example, in the absence of any reason for applying any one of the possible systemic principles to the norm that requires the wearing of phylacteries, the question of whether that norm is *de-oraita* or *de-rabbanan* is insignificant.

---

120. See Bava Kama 15a and Tosafot ad loc., s.v. *ḥishvah.* Or cf. the statement of the *baraita* (Shabbat 62a, Nedarim 55b): *Ha-ro'in yoẓe'in be-sakkin, ve-lo ha-ro'in bilvad ameru ella kol adam, ella she-darkan shel ro'in laẓet be-sakkin* ("shepherds may go out [on the Sabbath] in sackcloth, and not only shepherds, but everyone, but shepherds normally go out in sackcloth"). In Nedarim the conclusion reads: *ella she-dibberu ḥakhamim ba-hoveh* ("but the sages spoke of the common").

121. Leviticus 11:3.

122. In Ḥulin itself (42a) they are defined as *Halakhah le-Mosheh mi-Sinai* (see Rashi ad loc., s.v. *shemoneh esreh).* That category is, at least according to Maimonides (see above n. 25), *de-rabbanan,* and not *de-oraita.*

123. Deuteronomy 25:3.

124. Mishnah Makkot 3:10, 22a.

125. Cf. Rava's statement in Makkot 22b, in n. 5 above.

Only if there were some reason to apply one of the principles we have been discussing in this chapter to the norm requiring the wearing of phylacteries would the actual category of the obligation to wear phylacteries become significant.

Finally, then, to the list of possible areas of dispute that may lie at the source of a disagreement between legal scholars (see p. 12), we may now add many more: whether the norm concerning which there is dispute is *de-oraita* or *de-rabbanan;* whether it is a norm to which should be applied one of the systemic principles governing that category of *mizvot;* and if so, which of the possible systemic principles that are theoretically applicable ought to be applied in this specific case. In all of these areas, as we have seen, there can be wide disagreement between the recognized authorities of the system, with no resultant vitiation of the system, since the system itself allows such divergencies to coexist.

Chapter Three

Some Aspects of Decision-Making

The process of legal decision-making involves the judge or arbiter in questions of two types, questions of law and questions of fact, each of which must be understood in two different senses.[1]

In its first sense, a question of law is one which the arbiter "is bound to answer in accordance with a rule of law—a question which the law itself has authoritatively answered" (p. 66). In this sense, a question of law is one concerning which the law is absolutely clear and unambiguous, and concerning which it is equally clear that it is dealt with by the rule of law, "to the exclusion of the right of the court [arbiter] to answer the question as it [he] thinks fit in accordance with what is considered to be the truth and justice of the matter" (p. 66). That is, a question of law in the first sense is one about which there is absolute certainty concerning the applicability of the specific rule of law, a certainty that compels the arbiter to decide according to its dictates, regardless of any other consideration. Thus, a question about the *kashrut* of an animal that has been bludgeoned to death is a question of law in this sense. The rule of law that requires ritual slaughter is clear and unambiguous, and the *kashrut* of the animal in question is clearly dealt with by the rule of law,

1. Much of the material for the first portion of this chapter is based upon *Salmond on Jurisprudence*, 12th ed., by P. J. Fitzgerald (London: Sweet and Maxwell, 1966), pp. 65–75. Direct quotations from that work will be indicated by quotations marks and parenthetical page references, but not by separate footnotes. Salmond includes a third sense that is not applicable to an analysis of the halakhic system (p. 67).

and no consideration of the arbiter can be considered decisive in declaring the animal *kasher* in the absence of compliance with the rule of law.

A question of fact in the first sense is any question that is not a question of law in the first sense, i.e., any question that "has not been predetermined and authoritatively answered by the law" (p. 66). There can be no question of fact about a question of law in the first sense. The *kashrut* of a newly discovered species of fowl would be a question of fact in the first sense, since the question would not have been predetermined by the law. That no fish without fins and scales can be considered *kasher* is a matter of law in the first sense.[2] Whether a swordfish has fins and scales is a question of fact in the first sense, since it is a question that has not been authoritatively answered by the law. In addition, all questions of fact in the second sense (as yet undefined) are also questions of fact in the first sense.

A question of law in this first sense, then, is, by definition, a question about which a rule of law addresses itself clearly and unambiguously;[3] it is a question about which there can be no legitimate controversy concerning the correct answer.

A question of fact in the first sense, on the other hand, does allow for legitimate controversy, insofar as it is, by definition, a question that has not been authoritatively answered by a rule of law. Both the examples of questions of fact in the first sense just given have, indeed, been matters of legitimate controversy.[4]

In its second sense, "a question of law is a question as to what the law is" (p. 66). If, in its first sense, a question of law is predicated on a clear and unambiguous rule of law which offers a definitive answer to the matter in question, a question of law in its second sense arises out of uncertainty about the meaning of the rule of law. That is, questions of law in the second sense are predicated on rules of law that are *not* totally clear and unambiguous, but whose meanings are open to doubt. The doubt may center around imprecisely defined terms or provisions that

2. Leviticus 11:9, and assuming that the terms *senappir* and *kaskeset* there mean "fins" and "scales." If, in fact, the meaning of these terms were legally ambiguous, the question would be one of law in the second sense.

3. This, of course, does not necessarily imply that such rules of law cannot be amended or abrogated. The matter of amendment or abrogation might involve one in the area of concern of the preceding chapter insofar as it might be important to determine whether a given rule of law is *de-oraita* or *de-rabbanan*. Other aspects of the process of abrogation or amendment will be dealt with later.

4. Yom Tov Lippman Heller (1579–1654) declared turkey not to be *kasher*, against the opinion of most others. In more modern times, Rabbi Isaac Klein declared swordfish *kasher* in his analysis of that question of fact.

are insufficiently detailed. That the Jewish legal system recognizes a category of people called *mamzerim,* and contains a provision concerning them, viz., *Lo yavo bi-kehal ha-shem,*[5] cannot be gainsaid. The Torah, however, contains no precise definition of the term *mamzer,* nor any unambiguous statement that would authoritatively explain the meaning of the provision *Lo yavo bi-kehal ha–shem.*[6] Thus, when the issue first arose, it was a question of law in the second sense, i.e., "a question as to what the law is" (p. 66).[7] Actually, questions of this sort are, at one and the same time, questions of law in the second sense and questions of fact in the first sense. "If the whole law could be definitely ascertained, there would be no questions of law in this [second] sense; but all questions to be answered in accordance with the law would still be questions of law in the former [first] sense" (pp. 66–67).

Regarding questions of law in this sense, "the business of the court [arbiter] is to determine what, in its own judgment and in fact, is the true meaning of the words used by the legislature [legislation]" (p. 67). Thus, the arbiter plays an active role in the determination of the law regarding questions of law in the second sense, while he has no such function regarding questions of law in the first sense. Moreover, once the judgment of the arbiter becomes a factor in the determination of the law, absolute objectivity becomes improbable, and perhaps impossible.

When a question of law in the second sense has been authoritatively answered, either by judicial determination or by whatever method the legal system allows for authoritative decisions, it ceases to be a question of law in the second sense and becomes a matter of law in the first sense. Future questions which clearly fall within the purview of the rule of law, as now authoritatively defined, must be answered in accordance with that rule of law "to the exclusion of the right of the court [arbiter] to answer the question as it [he] thinks fit in accordance with what is considered to be the truth and justice of the matter" (p. 66), since both "truth" and "justice" have been authoritatively determined. If the term *mamzer* has been authoritatively defined, clearly and unambiguously, by

---

5. Deuteronomy 23:3.

6. Part of the ambiguity of the provision *Lo yavo bi-kehal ha-shem,* of course, lies in the ambiguity of *yavo* and *kehal ha-shem* themselves.

7. Caution: Reading the clause "when the issue first arose" to imply a time significantly later than the time of the promulgation of the law itself is only a possible reading, not a necessary one. It is theoretically conceivable that this question of law was dealt with on the abstract level (i.e., not arising out of an actual case) at the time of the promulgation of the law. Questions of law of this nature are often given as proofs of the extreme antiquity of the Oral Law. See, for example, H. Albeck, *Mavo la-Mishnah* (Tel Aviv: Devir, 1958), pp. 3–24. A viable legal system would have had to have confronted such questions of law at an early stage.

the halakhic system (according to whatever means it allows for such decisions), and if the meaning of the provision *Lo yavo bi-kehal ha-shem* has been equally authoritatively determined, the arbiter has no legal option but to apply the provision in any case when the person involved in the question is included in the category of *mamzer.* At that point, the arbiter is no longer involved in the determination of the law, but only in its application.

The meaning of question of fact in the second sense of the term is "any question except a question as to what the law is" (p. 68). Anything that is a question of fact in the second sense is also a question of fact in the first sense. The examples of questions of fact in the first sense listed above[8] could be either questions of law in the second sense or questions of fact in the second sense, depending on the nature of the problem. If it were clear, for example, that swordfish possess both fins and scales, but unclear whether the law accounts scales that fall off as the fish matures as meeting the legal requirement of scales, the *kashrut* of swordfish would be a question of law in the second sense and of fact in the first sense. If, on the other hand, the legal meaning of scales were clear, but the very existence or nature of the scales of swordfish were the issue, it would be a question of fact in the second sense as well as in the first.

"There is, however, a narrower and more specific sense, in which the expression question of fact does not include all questions that are not questions of law, but only some of them. In this sense a question of fact is opposed to a question of judicial discretion. The sphere of judicial discretion includes all questions as to what is right, just, equitable, or reasonable—so far as not predetermined by authoritative rules of law but committed to the *liberum arbitrium* of the courts [arbiters]" (p. 68). Questions of fact in this restricted sense, which is closest to the common use of the term, are those questions "seeking to ascertain the truth of the matter" (p. 69). The determination of the existence of fins and scales on swordfish would be such a question of fact. Ascertaining whether a criminal act of which one stands accused was witnessed by two witnesses would be such a question of fact. In this sense, then, "matters of fact are capable of proof, and are the subject of evidence adduced for that purpose. Matters of right and judicial discretion are not the subject of evidence and demonstration, but of argument, and are submitted to the reason and conscience of the court [arbiter]"(p. 68).

One further distinction concerning questions of fact must be borne in mind, viz., the difference between primary and secondary facts. "Pri-

8. P. 50.

mary facts are proved by oral, documentary and other evidence; secondary facts can be inferred from primary facts" (p. 70). That businessman X stood in the doorway of his place of business brandishing a rifle is established primarily by the oral testimony of eyewitnesses; that this act indicated his refusal to allow a certain class of people access to the premises of his place of business is an inference from the primary fact, i.e., a secondary fact. The importance of the distinction lies in the relative importance that is attached to the opinions of two different arbiters who might be involved in a matter at different times. The arbiter before whom the evidence establishing the primary facts was offered is clearly in a stronger position vis-à-vis those facts than any other arbiter. The same, however, cannot be said regarding the inferences to be drawn from the primary facts, i.e., the secondary facts. Concerning these latter facts, since they are inferred, a second arbiter is in no weaker a position than the original arbiter.

It is logical that, to the degree that a legal system seeks to become increasingly definitive, its development "represents the transformation, to a greater or less extent, of questions of fact and of judicial discretion into questions of law, by the establishment of authoritative and predetermined answers to these questions" (p. 71). The more restricted the number of matters that are questions of fact or matters of judicial discretion, the more definitive the system, and the fewer the chances for arbitrariness or judicial capriciousness.

On the basis of this hypothesis, it follows that the closer one gets to the beginning of a legal system, the greater are the number of questions of fact and matters of judicial discretion to be found within the system. If, in its earliest formulation, for example, the system forbids the act of murder, but gives an insufficiently clear definition of the act, then whether or not the act that is commonly called "manslaughter" today should be considered "murder" is a question of fact in the first sense (and also a question of law in the second sense). With the development of the system, however, the term *murder* comes to be defined with enough precision to transpose the above question from one of fact to one of law in the first sense. Verification of the act itself as having taken place remains a question of fact in the second sense. The imposition of a penalty might or might not be a matter of judicial discretion. If the system defines the parameters of legitimate punishment (e.g., execution, imprisonment, or parole), but does not define its imposition specifically, the matter of punishment is one of judicial discretion, to be exercised by the arbiter as he deems right and appropriate, within the sanctioned parameters. If, however, the system prescribes a specific punishment for the act (e.g., mandatory execution or mandatory life imprisonment), the matter of punishment is no longer a matter of judicial discretion, but a question of law in the first sense.

Within the developing system, the sphere in which the transposition of matters from the realm of fact to the realm of law primarily takes place is in the sphere of judicial discretion. But there are occasions when "even questions of pure fact are similarly transposed into questions of law" (p. 72). This phenomenon takes place primarily in the institution of legal presumptions, "whereby one fact is recognized by law as sufficient proof of another fact, whether it is in truth sufficient for that purpose or not" (p. 73). Thus, for example, within the halakhic system, a non-Jewish girl above the age of three is presumed not to be a virgin.[9] Legal presumptions themselves are of two sorts. The first calls for the inference of one fact from another, "even though this inference could be proved to be false" (p. 73). The example above is such a presumption, as would be the presumption *Ḥazakah ein adam oseh be'ilato be'ilat zenut* ("it is presumed that a man does not engage in intercourse promiscuously")[10] or the presumption *Ḥazakah ein adam tore'aḥ bi-se'udah u-mafsidah* ("it is presumed that no man would go to the trouble of arranging a festive meal for naught").[11] In presumptions of this sort, facts are totally irrelevant to the matter of law, except insofar as the primary fact (i.e., that the girl is non-Jewish and above the age of three, that an act of intercourse has taken place, or that a festive meal was held) must be substantiated. Presumptions of the second kind require an inference "even though there is no sufficient evidence to support it, provided only that there is no sufficient evidence to establish the contrary inference" (p. 73). The classical example of this type of presumption is the presumption of the innocence of the accused unless he is proven guilty, that is, the accused is assumed to be innocent even in the absence of sufficient proof of innocence, so long as the prosecution cannot provide sufficient evidence of his guilt. In presumptions of this sort, facts are

---

9. Attention ought to be drawn here again to the distinction between legal and historical sources of law. Theoretically, one might trace the legal origin of this presumption back to the era in which it was not a question of law at all, but one of fact. Once it has been transformed from fact into law, by a means acceptable to the system, it becomes a legal source. Though historical sources may have led to its incorporation into the system as a legal presumption, they themselves are legally insignificant. Thus, for example, it would be legally irrelevant that its incorporation into the system as a legal presumption was predicated on a reflection (whether true or untrue) of the sexual mores of non-Jews, or predicated on the hatred of Jews for non-Jews. See Kiddushin 78a, and Rashi and Ritba ad loc.

10. Yevamot 107a, et al.

11. Ketubbot 10a, Kiddushin 45b.

important to rebut, but not to establish, the presumption. Thus, in the institution of legal presumptions, questions of fact in the second sense (as well as the first sense) become matters of law in the first sense.

There is yet one further institution in which questions of fact are transposed into matters of law, regardless of actual truth or fact, and that is the institution of legal fictions. The utilization of legal fictions was more common to older legal systems than it is to modern systems, and was particularly prevalent in systems that were rigidly opposed to change. A legal fiction is a deliberate departure "from the truth of things" (p. 73). Adoption is a legal fiction in that the "adoptive child who is not in fact the child of its adopting parent, is deemed to be such" (p. 74). The institution of the *eruv teḥumin* is a legal fiction which affirms that one's domicile for the Sabbath is legally at some place other than its actual location.[12]

While it is surely the case that legal systems tend to restrict the number of questions of fact or judicial discretion by transforming them into matters of law, it is possible for matters that have already become matters of law in the first sense to revert to an earlier stage. Thus, for example, the abolition of a mandatory sentence for a given offense results in the reversion of a matter of law to a matter of judicial discretion. Similarly, the abrogation of a legal presumption results in the reversion of a matter of law to a question of fact. For example, the redefinition of the term *harmful drugs* to exclude marijuana, when, in fact, it was formerly included in that term as a matter of law in the first sense, results in the reversion of a matter of law in the first sense to a question of law in the second sense.[13]

Thus far we have dealt primarily with general definitions of relevant terms and with the phenomenon of the possible transposition of matters of law and fact from one category to another, and we have given brief examples from the halakhic system as well as from other systems. To the end of this chapter are appended several more examples from halakhic literature, each followed by an analysis of the processes used. These examples indicate both the applicability of the general terms and the applicability of the process of transposing matters from one category to another to the halakhic system.

One of the things which distinguishes the halakhic system from other systems, at least after the dissolution of its supreme court, the Sanhed-

12. See above, chap. 2, n. 35.

13. These examples consist of *legal statements,* and do not deal with the *reasons* which may motivate arbiters to transform questions of law into questions of fact or judicial discretion. That subject will be dealt with later.

rin, is the absence of a universally recognized body or individual possessing the authority to transform questions of fact or judicial discretion into matters of law in the first sense. This is not meant to imply that the process has ceased, but only that such transformations are not as definitive as they are in other systems. All of the systemic principles used by the Talmud itself to resolve disputes between sages or schools[14] are themselves no more than the result of the elevation of matters of judicial discretion to matters of law in the first sense. Yet, as we shall soon see, even though these principles are presented as if they were matters of law in the first sense there is still implied a range of judicial discretion within the halakhic system which is generally broader than in other systems. Furthermore, questions of law in the second sense about which there is a legitimate controversy,[15] and concerning which there is no clear consensus elevating one of the positions to a question of law in the first sense, remain matters of judicial discretion. That is, they are "questions as to what is right, just, equitable, or reasonable—so far as not predetermined by authoritative rules of law" (p. 68). The arbiter remains free to determine the law in accordance with any of the legitimate positions, and his decision constitutes his legitimate exercise of judicial discretion. Should a different arbiter render a different decision, both decisions would be legitimate and valid, reflecting only different perceptions of "what is right, just, equitable, or reasonable" under the circumstances. The later decision does not negate the validity of the earlier decision. It is, indeed, the exercise of this legitimate judicial discretion that is taking place when modern arbiters *(posekim)* render conflicting decisions on questions of law in the second sense, each supporting his own position by quoting earlier authorities whose views seem to coincide with his own.[16]

That this broad definition of judicial discretion is not only defensible within the halakhic tradition, but perhaps even too conservative, is clearly demonstrable. Following are two readings of the fifth *mishnah* in Eduyyot, chapter 1. The printed version reads:

---

14. For example, that the law follows the School of Hillel except in specified cases; or that the law is according to Rava, as opposed to Abayee, except in six specific cases; or that the law is according to R. Akiva or R. Yosé when either disagrees with one other sage, but according to the majority when either disagrees with more than one.

15. I.e., such that none of the positions can be legally demonstrated to be untenable or false. In talmudic parlance, a *maḥaloket* ("disagreement") which, upon analysis, does not result in a *teyuvta* ("refutation").

16. The question of his right to ignore all of the positions in favor of one of his own, or to ignore the consensus favoring one position that may have developed, will be discussed further on.

> Why is the minority opinion recorded together with the majority opinion, since the law is according to the majority? It is recorded so that if some court favors the minority opinion and decides in accordance therewith *(ve-yismokh alav)*, no other court may overturn the decision of the earlier court [i.e., the court that adopted the minority opinion], except if it is greater than the earlier court in wisdom and number.[17]

This is the reading of the *mishnah* to which Maimonides clearly refers, for he explains:

> The intent of this *mishnah* is that when some court establishes a precedent in accordance with the minority view, no other court may disagree and determine the law according to the majority opinion, save if it be greater in number than the court that has already established the precedent according to the minority opinion, and greater than it in wisdom.[18]

According to this reading, then, the subject of concern in this *mishnah* is the right of a later court to overturn the decision of the earlier court favoring a minority position. The *mishnah,* however, does not question the right of the earlier court to establish such a precedent on the basis of its legitimate exercise of judicial discretion, even though that exercise involved ignoring the systemic principle that ostensibly dictates that the law ought to follow the majority. The *mishnah* implies, therefore, that an arbiter has an indisputable right to exercise his judicial discretion in a matter of legitimate disagreement. This is so even in a case where this right had, apparently, been limited by a wide consensus that had transformed the precedent-setting decision into a matter of law in the first sense. In other words, the transformation of a matter of judicial discretion into a matter of law in the first sense is valuable as a guide for the arbiter, but does not necessarily predetermine his decision.[19]

The variant reading of the *mishnah* follows:

---

17. The meaning of the phrase "greater than the earlier in wisdom and number" is a matter of considerable dispute, but not relevant to this point.

18. *Commentary to the Mishnah* (found in the printed editions of the Babylonian Talmud), Eduyyot 1:5.

19. Not discussed in this context, admittedly, are the grounds on the basis of which the precedent-setting court ignored the guidance of the systemic principle and opted for the minority opinion. We shall turn to that subject at a later point.

> Why is the minority opinion recorded together with the majority opinion, since the law is according to the majority? It is recorded so that if some court favors the minority opinion, it may base itself upon it *(yismokh alav)*; since no court may overturn the decision of another unless the latter is greater than the former both in wisdom and number.[20]

The interpretation of Rabbi Abraham ben David (Ravad II, 1125–1198) indicates clearly that he had this reading.[21] Understanding his discussion, however, requires that the version of the Tosefta be quoted.[22] The Tosefta reads:

> The law always follows the majority. The minority position is mentioned together with the majority position only to indicate that it is unacceptable *(levattelan)*. Rabbi Judah claims that the minority position is mentioned together with the majority position so that if the circumstances *(sha'ah)* should require it [i.e., the minority opinion], they [i.e., later arbiters] may base themselves upon it.

The Ravad offers a two-pronged interpretation of the Tosefta.

> The language of the Tosefta, "so that if the circumstances should require it, they may base themselves upon it," implies, apparently, that the latter court may not base its decision upon the minority opinion except in a time of dire need—for no court may overturn the decision, etc. I.e., even in time of dire need, the latter court would not have been empowered to permit that which the earlier court had forbidden, were it not for the fact that the minority opinion [which itself disagreed with the majority opinion] had been recorded, since no court may overturn an earlier decision, etc.
>
> *But it is also possible* to claim that the reason [for the inclusion of the minority opinion] of the Tosefta is independent [i.e., not an explanation of the *mishnah*, but a disagreement with it]. And the reason of the *mishnah* is independent, implying that if a latter court feels that the law ought to be in accordance with the earlier minority view, it may base itself upon it. That is to say, the latter court may determine the law in accordance with the minority position, as we

20. Found in the Parma manuscript, De Rossi 138; Cambridge (Loew) manuscript; and as we shall soon see, in R. Abraham ben David. See also *Melekhet Shelomo* (in standard editions of the Mishnah), ad loc.

21. His interpretation is found in the printed editions of the Babylonian Talmud.

22. Eduyyot 1:4.

> find, in fact, in a number of places that *amora'im* [who are later] determine the law in accordance with earlier minority opinions, even though those opinions were disagreed with by the majority. But if the latter had not found the earlier minority opinions, they could not have decided on their own to override (lidḥot) the earlier opinion, since no court may overturn, etc. However, since they could find the early minority opinion which disagreed with the majority, they had a basis on which to make their judgment—and this is the reason [for the inclusion of the minority opinion] according to the *mishnah* [in disagreement with the Tosefta]. And the reason of the Tosefta is independent, as we have explained above. And this latter explanation is primary *(ve-zeh ikar)*.

Both of the explanations of Abraham ben David affirm the right of later arbiters to exercise legitimate judicial discretion even in the face of a systemic principle which apparently sought to remove those matters from the realm of judicial discretion to the realm of matters of law in the first sense. The first explanation restricts the legitimate exercise of judicial discretion to circumstances of "dire need," a term not easily defined. The second, however, is a very liberal interpretation of the right of arbiters to exercise judicial discretion. It permits the exercise of judicial discretion whenever there is a legitimate *maḥaloket* ("disagreement"). If there are sufficient reasons of right, justice, equity, or reasonableness to sway the arbiter to the minority position, the exercise of judicial discretion, even in opposition to the systemic principle which favors the majority, is legitimate.

The Me'iri, in his commentary to Eduyyot, adopts the second position of Abraham ben David.[23] "If, occasionally, some court of importance favors the view of the minority and establishes a precedent according to that position, they are so entitled." Finally, Rabbi Samson of Sens (late 12th–early 13th cent.), in his commentary to Eduyyot, adopts Abraham ben David's second position and adds the following comment:

> Even though the minority opinion was not accepted in the earlier time, and the majority did not agree with it, when the later generation arises and its majority agrees with the minority position, the law ought to be as they say, for the entire Torah was given to Moses with valid arguments for declaring unclean and valid arguments for declaring pure.[24]

23. *Beit ha-Beḥirah on Horayot and Eduyyot*, ed. A. Sofer (Jerusalem: Kedem, 1976), p. 180.
24. See above, n. 21.

Thus, clearly, whichever reading of this *mishnah* is correct, the weight of opinion favors a broad interpretation of the concept of judicial discretion. In addition, interestingly, the quotations above indicate how wide the range of judicial discretion is, extending even to the possibility of ignoring the systemic principle that dictates that the law follows the majority *(yaḥid ve-rabbim halakhah ke-rabbim)*, which, of all of the systemic principles that are able to transform matters of judicial discretion to matters of law in the first sense, is the only one defined by some as *de-oraita*.[25]

It seems accurate, therefore, to understand the term *maḥaloket* as the existence of differing but equally legitimate positions whose existence can constitute the grounds for the legitimate exercise of judicial discretion. A critical realm with regard to the exercise of judicial discretion within the halakhic system, therefore, would be in a *maḥaloket* concerning the proper categorization of a rule of law as *de-oraita* or *de-rabbanan*. Each arbiter would, for example, determine for himself the proper category to which he would assign the rule of law in question by means of the exercise of his judicial discretion, each basing himself upon the *maḥaloket* of Maimonides and Naḥmanides regarding the categorization of rules of law deduced by means of the commonly accepted exegetical principles. Since the differing views of Maimonides and Naḥmanides constitute a legitimate *maḥaloket*, differing decisions of later arbiters about a given rule of law would also reflect nothing more nor less than the legitimate exercise of the judicial discretion of each of them. In addition, the choice of which of the systemic principles that govern the relationship between matters *de-oraita* and *de-rabbanan* to apply in a given case would most often also be a matter of judicial discretion, since, as has been demonstrated in the previous chapter, there are no objective criteria that govern this application. Thus, in the absence of clear agreement by the vast majority of *posekim* about which particular systemic principle should govern a particular rule of law *de-rabbanan* in relationship to relevant rules of law *de-oraita*, each of three different arbiters could legitimately conclude that it is right and reasonable that

---

25. See *Talmudic Encyclopedia* (Hebrew) (Jerusalem: Talmudic Encyclopedia Publishers, 1959), 9:255–318. These principles which transform matters of judicial discretion into matters of law in the first sense by predetermining whose view should be decisive in any given dispute among sages—but which are themselves a matter of dispute—are themselves, therefore, matters of judicial discretion. Such principles serve as indicators of consensus or precedent, but are not definitive systemically. See Tosafot, Kiddushin 62b, s.v. *ve-amar Rabbi Ḥaninah*, and *The Responsa of Rabbi Isaiah the Elder*, ed. Rabbi A. J. Wertheimer (Jerusalem: Institute for the Complete Israeli Talmud, 1967 [5727]), responsum 1 (6), p. 48.

the law in question should be governed by a different one of the three possible systemic principles discussed above (chap. 2). Moreover, each of these differing positions would reflect no more nor less than the legitimate exercise of judicial discretion.

One implication of the right of different arbiters to exercise judicial discretion as they see fit is that divergent behaviors, not only divergent theoretical positions, are systemically legitimate within the halakhic system. And this, too, is clearly demonstrable from the traditional sources. In the interpretation of an interesting play on words, based on Deuteronomy 14:1, in which *titgodedo* is construed as *aguddot* ("factions"), causing the verse to mean "you should not create factions," Abayee and Rava give different explanations of factionalism.[26] Abayee contends that the prohibition against creating factions applies to two courts in the same locale, one deciding, for example, according to the School of Shammai, and the other according to the School of Hillel. If, however, the two courts were in two different locales, divergent behaviors would be legitimate. In objection, Rava maintains that the example of Beth Hillel and Beth Shammai is the equivalent of two courts in the same locale. Thus, if Abayee were correct, the divergent behaviors which resulted from their disagreements should be considered as the creation of factions, and that is surely not the case. Rava, therefore, explains that the prohibition against creating factions applies only to one and the same court in one locale, i.e., half of the arbiters deciding according to the School of Shammai, and the other half according to the School of Hillel. Two different courts, however, even within the same locale, are legitimately entitled to render different decisions, based upon their right of judicial discretion, although those differing decisions will result in different behaviors within the same locale.

The Meiri decides in favor of Rava's position,[27] as do most of the *posekim*, adding as a rationale that "it is impossible that they should all always agree with one position."

The impression often exists, and not only among laymen, that if one could but plumb the sources to their depths, there is no question to which *the halakhah* cannot provide its *definitive* answer.[28] Indeed, halakhic decisions, particularly in modern responsa, often appear to be composed primarily of statements of law in the first sense. Yet, upon analysis, it turns out that the arbiter has elevated a question that is in

---

26. Yevamot 14a.

27. *Beit ha-Beḥirah on Yevamot*, ed. Samuel Dikman (Jerusalem: Institute for the Complete Israeli Talmud, 1963 [5722]), p. 63.

28. See below, p. 95, the opinion of the sage quoted by R. Zeraḥi'ah ha-Levi.

reality a question of law in the second sense, fact, or judicial discretion to the plane of statement of law in the first sense. The phenomenon is clearly understandable, since the arbiter is not duty-bound to explicate in infinite detail either his understanding of the questions of fact involved or the fact that he has exercised his legitimate right of judicial discretion by accepting one or another position regarding a question of law in the second sense. We have seen how a system which, by historical accident or design, lacks an organ for the definitive elevation of matters to the level of matters of law in the first sense retains an extraordinarily wide range of areas for the exercise of judicial discretion. Moreover, the exercise of that discretion by any given arbiter in no way restricts the right of other arbiters to exercise their equally legitimate right to arrive at different conclusions.

The most far-reaching statement of this right can be found in Maimonides. He writes: "The High Court which has deduced something as it deems appropriate on the basis of recognized exegesis, and acted accordingly; yet a later court perceives some reason for overturning that decision—the later court may do so, and may determine the law as it sees fit."[29] The purpose of exegesis is to clarify the meaning of the law or to determine the law in cases for which the law does not provide a predetermined answer, i.e., to answer questions of law in the second sense and, apparently, transform them into statements of law in the first sense. Yet, claims Maimonides, such a transformation, even when carried out by the High Court [i.e., the most authoritative], does not constitute an irrevocable predetermination of the law for the future. Nor is it essential, according to Maimonides, that the overturning of the High Court's decision be predicated on the existence of a *maḥaloket* on the exegesis. Maimonides' declaration, therefore, amounts to the claim that questions of law in the second sense are never definitively elevated to matters of law in the first sense, but remain open to reconsideration by later courts on the basis of whatever considerations the later court deems appropriate.[30]

This far-reaching statement by Maimonides is apparently at variance with the systemic principle that later scholars *(amora'im)* are not at liberty to disagree with earlier scholars *(tanna'im)*. That is, it is at variance with the principle that declares that the statement of the earlier scholars predetermine the law in all identical cases which may arise in the future (assuming the absence of a *maḥaloket* among the *tanna'im*). R. Joseph Caro notes the problem and offers a solution, as follows:

---

29. *Mishneh Torah*, Hilkhot Mamrim 2:1.

30. Maimonides distinguishes between laws deduced by exegesis and those based upon rabbinic *takkanot* or *gezerot*.

> If you wonder, therefore, why the *amora'im* do not disagree explicitly with the *tanna'im*, as they clearly do not, as indicated by the frequent objections raised to the views of *amora'im* by the quotations of tannaitic statements [implying that any clearly demonstrable contradiction by the *amora'im* of the universally held tannaitic view would invalidate the *amora's* position because it contradicts a matter of law in the first sense], but must be able to substantiate the legitimacy of their position by claiming that they are in agreement with some *tanna* [i.e., that the tannaitic position is not universal, and therefore, not a question of law in the first sense], or else the quotation from the *tanna* constitutes a refutation *(kashya)* of his position, when according to our teacher [Maimonides] they are entitled to disagree with the positions of *tanna'im* [i.e., even universal tannaitic traditions]? It is possible to answer that from the compilation of the Mishnah on, they [i.e., the post-tannaitic sages] accepted upon themselves the principle that later generations may not disagree with former generations. And thus, too, after the compilation of the Gemara, such that after its completion no man is entitled to disagree with it.[31]

Careful reading of Caro's statement indicates that there is no theoretical disagreement between him and Maimonides. Caro grants that questions of law in the second sense are never definitively elevated to matters of law in the first sense. The fact that *amora'im* do not disagree with universal tannaitic statements or that later generations do not disagree with an undisputed statement of the Gemara is because later generations have chosen, by unspoken agreement, not to exercise their legal right. Yet, it should be noted, even Caro does not restrict the realm of judicial discretion of later arbiters when a given matter is one of *maḥaloket* among the earlier arbiters. One could clearly deduce from his statement that later arbiters could adopt one of the legitimate positions of a *maḥaloket* among the *amora'im,* in the same way that the *amora'im* could opt for the view of one of the positions of a *maḥaloket* among the *tanna'im.*[32]

---

31. *Kesef Mishneh* to *Mishneh Torah,* Hilkhot Mamrim 2:1.

32. Assuming that Caro's answer is systemically accurate, it would be theoretically possible for later generations to abrogate the transformation of those matters to questions of law in the first sense by application of the systemic principle *Hem ameru ve-hem ameru* (see above, p. 28) and cause, thereby, their reversion to questions of law in the second sense, to which Maimonides' theoretical statement would apply.

Though we have asserted above that the appearance of halakhic decisions as composed primarily of statements of law in the first sense is an understandable phenomenon, it must now be clear that viewing halakhic statements in their proper categories, as statements of law or of fact or of judicial discretion, sheds an entirely different light on the nature of the decision-making process. If should now be clear, for example, that a proposal for the modification or the abrogation of an apparently definitive answer to a question, which answer is based upon considerations *other* than matters of law in the first sense, cannot be equated with a similar proposal for the modification or abrogation of an answer that is based upon considerations of matters of law in the first sense.

Furthermore, the importance of proper categorization of legal statements is not restricted to matters of law in the second sense that appear to be matters of law in the first sense. Proper categorization is equally important for matters of fact that appear to be matters of law in the first sense. For, while it is the case that legal presumptions enjoin one to deduce one fact from another even in the absence of proof, or, at least, in the absence of contrary proof, it does not mean that their acceptance systemically was not originally predicated upon a factual or reasonable basis. That is, presumptions (contrary to legal fictions) did not originate as deliberate departures from facts. It is possible, therefore, to reopen the question of the factualness or reasonableness of a legal presumption, assigning it either to that category of presumption in which proof to the contrary constitutes rebuttal or to questions of fact. The legal contention would be that the factualness or reasonableness of the presumption is no longer sufficiently clear to warrant the assumption of one fact on the basis of another. That the reason for the present lack of clarity may lie in changed social or economic conditions, for example, would be legally incidental, although, consciously or unconsciously, it may influence the arbiter of the necessity for a reexamination of the factualness or reasonableness of the presumption.

One example from the Middle Ages will demonstrate that such a process has actually taken place. The law presumed that a wife would not have the audacity to lie about her husband in his presence, particularly if the matter of the lie was one about which he would know the truth.[33] If one affirms the presumption, it would follow that a woman who claimed in her husband's presence that he could not achieve an

33. *Ḥazakah ein ishah me'izzah panehah bifenei ba'alah* ("there is a presumption that a woman would not be audacious in the presence of her husband") (Nedarim 91a). Thus, she would not lie, claiming that her husband had divorced her when he had not. She might however, lie about the strength of his ejaculations *(yoreh ke-ḥeẓ)*, since he himself could not be certain (see Nedarim 90b).

erection would have been believed, since it was presumed that she would not have the audacity to lie about it. Yet no less an authority than Rabbi Me'ir ben Baruch of Rothenburg questioned whether the presumption ought not to be reexamined with regard to its factualness and reasonableness. In one of his responsa, concerning just that issue, he claims:[34] "In these times *(dorot)*, when there are lewd women *(peruẓot)*,[35] it is not appropriate (*ein ra'ui*) to believe her."

Rabbi Me'ir of Rothenburg questioned the factualness of the presumption. That his doubt concerning its factualness is based on a sociological reality which he considered different from that of the period in which the presumption was promulgated provides historical insight into the factors that motivated the reopening of the question, but is legally insignificant except insofar as its truth will buttress or rebut the contention that the presumption should no longer be allowed as legally decisive. In Chapter 9 we shall deal extensively with the nexus between historical and legal sources, and in that discussion we shall again quote this responsum of Rabbi Me'ir of Rothenburg.

Thus far we have discussed the importance of the proper categorization—as matters of law in the second sense—of legal statements that appear in the responsa as though they were already clear matters of law in the first sense, as well as the proper categorization of matters of fact that have been elevated in the responsa to matters of law in the first sense. Finally, we must now stress that even matters of law that are *in fact* matters of law in the first sense are not all cut from the same cloth. There are matters of law in the first sense that have always been matters of law in the first sense. Biblical verses, for example, that are linguistically clear, unambiguous, and definitive are generally and always have been matters of law in the first sense. Most matters of law in the first sense, however, have not always been so; rather, they were elevated to that status from their original status of questions of law in the second sense. Nor are even these all identical, for the process of their elevation is a crucial factor in distinguishing between them. If they were transformed into matters of law in the first sense by a process of purely philological exegesis,[36] that is, by a philologically sound explanation of an ambiguous word or phrase in the norm, an explanation of the *peshat*

34. *Responsa of R. Me'ir of Rothenburg* (Crimona, 1557; offset ed. Jerusalem, 1969), no. 271.

35. Variant reading from *Darkei Mosheh* to *Tur, Even ha-Ezer* 154:8: "audacious and strong-willed" *(ḥaẓufot ve-azzot)*.

36. For example, the process by which *na*, regarding the paschal lamb (Exodus 12:9), comes to be defined as "rare." See *Mekhilta, Bo, parashah* 6, Horovitz-Rabin ed. (Jerusalem: Bamberger and Wahrman, 1960), p. 20.

("actual meaning") of the word or phrase, they are definitive matters of law in the first sense. Similarly, if the question of law in the second sense was transformed into a matter of law in the first sense by a process of exegesis which, though not strictly purely philological, nevertheless reflects universal consensus,[37] the legal implication would be that the question so transformed has become a definitive matter of law in the first sense.

If, however, that which determined the transformation of the question of law in the second sense was merely a majority consensus of opinion favoring one view over one or more other views in an area of judicial discretion, the definitiveness of the transformation would be more open to question. And even this kind of transformation can take place under several different kinds of circumstances. It can result, for example, from the adoption of one position by a majority of *posekim* in the exercise of their judicial discretion, that is, by the proliferation of precedents favoring one opinion, even in the absence of any systemic principle that would suggest that particular choice above any other. It could result, on the other hand, from applying a systemic principle that restricts the realm of judicial discretion (e.g., *Halakhah ki-setam mishnah*, "the law follows the view of an anonymous *mishnah*") but which systemic principle is itself a matter of judicial discretion, that is, one concerning which there is a *maḥaloket*. In this case, of course, the weight of precedent favors applying the systemic principle, which itself undoubtedly became a systemic principle as a result of the former process.[38] That which would govern the arbiter's decision to ignore either the majority consensus or the systemic principle would be the grounds that permit either overturning or ignoring precedent (a subject we will examine later).

The above is not meant to imply that change is impossible in those questions of law in the first sense that are based upon philological exegesis or that reflect universal consensus, but only that such change would be governed by the systemic principles that deal with definitive matters of law (another subject to be examined later). However, since any matter of law in the first sense concerning which the question of modification or abrogation arises must, by definition, be either *de-oraita* or *de-rabbanan*, it is axiomatic that the systemic principles that govern the

---

37. Acceptance, for example, of the term *peri eẓ hadar* ("the fruit of a lovely tree" or "the lovely fruit of a tree") (Leviticus 23:40) as meaning *etrog* ("citron") (*Sifra, Emor,* chap. 16:4); or of *le-ot al yadekha* ("a sign upon your hand") and *le-totafot bein einekha* ("frontlets between your eyes") (Deuteronomy 6:8), as referring to *tefillin* (phylacteries), *Sifre Deuteronomy, piska* 35:8, L. Finkelstein ed. [New York: Jewish Theological Seminary of America, 1969], p. 63.

38. See above, no. 25.

relationship between the two categories will be relevant to the discussion (see the discussion in Chapter 2).

Appendix

As indicated in the text of the chapter, these appendices are intended to demonstrate how the concepts we have been discussing apply to the halakhic system. Each selection is followed by analysis in terms of those concepts. It should be stressed that these analyses are not exhaustive, merely demonstrative. The selections have been chosen to reflect the different genres of rabbinic literature: classical, medieval, and modern. Every effort has been made to select relatively noncomplex matters, so that the demonstration of the concepts is not lost in a labyrinth of explanations.

1. *Mishnah Berakhot 1:1*

> When may one begin to recite the *Shema* in the evening? From the time when the priests enter to eat their *terumah* [consecrated foods] until the end of the first watch [of the night], according to R. Eli'ezer; but the sages say, until midnight. Rabban Gamli'el says, until the morning star arises.

This passage reflects a *maḥaloket* about a question of law in the second sense. That question seeks to clarify the insufficiently detailed provisions of the law requiring the evening recitation of the *Shema*, namely, its *termini*. The passage assumes the obligation to recite the *Shema* as a matter of law in the first sense. Interestingly, the first section of *gemara* that follows this *mishnah* asks, in essence, for some indication of the legitimacy of this question of law, i.e., for the articulation of the unclear or ambiguous norm that the *mishnah* presupposes through an answer to a question of law in the second sense. The *gemara* asks: "What was the *tanna* referring to that prompted him to ask the question, 'When may one . . . ?' . . . He was referring to the phrase [Deuteronomy 6:7]: '. . . when you lie down and when you rise up.' " The key word in the *gemara*, which indicates the ambiguity being addressed in the *mishnah*, is *be-shokhbekha* ("when you lie down"). The *mishnah* assumes *be-shokhbekha* to imply an obligation to recite the *Shema* in the evening,[39] but is in doubt

39. N.B. It does not prove that the word means "an obligation to recite the *Shema*." In theory, therefore, one could argue that even the obligation to recite the *Shema* in the evening is a question of law in the second sense.

concerning the temporal parameters of the time "when you lie down."[40]

The *mishnah*'s treatment of the *terminus a quo* records no *maḥaloket*. Its definition of that *terminus* as "the time when the priests enter to eat their *terumah*" provides, therefore, a definitive answer to this question of law in the second sense, and transforms it into a matter of law in the first sense. This assumes, of course, that the time defined by the phrase "when the priests enter to eat their *terumah*" is clear. Obviously, it must have been clear to those who promulgated the definition, but it may not be clear to their successors. Thus, if it were, indeed, the case that the time defined by the phrase were a matter of *maḥaloket* to the successors, or if the meaning of the words themselves had become unclear and ambiguous, the determination of the meaning of the phrase would involve either a question of judicial discretion or a question of law in the second sense. Assume, theoretically, that a *maḥaloket* existed between a view that equated "the time when the priests enter to eat their *terumah*" with the appearance of the stars and another view that defined it as sunset. Assume further that the weight of opinion favored the first view, but that it had never been systemically transformed into a matter of law in the first sense, and had remained a matter of judicial discretion. A statement by an arbiter that the *terminus a quo* for the recitation of the evening *Shema* was the appearance of the stars, without careful explanation of how he arrived at that decision, might give the false impression that his statement was as much a matter of law in the first sense as the norm it sought to clarify, namely, the obligation to recite the *Shema* in the evening.

Regarding the *terminus ad quem*, the legal source does not provide a definitive answer. Thus, this question of law in the second sense is not transformed into a matter of law in the first sense. Assuming that each of the positions stated in our *mishnah* is legitimate (i.e., not subject to clear refutation on the basis of matters of law in the first sense), the determination of that *terminus* remains a matter of judicial discretion. This is not to say that, in its later development, the halakhic system did not particularly favor one of these opinions around which a majority consensus or the weight of precedent centered, but only that it was never definitively elevated to a matter of law in the first sense. Thus, in the absence of a careful delineation of the opinions he rejects as well as those he accepts, the arbiter is again running the risk of implying that the question is one of law in the first sense, when, in fact, it is one of judicial discretion.

---

40. The possibility that *be-shokhbekha* ("when you lie down") also implies physical position at the time of recitation is dealt with in the Mishnah and Gemara in another place.

The various positions regarding the *terminus ad quem* may themselves contain ambiguities. Thus, for example, R. Eli'ezer's position depends upon whether he considers the night to be divided into three or four watches.[41] This is a question of fact in the second (as well as the first) sense. If his position can be deduced from documentary evidence, for example, that fact is a primary fact, which ought to compel two different arbiters to reach the same factual conclusion concerning his position. If, on the other hand, his view on the question of the number of watches in the night could be deduced only from some oblique reference in another context, even though this reference can be plausibly interpreted to imply his position on the question of fact, it would be a secondary fact, and two different arbiters need not draw the same conclusion. Even if this had been the case, it would have been possible for two arbiters to have differed in the following ways: (1) one could have exercised his judicial discretion in favor of R. Eli'ezer's position on the *terminus ad quem,* and the other could have exercised his judicial discretion in favor of the position of Rabban Gamli'el; (2) both could have ruled in favor of R. Eli'ezer, with one deducing that R. Eli'ezer's position regarding the number of watches in the night was three, and the other deducing that it was four. In that case, the former would have posited the *terminus* at the end of the fourth hour of the night (assuming a twelve-hour night), and the latter would have posited it at the end of the third hour of the night. Thus, the two could have disagreed not only by exercising their right of judicial discretion in favor of different solutions, but also by proposing different resolutions to the question of fact.[42]

2. *Gemara Bavli, Kiddushin 45b*

Introductory Note: It is a matter of law in the first sense that a man may betroth his minor daughter to whomsoever he sees fit.[43] It is, however, a

41. See Berakhot 3a.

42. The position of the sages brings into focus another factor of the legal system, that is, *sevara* ("reason," or "reasonableness"). This factor will be discussed later, yet it is interesting to note here that the Gemara affirms that the position of the sages is unreasonable (see Berakhot 4a) insofar as their position does not correlate with any plausible definition of the term *be-shokhbekha,* which could reasonably mean either that time span during which people generally adjourn to bed or that time span during which people adjourn to bed and are asleep. The implications concerning the effect of sociological reality, even subconsciously, on legal reasoning are here clearly intimated. Surely no American in the twentieth century would consider the possibility that people might generally adjourn to bed as late as midnight to be an unreasonable position.

43. This matter of law is based, primarily, on the verse in Deuteronomy 22:16. In fact, it may be questionable whether it is really a matter of law in the first sense, but the talmudic passage to be discussed assumes it to be so.

question of law in the second sense whether, if she was betrothed without his knowledge, that betrothal has any legal status (e.g., would it require a writ of divorce for its dissolution?). The source of the doubt lies in the possibility that the father may have acquiesced to the betrothal upon hearing of it (*shemma nitrazzah ha-av ba-kiddushin*), thus giving the betrothal legal status. The question is a matter of *maḥaloket.*

> A man was determined to betroth his daughter to one of his relatives, and his wife was determined that she should be betrothed to one of her relatives. His wife badgered him until he agreed that the daughter would be betrothed to one of her relatives. While [invited guests of both families] were feasting [at a party given in honor of the betrothal, which had not yet taken place], one of his relatives betrothed her in an upper chamber. Abayee said: "It is written, 'The remnant of Israel neither acts corruptly nor speaks lies' [Zephaniah 3:13]." Rava said: "There is a presumption that a man does not labor *(tore'aḥ)* to prepare a feast in vain (*u-mafsidah*)." What is the difference between the views? The difference would be reflected in a case in which no labor of preparation was involved.

Lines 1–7 establish the primary facts of the case, which are ostensibly provable by means of some type of evidence. The implied question of law in the second sense is whether the circumstances of this case are such that the *maḥaloket* concerning the possible legal status of the betrothal based on the father's possible acquiescence to the betrothal by his relative applies (i.e., whether the case involves a matter of judicial discretion between the different positions of the *maḥaloket*), or whether the circumstances of this case are so different from the grounds of that *maḥaloket* that the matter is not one of judicial discretion, but rather one of law in the first sense.

In lines 8–11 two sages answer that the latter is the case, and that there can be no doubt that the act of betrothal that took place in the upper chamber is null and void. Both base their decisions on presumptions of law which, whether factually true or not, are legally valid. Thus, for Abayee, the presumption that Jews do not act deceitfully or lie is sufficient proof of the fact that the father did not acquiesce to the betrothal of his relative, since such acquiescence would imply either that the whole affair had been deceitfully plotted or that he had lied to his wife in agreeing that the daughter would be betrothed to one of her relatives.[44] For Rava, the effort (presumably the physical and financial effort) involved in preparing the party compels one to assume that the father had not acquiesced to the betrothal, based upon the presumption that no man would make such an investment in vain.

The final three lines of the selection indicate clearly the difficulty of determining the nature of a legal presumption. Were it not for the final three lines, there would be few grounds on which to base a determination in this case. Yet the text makes clear that, for Abayee, the presumption he invokes is of the nonrebuttable type as far as he is concerned, since it applies not only in the face of the father's original desire, but also in the absence of the labor of the feast. For Rava, on the other hand, Abayee's presumption is clearly of the rebuttable type.[45]

3. *Iggerot Mosheh (Responsa of Rabbi Moses Feinstein), Yoreh De'ah, no. 139*

Introductory Note: It is common in responsa for the recipient to be addressed in the third person. In the following translation, however, I have used the second person in order to make the responsum more comprehensible.[46]

Concerning a Teaching Position among Conservatives

> Concerning the position which you accepted among the heretics (*ha-koferim*) to be the principal of a Talmud Torah for young boys and girls, concerning which the directors of Yeshivat Beit Yehuda[47] have said that you have not acted appropriately (*lo yafeh asah*): It is the case that even in that manner in which it would be appropriate to accept such a position, that is, that you study with them the Torah of God, and pray properly with them, and in a different place,[48] in which case it would be acceptable to take such a position, since it is necessary to teach

44. Note to what extent Abayee considers the legal presumption to be of the first type of presumption, i.e., the type with regard to which facts are irrelevant. The father's original intention to betroth his daughter to his own relative might otherwise be considered "sufficient evidence to establish the contrary inference" (p. 73).

45. What is left unclear, admittedly, is Abayee's classification of Rava's presumption and Rava's classification of his own presumption.

46. The original text will be found in *Iggerot Mosheh* (New York: Balshon Press, 1959).

47. Evidently, the name of the non-Conservative institution in which the man to whom the responsum is addressed (Mr. Samuel Kaplan) was also employed as a teacher.

48. The continuation of the responsum implies quite clearly that this clause means that the Conservative school is not housed in the Conservative synagogue itself.

Torah also to their [the heretics'] children so that they might grow up to [the observance] of Torah and *mizvot* as fit Jews (*ki-hudim kesherim*), it is nonetheless inappropriate for the directors of the yeshiva to accept such a teacher to teach in the yeshiva as well. For there are grounds to suspect that the students of the yeshiva will think that it is good to teach there [in a Conservative school], for their rabbi is also a rabbi there, and this may result, God forbid, in terrible consequences (*kilkul gadol*). But considering what you have written, that they recite some prayers from an abridged prayer book and not according to the order of the prayer, and also that they do not recite all of the benedictions of the *Amidah,* it turns out that instead of educating them to the *mizvah* of prayer, they are being educated to forbidden acts, for any of the benedictions of the *Amidah* prevent its recitation from being acceptable if omitted (*she-kol birkhot shemoneh esreh me'akkeven zeh et zeh*), and surely so if the benediction itself is not according to the decree of the men of the Great Assembly, and surely if it takes place in that building itself, [under these conditions] it is obviously forbidden to accept such a position even if, occasionally, you might influence a few positively. And surely this is so since, contrarily, there is greater danger that the opposite might happen, for, God forbid, sectarianism (*minut*) is attractive, and you must sever yourself from this sectarian path, see Avodah Zarah 17a.

This entire passage seeks to answer a question of law in the second sense, namely, the permissibility of teaching in a Conservative Talmud Torah. The response, however, consistently confuses matters of law in the first sense with questions of fact, and even with matters of opinion.[49] The respondent clearly implies that if it were not for the "missionary possibilities" inherent in teaching in a Conservative institution, the prohibition would be certain (i.e., a matter of law in the first sense). The question really centers around the positive merits of the "missionary

49. The term *matter of opinion* was not dealt with in the body of this chapter. "Matters of fact" are different from "matters of opinion" in that the former are questions "capable of being answered by way of demonstration" (p. 69), while the latter are questions or matters which "cannot be so answered" (p. 69). "The answer to a question of opinion may be a matter of assessment or evaluation which can neither be proved by evidence *nor determined by law, since the law may not provide criteria for assessment*" (pp. 69–70; emphasis added). Matters calling for such evaluation often fall within the purview of arbiters, and must be recognized as doing so.

possibilities" as opposed to the possible drawbacks. Thus, in lines 5–12, the criteria on the basis of which one could grant permission to teach in such an institution are outlined. The primary fact which complicates the question for the respondent is the other position held by the person involved. Note, however, that the primary grounds for the possible prohibition is that Conservative Jews are heretics. That fact is stated as undisputed and as though it possessed legal, not merely theological, significance. No note is made of the possibility that such a characterization of Conservative Jews is, at best, a *maḥaloket*, and conceivably a matter of opinion.[50]

Systemically, lines 14–17 establish the primary facts that lead to the resolution of the question of law.[51] What is left undiscussed, and what could, in reality, be a source of *maḥaloket* between arbiters, is the question of the probability of the realization of the "suspicion" with its resultant "terrible consequences." And even that question is two-pronged, for two arbiters may agree on the degree of the probability of the "suspicion" becoming a reality, and disagree on the question of the probability of that reality resulting in "terrible consequences." Furthermore, it may be either a matter of judicial discretion or a matter of opinion whether, for example, a fifteen percent chance of "terrible consequences" outweighs a twenty percent chance of positive "missionary possibility." Thus, the inferences drawn from the primary facts are not legally undisputable, and contrary inferences are possible even if one accepts the validity (i.e., the factualness) of the primary facts. The respondent is not oblivious to these problems, however, as indicated in lines 28–33, where he reveals his own opinion that the chance of "missionary success" does not outweigh the dangers of being lured into "sectarian paths." It is unclear, however, whether he intends these

---

50. I would surmise, of course, that Rabbi Feinstein would point to the widespread denial of the Mosaic authorship of the Torah by Conservative Jews and their apparent lack of commitment to *halakhah* as bases for the contention that they are heretics (see, for example, Mishnah Sanhedrin 11:1). I have stated the two together because, I suspect, Rabbi Feinstein would posit a cause-effect relationship between denial of the Mosaic authorship of the Torah and lack of commitment to *halakhah*. Were only the former true, he would probably not consign Conservative Jews to the heretic category—*Halevai oti shakhehu ve-et Torati shameru* ("would that they might forget Me, but observe My Torah"). What he ignores, however, is the possibility that there may be legitimate *maḥaloket* between him and the Conservative movement about the nature of the halakhic process, such that neither he nor they are heretics. One questions not his right to exercise his judicial discretion as he deems appropriate, but, rather, the appropriateness of postulating a question of fact as if it were a matter of law in the first sense.

51. I.e., it is theoretically demonstrable by some type of evidence that "the students of the yeshiva . . . and this may result in terrible consequences."

statements to be understood as demonstrable (primary), thereby compelling the same conclusion by other arbiters; or an expression of opinion, not compelling others to reach the same conclusion.

Suffice it to say, concerning lines 21–27, that a pure matter of opinion (an educational opinion) is being treated as a matter of law in the first sense. The implication of these lines is clearly that the law permits a certain flexibility for the sake of education. The respondent, however, states his opinion on the educational question—of the likelihood of attaining the desired goal of Torah and *mizvah* observance via the use of abridged prayer books with modified wording and omissions—in terms that appear to be legal rather than what they really are, mere opinion. Someone with a different educational perspective might favor a different educational position on the issue, and thus draw a different legal conclusion to the question, no less legitimate than that drawn by this respondent.

4. A. *Mishnah Sanhedrin 4:1, 33b*

In capital cases all may argue for acquittal, but not all may argue for conviction. *Gemara:* "All" implies even the witnesses. Shall we therefore claim that the *mishnah* reflects the view of R. Yosé, the son of R. Yehudah, and not the view of the sages, as implied by the following *baraita:* "No witness may argue against the accused [Numbers 35:30][52] either for acquittal or for conviction. R. Yosé the son of R. Yehudah says, 'He may argue for acquittal but not for conviction.' [Thus "all" in the *mishnah,* as interpreted by the *gemara* to mean "witnesses," follows the view of R. Yosé and not the sages, since it allows the witnesses to argue for acquittal, which the sages would forbid.] Rav Papa claims that the *mishnah* refers to one of the students,[53] and is, therefore, a universal opinion.[54]

B. *Sanhedrin 17a*

Rabbi Abahu says that we create even-numbered courts from the outset in cases where judges are added.[55] Is this not obvious? It is

52. The translation of the verse reflects the way it is being interpreted in the source, not its *peshat*.

53. Who were commonly present in the court or academy when the cases were being tried.

54. I.e., one with which the sages would also agree.

55. I.e., in cases where one of the original judges claims, "I don't know" how to decide or argue this case. In such cases, two additional judges are added to the court, thus creating an even-numbered court. E.g., if eleven judges argue for acquittal, eleven argue for conviction, and one says "I don't know," two additional judges are appointed, bringing the total number of participating judges to twenty-four.

stated explicitly to prevent the claim that the judge who said "I don't know" could still be considered part of the court, such that if he later made a claim he could be listened to. Thus, the explicit statement indicates that the judge who said "I don't know" is considered as though he were not present, and if he presents an argument he is ignored [and is considered as if he were one of the students].[56]

C. *Tosafot Sanhedrin 33b, s.v. eḥad*

[The claim that the word "all" in the *mishnah* refers to students] is puzzling, since the Talmud claims at the end of the first chapter [B above] that if one of the judges says "I don't know," and then expounds some reason, he is ignored, and is considered as no more than one of the students. [I.e., the apparent implication of B being that he is ignored whether he argues for acquittal or conviction, which is defined in B as being "one of the students," thus creating a contradiction between A and B.] But one could claim that there [in B] the reference is to an argument for conviction, and here [in A] to an argument for acquittal [thus eliminating the contradiction between A and B].

D. *Me'iri to Sanhedrin 17a*[57]

Our contention concerning one who has said "I don't know," that he is as though not present, that he is ignored even if he retracts and proffers an argument, for having said "I don't know" is the equivalent of having absented himself, applies only, however, to a retraction followed by an attempt to argue for conviction; but if he argues for acquittal he is surely not ignored, for even concerning one of the students it has been said that he may argue for acquittal, and be brought up to sit with the court that day, although he cannot argue for conviction.[58] [Thus, it is unthinkable that the original judge, whose status is certainly higher than that of a student, should be denied rights equal to those of a student.]

E. *R. Me'ir ha-Levi Abulafia (Ramah) to Sanhedrin 17a*[59]

. . . and the one who had originally claimed "I don't know" later professed a reason for acquittal that did not seem cogent to the other judges. And if we considered him to be part of the court, even though his argument did not seem cogent to the others, he would of necessity

---

56. The bracketed clause is missing both in extant manuscripts and in printed editions of the Talmud. It is added here in order to facilitate the understanding of C, according to which the clause is part of B.

57. Isaac Ralbag, *Beit ha-Beḥirah on Sanhedrin* (Jerusalem, 5731[1971]),p. 50.

58. Mishnah Sanhedrin 5:4, 40a.

59. *Yad Ramah on Sanhedrin* (New York, 5713 [1953]), p. 36.

have to be counted for the vote as well. [Were it not for R. Abahu's statement in B] it might have been claimed that he, indeed, should be counted among the acquitters . . . [but his statement] comes to teach us that he is as though not present, and is not counted. And this is all the more true when he professed an argument for conviction that did not seem cogent to all or most of the other judges. Surely then he is not counted among the convicters, for having said "I don't know," he is discounted from the court and acquires the status of a student. And just as a student is unattended, even when he argues for acquittal, except if his claim has substance . . . this one who claimed "I don't know," too, even though he later argued either for acquittal or for conviction, is ignored if his argument does not seem cogent to the others, and is not counted. Yet there are some legalists who contend that the statement here which claims that he is ignored implies that he is ignored entirely. That even when he presents a cogent argument it is ignored. But they are then faced with the problem of his apparent inferiority even to students . . . and are forced to explain that the reference here is restricted to a case in which he presents a cogent argument for conviction in which, since he had said "I don't know," he becomes as one of the students concerning whom it is taught[60] that if one of the students says he has an argument for conviction, he is silenced.

F. *R. Isaiah d'Trani the Latter (Ri'az)*[61]

Since he said "I don't know," and others had to be appointed in his stead, he is no longer considered as one of the judges and is not counted among them in this case in anything he might say.

G. *Maimonides, Mishneh Torah, Sanhedrin 11:1*

In capital cases all may argue for acquittal, even students, but only the judges may argue for conviction.

H. *Ibid., Testimony 5:8*

Any witness who has testified in a capital case may not render judgment in the case of that accused, and may not argue either in his defense or against him.

I. *Ibid., Sanhedrin 8:2*

In a court of three . . . if one says innocent, one says guilty, and the third says "I don't know," or if two said innocent or guilty and the third said "I

60. See above, n. 58.

61. Jacob Lifshitz, *Kuntres ha-Re'ayot,* in *Sanhedrei Gedolah* (Jerusalem: Harry Fischel Institute, 5732 [1972]), vol. 5, p. 20.

don't know," two judges should be added, thus resulting in five considering the issue.

J. Hassagot ha-Ravad (R. Abraham ben David) to Maimonides' Mishneh Torah, Sanhedrin 8:2

I see from the Talmud that the one who claimed "I don't know" is no longer counted, and is ignored if he offers a reason. Thus, after adding the additional justices, there are only four [considering the case].

K. Maimonides, Mishneh Torah, Sanhedrin 9:2

A capital court which was divided . . . the one who said "I don't know" is as though not present, since he cannot retract and argue for conviction. Thus, after the addition, there are twenty-four judges, beside the one who was doubtful (*zeh she-nistappek*).

This lengthy list of sources demonstrates several things quite clearly about the halakhic process. First, all the sources from B on accept the position of Rav Papa in A. In this, they follow a systemic principle that favors a universal explanation of a *mishnah* above a disputed explanation. This is not to deny, however, that an arbiter could exercise his judicial discretion in favor of the first explanation of the *mishnah* if circumstances so warrant. That is, the question of law in the second sense [the meaning of the word "all"] has not attained the certainty of a matter of law in the first sense.

Even if one accepts Rav Papa's explanation of the *mishnah*, sources C through F, and H through K, indicate that within the halakhic system, as in other systems, questions of law in the second sense may arise out of an apparent inconsistency or contradiction between matters which seem to be of law in the first sense. In this case, it is source B that gives rise to such a question of law, even if one accepts Rav Papa's explanation of the *mishnah* as definitive.[62] The question concerns the status of the judge who has said "I don't know" vis-à-vis his right to retract. B seems to imply that he may not do so under any circumstances (because he is now like a student),[63] while A affirms the right of a student to argue for

62. A further problem that these sources allude to is that of the place of variant readings in the halakhic process. In essence, that is the problem, on one level, of the nexus between critical textual scholarship and the halakhic process. The statement of the Tosafot (C) presupposes a reading in B which equates the judge who says "I don't know" with a student, thus creating the contradiction between A and B. That issue will be discussed in Chapter 11. Our case is only an allusion to the problem, however, because the question is raised even by sources that do not necessarily presuppose the reading of the Tosafot (D and E, for example.)

63. Cf. F.

acquittal. To what degree, then, was the judge who said "I don't know" compared to a student, and how literally was the analogy to a student applied to him?

Sources C and D employ the common process of differentiation, by means of which a distinction is made in the subject matter of the conflicting norms. The distinction resolves the difficulty. Thus, in our case, C and D posit that A deals exclusively with the argument for acquittal, and B with the argument for conviction. That is, B does not, in fact, imply anything about students not already stated in A, which claims that they may argue for acquittal but not for conviction. It should be noted that the language of B does not correlate with the content of C and D as well as the language of A. The fact that the language of one source [in this case, B] does not correlate perfectly with the proposed differentiation [in this case, C and D] is quite common to the process of differentiation, and buttresses again the contention that the legal process is not necessarily to be equated with the *peshat* of a legal statement. While D reaches the same conclusion as C, it should be noted that D is based more on "reason" than on an apparent contradiction between sources.[64] The source quoted by D supports the "reasonableness" of the distinction, but is not the source of the distinction.

Source E eliminates the necessity of introducing the element of argument for conviction alone into B, undoubtedly because Abulafia felt that the language of B could not reasonably bear such an interpretation. Instead, he posits that the comparison of the judge who says "I don't know" to a student is accurate but incomplete, that is, just as the claim of a student must be considered "reasonable" by the justices before it is attended to, so must be the claim of the judge who said "I don't know." The comparison is incomplete, however, insofar as the student may argue only for acquittal, while the "ignored judge" may argue both for acquittal or conviction, if his argument seems cogent to the others. Those who understand the term *ignored* to be independent of cogency are forced to affirm that B refers only to arguments for conviction, contrary to its apparent meaning. Thus, E refrains from forcing the language of B by introducing a heretofore unmentioned element, namely, cogency.[65]

64. This would lead one to believe that the Me'iri did not have the bracketed section of B in his text of the Talmud.

65. Furthermore, Abulafia's contention (ll. 12–14) that the student's argument for acquittal must be considered cogent by the judges, while seemingly based on Mishnah Sanhedrin 5:4, is actually not uncontestable, the language of that *mishnah* being very difficult.

Source F presents both the simplest and the most difficult resolution to the problem. Simplest in its straightforwardness and consistency with the language of B, and the most difficult in its ignoring of the problem posed by A.[66]

Sources G through K are taken from the legal code of Maimonides and a commentary thereon.[67] G and H codify Maimonides' exercise of judicial discretion against the explanation of R. Yosé ben Yehuda, and in favor of Rav Papa in A.

Source I clarifies that for Maimonides, at least in monetary cases, the judge who said "I don't know" remains an active member of the court, with the apparent right to retract, to voice any opinion he sees fit, and be counted for the verdict. Source K puts Maimonides in the camp of C and D regarding the conflict between A and B, in codified form. Note, however, the ambiguity of the final sentence of K regarding the number of judges who apparently have a vote on the case.

Finally, source J reflects R. Abraham ben David's disagreement with Maimonides on the status of the judge who said "I don't know." Bearing in mind that Rabbi Abahu's statement in B is located in a general section dealing with capital cases, but that it is not clear that it is in that specific context that the statement was made, one can clearly see grounds for the disagreement between Maimonides and the Ravad. Maimonides restricts the application of Rabbi Abahu's statement to the context in which it appears, and the Ravad supposes that Rabbi Abahu's statement was intended as a general statement of the status of a judge who claimed "I don't know," and that it is not restricted to the specific context in which it appears. Thus, from all indications, the position of Rabbi Abraham ben David is the same as Rabbi Isaiah d'Trani's position in F.

Even though Maimonides' codified positions do not favor the opinions reflected in E and F, there is no theoretical reason why they should be excluded from the opinions among which an arbiter might choose in the legitimate exercise of his right of judicial discretion. The range of positions among which an arbiter can choose in the exercise of this right is wide indeed, and none can be called illegitimate. One ought not to be

66. This is not to say, however, that his view is indefensible. Clearly, the Ri'az did not have the bracketed clause in B in his Talmud text, or he could not have ignored the problem which it raises. Granting that, however, he can maintain that judges who say "I don't know" and students are totally separate categories, bearing no logical relationship to each other. Thus, the inability of such a judge to retract even for acquittal does not indicate inferiority of status as compared to students, since the categories are not comparable.

67. Since it was impossible to hold trials of capital cases in rabbinic courts during the Middle Ages, Caro is silent on the subject in the *Shulḥan Arukh*. His comments on the subject are limited to his explications of Maimonides in his *Kesef Mishneh*.

misled by the fact that none of the sources in this list (with the exception of E) even intimates that judicial discretion is being exercised by its author. A comparison of sources relevant to any given subject will regularly reveal that the authors are exercising the right of judicial discretion even though the statements appear, on the surface, to be of law in the first sense.

Chapter Four

On Judicial Discretion and Precedent

A legal system that allows its judges and arbiters the range of judicial discretion indicated in the preceding chapter is, by that latitude alone, likely to cause doubt and anxiety for its arbiters in the exercise of that discretion. The number of issues involving the exercise of judicial discretion that may have to be addressed in the resolution of even the simplest question is potentially enormous. When this fact is coupled with the knowledge that the *posekim* of the halakhic system are directed by the feeling that their decisions must reflect not their personal opinion, but the will of God as mediated through their opinion,[1] the sources of tension and anxiety expand to include religious and theological, as well as strictly legal, considerations. When all of the considerations, in turn, are joined to the systemically legitimate principle that later generations are inferior to earlier generations,[2] the number of anxiety-produc-

1. See above, pp. 9–10, and below, chap. 5, for a more detailed discussion of this factor.

2. The most straightforward expression of this idea is found in the Talmud itself: "If the earlier generations (*rishonim*) are as angels, we are as human beings; but if they are as human beings, we are as asses" (Shabbat 112b). Whichever position one adopts, the inferiority of later generations remains the same. Certain of the passages examined in this chapter will illustrate the idea again. It should be noted here that the concept of the superiority of earlier generations is systematically valid even if it may not be true either generally or in specific cases. The fact that halakhic arbiters have perceived it to be true is far more important systemically than its objective verifiability. Obviously, the validity of a claim such as Caro's, that later generations accepted the principle that they could not disagree with former generations (see above, p. 63), is predicated on the assumption that those earlier generations were somehow superior.

ing factors that intrude upon a *posek* is increased even further—particularly if he is actively contemplating a decision at variance with common practice or precedent.

For guidance in the resolution of these complexities, an arbiter will naturally look to the system itself. Is there an established procedure for deciding between conflicting systemic principles? Between the two or more positions of a *maḥaloket?* To what degree is the *posek* bound by precedent? By widespread consensus? By universal consensus? Is there, perhaps, some systemic principle that can itself guide him in dealing with these matters?

Throughout this chapter, the term *precedent* will be used to mean any judicial decision or any statement expressing a legal opinion that can be used as a guide in the determination of future cases. These will include the results of cases already adjudicated,[3] deductions of other arbiters that are based upon the actions of recognized rabbinic sages,[4] and legal opinions rendered in or deduced by others from the theoretical writings of halakhic legalists.[5] To a large extent, we adopt the position that the halakhic system sees "no difference of kind between precedent[6] and any other expression of legal opinion."[7]

In order to comprehend fully the thrust of the preceding sentence, we must note that, as Salmond wrote, "the phrase 'the doctrine of precedent' has two meanings. In the first, which may be called the loose meaning, the phrase means merely that precedents are reported, may be cited, and will probably be followed by the courts. . . . In the second, the strict meaning, the phrase means that precedents not only have great authority but must (in certain circumstances) be followed."[8] Elon, however, has shown that precedents of the second type (i.e., authoritative precedents) do not exist within the halakhic system.[9] That is not to say, of course, that precedents do not speak with great authority, but only that they are not absolutely authoritative.

There is, actually, a systemic principle that bears upon the resolution of the conflicts of *posekim.* Yet it must be noted at the outset that this principle does not mollify the tension and anxiety implicit in the deci-

3. See Elon, *Jewish Law,* 2:772 ff.
4. *Ibid.,* 2:779 ff.
5. I.e., their commentaries on classical texts or legal writings, but not case-law.
6. I.e., in its technical sense, precedent that is based upon actual cases.
7. Fitzgerald, *Salmond,* p. 141. The halakhic system recognizes no difference in kind, although it may recognize differences of degree between them. See, for example, in Elon, *Jewish Law,* 2:796, sources favoring case law above theoretical writings, and *ibid.,* 3:1215 ff., which includes sources reflecting the opposite position.
8. Fitzgerald, *Salmond,* p. 142.
9. Elon, *Jewish Law,* 2:797–804.

sion-making process; if anything, it exacerbates the problem. Nonetheless, according to most, it is the *sine qua non* of the system. As succinctly stated in the Talmud, it reads: *Ein lo la-dayyan ella mah she-einav ro'ot* ("a judge must be guided by what he sees"). It is to the explication of this principle and to an examination of its relationship to the persuasive authority of precedent that the remainder of this chapter is devoted.

The principle is stated three times in the Babylonian Talmud, each repetition reflecting a broadening of its meaning. In the first context the words are interpreted literally: The principle is quoted in order to direct the judge to guide himself by the appearance of the blood (the question of fact in the second sense to be determined is whether the blood before him is menstrual blood or not) as it appears to him at the time the decision is being made.[10] He should not concern himself with the possibility that he might render a different judgment if the blood were moist rather than dry, because *Ein lo la-dayyan ella mah she-einav ro'ot.*

The second context in which the principle appears concerns the possibility that the awesome responsibility of judgment, including the possibility of Divine punishment in the event of a gross miscarriage of justice, might persuade qualified judges to refrain from making any judgments at all.[11] In response to such a possible claim, the talmudic passage offers the assurance that so long as his decisions are just and are made on the basis of the matters before him, he need not worry about the possible punishment for a miscarriage of justice, since *Ein lo la-dayyan ella mah she-einav ro'ot.*

The third statement of the principle is the most important for the present discussion. The Talmud reads:[12]

> Rava said to Rav Papa and to Rav Huna the son of Rav Yehoshu'a, "If one of my decisions comes before you,[13] and it seems to you to be refutable, don't tear it up until you come to me. If I have some reason,[14] I will tell you; and if not, I shall retract. If the same thing happens after I die, do not tear it up; but also do not use it as a paradigm on the basis of which to determine other similar cases (*u-migmar nammi la tigmeru mineih*). You should not tear it up, since were I alive I might have been able to explain it to you. You should

10. Niddah 20b.
11. Sanhedrin 6b.
12. Bava Batra 130b.
13. The Rashbam (printed in all standard editions of the Talmud) interprets this to mean "a decision I wrote out and gave to the man as proof of my decision."
14. I.e., if I can demonstrate that your argument against my decision is invalid for some reason.

> not use it as a paradigm, for a judge must be guided by what he sees."

Rabbi Samu'el ben Me'ir (Rashbam, ca. 1080–1174) makes quite clear in his commentary on this passage[15] that Rava's statement intimates an expansion of the principle beyond that indicated in the first of the talmudic passages referred to above. The Rashbam writes that in Rava's statement the principle applies "to a matter of judgment based on logical reasoning (*sevara*) as well, in which the judge must be guided by the dictates of his mind (*mah she-libbo ro'ehu*)."

As the passage implies, Rava was the teacher of Rav Huna and Rav Papa. We can assume, therefore, that since a student stands in a special relationship to his teacher, and vice versa[16]—that is to say, if there is any circumstance in which a later arbiter would be bound by an authoritative precedent, it is one in which the student-teacher relationship prevailed—the passage proves beyond a doubt that the concept of authoritative precedent does not exist in the halakhic system.

Yet the contention that there is no such thing as authoritative precedent in the halakhic system must be clearly distinguished from the obligation of the student to abide by his teacher's decision in the specific case in which the student found his teacher's legal reasoning refutable and erroneous. The extent of the student's obligation to abide by his teacher's decision in the specific case is made clear by Rabbi Nissim ben Re'uven Gerondi (Ran, ca. 1310–1375) in his comments on this passage.[17] He begins by deducing, on the basis of a different talmudic passage,[18] that in our passage the student detected an error by his teacher concerning a clear and unambiguous matter of law *(devar mishnah)*.[19] Thus, Gerondi concludes:

> Rava's statement that "after death you should not tear up my decision" implies that even concerning a mistake of this nature [i.e., *devar mishnah*], a student is obligated to honor his teacher and refrain from reversing his decision in that case itself; even though, by law, it could be reversed. This applies, however, only to that

15. Bava Batra, 131a, s.v. *ve-al tigmeru*.
16. See, for example, Mishnah Bava Meẓi'a 2:11, Sanhedrin 5b, and Eruvin 62b.
17. *Ḥiddushei ha-Ran*, Bava Batra, ed. A. Sofer (Jerusalem: Alexander Kohut Foundation, 1963 [5723]), p. 428.
18. Sanhedrin 6a.
19. The basis of his deduction is Rava's claim that he would retract his decision if he could not refute his students' argument against it. The right of an arbiter to retract his decision in a particular case is restricted, according to the passage in Sanhedrin, to an error in a *devar mishnah*. In any other type of error, the decision in the particular case stands.

specific case. But if another case should come before him [i.e., the student], even though it is identical to the case adjudicated by his teacher (*af al pi she-hu shaveh lo mammash*), he is entitled to judge as it seems to him, since a judge must be guided by what he sees.

Rabbi Me'ir ha-Levi Abulafia (ca. 1170–1244) adds another dimension to the implications of Rava's statement. He writes: "You should not use it as a paradigm, since a judge must be guided by what he sees. Therefore, you should judge future cases as it seems appropriate to you. But do not tear up my decision, since perhaps some other arbiter will come along who will offer a reason for it, resulting in its resubstantiation."[20] Thus, the reasoned refutation of an opinion does not result in its obliteration from the range of possible decisions open to future arbiters. Rather, it remains a viable option for a future arbiter, who, in the exercise of his right of judicial discretion, and guided by what he sees, may consider it appropriate. According to Abulafia, therefore, the rejection of the original decision results, not in its abolition, but in the creation of a legitimate *maḥaloket* (in which the existence of two legitimate opinions becomes the grounds for the exercise of judicial discretion).

The principle *Ein lo la-dayyan ella mah she-einav ro'ot*, therefore, is the systemic legitimization of the right of judges to exercise judicial discretion as they deem appropriate. Even more, the principle demands of *posekim* that they do more than merely recognize the existence of their theoretical right to exercise judicial discretion; it demands of them that they, *in fact*, exercise their right. It elevates the right to exercise judicial discretion to a systemic imperative. Note how closely the following statement of an early halakhic commentator on the principle both parallels Salmond's definition of judicial discretion and at the same time elevates it to a systemic imperative. Salmond writes: "The sphere of judicial discretion includes all questions as to what is right, just, equitable, or reasonable . . . committed to the *liberum arbitrium* of the courts."[21] And the early commentator writes: "Arbiters must depend upon and judge according to what seems to them to be true (*emet*)."[22]

Having demonstrated the elevation of the concept of judicial discretion to a systemic imperative, I now propose to deal with the preeminent

20. *Yad Ramah* (Warsaw, 1895), Bava Batra, chap. 8, par. 135.
21. Fitzgerald, *Salmond*, p. 68.
22. Moses Hershler and Ch. Ben-Zion Hershler, eds., *Perush Kadmon to Bava Batra* (Jerusalem, 1971 [5731]), p. 29.

position of that imperative as a guide to *posekim* in grappling with the anxiety-producing factors to which I referred at the beginning of this chapter. In the process, I shall reinforce my earlier contention that (a) although this principle bears upon the resolution of the conflicts of *posekim*, it at the same time exacerbates them, and (b) the principle is, nonetheless, a *sine qua non* of the halakhic system.

A responsum of Rabbi Abraham, son of Maimonides (1186–1237), provides a most explicit indication of its preeminence. He wrote:[23]

> In sum: I affirm that a judge who is guided in his decisions only by that which is written and explicit is both weak and timid, and such a course will result in the annulment of the dictum *Ein lo la-dayyan ella mah she-einav ro'ot*. But that is not as it should be. Rather, the matters that are written constitute the foundation; and it is the obligation of the one who is judging a case or rendering a decision to ponder (*lishkol*) them in every matter that comes before him, to draw analogies between the case and things comparable to it, and to extrapolate *(lehoẓi anafim)* from those foundations. For the many precedents, which encompass a percentage of the laws, were not recorded in the Talmud for naught, but also were not intended to dictate the decision in accordance with what is mentioned there. Rather, they are intended to facilitate the ability of the sage, who has heard them many times, to engage in the exercise of discretion (*shikkul ha-da'at*) and to render actual decisions appropriately. And even if the abrogation of the law concerning a neighbor's right of acquisition if the neighbor has moved to a different city were explicit in the Talmud,[24] the judge would be required to weigh both sides of the issue in this case; and all the more so is that the case, since its abrogation under those circumstances is the reasoned opinion (*sevara*) of later sages, arising from concern for social welfare (*tikkun ha-olam*).[25]

Rabbi Abraham Maimuni clearly postulates that the principle *Ein lo la-dayyan ella mah she-einav ro'ot* is the closest possible thing to an ultimate systemic principle. A judge's absolute reliance upon precedent, elevating it to the level of authoritative precedent, results in the not only undesirable but also unacceptable abrogation of the basic systemic

---

23. *Responsa of Rabbi Abraham, Son of the Rambam*, ed. A. Freiman (Jerusalem: Mekiẓe Nirdamim, 1937), respomsum 97. pp. 147–48.

24. I.e., *bar meẓer;* see Bava Meẓi'a 108a and b. The laws of *bar meẓer* (preemption) are the specific issue being dealt with in the responsum under discussion.

25. See Maimonides, *Mishneh Torah,* Hilkhot Shekhenim 14:3.

imperative principle that *Ein lo la-dayyan ella mah she-einav ro'ot,* which dictates that *posekim* must exercise their right of judicial discretion whenever appropriate. The precedents of the halakhic system are intended to guide arbiters not only by what they say explicitly, but also by serving as paradigms *par excellence* of the methodology according to which previous masters balanced such precedent against what they themselves saw. Even an explicit talmudic statement is not sufficient to deny an arbiter the right to exercise his judicial discretion in the way he deems best suited to the specific issue before him. Precedents will probably be followed, not because they are absolutely authoritative, but because careful consideration of them is most likely to guide the present arbiter in the same way that earlier arbiters were guided. Nevertheless, if a later judge sees significant and crucial differences between the cases that established the precedent and the case before him, he is duty-bound, notwithstanding the similarities between the cases, to follow the dictates of his reason, and he must depend upon and judge according to what seems to him to be true. The refusal of a judge to allow himself to be guided by what he sees places him in the category of the weak and timid. Implicit in Abraham Maimuni's words is the intimation that the weak and the timid are not only not the best guarantors of the viability of the system, but, indeed, its worst guarantors.

The passages yet to be discussed in this chapter will reinforce Maimuni's view and will clarify some of the factors that must be included in the concept of what the judge sees. Having opted for a broad definition of the term *precedent,* it should be noted that one of the factors in the judge's consideration must be the literary context of the precedent-statement.[26] Bearing this fact in mind, the following passage from Rabbi Menaḥem ben Shelomo ha-Me'iri (1249–1316) is relevant to further explication of the principle under discussion.[27]

> [Decisions intended to be acted upon *(halakhah le-ma'aseh)* are not to be deduced except from] decisions rendered by *amora'im,* for their statements were made only after careful consideration (*iyyun*). Indeed, some of the talmudic sages used to order their students that when they heard the teacher say of something that it is the law, they should not deduce actual practice from it, unless he has stated that it is law and is intended to be acted upon. . . . And this matter is

---

26. See above, p. 82, and n. 7.

27. *Beit ha-Beḥirah to Bava Batra,* ed. A. Sofer (New York: Kedem Publishers, 1956) p. 537, referring to Bava Batra 130b. Cf. his response to his questioners in *Teshuvot Rabbenu ha-Me'iri* (Jerusalem, New York: Ma'ayan Hachochma, 1957 [5718]), p. 46.

> one that the wise should implant firmly in their hearts. And this claim is based upon my observation that this generation is failing in such matters. For whenever some decision or case comes to our attention, and is such that by talmudic law and on the basis of *halakhah* it should be judged as forbidden or allowed, innocent or guilty, fit or unfit, impure or pure, they [i.e. arbiters in the Me'iri's day] disagree [with the clear implications of the Talmud], basing themselves on the haggard hair-splitting (*nimmukei bela'ot*) of novellae and *tosafot* and anthologies of quotations (*likkutin shel leshonot*). Yet they shriek like a crane,[28] "Look what I found that so-and-so wrote," without either knowing or paying heed to whether or not it was said correctly, and without basing themselves upon the Talmud. They pay no heed either to the identity of the speaker or to what he said. And if, occasionally, they are motivated to take note of the identity of the speaker and they chance upon one of the greats of instruction (*gedolei ha-hora'ah*), then what he said becomes absolutely definitive no matter what its content. They pay no heed to whether or not it is true, or whether it was stated as a definitive decision (*pesak muḥlat*) or by way of commentary or reconciliation of a difficulty. I have found many failing in such matters in my generation . . . and that is the implication of the Talmud's later statement: "Shall we depend upon the forced resolution to a problem (*Atu anan a-shinnuyah neikom ve-nismokh*)?"[29] That is, that we should put aside clear talmudic passages or a *baraita* because of some reconciliation (*teruẓin*). If such can be said of *tanna'im* and *amora'im*, then let the *ge'onim* and rabbis forgo their honor, for any statement of theirs that comes to our attention and seems either novel or strange (*be-ḥiddush o be-zarut*) will be accepted by us only insofar as it is supportable by talmudic proofs or if it seems acceptable because of its eminent reasonableness. . . . Now, then, regarding all matters of decision-making and give-and-take, it is not appropriate to render decisions according to what may be found written by some scholar or codifier or commentator who has rendered a very novel opinion, whether for leniency or stringency, except if it is accompanied by proof.

Heeding the Me'iri's own proviso that one should consider the forum in which a comment appears, and, therefore, aware that this comment does not come from a work of halakhic philosophy, and discounting the hyperbole of the statement, we maintain that it nonetheless has impor-

28. Cf. Kiddushin 44a.
29. Bava Batra 135a.

tant implications for the present discussion. For to require proofs and to test the reasonableness of judicial opinions means no less than to exercise the right of judicial discretion appropriately. The claim that an opinion that can be disproved or that seems untenable from the perspective of reason does not constitute a precedent that ought to be followed affirms that opinions contrary to the one being questioned and that are based either upon clear proofs or upon reason constitute legitimate grounds for the exercise of judicial discretion. If this is the case, it follows that, ultimately, *Ein lo la-dayyan ella mah she-einav ro'ot*.

Furthermore, one of the complaints the Me'iri levels against his contemporaries is very familiar. It can only be the sense of his own inferiority that moves the average arbiter to elevate the statements of great legalists of the past to the plane of authoritative precedent without consideration of the content of their statements. But it is against such blind sanctification of written or codified opinion that the Me'iri argues so vehemently. Moreover, implicit in his statement is the contention that the great legalists of the past earned their reputations by the brilliance and the cogency of their arguments, by the methods they employed in judging in accordance with what they saw, and by their acumen in the exercise of judicial discretion. The conclusion is inescapable that the methods of inquiry and the force of intellect brought by the great men of the past to their task must be called into play by the arbiters of the present as well. If they are not brought into play, the arbiter becomes nothing more than a purveyor of ostensibly authoritative precedent—a category the very existence of which we have already demonstrated to be inimical to the viable functioning of the halakhic system.

It should be stressed, as well, that the Me'iri does not suggest that only statements made by the *ge'onim* and rabbis in "the forced resolution of a problem" be subjected to critical analysis, he maintains that "any statement of theirs that comes to our attention" should be subjected to the same examination. When the Me'iri asserts that even "the forced resolution of a problem" by *tanna'im* or *amora'im* cannot supersede clear talmudic passages or a *baraita*, he does so to indicate the caliber of people whose opinions require scrutiny; it is not meant to be exhaustive regarding the nature of the statements that require scrutiny. This is made exceptionally clear by the conclusion of the Me'iri's statement: "Regarding all matters of decision-making and give-and-take, it is not appropriate to render decisions . . . except if it is accompanied by proof."[30]

---

30. See also Abayee's statement about R. Ḥanina and Rav Minyumi's statement re Rav Yosef (Ketubbot 81b); and Rav Aḥa b. Ya'akov's statement re a decision of Rav Sheshet (Yevamot 97b). Both are quoted by the Me'iri in *Beit ha-Beḥirah to Bava Batra*, p. 538.

Having dealt thus far primarily with the pivotal importance of the systemic principle *Ein lo la-dayyan ella mah she-einav ro'ot,* we can now turn our attention to a discussion of another aspect of it, namely, the question of the *degree* to which an arbiter *is* bound by precedent and the weight of opinion. In essence, this will involve us in the further study of the systemic elevation of matters of judicial discretion to matters of law in the first sense (i.e., matters of law that are clear and unambiguous). We must bear in mind, however, that even when matters of judicial discretion are thus elevated, they still do not become absolutely definitive, authoritative precedents, since, as we have demonstrated, there is no such category within the halakhic system.[31]

There is one talmudic section that offers definitional guidance, in talmudic parlance, concerning matters of law in the first sense and matters of judicial discretion.[32] However, understanding this section and the commentaries upon it requires knowledge of the specific context of the discussion, even though the context is not particularly relevant to the present discussion. The material deals with the question of which cases of completed adjudication may be overturned with the result that any actions that may have already taken place can be reversed, and the question of what, in a case of irreversible judicial error, should be the liability of the judge in the matter of restitution. The Talmud in Sanhedrin reads:

> Rav Sheshet said in the name of Rav Asi: "[If a judge] erred in a matter explicit in the Mishnah (*devar mishnah*), his decision is reversible. [If he] erred in a matter of *shikkul ha-da'at,* his decision is not reversible." Ravina said to Rav Ashi:[33] "[Does the category of *devar mishnah* apply if] he erred concerning statements of Rabbi Ḥiyya and Rabbi Oshai'a?"[34] He answered him affirmatively. "[Does it apply] even to Rav and Samu'el?"[35] He answered him affirmatively. "Does it apply even to you and me?" He answered: "Yes, even to you and me. Are we reed-cutters in the marsh?"[36]

31. See above, pp. 82 f. Yet to be discussed at length is the status of matters *de-oraita* vis-à-vis these problems.
32. Sanhedrin 33a.
33. See below, n. 56.
34. Traditionally, the compilers of the Tosefta, a collection of tannaitic statements roughly similar to the Mishnah. Only the compilation of Rabbi Judah the Prince, however, is recognized as *the* Mishnah. All other collections are secondary to it in importance and authority.
35. Outstanding scholars and founders of the academies in Babylonia during the first generation of *amora'im* (the first half of the third century C.E.).
36. I.e., of no importance or consequence.

> What, then, is *shikkul ha-da'at?* Rav Papa said: "[It occurs,] for example, when two *tanna'im* or two *amora'im* disagree with each other, and the law has not been determined according to either opinion, but the general practice (*sugya de-alma* or *sugya di-shema'atin*) follows one of the positions, and the judge acted according to the other. That is *shikkul ha-da'at*.

In the following selection, Rabbi Menaḥem ha-Me'iri offers an explanation of the terms used in the passage and spells out the implications that can be derived from it. He writes:[37]

> The concept of error in a matter explicit in the Mishnah (*devar mishnah*), which has been mentioned, is not restricted to the Mishnah alone, but includes even a *baraita* or the Tosefta, and even the words of *amora'im,* [and is defined as] a matter which is mentioned explicitly in the Talmud with no difference of opinion, or one concerning which there is a disagreement but which has been decided within the Talmud according to one of the positions. And an error in *shikkul ha-da'at* refers to a disputed issue in the Talmud which has not been internally decided according to one of the positions, but concerning which there is widespread agreement (*nitpashet minhag ha'olam*) favoring one of the positions, without any decision within the Talmud, and the judge decided according to the other opinion, offering neither proof nor reason for his decision.
>
> But any matter that is not mentioned in the Talmud at all, or is mentioned in the Talmud without final decision and concerning which there is no widespread agreement favoring one position, even if one of the *ge'onim* or one of the latter sages decided according to one opinion, but without explicit proof (*re'ayah berurah*), [whatever decision the judge renders] cannot be considered an error at all. And surely this is so concerning a matter which is disputed among *posekim*. If, however, the judge's decision is refutable by explicit proof, it is an error in a matter explicit in the Mishnah (*devar mishnah*). And if the judge's decision can be refuted by referring to widespread agreement favoring a different position, it is an error in *shikkul ha-da'at.* Furthermore, if the judge offers proof for his position [even against the position to which there is widespread agreement] or refutes the proofs of earlier authorities,

37. *Beit ha-Beḥirah to Sanhedrin,* ed. Isaac Ralbag (Jerusalem, 1971 [5731]), p. 122a, referring to Sanhedrin 33a.

> his decision is not considered an error. Indeed, in several matters we have seen that the greatest sages of the *ge'onim* and the rabbis have erred, and their positions can be refuted from the Talmud itself; and how could we, under those circumstances, consider a judge who does not act according to their decision in error?
> There are those, however, who disagree, claiming that any matter concerning which the *ge'onim* have rendered a decision should be considered as though it were talmudically determined,[38] but that claim need not be heeded at all *(ve-ein la-ḥush le-divreihem bi-khelal).*

Since the explanation of the Me'iri is not only defensible but compelling and cogent, it is systemically accurate to assert that the Hebrew term *devar mishnah*—which we have translated in this quotation as "a matter explicit in the Mishnah," although, as we have seen in the quotation from Sanhedrin, the term is not meant to be restricted to such matters in the Mishnah alone—is the equivalent in the halakhic system of a matter of law in the first sense. That is, a *devar mishnah* is a matter concerning which the talmudic law is clear and unambiguous, and which, therefore, compels the arbiter, under most circumstances,[39] to decide according to its dictates, regardless of any other consideration.[40] The number of matters of law in the first sense within the halakhic system is thus restricted to undisputed talmudic statements, or to those matters that, though matters of dispute among sages in the Talmud, have been ultimately decided within the Talmud itself.

Secondly, it is equally accurate to assert that, as used in this quotation, the term *shikkul ha-da'at* is equivalent in the halakhic system to the category of judicial discretion. That is, it encompasses "all questions as to what is right, just, equitable, or reasonable—so far as not predetermined by authoritative rules of law but committed to the *liberum arbitrium* of the courts."[41] Halakhically, all matters that are not *divrei mishnah* are *shikkul ha-da'at*.

The very fact, however, that the passage from Sanhedrin deals with

---

38. Thus a judicial decision at variance with the geonic opinion would be an error in a *devar mishnah*.

39. The proviso is added both in recognition of the Maimonidean position (see above, p. 62), and in anticipation of a future discussion of the types of considerations that might allow an arbiter to render a decision contrary to a matter of law in the first sense (see below, chaps. 9 and 11).

40. See above, p. 49.

41. See above, p. 52, and Fitzgerald, *Salmond*, p. 68.

the possibility of judicial error in a matter of judicial discretion indicates clearly that the *halakhah* must contain a systemic principle that limits the exercise of judicial discretion in some way. And, indeed, the central systemic consideration with regard to such limits is the weight of precedent.

As the Me'iri implies, widespread agreement with one position in a matter of judicial discretion puts the full weight of precedent behind that position, and, as a general rule, dictates that the arbiter abide by it. If that were not the case, it would be impossible to speak of an error in judicial discretion. Yet it must be stressed again that even the full weight of precedent does not elevate the position it favors to an absolutely definitive matter of law in the first sense. The right of the judge to exercise his discretion in favor of the nonprecedented position is restricted only if he is unable to offer any cogent reason or evidence for his rejection of the precedented position. If he can offer them, his right to exercise his judicial discretion as he sees fit is, in fact, undeniable. In such a case, his decision favoring the nonprecedented position cannot be considered systemically erroneous, even if others may disagree with his reason or evidence, for *Ein lo la-dayyan ella mah she-einav ro'ot*.

A position similar to that of the Me'iri is offered by Rabbi Solomon ben Abraham Adret (Rashba, ca. 1235–1310), although he places greater emphasis on the weight of precedent than on the right of arbiter to overturn it. He writes: "The words of the earlier sages (*rishonim*) are to be heeded . . . and the words of the earlier sages, the sages of the earlier generations, based on reason (*sevara*), should not be put aside without proof."[42]

The systemic processes of *halakhah* that we have been discussing remain as valid for the modern period as for the past. It ought to be borne in mind, however, that the weight of precedent, which could not be easily ignored even during the Middle Ages, is still weightier in the modern period, especially in those cases where a widespread agreement favoring one of the positions in a matter of judicial discretion has persisted.

In light of the tendency of legal systems, as they develop, to limit areas of judicial discretion in favor of matters of law in the first sense,[43] it is not unanticipated that we find the same tendency operative in the halakhic system as well. Moreover, the degree to which the recognized greats of the legal tradition acquiesce in this development, or fight against it, gives us an indication of what each conceived to be the best

42. *Responsa of Rashba* (Benei Berak, 1958 [5718]), pt. 2, no. 322.
43. See above, p. 53.

way of ensuring the viability of the system. To the degree that some advocate the retention of maximal and expanding realms of judicial discretion and theoretical flexibility within the *halakhah,* they indicate their conviction that its viability is ensured by openness and nonuniformity. If, on the other hand, others reject this view and favor the imposition of uniformity through the elevation of increasing numbers of questions to the realm of matters of law in the first sense, they are arguing for definitiveness as the best guarantor of the viability of the system. Since both positions, in their extreme forms, are problematic—the former because of the danger of legal chaos, and the latter because of the danger of the stultification of the system—one seeks to discover how the masters of the past have balanced these opposing forces.

Since we have already demonstrated that the term *devar mishnah* is the halakhic equivalent of a matter of law in the first sense, and that the term *shikkul ha-da'at* is the halakhic equivalent of the category of judicial discretion, we must turn our attention to the halakhic sources that deal with the restriction of the category of *shikkul ha-da'at* in favor of the category of *devar mishnah;* that is, to the sources that deal with the question of the elevation of matters of *shikkul ha-da'at* to the status of *devar mishnah.* It is from these sources that we should be able to discover how the masters of the past have balanced the opposing forces of the weight of precedent and judicial discretion.

Furthermore, we must bear in mind that the authors of post-talmudic halakhic literature are generally divided into three groups: *ge'onim, rishonim, and aḥaronim.* The term *ge'onim* refers to the sages who headed the Babylonian academies from the close of the Talmud until the eleventh century; *rishonim* ("early ones") refers to the sages who lived in the period between the end of the geonic period and the publication of the *Shulḥan Arukh* in the sixteenth century; and *aḥaronim* ("later ones") refers to the sages of the period from the publication of the *Shulḥan Arukh* until the present. Since we have already referred to the systemic principle that affirms the inferiority of later generations to earlier generations, it is clear that the earliest indications of the elevation of matters of judicial discretion in the Talmud to the level of matters of law in the first sense should first be sought in the attitude of the *rishonim* to the *ge'onim.* It is to an examination of these sources that we now turn.

As early as the middle of the twelfth century we find evidence that, in the opinion of some, elevation of matters of judicial discretion to the level of matters of law in the first sense had already taken place, to the virtual elimination of all legitimate exercise of judicial discretion. Rabbi Zeraḥiah ben Isaac ha-Levi Gerondi, whose *Sefer ha-Ma'or* was completed during the last part of that century, quotes such a view. He writes:

> I have heard in the name of one of the sages of the preceding generation that the category of error in *shikkul ha-da'at* no longer exists, for all laws are now authoritatively determined for us *(pesukot be-yadeinu)* either from the Talmud or from the *ge'onim* who followed the Talmud. Therefore, one can no longer find an example of an error in *shikkul ha-da'at*. Rather, all who err, err in a *devar mishnah*.[44]

According to this anonymous sage, the concept of the legitimate exercise of judicial discretion had already passed out of existence. Rabbi Zeraḥiah ha-Levi himself, however, immediately challenges that position. He continues:

> But this view seems untenable to me. Rather, anyone whose error cannot be clearly demonstrated (*mitbareret*) from the Mishnah or the Talmud explicitly, beyond all doubt, is not erring in a *devar mishnah*, but in *shikkul ha-da'at*. . . . [Any case in which] it is impossible to demonstrate the error clearly from our Mishnah or our Talmud explicitly, is an error in *shikkul ha-da'at*. And any decision rendered by the *ge'onim*, after the closing of the Talmud, as an expression of preference for one view over another not based upon clear and authoritative law from the Talmud, has the status of general practice *(ke-sugyan be-alma havei)*, and one who errs in it has erred in *shikkul ha-da'at*, but has not erred in *devar mishnah*.

Rabbi Zeraḥiah ha-Levi clearly opts for restricting the elevation of increasing numbers of questions of judicial discretion to matters of law in the first sense. Equally clear, however, is the fact that the opinions of the *ge'onim* possess sufficient authority that ignoring them in favor of another opinion constitutes an error, if only in *shikkul ha-da'at*.

Since the talmudic passage to which Rabbi Zeraḥiah's comments refer is concerned primarily with the liability of a judge to make restitution for an error in judgment,[45] it is difficult to determine what weight he would attach to a geonic decision in the event that the judge ignored it on the grounds that it seemed to him either unreasonable, refutable, or not clearly proven. The most that ought to be deduced at this point is his obvious preference for the retention of *shikkul ha-da'at* as a halakhic category.

There are, however, several other sources that bear directly upon the

---

44. *Ha-Ma'or ha-Gadol* on Alfasi to Sanhedrin, chap. 4, p. 12a, s.v. *bava revi'a*.
45. Sanhedrin 33a; see above, p. 90.

question of the weight of geonic opinion that a later *posek* finds either unreasonable, refutable, or unproven. Implicit in these sources, too, is the preference of their authors for retaining the category of *shikkul ha-da'at* and for restricting the elevation of matters of judicial discretion to the level of *divrei mishnah*.

Regarding the authority of geonic decisions that are not clearly proven, Maimonides writes:[46]

> In general I would claim that any statement (*ma'amar*) by the *ge'onim*, well known for their decisions (*ha-mefursamim be-hora'ah*), of blessed memory, for which we can find no clear proof, should not be shunted aside, nor should we claim that its author was in error. Rather, we should claim that perhaps he had some proof. But it is undesirable (*ein ra'ui*) for us to rely upon it. Nor should we act in accordance therewith until his reason has been clarified. And our sages, of blessed memory, have already explained this fundamental principle to us when they said: "You should not tear it up, but you should not use it as a paradigm."[47]

Maimonides refused to attach special status to geonic statements. He applied to them the same analytical criteria that Rava advocated that his pupils apply to *his* own statements. Yet Maimonides is, at the same time, extremely careful to avoid dismissing an unproven geonic statement summarily, never calling such an opinion erroneous. What is crucial to our argument, however, is his affirmation that one should not be governed by such an opinion, even though one is obliged to assume that its author had a reason for making it. Equally important is the fact that for him the unproven geonic decision remains within the realm of possible choices for some future judge who, finding support for it, and guided by what he sees, is inclined, in the legitimate exercise of his judicial discretion, to accept it above other opinions. If anything can be considered sacrosanct, for Maimonides, it is the right of arbiters to be guided by what they see and to exercise *shikkul ha-da'at*.[48]

In an answer to a query addressed to the Babylonian academies by the North African community of Kairouan, the right of judicial discretion is also applied to questions where there is *disagreement* among *ge'onim*. The question and the geonic response read:[49]

---

46. *Teshuvot ha-Rambam*, ed. Jehoshua Blau, vol. 2 (Jerusalem: Mekiẓe Nirdamim, 1960), responsum 310, p. 576.

47. Bava Batra 130b; see above, p. 83.

48. Compare the Maimonidean responsum with Abulafia's comment on the passage from Bava Batra 130b, on p. 85 above.

49. *Teshuvot ha-Ge'onim*, ed. A. Harkavy (Berlin, 1887), no. 347, p. 175.

> What ought to be done in a case where two geonic responsa disagree with each other, and each litigant or judge adopts one of them? . . . If it is possible to ask from the High Court which is extant at that time,[50] it should be asked, and its decision should be honored, since it shall have judged the case and you have none other than the judge of your own time.[51] . . . But when it is impossible to bring the matter before the High Court, and there are two different geonic responsa, the judge must do as he sees fit (*mah she-hu ro'eh*), and as his heart dictates (*makhri'a*), for he must be guided by what he sees.

Thus, neither Rabbi Zeraḥiah ha-Levi nor Maimonides was prepared to allow the recognized authority of the *ge'onim* and the systemically assumed inferiority of the *rishonim* to them to result in the *ipso facto* elevation of their decisions to matters of law in the first sense. For Rabbi Zeraḥiah ha-Levi this is reflected in the assertion that an error in judgment, in which the error results from failure to take a geonic decision into account, is an error in *shikkul ha-da'at*, and not an error in a *devar mishnah*. For Maimonides, it is reflected in the fact that when a later *posek* ignores a geonic opinion for which he can find no clear proof, he has not erred even in a matter of *shikkul ha-da'at*. Furthermore, as we have seen in the geonic responsum, it remains within the realm of the legitimate exercise of judicial discretion for a judge to choose as he sees fit between conflicting geonic opinions, especially when there is no weight of precedent favoring one or the other of the conflicting opinions.

As yet unexamined, however, is the status of a geonic statement unknown to the arbiter at the time of adjudication, but which becomes known to him subsequently, as well as the right of an arbiter to disagree with or refute a geonic statement, even if the statement is accompanied by some apparently clear proof or reason. A lengthy passage of Rabbi Asher ben Yeḥi'el (Rosh, ca. 1250–1327), containing a quotation from Rabbi Abraham ben David (Ravad, 1125–1198), addresses itself to these questions.[52] The Rosh begins by quoting the passage from Rabbi Zeraḥiah ha-Levi discussed above.[53] Following that he writes:

---

50. It seems doubtful that the reference is to the actual Sanhedrin. More likely, the reference is to some court widely recognized as authoritative. If, in fact, the former is intended, this passage implies an even broader scope for judicial discretion than is being claimed presently.

51. Cf. Rosh ha-Shanah 25b.

52. *Piskei Rosh*, Sanhedrin 4:6.

53. See above, p. 95.

And the Ravad wrote concerning the words of the Ba'al ha–Ma'or [Rabbi Zeraḥiah ha-Levi] that "the anonymous sage is correct if the judge erred regarding geonic decisions that were unknown to him, such that had he known them he would have retracted. Surely such a case is an error in a *devar mishnah.* And I am inclined to say that even if the judge had disagreed with the decision of the *ga'on,* because his own opinion was not according to the view or explanation of the *ga'on,* this, too, is an error in a *devar mishnah.* For we may no longer dispute the words of a *ga'on* from our own opinion, explaining a matter in some other way, such that the law will be different, except in the case of some universally recognized problem (*kushya mefursemet*), and such do not exist."

But I [the Rosh] say that surely anyone who erred regarding a geonic decision because he had not heard their view, but when he heard the geonic decision he agreed with it, has committed an error in a *devar mishnah.* And the same is true not only of geonic decisions, but also of those of the sages of every succeeding generation, for they are not reed-cutters in the marsh.[54] Thus, if a judge decided a case not in accordance with their position, and, upon hearing their view, agreed with it and conceded that he had erred, that error is one of *devar mishnah* and is reversible.

But if the judge did not agree with their opinion, and adduced proofs for his own position that were acceptable to his own generation, then the principle "Jephthah in his generation is as authoritative as Samuel in his, for one has no other judge than the one who exists in his own day"[55] applies, and he may refute their opinions. For any opinions not stated clearly (*mevo'arim*) in the Talmud edited by Rav Ashi and Ravina, a man may refute and rebuild, even to the extent of disagreeing with the *ge'onim.* Indeed, that is the meaning of Rav Huna's statement to Rav Sheshet, "Does the category of *devar mishnah* apply even to statements made by you and me?"[56] To

54. Sanhedrin 33a; see above, n. 36.

55. Rosh ha-Shanah 25b; see above, p. 96, the responsum to Kairouan; and see below, chap. 5.

56. Sanhedrin 33a. The printed editions of the Talmud read "Ravina to Rav Ashi." The reading of the Rosh should probably be "Rav Hamnuna to Rav Sheshet," as is the reading of the Alfasi and Abulafia (cf. Rabbinovicz, *Dikdukei Soferim,* Sanhedrin 33a, letter *gimmel).* Rabbi Yom Tov Lippman Heller, in *Pilpula Ḥarifta* (printed in standard editions of the Talmud) to the Rosh (to Sanhedrin 33a), letter *ayin,* deduced that the Rosh's reading allowed him to affirm that postgeonic scholars could disagree with the *ge'onim.* Heller maintains, however, that the view of Rabbi Abraham ben David is based on the reading

which he replied, "Are we reed-cutters in the marsh?" That is to say, if we, on our own (*mi-da'atenu*), have introduced something new which is not found either in the Mishnah or the Gemara, and a judge who was unaware of our opinion decided differently, yet when he heard our opinion he agreed with it, that judge has erred in a *devar mishnah* and may reverse his decision. But it is obvious that that judge may disagree with their [the geonic] decision, just as later *amora'im* disagreed at times with earlier *amora'im*. And most surely this is so, for we affirm the fundamental importance of later views (*tofesin divrei ha-aḥaronim ikar*), since they were aware of the position (*sevarat*) of the earlier ones as well as their own, and weighed both of the positions, thus getting to the bottom of the matter (*ve-amedu al ikaro shel davar*) before rendering final judgment. And evidence for this can be adduced from the fact that we do not render legal decisions on the basis of the Mishnah but from the words of *amora'im*,[57] even though the *tanna'im* were greater than the *amora'im*.

And in a circumstance in which two greats (*gedolim*) disagree, a judge should not say, "I will decide according to whomever I wish"; and if he does so, that is a false judgment (*din sheker*). Rather, if he himself is a great scholar who has studied and is capable of cogent reasoning (*gamir ve-savir*), and qualified to decide in favor of one of the opinions by clear and incisive (*berurot u-nekhoḥot*) proofs, he is entitled to do so; even if some other sage has decided differently, he may refute his position with proofs and disagree with him, as I have written above. And surely if he has support from one of the original conflicting positions.

. . . And if the arbiter (*posek*) does not know about the disagreement between the *ge'onim*, and it later comes to his attention, if he is unqualified to decide between them, or cannot do so, then, if one of the opinions is favored by most of the sages and he acted according to the second, that is an error in *shikkul ha-da'at*. And if it is impossible to verify the position of most of the sages (*ve-im i efshar la'amod al ha-davar*), then his decision is not considered in error; rather, it is acceptable (*mah she-pasak pasak*).

"Ravina to Rav Ashi," which, since they mark the conclusion of the talmudic period, he interprets to mean that the right of later scholars to disagree with earlier scholars ends with Ravina and Rav Ashi. The tone of both the Talmud and Rabbi Asher b. Yeḥi'el, however, favors the broader interpretation.

57. Niddah 7b; Bava Batra 130b, Rashbam, s.v. *ad she-yomar, et al.*

This passage indicates universal agreement that an opinion of an earlier authority of stature, the contents of which were unknown to the arbiter at the time of the arbitration, but which became known to him after the completion of the adjudication, may have the status of a *devar mishnah* (i.e., a matter of law in the first sense). The disputes between the various *rishonim* center around the circumstances under which it may or must be so considered.

A careful reading of the position of Rabbi Abraham ben David indicates that his opinion is more dissimilar to that of the anonymous sage quoted by Rabbi Zeraḥiah ha-Levi than similar to it. Whereas the anonymous sage maintains that the category of *shikkul ha-da'at* no longer exists, the Ravad affirms that only the clear and undisputed view of the *ge'onim,* whether or not known to the arbiter at the time of decision, has the status of a matter of law in the first sense. His position, however, in no way impinges upon the right of an arbiter to the legitimate exercise of his judicial discretion in the case of a dispute between *ge'onim.* In that regard, the Ravad is consistent with his own position regarding the right to exercise judicial discretion even in matters that are disputed among *tanna'im.*[58]

Attention should be drawn, as well, to those things that are either unclear or not addressed at all in this statement of the Ravad. First, he is silent concerning the elevation of undisputed opinions of postgeonic *posekim* to matters of law in the first sense, so that later *posekim* would no longer be entitled to disagree wtih them and render a different decision. It is conceivable that he would place *ge'onim* in a separate class from postgeonic *posekim,* but also possible that he would claim that later arbiters attain the same status as *ge'onim* with regard to the elevation of their undisputed opinions to matters of law in the first sense after the passage of some length of time. Second, it is unclear whether his statement that universally recognized problems regarding geonic positions do not exist is intended as a temporal statement, implying that, although they do not exist at present, they may exist in the future and would then be grounds for disregarding the present undisputed geonic position; or whether it is intended as a definitive legal statement, implying that such universally recognized problems not only do not exist, but cannot exist.

The view of Rabbi Zeraḥiah ha-Levi Gerondi also requires careful scrutiny in order to ascertain exactly what it does affirm and what it does not affirm.[59] Since it is possible that the statement of the Ravad deals

58. See above, p. 58.
59. See above, p. 95.

with a geonic decision that is not an expression of preference for one view expressed by the Talmud over another view expressed by the Talmud, but rather a decision on a new issue to which there is no clear reference in the Talmud whatsoever, it is not clear that there is any difference of opinion at all between him and Rabbi Zeraḥiah ha-Levi. Each is silent concerning the issues addressed by the other. If Rabbi Abraham ben David's statement, however, refers to a geonic decision that *is* an expression of preference for one talmudic view over another, one clear dispute between him and Rabbi Zeraḥiah can be discerned. The Ravad would maintain, in that case, that the undisputed geonic statement of preference for one position in an earlier matter of judicial discretion elevates that issue from the plane of judicial discretion to the level of a matter of law in the first sense; Rabbi Zeraḥiah ha-Levi, on the other hand, would affirm that the geonic position does not elevate the question to a matter of law in the first sense but, rather, lends to the position adopted by the *ge'onim* the weight of precedent. In most circumstances, the difference between the two positions would be purely theoretical; practical differences would be reflected only in consideration of the grounds that would be sufficient to overturn or ignore the geonic decision. For the Ravad, they would have to be grounds that permit overturning a *devar mishnah* (to be discussed later), and for Rabbi Zeraḥiah ha-Levi, they would have to be grounds that permit ignoring precedent.

Furthermore, as we have noted, the statement of Rabbi Zeraḥiah ha-Levi neither affirms nor denies the right of future arbiters to disagree (ie., not erroneously) with a geonic position for cause. That is, he does not address himself to the possibility that the arbiter might knowingly overturn a stated preference of the *ge'onim* on the basis of reasoned proofs or on the basis of refutations of the reasons that led the *ge'onim* to favor the position their statement reflects. Regarding later *posekim*, however, his position affirms, by obvious implication, that the status of their statements cannot be greater than the status of statements of the *ge'onim* (i.e., that they cannot be elevated to matters of law in the first sense, and therefore that an error would be, at most, an error in *shikkul ha-da'at*).

In addition to his affirmation that it is possible for the position of an earlier authority to later attain the status of a *devar mishnah,* the view of Rabbi Asher ben Yiḥi'el is also clear on those issues concerning which the others are either silent or ambiguous. According to him, the "reed-cutters in the marsh" clause applies to the sages of every generation, whose opinions, therefore, may acquire the status of *divrei mishnah*. More importantly, Rabbenu Asher affirms the right of later arbiters to disagree with earlier opinions, not only in the exercise of judicial discretion between conflicting earlier opinions, but even in the refutation of undisputed earlier opinion. He does not deny the inferiority of later scholars to earlier ones, but affirms clearly that the law is determined for each age by the scholars of that age, who are authoritative for that age regardless of their absolute stature in comparison to earlier sages. The only matters that have acquired the status of matters of law in the first sense are those that are unequivocal in the Talmud itself.

In the course of his analysis, the Rosh has recourse to yet another systemic principle, that is, that the law follows the latter ones *(hilkheta ke-vatra'ei),* the meaning of which, according to him, not only clarifies but buttresses his position. The law follows later opinion, he maintains, because, by definition, later authorities carefully consider the positions of earlier authorities before rendering their own. Thus, if they allow themselves to override or supersede the position of the earlier authorities, such an action would be the result of that consideration, and therefore acceptable. Furthermore, assuming that the logic perceived by the Rosh does underlie the principle that the law follows the latter ones, we can comprehend the reason for accepting an earlier opinion as a matter of law in the first sense if it was unknown to the judge at the time of judgment. Since the judge's decision was reached without consideration of the earlier opinion, the principle that the law follows the latter ones does not apply to it.

The Rosh, however, adds an important condition to according the status of a *devar mishnah* to a previously unknown earlier opinion. For him that status would apply to a previously unknown earlier opinion only if the later judge found in it convincing grounds for the reversal of his own decision. It does not become definitive to the degree that the later arbiter no longer possesses the right to disagree with it in favor of his own position. Rather, if, upon considering the previously unknown earlier opinion, the later arbiter finds it either refutable or unconvincing for some reason, he retains the right to disagree with it and adjudicate as he sees fit. In this circumstance, however, the principle that the law follows the latter ones is applicable to his final decision.

While arguing very emphatically for the retention of maximal judicial discretion and against their elevation to the level of matters of law in the first sense, Rabbi Asher ben Yeḥi'el does not ignore the issue of the weight of precedent. He stipulates, with equal emphasis, that the broad rights of discretion that he supports are predicated on the assumption that the final decisions are based on reasoned opinions and "clear and incisive proofs." Decisions that ignore precedent cannot be made capriciously, and any such decision would constitute a vitiation of the pivotal systemic principle that the judge must be guided by what he sees. In the absence of clear and defensible arguments in favor of his own position (assuming that is one that is in opposition to the weight of precedent), the weight of precedent prevails: To ignore it is to be guilty of an error in *shikkul ha-da'at*.

While the statements of the Rosh and the Ravad are certainly different in tone and emphasis, it is possible that they are not as substantively different from each other as would appear. It is conceivable that for the Rosh, the "clear and incisive" refutations of earlier opinion that warrant overriding precedent are not functionally different, in most cases, from the "universally recognized problems" with geonic positions, which, at least according to one explanation of the Ravad, are to be understood temporally, and which would qualify as grounds for overriding geonic traditions.

In sum, then, the weight of opinion among *rishonim* seems clearly to favor the retention of broad judicial discretion over the elevation of increasing numbers of matters to the level of law in the first sense, although differences of stress and circumstances are obviously discernible among their statements. What remains to be discussed are the attitudes that prevailed upon the flowering of codification, so that we can ascertain whether this new source of law brought with it a change in the development of the halakhic process.[60]

It should be noted at the outset of this discussion, however, that the circumstances that gave rise to the development of the codes[61] are, from a systemic point of view, of only historical interest. The codes themselves are legal sources of the system; the factors that gave rise to them are historical sources.

Both the *Mishneh Torah* and the *Shulḥan Arukh* engendered considerable controversy. From a systemic perspective, most of the opponents of these works question the right of their authors to limit the exercise of judicial discretion in favor of the elevation of more and more matters to the level of law in the first sense.

The vehement reaction of Rabbi Abraham ben David (Ravad, 1125–

60. Emphasis will center on Maimonides' *Mishneh Torah*, on which he worked for ten years, beginning in 1177; and Caro's *Shulḥan Arukh*, which was completed in 1563. For further detail on the subject in general, see Elon, *Jewish Law*, 3:977–1185, and his entry "Codification of Law" in the *Encyclopaedia Judaica* (Jerusalem: Keter Publishing House, 1972).

61. See Elon, *Jewish Law*, 3:955–57.

1198) to the Maimonidean code is well known and often quoted. He wrote:

> He [Maimonides] thought he was doing a service (*savar letakken*), but he did no service. For he abandoned the method of all the authors who preceded him insofar as they brought proofs for their positions, and quoted statements in the names of their authors. And this method was of great use [to the judge], since it might often seem appropriate to him to forbid or allow on the basis of some source, and had he known that there was someone great who had favored another opinion, he might have retracted. But now [if guided by Maimonides' work], I do not know why I should retract from my own tradition and my own proof because of this author's code. If the one who disagrees with me is greater than I, good and well; but if I am greater than he, why should I nullify my position because of his? Furthermore, there are issues on which the *ge'onim* disagree with each other, and this codifier selected the position of one of them, and entered it into his code. But why should I depend upon his selection when it does not seem correct to me, and I cannot know [on the basis of the code] who disagrees with him, and whether he is worthy to disagree or not?[62]

The statement of the Ravad makes very clear his belief that no code, no matter what its author's intention, can be construed as anything more than a record of its author's exercise of judicial discretion; a code records the author's decisions, but in no way elevates those decisions to matters of law in the first sense. Any other qualified arbiter retains the right to exercise his own judicial discretion as he sees fit, either agreeing or disagreeing with the codified position. A codified view constitutes a precedent, with the same authority as, but no more than, any other precedent. The fact that a code is composed and published in the form of definitive statements that appear to be either undisputed or clearly demonstrable blurs the distinction between matters of law in the first sense and questions of legitimate judicial discretion, and consequently does not constitute a service to the halakhic process.

Similar expressions of aversion to the idea of codification in general both precede and follow the composition of the *Shulḥan Arukh*, in addition to specific objections to the method adopted by Caro in reach-

62. *Hassagot ha-Ravad* to Maimonides' *Introduction to the Mishneh Torah*.

ing his decisions.[63] Rabbi Israel Shakhna recounts the following concerning his father, Rabbi Shalom Shakhna (d. 1558):[64]

> Many times I, together with other of his students, requested of him that he become a *posek*.[65] In answer, because of his great piety and humility, being more humble than any other man on earth,[66] he used to say: "I know that nobody will render a decision other than my opinion, since the law is as the latter one, and I do not want the world to depend on me." He meant, for example, an instance in which there is a disagreement among scholars, and he would decide in favor of one position *(yakhri'a)* or, at times, disagree; and the judge must be guided by what he sees. Therefore, let each one do as the time requires (*ke-fi hora'at sha'ah*), guided by his heart.

Admittedly, Rabbi Shalom Shakhna's position is extreme. If it had been followed universally, the number of sources of law in the halakhic system would have been severely restricted, to the ultimate detriment of the system. His unwillingness to commit his opinions to writing does, however, indicate a keen awareness of the power of the written opinion in general, and especially of the written opinion of a recognized authority, to elevate that opinion to the level of a matter of law in the first sense. At the same time, his reticence forcefully affirms the centrality of judicial discretion within the halakhic system. Indeed, the conclusion of his statement constitutes as strong an affirmation of the pivotal nature of the principle *Ein lo la-dayyan ella mah she-einav ro'ot* as did that of Abraham Maimuni approximately three hundred years earlier.[67]

Rabbi Moses ben Israel Isserles (Rema, 1525–1572) was working on a code of his own when Caro's work came to his attention. (He modified his own code to glosses on Caro's work.) Nevertheless, he indicates his feelings about the authority of codes generally, and about his own work specifically, in the following comment:[68]

---

63. I.e., he ignored the systemic principle *hilkheta ke-vatra'ei* ("the law follows the later authorities") by deciding on the basis of the positions of the Alfasi, Asher b. Yeḥi'el, and Maimonides. See Isserles' *Introduction to Darkei Mosheh* on *Tur* (Jerusalem: El Hamikorot, 1958 [5718]), quoted by Elon, *Jewish Law*, 3:1127–28.

64. *Responsa of Rema*, ed. Asher Ziv (Jerusalem, 1970), no. 25, p. 156b.

65. I.e., that he commit his decisions to writing in some form, although not necessarily in the form of a code.

66. Numbers 12:3.

67. See above, p. 86.

68. Introduction to Isserles' *Darkei Mosheh*.

> If I were to write my opinion anonymously, definitively, rather than as the expression of my own opinion (*be-derekh bari ve-lo be-shemma*), then, perhaps, those who come after me would depend on it. For they might think that it was said by one who lives among the lions,[69] and would fear greatly to say that a given statement seemed difficult, as though disagreeing with the Torah of Moses itself.[70] Therefore, I have decided to add my own name to my own words. Thus, it is within the legitimate rights of anyone to disagree with my statements. Yet he who wishes to depend on me, let him come and do so. And any perversion which may result (*ḥet asher yeḥeta*) shall be the responsibility of him who depended on me, since it shall have been his choice to determine whether my positions were correct or erroneous. Ultimately (*mi-kol makom*), a judge must be guided by what he sees.

Thus, even the glossator *par excellence* to the *Shulḥan Arukh* affirms that the codified position is actually no more than an additional datum which the arbiter is duty-bound to consider in the exercise of his judicial function. Ultimately, however, he must be guided by what he sees.

Yet it cannot be denied that the authority of the codes, and particularly of the *Shulḥan Arukh,* became very weighty indeed. There were many *posekim* who were guided by the *Shulḥan Arukh* exclusively, elevating all its decisions virtually to the level of matters of law in the first sense. Those who disapproved of this development did not argue so much against the specific decisions of the *Shulḥan Arukh* as against its unqualified acceptance, maintaining that this constituted an unwarranted vitiation of the halakhic system, and even, at times, resulted in error. As for those who approved, their words deserve careful scrutiny to determine the grounds for their approval, in order to ascertain whether the two positions reflect substantive disagreement or, rather, a difference of emphasis.

In the seventeenth century, Rabbi Samu'el Eli'ezer ben Judah ha-Levi Edels (Maharsha, 1555–1631) castigates those who rely exclusively on the *Shulḥan Arukh.* He writes:[71]

---

69. Probably based on the verse in Psalms 57:5, and meant to encompass the conclusion of the verse as well, from which one can deduce the attitude toward the words of great scholars. It reads: "Their teeth are like a spear and arrows, their tongue a sharp sword."

70. I.e., disagreeing with an explicit statement of the *grundnorm,* which is, to the degree that anything is, an unequivocal matter of law in the first sense.

71. In *Ḥiddushei Halakhot ve-Aggadot* (in printed editions of the Talmud), Sotah 22a, s.v. *yera.*

In these times, those who determine the law (*morin halakhah*) from the *Shulḥan Arukh* cannot know the reason for each of the matters if they do not first analyze the matter from the Talmud, the study of which is itself like serving scholars (*she-hu shimmush talmidei ḥakhamim*), and err in their decisions. Such are included in the category of "the destroyers of the world."[72] and ought to be rebuked (*ligor*).

It is interesting to note that Rabbi Abraham Zevi Hirsch ben Jacob Eisenstadt (1813–1868), author of *Pitḥei Teshuvah*, adds the following postscript to Edels's statement:[73]

And it is possible that the Maharsha's statement applies specifically to his own time, during which none of the commentaries (*ḥibbur*) to the *Shulḥan Arukh* had yet been composed. But today, in light of the composition of the *Taz*,[74] the *Shakh*,[75] the *Magen Avraham*,[76] and the other *aḥaronim*, such that the reason for each law [in the *Shulḥan Arukh*] is explained on the spot, it is permissible to render decisions on the basis of the *Shulḥan Arukh* and the *aḥaronim*.

Eisenstadt is not denying the validity of Edels's claim; on the contrary, he is affirming its validity. His primary contention is that Edels's objection has been met by the composition of the commentaries to the *Shulḥan Arukh*, the purpose of which was to clarify the sources of the law, to examine the reasons because of which Caro exercised his judicial discretion as he did, to discuss possible conflicting opinions, and to quote later opinions. The commentaries, he claims, restored the steps in the halakhic process that were deleted in the final texts of the codes, and by this process of restoration legitimized the use of the *Shulḥan Arukh*, together with the commentaries, as a basis for decision-making. To the extent that the commentaries on the *Shulḥan Arukh* agree with its decisions, explaining the sources of and the reasons for those decisions, the decisions attain nearly universal acceptance—not because they are the only possible decisions, but because they are now presented as the result of the reasoned and appropriate exercise of judicial discretion.

---

72. I.e., those who do not do a service but, rather, cause harm. Cf. Sotah 22a.

73. *Pitḥei Teshuvah, Yoreh De'ah* 242, no. 8.

74. *Turei Zahav*, by Rabbi David ben Samuel ha-Levi (1586–1667), son-in-law of Rabbi Joel Sirkes (Baḥ). The Taz on *Oraḥ Ḥayyim* is published under the title *Magen David*.

75. *Siftei Kohen*, by Rabbi Shabbetai ben Me'ir ha-Kohen (1621–1662).

76. By Rabbi Abraham Abele ben Ḥayyim ha-Levi Gumbiner (ca. 1637–1683).

When the commentators agree with the decisions of the *Shulḥan Arukh,* they reinforce them by adding even greater weight of precedent to those decisions. To the extent that the commentaries disagree with the decisions of the *Shulḥan Arukh,* those decisions again become legitimate grounds for the exercise of judicial discretion.[77]

The idea that the authority of the codes rests on the weight of precedent that their widespread acceptance has established for them is reflected as early as the fifteenth century, even before the publication of the *Shulḥan Arukh.* The well-known Ashkenazic authority Rabbi Israel ben Petaḥiah Isserlein (1390–1460) wrote:[78]

> Concerning your query regarding the right of contemporary rabbis to be lenient regarding some matter concerning which the codes (*ḥibburim*)[79] have written that it is forbidden: Obviously, they do not have that authority. And how is it conceivable that one could be arrogant enough *(she-yemalle le-ish levavo)* to disagree with the codes which have been so widely accepted (*she-nitpashetu*) among Jews, except if he has a tradition from his most outstanding teachers that the decision of the codes is not accepted (*de-lo nahagu hakhi*), as we do have in a few instances. But to disagree on the basis of one's own reason, surely not.

According to Isserlein, the widespread acceptance of the codes lends so great a weight of precedent to their statements that they cannot be

77. In such a case, the weight of precedent may or may not favor one or the other of the positions. Note how Yeḥi'el Micha'el ben Aaron Isaac ha-Levi Epstein (1829–1908), author of the *Arukh ha-Shulḥan,* demonstrates the interrelatedness of systemic principles. In *Ḥoshen Mishpat,* sec. 25, par. 12, he writes: "If there is a dispute among *posekim,* and the judge is not sufficiently qualified *(gadol be-Torah)* to decide among the opinions with his own proofs, and there is no widespread weight of precedent *(ve-sugya de-alma lo nitpashtah)* concerning the matter favoring one position . . . if it is an area of prohibition from the Torah itself *(issur de-oraita),* he should decide in favor of the stricter position, while a rabbinic prohibition *(issur de-rabbanan)* should be decided in favor of the more lenient position (see above, p. 25). . . . If, however, there is widespread agreement with one position, the other being affirmed only by a small minority *(be-makom she-posekim rabbim ḥolekim al ha-yaḥid),* he should follow the majority whether for leniency or severity."

Intertwined, depending on the circumstances, are: (1) the right of a qualified arbiter to render his own reasoned decision, even opposing precedent; (2) the authority of the weight of precedent, regardless of the category (i.e., *de-oraita* or *de-rabbanan*) of the question involved; and (3) the application of appropriate systemic principles, depending on the category of the question involved.

78. *Terumat ha-Deshen,* ed. Isaac Wolf (New York: Sentry Press, 1968), *Ketavim u-fesakim,* no. 241.

79. While Isserlein could be referring to the Alfasi and Maimonides, it is equally likely that he uses the term broadly to include *sifrei pesakim* (books of legal decisions), such as the Rosh, the Ravan, the *Or Zaru'a,* etc.

ignored, except for compelling reasons—and then only by eminently qualified legalists. By the same token, however, his statement clearly implies that when the reasons *are* compelling, eminent legalists may indeed disregard the precedent of the codes. Worthy of note, as well, is the fact that Isserlein's statement does not address itself to a disagreement between scholars or codes. Apparently, the right of judicial discretion, tempered by the weight of precedent, remains unassailable under those circumstances.

With the steadily increasing acceptance of the definitive nature of the *Shulḥan Arukh,* the responsa of some arbiters, insofar as these men allowed themselves to disagree with the *Shulḥan Arukh,* indicate the pressure to which they were subject. At the same time, the very fact that they do allow themselves the right to disagree affirms their belief in the arbiter's systemic right to the legitimate exercise of his judicial discretion.

Responsa by Rabbi Joshua Hoeschel ben Joseph of Cracow (*Penei Yehoshu'a,* 1578–1648) regarding an *agunah* (i.e., a woman ineligible to remarry) whom he had declared eligible to remarry, contrary to the opinion expressed by Caro, contains examples of the conflict. He wrote:

> From the beginning of my response I knew that contemporary sages (*ḥakhmei ha-dor*) would not agree with me. For it is the nature of the present era that no reliance be placed on one who disagrees with anything written in books, even those of the very latest authors (*batra de-batra*), even if all indications are clearly against it (*afillu kol ha-ruḥot she-ba-olam ba'ot ve-noshevot bo*), though he [the disputer] may speak pearls.[80]

Later in the exchange which followed his original answer he continued:

> And concerning the *Beit Yosef* [Caro] I am greatly anguished, for he did not indicate that the view [of the earlier *posekim*] was unclear; rather, he wrote that their words clearly indicated that one must be concerned with the possibility of lending significant amounts of clothing [an element in the response of the *Penei Yehoshu'a*]—and that is very surprising. By God, if the contemporary *posekim* would say that, I would pay them no heed, for they place a stumbling block through their words by relying on prophecy [i.e., stating as

80. *Responsa Penei Yehoshu'a* (Lemberg, 1860), pt. 2, *Even ha-Ezer,* no. 47, 25b.

clear that which earlier authorities have left unsolved or unaddressed].[81]

He states further:[82]

Indeed, I surely know that even if Joshua the son of Nun had said it, he would not have been heeded, according to the custom of the sages of our country. Any matter printed in the *Shulḥan Arukh*, cannot be changed, God forbid, as though it were the Torah of Moses. Even concerning matters which are demonstrably wrong (*devarim ha-mukhraḥim*), we must put a large elephant through the small eye of a needle,[83] in order not to concede, God forbid, to any sage who has explained differently (*she-ḥiddesh davar*). . . . And not only that but . . . concerning a senseless statement, we must attribute its senselessness to our own intellectual shortcomings. . . . If so, if I find something permitted in the *Shulḥan Arukh* which seems forbidden to me on the basis of some strong objection, am I duty-bound to permit what is forbidden or pay from my own pocket, Heaven forfend, because of that view? But rather, a judge must be guided by what he sees, and Jephthah in his generation, etc. . . . for there can be no favoritism regarding the words of the living God.

The widespread acceptance of the *Shulḥan Arukh* is one thing, but the elevation of each and every one of its decisions to the inviolable status of a matter of law in the first sense is quite another: To do this is to equate a latter-day code with the Torah itself. Worse, to do this presupposes the author of the code to be virtually infallible, and, consequently, necessitates denying one's own intellectual capabilities should one conclude that the *Shulḥan Arukh* is wrong. In the final analysis, claims the *Penei Yehoshu'a*, such total abdication of one's rights negates the systemic principles that empower the sages of every generation to render authentic and authoritative decisions as they deem appropriate and necessary and any sage audacious enough to exercise his traditional rights may be assured that his efforts, even if absolutely defensible, will be vilified and rejected.

In the eighteenth century, too, one can find strongly worded affirmations of the rights of *posekim* to make judgments independent of the

81. *Ibid.*, no. 50, 27d.
82. *Ibid.*, no. 52, 29a.
83. Berakhot 55b and Bava Meẓi'a 38b.

Shulḥan Arukh. The most vocal defender of such rights was Rabbi Jacob Emden (1697–1776). In the introduction to his commentary on the Mishnah, *Leḥem Shamayim*, he states his position theoretically, without specifically mentioning the *Shulḥan Arukh*. After a lengthy discourse on the brilliance of earlier authorities, he reaffirms the obligation of later scholars to subject the words of those who preceded them to careful and critical scrutiny. He wrote:

> Even the smallest of the small can find justified objections against the greatest of the great. And there can be no favoritism in Torah. Indeed, the work of Heaven is an obligation incumbent upon every man who is competent and qualified, each according to his ability. . . . Therefore, let no man exempt himself with an erroneous claim, in order to make his task less burdensome, to be beguiled by the inclination to transgress by virtue of the false contention that one who questions the words of the ancients, those after the close of the Talmud, is as though he commits a heinous offense, as though he eats from the Tree of Knowledge.[84]

Abdicating one's obligation to be critical of earlier authorities on the beguiling grounds of their supreme superiority is an offense disguised as humility and deference. Emden never shirked his own responsibility vis-à-vis the *Shulḥan Arukh*, and he gave the fullest expression of his position in an exchange of letters with Rabbi Israel Zamosc in 1764, twelve years before his death. Interestingly, his declaration of independence from the *Shulḥan Arukh* appears in an instance in which he actually supported it. The specific subject is the applicability of *orlah* (i.e., the prohibition against eating the fruit of a tree for its first three years)[85] to engrafted trees outside of Israel. At one point in the argument he wrote:[86]

> In sum: I am aware of my worth, but have not found sufficient basis to disagree with the decision (*haskamah*) of the *Shulḥan Arukh*, even toward greater stringency; although I have not acceded to the words of even those a thousand times greater than myself in several places in my writings, when there are clear and compelling proofs (*she-ha-re'ayot makhriḥot ẓoveḥot ve-noẓeḥot*). In such cases there can

84. *Leḥem Shamayim*, ed. Rabbi J. Klein (Jerusalem: Ma'ayan Hachochma, 1958 [5718]), pp. 8 f.

85. Leviticus 19:23–25.

86. *Responsa of Yavetz* (=Jacob Emden) (Lemberg, 1884), pt. 2, end of no. 20, 12d. The entire exchange includes nos. 19–21.

> be no favoritism in Torah. Indeed, I heard from my father in the name of a great man, the author of *Ḥelkat Meḥokek,*[87] of blessed memory, that no man is entitled to render religious decisions until he is able to uproot and erase a paragraph from the *Shulḥan Arukh*. . . . And the *aḥaronim* have shown the way, that we show no favoritism toward the *Shulḥan Arukh* in an instance of compelling certainty (*be-makom hekhre'aḥ aẓum*). . . . And such has been the practice of the sages of every generation, that they have not allowed the decision of any code, either early or late, to take precedence over conclusive objections (*teshuvot niẓẓaḥot*). But God forbid that one should be lenient vis-à-vis a decision of the *Shulḥan Arukh* in a matter lacking definitive and compelling reason. . . . I do not deviate, either toward leniency or stringency, in the absence of clear compulsion (*ẓad ha-hekhre'aḥ ha-gozer*).

Later in the exchange Emden concluded:

> I show no favoritism in Torah, as my deeds in my writings demonstrate. I call an error an error, the overlooking [of a relevant source], overlooking, a defective text, defective, superfluousness, superfluous. To an astute and correct statement I say: "Well and nicely said (*kaftor va-feraḥ*)," even if it emanates from an inconsequential scholar. . . . If I err, the error is my responsibility, and I will accept the truth from any source whatsoever (*mi-mi she-amaro*).[88]

Emden's attitude toward Caro's code is a blend of deference and independence. The decisions of the *Shulḥan Arukh* have the clear status of precedent, based upon the work's widely accepted authority. But while precedent must not be easily ignored or overturned, the *Shulḥan Arukh* is not infallible; it is subject to error, either that of the author himself or that of an interpreter. The work of Torah demands that the *Shulḥan Arukh* be analyzed and scrutinized with no less care and criticism than works which preceded it. If and when compelling arguments can be raised in opposition to one of its decisions, such a decision is subject to the same systemic rules that apply to earlier sources. Moreover, analytical ability is reflected in the analysis itself, and is not dependent on either the name or the status of the analyst. Anything short of objectivity toward the arbiter or his analysis displays unwar-

---

87. Rabbi Moses ben Isaac Judah Lema (d. ca. 1670).
88. *Yavetz, loc. cit.*, no. 21, 13a.

ranted deference which, regarding Torah, is unjustified favoritism *(maso panim).*

Yet, as should even by now be clear, what is "compelling," "definitive," and "conclusive" to one is not necessarily compelling, definitive, or conclusive for another. The antagonists of Rabbi Joshua of Cracow and Rabbi Jacob Emden surely considered their own opinions no less compelling than those of Rabbi Joshua and Emden. Indeed, if disputants, after careful consideration of their antagonists' positions, continue to find their own views equally cogent, the result is a legitimate disagreement *(maḥaloket),* and in the final analysis, a judge must be guided by what he sees.

It is true, however, that by the time of the seventeenth century one also finds statements that emphasize the superiority of earlier scholars over later ones far beyond anything quoted so far, and that elevate the *Shulḥan Arukh* with the Rema almost to the level of authoritative precedent. Rabbi Menaḥem Mendel ben Abraham Krochmal (ca. 1600–1661) wrote: "After the publication of the great work of the author of the *Beit Yosef* and his *Shulḥan Arukh,* and following him the master [Rabbi Moses Isserles] in his glosses to the *Shulḥan Arukh,* and the widespread acceptance of their codes, their words are our exclusive guides (*Ein lanu ella divreihem*)."[89]

It cannot be denied, in sum, that the process of codification, and particularly the publication of the *Shulḥan Arukh* and the works of its glossators and commentators, marks a watershed in the development of the halakhic process. Yet, as relevant as this development may be, its importance should not be overstressed. The authority of the codes reflects more than anything else their acceptance as the repositories of the recorded and reasoned weight of precedent. As such, and consonant with the doctrine of precedent, they "will probably be followed by the courts."[90] But circumstances and considerations that are sufficient to warrant overturning an accepted precedent can warrant overturning a decision recorded in the *Shulḥan Arukh* too.[91] In the final analysis, only the systemic principle *Ein lo la-dayyan ella mah she-einav ro'ot* stands as the ultimate judicial guide.

89. *Responsa of Ẓemaḥ Ẓedek* (Amsterdam, 1675), no. 9, p. 15c.
90. See above, n. 8.
91. A detailed discussion and analysis of these factors is the subject of Chapter 9.

Chapter Five

On the Source and Scope of Rabbinic Authority

One of the underlying assumptions of the preceding chapters has been that the rabbis (sages, arbiters) of each generation are systemically empowered to fulfill the functions (i.e., to render the decisions and exercise the judicial discretion) that we have been discussing. Since that same assumption will underlie the remainder of this work as well, the present chapter will first explicate the systemic sources of that authority and second discuss its scope.[1]

The sources of rabbinic authority are of two types: The first is the original basis for that authority, and the second is the right of later generations of authorities to exercise the same authority as that of earlier generations.

All rabbinic authority is based, according to the rabbis themselves, on a biblical passage. In Deuteronomy 17:8–11, the Torah reads:

> When a matter of judgment is unknown to you . . . you should go up to the place that the Lord your God has chosen, and come to the levitical priests and to the judge who will exist during those days. Inquire, and they will tell you the matter of judgment. And you should act according to that which they will tell you. . . . According

1. The discussion is limited to the source of rabbinic authority with regard to its function as judge-arbiter. As for the possibility that the source of rabbinic authority with regard to its function as legislator (i.e., *ligezor u-lehatkin*) may be other than as outlined here, see Elon, *Jewish Law*, 2:395–98.

> to the instruction which they will render and the judgment which they will stipulate should you do. You should not deviate from what they tell you either to the right or to the left.

The central clause of this passage is "and to *(ve-el)* the judge who will exist during those days (*ha-shofet asher yihyeh ba-yamim hahem*)." To that clause, Rabbi Shimon ben Lakish comments succinctly: "You have none other than the judge of your own generation."[2] With a slight variation, the Babylonian Talmud reads:[3]

> Would it occur to anyone to think that one should go to a judge who is not in his own time? Rather, [the implication is] that one may not go to any but the judge in his own time, concerning which [Kohelet] says: "Say not, 'How is it that the earlier times were better than these?' "[4]

The Tosafot clarify the meaning of the quotation from Kohelet as follows:

> Since the earlier times were better than these, it follows that one should harken to the earlier ones (*rishonim*) more than the latter ones (*aḥaronim*). Do not say thus. For you have none but the judge of your own time.[5]

Interestingly, the rabbinic explanation of the verse from Deuteronomy is not free from the problems generally related to the issues of legal and historical sources. Since the sages do not stipulate that the judge of one's own time must be a priest,[6] it follows that they understood the letter *vav* of the word *ve-el* disjunctively. That this interpretation may not be the *peshat* of the verse is indicated by the following selection.[7]

> It is desirable *(mizṿah)* that the court contain priests and Levites.[8] Is it possible that [their inclusion] is obligatory to the extent of disqual-

2. *Midrash ha-Gadol* to Deuteronomy 17:9, ed. Rabbi Solomon Fisch (Jerusalem: Mossad HaRav Kook, 1972), p. 390. Cf. *Sifrei Deuteronomy*, ed. Louis Finkelstein (New York: Jewish Theological Seminary, 1969), sec. 153, p. 206, 1. 13, and note to 1. 14.
3. Rosh ha-Shanah 25b.
4. Kohelet 7:10.
5. Rosh ha-Shanah 25b, s.v. *she-ha-yamim*.
6. I.e., the sages do not understand the phrase *ha-kohanim ha-leviyyim* to mean levitical priests (priests from the tribe of Levi). See Finkelstein's note in his edition of *Sifrei Deuteronomy*, sec. 153, 1. 10, p. 206, s.v. *mizṿah*.
7. *Ibid.*, 1. 10.
8. See above, n. 6.

> ifying a court that does not contain them? The Torah says: "Or to the judge"—even though [the court] contains no priests or Levites, it is proper (*kasher*).

Clearly, the "desirable" state posited by the beginning of the passage implies recognition that, according to the *peshat*, the *vav* may be conjunctive. It is the sages themselves who attempt to reconcile the two possibilities by positing a conjunctive meaning as "desirable," while affirming that the legal meaning is disjunctive.[9] In point of fact, systemically speaking, the *peshat* of the verse is of only historical significance. Legally, only the conclusion that judges need not be priests is of any consequence.

Furthermore, even if one could demonstrate beyond doubt that the rabbinic interpretation of this verse, or any other, originated as a self-serving explanation designed to support their own claim to authority against other sects or groups which may have been contesting that authority, that fact would be legally irrelevant. Since, no matter what the reason, the halakhic system is Pharisaic-rabbinic, no interpretations deriving from other "halakhic systems"—the Sadducean-Karaitic system, for example—can have any claim to legitimacy within it. Only statements that are systemically acceptable as legal sources have a claim to normativeness. The validity of the arguments of any legal system is internal to that system, not external to it.[10]

Beyond the phrase "the judge who will exist during those days" the verse does not actually address the problem of the status of later sages in comparison to earlier ones.[11] The concept of the superiority of earlier scholars (whether or not such superiority is actual or merely supposed) called the authority of later scholars into doubt. In several *midrashim* the rabbis found it necessary to stress that the authority of later generations was equal to that of earlier generations, regardless of absolute qualification.

In his speech to the Israelites acquiescing to the appointment of a king, the prophet Samuel says, *inter alia:* "[It is] the Lord who has made

9. The *midrash* does not include a third possibility, viz., that the *vav* is explicative *(vav ha-perush),* implying that the levitical priests *are* the judges of every generation.

10. It should be noted, consequently, that a disagreement is illegitimate systemically when the view of one of the disputants is external to the system (i.e., based on some other system). Yet the very same disagreement would be systemically legitimate if both of the views were internal to the system. If, then, one position could be both internal and external to the system, the crucial issue becomes the clarification of the concepts of "internality" and "externality." That issue will be dealt with in the following chapter.

11. See the quotation from Tosafot on p. 116; as well as p. 81 above and n.2 to that page; and p. 89.

Moses and Aaron . . . and the Lord sent Jerubbaal, and Bedan, and Jephthah, and Samuel."[12] The juxtaposition of three great leaders and three mediocre leaders inspired the following rabbinic exegesis, of very great systemic significance.[13]

> "[It is] the Lord who has made Moses and Aaron," and Scripture states further: "and the Lord sent Jerubbaal, and Bedan, and Jephthah, and Samuel." Jerubbaal is Gideon;[14] Bedan is Samson;[15] Jephthah is as implied by his name.[16] And Scripture further states:[17] "Moses and Aaron among His priests, and Samuel among them that call upon His name."[18] Thus, Scripture has equated three lightweights *(kallei olam)* with three heavyweights *(gedolei olam)*,[19] to indicate that Jerubbaal's court is as authoritative *(gadol)* before God as the court of Moses, and Jephthah's court is as authoritative before God as the court of Samuel;[20] intimating that anyone who has been appointed a community leader *(parnas al ha-ẓibbur)*, even the lightest of lightweights, is equal to the noblest of nobles.[21]

---

12. I Samuel 12:6, 11.

13. Tosefta, Rosh ha-Shanah, Lieberman ed. (New York: Jewish Theological Seminary, 1962), 1:18. Cf. Rosh ha-Shanah 25a, Yer. Rosh ha-Shanah 2:9, 58b; *Kohelet Rabbah* 1:4.

14. See Judges 6:32, 7:1. The biblical narration of Gideon's feats is found in Judges 6:1–8:28.

15. "Why was he called Bedan? Because he came from the tribe of Dan" (Rosh ha-Shanah 25a). See Judges 13:2–16:31.

16. Judges 11:1–12:7.

17. Psalms 99:6.

18. This verse is quoted to prove that Samuel is to be classified in the same category (i.e., great) as Moses and Aaron, rather than with the other three.

19. This statement is probably meant more as a comparison to the three heavyweights than as a statement of their individual worth. While one could categorize Samson and Jephthah as inherently lightweights, the biblical account does not support such a categorization of Gideon.

20. Rosh ha-Shanah 25b: *Yeruba'al be-doro ke-Mosheh be-doro, Bedan be-doro ke-Aharon be-doro, Yiftaḥ be-doro ki-Shemu'el be-doro* ("Jerubaal in his generation is as Moses in his, Bedan in his generation is as Aaron in his, and Jephthah in his generation is as Samuel in his"). Yer. Rosh ha-Shanah 2:9: *Beit dino shel Gidon ve-shel Yiftaḥ ve-shel Shimshon shekulim ke-neged Mosheh ve-Aharon u-Shemu'el* ("The courts of Gideon, Jephthah, and Samson are comparable to those of Moses, Aaron, and Samuel, respectively").

21. Edels maintains that the *kal she-ba-kallim* ("lightest of the light," i.e., the least significant) means Jephthah, who was the offspring of a harlot and whose appointment was not by God; and that *abbir she-ba-abbirim* ("mightiest of the mighty") means Samuel, who is equated to Moses and Aaron combined. Thus, the most extreme statement of the equality of later generations to earlier ages is embodied in *Yiftaḥ be-doro ki-Shemu'el be-doro* ("Jephthah in his generation is as Samuel in his"). This contention explains, as well, why Jephthah is listed out of chronological order, since he preceded Samson. See Maharsha (Samuel Eliezer ben Judah ha-Levi Edels, 1555–1631, Poland) to Rosh ha-Shanah 25b (in his *Ḥiddushei Halakhot ve-Aggadot*, found in standard editions of the Babylonian Talmud).

Given the nonphilosophical and nontheoretical nature of most halakhic literature, one would be hard-pressed to find a clearer or more definitive affirmation of the right of later sages to assume the status of earlier sages, systemically if not objectively. Any system that places its earlier authorities on so high a pedestal that its later sages are impeded from exercising equal systemic authority hastens its own demise as a viable system. The very fact that the sources quoted thus far in this chapter stress the generational nature of authority is itself an intimation of the sages' cognizance of the fact that the legal system must continue to develop from generation to generation. But if that is to be the case, the system cannot allow itself to become frozen at any given generational level without destroying itself. To maintain its viability the system must recognize the authorities of each succeeding generation as legitimate and authoritative for their own time. To recognize the greatness of the early sages and be guided by their wisdom and insight is one thing; to immobilize oneself because of one's actual or possible inferiority is detrimental to the very system which, in their greatness, the early sages sought to ensure:

> Rabbi Abba bar Kahana (and some transmit it in the name of Rabbi Ada bar Huna) said, "It is written; 'A generation passes and a generation comes.'[22] Let the coming generation always be in your esteem as the generation that has passed. Do not say, 'Were Rabbi Akiva alive I would study the Bible before him.[23] Were Rabbi Zeira alive I would study Mishnah before him.'[24] And thus did he [Kohelet] say: 'Say not, "How is it that the earlier times were better than these?" '[25]—[for] you have none other than the judge of your generation."[26]

It has no doubt been noted that with the exception of the discussion of the *grundnorm*,[27] our analysis of the halakhic system has, thus far, made scarce mention of God. While this fact may seem astonishing at first glance, it is comprehensible upon analysis. First, as we shall see, the halakhic system, though positing a Divine *grundnorm*, does not allow

22. Kohelet 1:4.
23. See Menaḥot 29b for indications of Rabbi Akiva's prowess as a biblical exegete.
24. He was punctilious in the transmission of accurate traditions and always stated them in the name of their authors. Yer. Kiddushin 1:7, 61a, *et passim*.
25. Kohelet 7:10.
26. *Midrash ha-Gadol* to Deuteronomy 17:9, Fisch ed., p. 391. Cf. *Kohelet Rabbah* 1:4 and *Midrash Samuel* 15.
27. See above, chap. 1, particularly pp. 7–10.

direct or mediated Divine intervention to play an active part in its later development.[28] Second, even the indirect role that God may be perceived to have within the halakhic system cannot be either quantified or proven; and if it can be neither quantified nor proven, it must, by definition, be either denied completely or else held to be a matter of subjective evaluation.

Which of these one holds to be true depends primarily upon one's personal perspective. The fact, for example, that history may be objectively analyzed in terms of economics, sociology, power, coincidence, or a plethora of other factors (either alone or in combination) does not prevent one from interpreting these factors as expressions of the Divine will, if that is one's theological inclination. One who is not so inclined can interpret history without any recourse at all to God's place in it (except, of course, insofar as the affirmation of God's place in history is itself a factor in the analysis of any given historical period). But one can no more demonstrate that all of human history is Providential to one who lacks a theological perspective than one can demonstrate that all of human history is no more than coincidence to one possessed of a theological perspective. To the theologically oriented the idea that God works through history may constitute a given, so self-evident that it requires no proof. For the non–theologically inclined, the opposite is the case. None of this is to say, of course, that each could not understand the other's position—and perhaps even appreciate it.

Similarly, the place one assigns to God in the halakhic process depends upon one's personal perspective. The ascendancy of the Pharisees over the Sadducees, the Hillelites over the Shammaites, the Akivaites over the Ishmaelites, the Mishnah of Judah the Prince over all other collections, the Babylonian Talmud over the Palestinian Talmud, the Rabbanites over the Karaites; the acceptance of the Alfas, Asher ben Yeḥi'el, and Maimonides as *posekim par excellence;* and the authority acquired by the *Shulḥan Arukh*—all of these can be and, indeed, have been interpreted as being the result of historical circumstance, coincidence, economics, politics, power, and a plethora of other factors (either alone or in combination). But, as with history in general, it is one's personal theological perspective that determines whether one sees the operation of these factors as accidental or Providential. If accidental, God's real place in the halakhic system is virtually nil; if Providential, it is all. Thus, it is the theological perspective of the individual that is the central determinant of that person's evaluation of God's place within the halakhic system. It is important to note, moreover, that to those who

28. The validity of the contention will be demonstrated below, p. 123.

affirm that God is *all* in the system, frequent mention of Him is superfluous, since every step of the system is Providentially supervised. If, on the other hand, He has no place within the development of the system, any mention of Him is intellectually dishonest.

What must yet be addressed, however, is whether or not the system itself prescribes a particular theological position as a *sine qua non* for its authorities.[29]

The above theological digression is, in reality, the preface to a discussion of the scope of rabbinic authority, for the scope of that authority, while primarily of concern to us legally, was a source of great theological difficulty for those upon whom it rested, for it bore upon their perception of the place of God in the halakhic system, particularly with respect to the wide latitude that, we have seen, was available to them in the area of legitimate differences of opinion and the exercise of judicial discretion.

The end of the passage that served as the primary source of rabbinic authority, Deuteronomy 17:8–11, also served as the basis for rabbinic discussion of the scope of that authority. The sentence "You should not deviate from what they tell you either to the right or to the left" is interpreted in the *Sifrei* as follows: "Even if they decide concerning that which seems to you to be clearly right that it is left, or concerning that which is clearly left that it is right, obey them."[30] In his *Commentary* on the same verse Naḥmanides wrote:

> Even if you think that they are in error, and the matter seems as straightforward to you as your knowledge between your right hand and your left hand, do as they command. Do not say, "How shall I eat [completely forbidden] fat?"[31] or "[How] shall I execute this innocent man?"[32] Say rather: "Thus did the Master, who commanded concerning the *miẓvot*, command me, that I should comply concerning all of His commandments with everything which those who stand before Him in the place that He chose may instruct. He gave me the Torah [to be obeyed] according to their interpretation (*al mashma'ut da'atam*), even if they are mistaken . . . according to whatever they might say in explanation of the Torah, having received its explanation in a direct chain of tradition to Moses from the Almighty, or having explained thus on the basis of the Torah's

29. See below, chap. 6.
30. *Sifrei Deuteronomy*, Finkelstein ed., sec. 154, p. 207.
31. Leviticus 3:17.
32. Exodus 23:7.

clear or intended meaning (*le-fi mashma'ut ha-torah o kavvanatah*). For He has given the Torah [to be obeyed] according to their understanding thereof, even if it seems to you to be a reversal of the right with the left. And surely so when it appears to you that they say of the right that it is right. For the spirit of God is with *(al)* the ministers of His sanctuary, and He does not abandon those committed to Him (*ḥasidav*), who are forever preserved[33] from error and stumbling-block.

As the rabbis see it, then, the scope of rabbinic authority extends even to the most extreme theoretical possibility, that of an apparently gross miscarriage of the will of God, the making of what is ostensibly "right" into "left." The traditional theological grounds for such authority is that the development of the *halakhah* is Providentially guided: Since His sages are guarded from error by Providence, even an apparent miscarriage of His will is His will.[34]

The establishment by the sages themselves of their right to interpret the Torah, and their definition of the extent of that right, demonstrate clearly that the validity of the system is internal to it; that is to say, the system is, on a very basic level, completely circular. First, the *grundnorm* of the system posits the supremacy of the Torah as the reflection of the word and the will of God. Subsequently, for whatever reason—economic, political, historical, Providential—the developing system recognized Pharisaic authority alone as normative. On the basis of this recognized authority, the Pharisees then interpreted the Deuteronomic passage to mean that, as the only empowered authorities, only they have the right to interpret the Torah normatively, even to the point of an apparently erroneous interpretation. Ultimately, therefore, it is the sages' own interpretation of the Torah that validates their right to do so, and that defines the scope of that right. Furthermore, the only validation of this interpretation is the fact that the system recognized them as the normative interpreters of the Torah. Ergo, we have a complete circle, beginning and ending with the systemic recognition of the sages as the normative interpreters of the Torah.

Obviously, if one were to deny that the system recognized the sages as the only normative interpreters of the Torah, it would follow that their claim to be so is either not true or, minimally, nondemonstrable.

33. Psalms 37:28.

34. The Yerushalmi (Horayot 1:1, 45d) is more circumspect than the *Sifrei*, restricting the scope of the sages' authority to their declaration: *Al yamin she-hu yamin ve-al semol she-hi semol* ("about the right that it is right and the left that it is left").

Yet any such argument against either the right of the sages to interpret or against the scope of that right is an argument from outside the system, and is, therefore, not valid systemically. Thus we come around once again to the fact that the validity of the system is internal to it.[35]

Having posited themselves as the sole normative interpreters of the Torah, it is not at all surprising that the sages developed systemic safeguards against any encroachment upon their prerogatives. Once the ascendancy of the Pharisees over competing sects was assured, the greatest danger to the system came from a source which, at first glance, seems astonishing, namely, from God Himself—either through direct or mediated revelation. Since, by definition, Divine revelation is not susceptible to systemic control, and since they could not deny the truth of Divine revelation, its systemic acceptance could wreak havoc with the ordinary functioning of the system and, ultimately, could destroy it.

Actually, with rare exceptions, recourse to Divine intervention has not been a significant legal issue throughout most of the history of the *halakhah*.[36] I will, therefore, treat the subject briefly here only to indicate that the safeguards alluded to above were, in fact, instituted by the sages.

On the basis of the words *elleh ha-mizvot* ("these are the commandments") in Leviticus 27:34, the rabbis opined that "no prophet may introduce something new (*lehaddesh*) from now on,"[37] and thus denied mediated revelation any further systemic authority.[38]

As for direct Divine revelation, the classical, and profoundly significant, passage that clearly denies systemic authority to any such claim in the future recounts a dispute between Rabbi Eli'ezer ben Hyrcanus and the sages concerning the susceptibility of a certain type of oven to ritual

---

35. The Supreme Court's right of judicial review is similarly circular. That is, the systemically recognized ultimate interpreters of the Constitution interpreted it to mean that they possess the right of judicial review. The only possible validation of that claim is their systemic recognition as the ultimate interpreters of the *grundnorm*. Any arguments against the constitutional right of the Supreme Court to exercise judicial review that base themselves on systems that do not recognize such a right within their own judiciaries would be legally insignificant because such arguments come from outside the system, and the system's validity is completely internal.

36. See Elon, *Jewish Law*, chap. 7, and particularly, 1:227 ff.

37. *Sifra, Be-hukotai* 13:7 and talmudic parallels in Shabbat 104a, Yoma 70a, Megillah 2b, and Temurah 16a.

38. Note that this rabbinic opinion restricted the prophetic right to introduce something new *(lehadesh)* from the time of the giving of the Torah onward, which includes the prophetic period itself. This fact becomes comprehensible when we understand that the rabbis posited a direct systemic chain from Moses through themselves. From a strictly legal point of view, the elimination of mediated Divine intervention is crucial only in the postprophetic stage.

impurity.[39] The sages affirmed that the oven was susceptible, and Rabbi Eli'ezer claimed that it was not. Yet the sages remained adamant, even in the face of Rabbi Eli'ezer's cogent arguments against their position. Rabbi Eli'ezer then had recourse to supernatural signs attesting the rectitude of his position: A carob tree uprooted itself, water flowed uphill, and the walls of the academy tilted. But it was all to no avail. At that point, Rabbi Eli'ezer said to them:

> "If the law is as I say, let it be proved from Heaven." A Divine voice was heard (*yaẓatah bat kol*) saying: "What do you want from Rabbi Eli'ezer! The law is according to his position in all cases!" Whereupon Rabbi Joshua stood up on his feet and exclaimed: "It [the Torah] is not in Heaven."[40] What is the meaning of "It is not in Heaven"? Rabbi Jeremiah explained, "After the giving of the Torah at Sinai we no longer pay any heed to divine voices. For the Torah already says: "Follow the majority."[41] [After this episode] Rabbi Nathan met Elijah and said to him, "What was the Holy One, blessed be He, doing at the time?" Elijah answered, "He was smiling and saying, 'My sons have defeated Me, My sons have defeated Me.' "

On the level of the present discussion, the passage clearly indicates the systemic inadmissibility of direct Divine revelation as a determinant of the law. Even more, its conclusion declares the rabbinic affirmation that God Himself acquiesced in His exclusion from the halakhic process. Having revealed His will at Sinai in the *grundnorm,* He Himself, according to the circular rabbinic argument, entrusted the interpretation of His will to the sages. Thus, the ultimate irony is that God's active participation in the halakhic process would constitute a vitiation of His own will.

The passage just quoted is also discussed by later authorities with regard to its implications concerning the theoretically unlimited scope of rabbinic authority and the problems arising from it, and it is to an examination of these implications that we turn now.

Rabbi Nissim ben Re'uven Gerondi (Ran, ca. 1310–1375) provides the clearest and most comprehensive explication of the implications of this passage. In one of his sermons he writes:[42]

---

39. Bava Meẓi'a 59b.
40. Deuteronomy 30:12.
41. Exodus 23:2.
42. *Derashot ha-Ran,* ed. M. Stern (Jerusalem, 1959 [5719]), no. 7, p. 24a.

> When disputes among the sages proliferated, the law would be established according to the majority position if the dispute was one between a minority (*yaḥid*) and the majority. But if the dispute was many against many or one against one, it would be resloved as the sages of that time deemed appropriate (*ke-fi ha-nireh*). For the determination of the law has already been entrusted to them, as it says:[43] "You should come to the levitical priests or (*o*)[44] to the judge . . . You should not deviate. . . ." Thus, permission is granted to the sages of every generation (*ḥakhmei ha-dorot*) to decide in a dispute among sages as they deem appropriate, even if the earlier ones were greater than they or more numerous than they.[45] And we are commanded to abide by their decision whether it is "true" or its opposite. And that is the implication of the matter of Rabbi Eli'ezer the Great in his dispute. As we say there in Bava Meẓi'a: "Rabbi Joshua stood on his feet and exclaimed, 'It is not in Heaven.' The Torah has already been given to Moses at Sinai, and it is written therein: 'Follow the majority.' " In truth, all of the sages saw that Rabbi Eli'ezer had determined the law correctly (*maskim al ha-emet*), more than they, and that the supernatural signs which he produced were all honest and legitimate (*amittiyyim ẓodekim*),[46] and that a decision in his favor was rendered from Heaven itself. Nonetheless, action on the law was according to their decision. For, since their reason (*sikhlam*) was inclined to declare the oven susceptible to ritual impurity, even though they knew that their decision was counter to the "truth," they would not agree (*lo raẓu*) to declare it unsusceptible to ritual impurity. Had they done so, they would have been violating the Torah, since their reason guided them to declare it susceptible to ritual impurity. For the determination of the law has been entrusted to the sages of each generation, and what they decide is what God has commanded.

The Ran repeats the same idea in another of his sermons amplifying the final portion of the above passage.

> And we believe *(betuḥim)*, concerning the *miẓvot* of the Torah and its laws, that so long as we abide by the decisions of the sages of the

43. Deuteronomy 17:8–11.
44. See the verse itself, and above, p. 117.
45. I.e., the systemic principle *Ein bet din yakhol le-vattel divrei bet din haveiro ella im ken gadol heimenu be-ḥokhmah u-ve-minyan* does not apply to this set of circumstances, since, in point of fact, the present sages are not abrogating an earlier decision, but exercising legitimate judicial discretion.
46. I.e., neither magic nor optical illusions.

> generation (*gedolei ha-dor*) we are fulfilling the will of the blessed God . . . even if we believe (*na'amin*) that they have decided contrary to the "truth."[47]

The scope of rabbinic authority knows no theoretical bounds. As the sole normative interpreters of the meaning of the Torah, Torah means whatever the rabbis say it means. And to whatever they say it means, in every generation, God agrees, even if, in some "objective" realm, He disagrees with their interpretation.[48]

If one concludes that, given the broad scope of rabbinic authority, it was possible for the halakhic system to develop in such a way that its later stages would bear no relationship to its earlier stages, one would be correct. The talmudic sages themselves recognized this possibility and gave eloquent expression to it in the well-known *midrash* dealing with Moses' ascent to Heaven to receive the Torah.[49] While in Heaven, Moses sits at the very back of a class being taught by Rabbi Akiva, who is, ostensibly, expounding upon the Torah of Moses (i.e., interpreting the *grundnorm*). Listening, Moses becomes very disheartened because he cannot understand what is being said. His spirit revives only when, in answer to a question, Rabbi Akiva responds that the source of one of his statements is the law which God gave Moses at Sinai *(halakhah le-Mosheh mi-Sinai)*. What the *midrash* is expressing here is the rabbis' recognition of the fact that the law as they know it is the result of their own interpretation of it, an interpretation that may at times be far removed from the original intention of the author. Yet they affirm with equal adamance that so long as their interpretation is ultimately grounded in the *grundnorm*, the later stages of the halakhic process constitute, not a vitiation of the system, but its legitimate growth.

The passages quoted thus far in this book have referred *inter alia* to the principle that the law is determined according to the majority. This assertion stems primarily from the biblical verse "Follow the majority," which is referred to in the passage from Bava Meẓi'a.[50] Furthermore, the

---

47. *Derashot ha-Ran*, Stern ed., no. 11, p. 39c.

48. Thus far, the discussion has been restricted to the scope of rabbinic authority as interpreters of the *grundnorm*, but not as abrogators or changers of the *grundnorm*. To the extent that we may find, in a later discussion, that the scope of rabbinic authority includes the possibility of abrogating or changing the *grundnorm* itself, we shall have to address the problem of *ultra vires* ("beyond the authority"), i.e., the possibility that that degree of authority allowed to the sages vitiates the supremacy of the *grundnorm*. Put theologically, the problem concerns the possibility that the sages, in fact, take the place, systemically, of God Himself, instead of remaining just the interpreters of His word.

49. Menaḥot 29b. Referred to above in n. 23 as containing an indication of the prowess of Rabbi Akiva as a biblical exegete.

50. Bava Meẓi'a 59b, Exodus 23:2; also see above, p. 124.

Deuteronomic passage that serves as the fundamental source of rabbinic authority assumes the existence of a supreme body possessing the right to render definitive decisions.[51] Yet both of these passages seem to be at variance with some of the conclusions we have reached in preceding chapters regarding the legitimacy of *maḥaloket*, the range of judicial discretion, the weight of precedent, and the validity even of divergent behaviors. Systemically, however, the primary difference between an era in which such a supreme body exists and an era in which it does not is that its existence makes it possible to elevate matters of law in the second sense, matters of fact, and questions of judicial discretion, definitively, to matters of law in the first sense. It is not that the inner systemic workings of the rabbinic process are different when such a body does not exist, for they are *not* different. The lack of a supreme body only means that it is impossible to elevate anything definitively to a matter of law in the first sense. Moreover, even in the era when a supreme body did exist, disputes, disagreements, and conflicts preceded the definitive determination of the law;[52] the existence of such a body did not eliminate dispute and conflict. Thus, if the development of the *halakhah* is not capricious, but Providentially guided, the implication is, clearly, that God Himself acquiesces in the existence of controversy in the interpretation of His will.

The basis of the first talmudic statement which bears on that subject is the following enigmatic verse from Kohelet:[53] "The words of the wise are as goads, and as well-driven nails [are the] *ba'alei asufot*;[54] they were given by one shepherd [or, Shepherd]."[55] The Talmud comments:[56]

> *Ba'alei asufot* are the sages who sit in groups (*asufot asufot*) and study the Torah. Some declare impure, others declare pure; some forbid, others permit; some disqualify, others declare fit. And lest one say, "How, then, shall I study Torah?"[57] the Scripture affirms, "They

---

51. Deuteronomy 17:8–11.

52. See Maimonides, *Mishneh Torah*, Hilkhot Mamrim 2:1, re the finality of definitive decisions; and above, p. 62.

53. Kohelet 12:11.

54. The translations of this ambiguous phrase vary greatly: "master of Assemblies," "masters of collections," "composed in collections." The words have been left untranslated, since the *peshat* of the phrase is irrelevant to the *midrash*.

55. See *Sifrei Deuteronomy*, Finkelstein ed., sec. 41, p. 86.

56. Ḥagigah 3b. Cf. Tosefta Sotah 7:10–12, *Avot d'Rabbi Nathan*, ed. Solomon Schechter (New York: Feldheim, 1967), Version A, chap. 18. Rashi (in his commentary to Ḥagigah 3b, s.v. *af hu*) attributes the *midrash* to Rabbi Elazar ben Azariah. Maharsha (in his commentary to Ḥagigah 3b, s.v. *af hu*) attributes it to Rabbi Joshua. The version of *Avot d'Rabbi Nathan* supports the attribution of Rashi.

57. I.e., "Of what use is it to study Torah, considering the obvious ambiguity of its meaning, as indicated by the proliferation of disputes?"

> were given by one shepherd."[58] One God gave them, one leader (*parnas*)[59] spoke them all from the mouth of the Master of all deeds, blessed be He, as it is written: "And the Lord spoke all of these things."[60] You too, therefore, make your ear like a grain-hopper, and acquire the understanding to comprehend the words of those who declare impure and those of them who declare pure, the words of those who forbid and those of them who permit, the words of those who disqualify and those of them who declare fit.

While the selection is not, admittedly, an explanation of why the situation that the sages deduced from the verse on Kohelet is or ought to be the case, it constitutes, at least, a very strong affirmation that conflicting opinions can be, at one and the same time, equally Divine. And that affirmation is expressed in the strongest possible rabbinic language, namely, the statement that the conflicting positions themselves were revealed by God to Moses. A bit of the metaphysical edge is removed from the passage by Rashi, who, with his usual brevity, intimates how it is possible for each of two or more conflicting positions to be Divine. He says: "Since all of the positions are stated with the intent to understand the Divine will (*me-aḥar she-kullam libban la-shamayim*), allow yourself to grasp, study, and comprehend all of the positions. And when you can distinguish which of them is most appropriate, set the law in accordance therewith."[61] Thus, the master of commentators affirms that the Divine nature of conflicting opinions is not a factor of their specific content, but of the purity of intent of those who express them. And what legitimizes any position, ultimately, is its having been stated "for the sake of Heaven" *(le-shem shamayim)*.[62] The substance of the position is not decisive, since "even concerning the Law given to Moses there are arguments in favor of both impurity and purity. [And rabbinic exegesis] on the basis of the words 'All of these things'[63] includes them all [as if] from the mouth of the Almighty; for the Divine word bears many interpretations (*mitḥallek le-khammah kolot*).[64]

---

58. Kohelet 12:11.
59. I.e., Moses.
60. Exodus 20:1.
61. Ḥagigah 3b, s.v. *aseh*.
62. Cf. Avot 5:17, and especially Obadiah Bertinoro's (15th cent. commentator on the Mishnah, found in standard editions of the Mishnah) second explanation of *sofah*.
63. Exodus 20:1. See above, p. 127, the quotation from Ḥagigah 3b.
64. Maharsha, Ḥagigah 3b, s.v. *nittenu*. Cf. Sanhedrin 34a: *u-khe-fattish yefoẓeẓ sela: mah pattish zeh mitḥallek le-khammah niẓoẓot, af mikra eḥad yoẓe le-khammah te'amim*. An interesting medieval philosophical twist is proffered by a commentator, probably Naḥmanides, in *Mehararei Nemerim* (Venice, 1599), Ḥagigah, chap. 1, p. 17a. He wrote: " 'They were all

Considering, however, the fact that in any given case a decision must be reached, as well as the fact that conflicting positions on a matter are recognized as equally Divine, both the manner in which a decision is finally reached and the implications of that final decision for the Divine nature of the *rejected* position become problematic. It is to these particular issues that a second talmudic passage addresses itself.[65]

> Rabbi Abba said in the name of Samuel: "For three years the School of Shammai and the School of Hillel argued. The former said: 'The law is according to our opinions.' The latter said: 'The law is according to our opinions.' A Divine voice was heard,[66] saying: 'The words of both are the words of the Living God (*Ellu ve-ellu divrei elohim ḥayyim*), but the law is in accordance with the School of Hillel.' "
>
> But if the words of both are the words of the Living God, on what basis did the School of Hillel merit that the law should be determined in accordance with its positions? Because they were gentle and kind, and used to include their own words plus those of the School of Shammai. They even used to place the words of the School of Shammai before their own.

Understood in a straightforward manner, the passage implies that none of the positions in a conflict is inherently or objectively correct or incorrect. All positions are both correct and incorrect; and all positions remain equally Divine, even after all but one have been rejected as normative guides to behavior. The actual determination of the law may be predicated on factors totally independent of the objective rectitude of the favored position. Indeed, just such an interpretation was given by Rabbi Yom Tov ben Abraham Ishbili (Ritba, ca. 1250–1330).[67] He wrote:

---

given by one Shepherd' means that since we usually comprehend a matter better by its negation *(hafakho)*—and we cannot comprehend it as well inherently *(me-aẓmuto)* as from its negation—God, therefore, wished to provide us with conflicting positions so that, when we encounter the correct explanation *(ha-sevara ha-amittit)* we will comprehend it thoroughly."

65. Eruvin 13b.

66. Evidently reflecting a position at variance with that of the selection from Bava Meẓi'a (above, p. 124). Attempts of the commentators to reconcile the apparent disagreement notwithstanding (e.g., Tosafot, Bava Meẓi'a, 59b, s.v. *lo*), the implication is that the refusal to permit direct Divine intervention in the halakhic process is a matter of judicial discretion, with the vast weight of precedent favoring the position which refuses such recognition. In theory, then, the same types of compelling reasons that could serve as grounds for rejecting precedent could be applied as well to accepting direct Divine intervention in the halakhic process.

67. Ritba, Eruvin 13b.

> The French sages, of blessed memory, asked how it is possible that "the words of both are the words of the Living God," when one forbids and the other permits. And they explained that when Moses ascended to Heaven to receive the Torah, he was shown concerning every single issue forty-nine indications to declare forbidden and forty-nine indications to declare permissible.[68] When he asked the Holy One, blessed be He, about this, He answered that it [the determination of the law] is entrusted to the sages of Israel, in every generation, and the decision should be according to them. Midrashically, this explanation is correct.[69] Philosophically, the phrase has an esoteric meaning *(u-ve-derekh ha-emet yesh ta'am sod ba-davar).*

The word of God may be susceptible to multiple interpretations, even contradictory ones, none of which is necessarily true or false. Only such a claim can make the statement that Moses was shown so many possible interpretations in Heaven itself comprehensible. Moreover, since no single explanation is objectively true or false, God Himself must acquiesce in whatever decision the sages of any generation may reach. The intent of the clause "in every generation" is, evidently, that God acquiesces in the decisions of each generation, even if the decisions of one generation are at variance with the decisions of another. Only the sages of each generation can determine the meaning of the word of God for that generation. Since the word of God has no objective meaning, it must, therefore, mean whatever the sages in any generation say it means.

A less metaphysical interpretation is offered by Rabbi Isaiah ben Abraham ha-Levi Horowitz (ca. 1565–1630). He writes:

> The words of both are the words of the Living God. When two *amora'im* disagree about a law or a matter concerning what is forbidden or what is permitted, each one supporting his position with some reason, there is no falsehood implied. For each one gives his own reason, one arguing to permit and the other to forbid; one comparing the matter in question to one thing, and the other to another. In such a case one can say, "The words of both are the words of the Living God," for occasionally the one reason applies, and occasionally the other. For the application of the appropriate reason varies on the basis of very minor changes.[70]

---

68. See Eruvin 13b.

69. What is midrashic is the purported dialogue between Moses and God. The contention that the law is entrusted to the sages of Israel of each generation is not midrashic.

70. *Shenei Luḥot he-Berit* (Jerusalem: Project for the Publication of the *Shenei Luḥot ha-Berit,* 1959), pt. IV, "Torah She-be-al Peh: Kelal Leshonot Sugyot," s.v. *af al pi she-ein,* p.

While closer to a more rationalistic understanding of the phrase, even this explanation affirms that none of the views in a conflict is objectively wrong. What may be right at one time and under one set of circumstances may be wrong at another. All positions constitute the words of the Living God.

It is not surprising that the talmudic passage should also be interpreted in ways that do not accord with its *peshat*. The *peshat* after all, makes the will of God difficult to understand by positing the complex idea that both A and not-A can be correct, an idea about which no less an authority than Rabbi Joseph Caro seems to have been bothered. He wrote:[71]

> I find the following surprising: If the law was not really as they said,[72] would it have been determined in accordance with their position on the basis of their characterological virtues (*ha-middot ha-tovot*) alone? Perhaps the intent of the passage is to ask: On what basis did they merit that their positions should always be correct (*she-yekhavvenu tamid ha-emet*), such that, by virtue of their being correct, the law was established in accordance therewith?

The clear implication of Caro's wonder is the denial of the possibility that the idea *Ellu ve-ellu divrei elohim ḥayyim* can be understood without embellishment: Two contradictory positions cannot both be correct. But in order to circumvent the admitted difficulties of the passage, he is forced to explain the selection in a way that is difficult to support textually, although easier metaphysically.

There is yet another interpretation that, while incorporating Caro's objection in a very subtle fashion, retains most of the implications of the more straightforward interpretation. Solomon Algazi (ca. 1610–1683) quoted the following in the name of Rabbenu Ḥananel:[73]

> The meaning of "The words of both are the words of the Living God" is as follows: The Holy One, blessed be He, demonstrated to Moses at Sinai forty-nine indications to declare pure and forty-nine indications to declare impure, but did not decide the matter. Rather,

---

10a. Cf. also Rashi, Ketubbot 57a, s.v. *ha km"l*. Horowitz offers mystical interpretations in the same work, pt. I, "Beit Ḥokhmah," p. 13c, s.v. *ma'alat ellu ve-ellu divrei elohim ḥayyim*, p. 60a. See Gershom G. Scholem, *The Messianic Idea in Judaism*, "Revelation of Tradition as Religious Categories" (New York: Schocken Books, 1971), pp. 301 ff.

71. *Kelalei ha-Gemara* (a commentary to *Halikhot Olam* [Warsaw, 1883] by Yeshu'a ha-Levi), p. 87a.

72. I.e., the School of Hillel in the above passage from Eruvin.

73. *Yavin Shemu'ah* (a commentary to *Halikhot Olam* and *Kelalei ha-Gemara* [see above, n. 71]), p. 88b.

> the determination was left to be carried out in accordance with the decision of the majority, as He wrote in the Torah: "Follow the majority."[74] Thus this, in essence, is the meaning of the Talmud's question: Since the words of both are the words of the Living God, and both views were stated to Moses on Sinai, although the Holy One, blessed be He, does not wish to decide in any matter, then on what basis did the School of Hillel merit that the law be determined according to their position from Heaven, via a *bat kol* [heavenly voice], when that very fact contradicts the contention that both are the words of the Living God, which means that the Holy One, blessed be He, does not decide Himself?

The interpretation here attributed to Rabbenu Ḥananel incorporates the thrust of Caro's objection by defining the idea *Ellu ve-ellu divrei elohim ḥayyim* to mean not that there is no one correct will of God, but that He, in essence, has withdrawn Himself from revealing His will, leaving its determination to the sages. The logical and philosophical problem is thus solved, but the practical result is no different from the earlier interpretations of the passage, insofar as God's refusal to make His own will known definitively is the equivalent of the contention that there is no definitive will of God. And if that is the meaning of *Ellu ve-ellu divrei elohim ḥayyim,* the meaning of the Talmud's question must be reinterpreted to mean: "Why, in the case of the School of Hillel, did God find it proper to ignore His own self-imposed withdrawal from active participation in the determination of His will by intervening in that school's favor?"

Even if one could claim that the idea "The words of both are the words of the Living God" can bear this interpretation (a doubtful claim at best), the talmudic text does not support the contention that the thrust of the question concerning the merit of the School of Hillel was meant to emphasize the heavenliness of the determination as opposed to the determination itself. Thus, in the absence of any defensible evidence to the contrary, the talmudic text must be allowed to speak for itself. It expresses the difficult philosophical and metaphysical hypothesis that in any controversy all positions are equally Divine and that none is inherently right or wrong. Whichever position is adopted by the sages of any generation becomes the will of God for that generation, by virtue of His own acquiescence. Even in an era in which there exists a supreme body possessing the right to render definite decisions, the decision elevates the favored position to the status of law in the first sense, but

74. Exodus 23:2.

does not negate the Divinity of the nonfavored positions. It is in this sense, then, that "The words of both are the words of the Living God, but the law is according to the School of Hillel."

Thus, it is accurate to say that the scope of rabbinic authority is, in theory, unbounded.[75] The meaning of the Torah in every generation, and with it the determination of the will of God for that generation, is entrusted to the hands of that generation. Rabbinic interpretation of the law is, as it were, the never-ending revelation of the will of God. There is no absolute in the content of the Divine will that is mediated through the decisions and opinions of those who are systemically recognized authorities of the halakhic process.

It should be clear that the exercise of rabbinic authority, as it is understood in this chapter, entails an awesome responsibility; for any declaration of opinion amounts to a declaration not just that such is the opinion of Sage X, but that, in the opinion of Sage X, such is the will of God. To be counted among those to whom is entrusted the authority to act as the "recipients" of the never-ending revelation of the will of God is not a matter to be taken lightly. One becomes more sympathetic to the tendency among recognized authorities to shy away from the acceptance of this responsibility, or, at least, to be very conservative in its exercise. One can more readily understand why the sages were motivated to define the age before which it was unlikely that one could be entrusted to exercise such authority responsibly;[76] or why, on the other hand, they were compelled to affirm that the shirking of that responsibility by those who were qualified to exercise it was as detrimental to the functioning and growth of the system as its irresponsible exercise.[77]

Given the almost unbounded scope of rabbinic authority, and the religious-theological significance of its exercise, it is logical that this discussion should proceed to an analysis of the qualifications and characteristics that the system demands of its recognized authorities.

---

75. See above, n. 48.
76. Avodah Zarah 19b.
77. *Ibid.*

Chapter Six

On the Qualifications of Authorities

The question "Who qualifies as a rabbinic authority?" requires a twofold answer, since there are academic qualifications that must be satisfied as well as nonacademic qualifications (i.e., those characteristics of personality and religious requirements that any rabbinic authority must possess). Indeed, it is our contention, to be demonstrated, that the possession of both kinds of qualifications is a necessary condition for recognition as an authority; neither alone is sufficient.

In his capacity as judge-arbiter, an authority can be called upon, theoretically, to decide four kinds of cases: (1) cases that require the determination of that which is forbidden and that which is permissible *(issur ve-hetter);*[1] (2) cases that involve judgments concerning civil monetary matters *(dinei mamonot);* [2] (3) cases that require the imposition of stipulated fines *(dinei kenasot);*[3] and (4) cases that involve capital crimes

1. These include, *inter alia,* almost all matters of ritual, Sabbath, festival, and holiday observance, *kashrut,* mourning, marriage, and divorce.

2. These include, *inter alia,* damages of all kinds, injury, debts, negligence, torts, and breaches of contract. The primary legal factor that distinguishes this category from the next is that the payment imposed on the guilty party is made in direct restitution for the offense, the amount varying according to the damage or injury.

3. These are restricted to the small number of instances where the Torah stipulates a specific penalty for a specific offense, the amount of which is legally fixed and never varies. See, for example, Exodus 21:32 and Deuteronomy 22:19, 28.

(dinei nefashot).[4] Since the third and fourth categories are not within the jurisdiction of rabbinical courts in the modern period, our analysis of the qualifications necessary for rabbinic authority will focus on the qualifications necessary for judging the first two categories. It should be noted, however, that the vast majority of cases modern authorities are called upon to determine concern the forbidden and the permissible; judgments involving civil monetary matters being restricted, primarily, to cases in which the litigants voluntarily agree to appear before the rabbinic court.

From the talmudic description of the ordination of Rav and Rabbah bar Ḥanah,[5] it is clear that the right to judge that which is forbidden and that which is permissible *(issur ve-hetter)* is called "the right to teach" or "to instruct" *(lehorot),* while the right to judge matters involving money *(dinei mamonot)* is called "the right to judge" *(ladun).*

The Mishnah stipulates that *dinei mamonot* are to be judged by a court of three;[6] and there is universal consensus (at least regarding loans and debts, the most common of monetary cases) that the three judges need not be experts *(mumḥin);* rather, they can even be nonexperts *(hedyotot).*[7] The Talmud[8] justifies the use of three nonexperts in the matter of loans on the grounds that "it is impossible that there not be among them at least one who has learned *(de-gamir).*"[9] Since, however, a nonexpert is clearly not an authority, it follows that learning itself is not a sufficient academic qualification for authority.

A *baraita* stipulates further that although monetary cases require a court of three, if one is a recognized expert *(mumḥeh la-rabbim)* he may judge them alone.[10] The passage that follows immediately upon this *baraita* sheds light on the qualifications of such a recognized expert.

> Rav Naḥman said, "I, for example, can judge monetary cases alone." Similarly, Rabbi Ḥiyya said, "I, for example, can judge

---

4. It is also true that certain legal considerations apply to all of the types of cases, with variations, for example, court procedures and the qualification or disqualification of judges and/or witnesses.

5. Sanhedrin 5a–b.

6. Sanhedrin 1:1.

7. A complicating factor, not relevant to the present discussion, but potentially germane to future analysis, revolves around the question of proper categorization—*de-oraita* or *de-rabbanan*—of the nonspecialist court's right to judge. If its right to judge is *de-rabbanan,* but *de-oraita* the requirement is for specialists to judge, we have here an instance of rabbinic modification of the *grundnorm.* In terms of the delineation of the academic qualifications of judges, specialists or not, however, the question of *de-oraita* or *de-rabbanan* is not relevant.

8. Sanhedrin 3a.

9. Rashi (Sanhedrin 3a, s.v. *de-gamir*) explains: "Who has heard the laws of loans from sages and judges."

10. Sanhedrin 4b–5a.

monetary cases alone." They [the sages in the academy] asked, Does "I, for example" [mean to imply] "who have studied (*de-gamirna*),[11] am capable of cogent reasoning (*savirna*),[12] and have received permission *(nakitna reshuta),*"[13] such that if one did not receive permission, his judgment would be unacceptable? Or, perhaps ["I, for example," refers only to the first two characteristics, such that] even though he did not have permission his judgment is acceptable.

The Talmud assumes that Rav Naḥman and Rabbi Ḥiyya each possessed three qualifications: Each was knowledgeable, each was capable of cogent reasoning, and each had been ordained, i.e., received permission. It assumes, further, that the first two qualifications are necessary conditions for being considered a recognized authority, questioning only whether the two are sufficient or whether ordination is also a necessary condition. The answer is deduced in the Talmud itself from the following incident, related in the continuation of the passage.

Mar Zutra the son of Rav Naḥman [who did not have permission to judge monetary cases alone] once judged a case [alone] and erred. He came before Rav Joseph,[14] who said to him, "If they agreed to accept whatever decision you rendered, you need not pay. If not, go and pay." From which can be conclusively deduced that his decision stands even though he had not received permission.

Since Rav Joseph did not instruct Mar Zutra to abrogate his decision, although the latter was operating without formal permission to judge monetary cases alone, it follows conclusively that ordination is not a necessary condition for acquiring the status of a recognized expert. Formal ordination guarantees its recipient exemption from compensating the injured party for an error in judgment,[15] but is not a necessary condition for recognition as an expert. This definitive statement by the Talmud has never been overturned.

Thus, one who is a recognized expert with regard to the right to judge

---

11. Rashi (Sanhedrin 5a, s.v. *de-gamirna*) explains: "Who have studied traditions (*she-mu'ot*) and laws from my teachers."

12. Rashi (*ibid.*, s.v. *ve-savirna*) explains: "I am able to add and reconcile various reasons (*te'amim*) on my own."

13. Rashi (*ibid.*, s.v. *ve-nakitna reshuta*) explains: "Have received permission [been ordained] by the Resh Galuta to judge monetary cases alone."

14. To ask him: (1) whether it was possible for his decision to stand, and (2) if so, whether or not he was obligated to recompense the party against whom he had erred.

15. Cf. the explicit statements of Rav and Samuel, Sanhedrin 5a; the passage on Sanhedrin 33a; and above, p. 90.

monetary matters *(ladun)* is one who is both knowledgeable *(gamir)* and capable of reasoning cogently *(savir)*.[16]

Rav Sherira Ga'on (ca. 900–1000) offers definitions of these terms along with an interesting and important addition.[17]

> An individual expert who has the status of Rav Naḥman in his generation is one who is proficient in Mishnah and Gemara, proficient in the exercise of cogent reasoning (*be-shikkul ha-da'at*),[18] has studied the laws for several years, and has been tried [tested] many times without having been found in error. Such a one is a *mumḥeh la-rabbim*. The basic meaning of *mumḥeh* is "experienced" (*menuseh*).

Rav Sherira's emphasis on the idea of "testing" intimates quite clearly that academic qualifications alone are not sufficient to accord one the status of *mumḥeh la-rabbim*. While they are necessary, they become sufficient only in combination with actual experience. One is never *declared* to be a *mumḥeh la-rabbim*, he acquires that status over a period of time in the course of which he demonstrates his right to be so classified. Thus, an "authority" is one whose actual experience in judgment is "recognized" as embodying the joint concepts of *gamir* and *savir*. While Rav Sherira does not say so explicitly, it seems reasonable to deduce from his words that such recognition is granted by the general opinion of a judge's peers and colleagues, since only they would be able to decide knowledgeably whether or not his many "tests" have been decided without error.[19]

---

16. Cf. the succinct statement by Rabbi Joseph Ḥaviva (15th cent.) in *Nimmukei Yosef* on the beginning of Sanhedrin (Rif, Sanhedrin, 1a, s.v. *dinei*): "Whoever is *gamir ve-savir* is called a recognized expert (*mumḥeh*)."

17. As quoted in *Piskei Rosh*, Sanhedrin 1:2. Also, Isaac ben Abba Mari in *Sefer ha-Ittur* (New York: American Academy for Jewish Research, 1955), pt. I, p. 79b, *Nimmukei Yosef* to Sanhedrin, loc. cit., and Jacob ben Asher in the *Tur, Ḥoshen Mishpat*, sec. 3.

18. The term is used here by Rav Sherira in its literal sense, "weighing of opinion," rather than its technical sense, "exercise of judicial discretion." The two meanings, however, are not radically different from each other, since the latter implies the ability to render judgment on the basis of all of the factors implied by the former. Thus, Rav Sherira explains the quality of being *savir* as the functional equivalent of the ability to engage in *shikkul ha-da'at*.

19. It is interesting to note that, particularly in modern times, some very well known scholars have refused to function as *posekim*, claiming that scholarship and the rendering of legal decisions do not necessarily go hand in hand. The claim can probably be understood in three ways. First, that the scholar may lack the actual experience as a *posek*, and therefore refuses to engage in decision-making. Second, that the scholar may possess the academic qualifications of authority but lack the nonacademic qualifications (see below, pp. 144 ff.). Third, that the scholar may not wish to see the results of his scholarship applied within the halakhic process and indicates this by refraining from decision-making.

The academic qualifications *ladun* are, therefore, *gamir* and *savir*, and experience. Formal permission is not a systemic requirement *ladun*. Ordination guarantees only that a judge who makes an error in judgment will be exempt from any obligation to compensate.

Since the Talmud states succinctly that "the right to teach, or instruct" *(lehorot)* implies "*gamir* and *savir*,"[20] the academic requirements for judging that which is forbidden and that which is permitted *(issur ve-hetter)* would seem to be identical to those for judging monetary cases alone *(dinei mamonot)*. With regard to monetary matters these qualifications are sufficient. It is to the question of their sufficiency for *issur ve-hetter* that we now turn.

The primary talmudic source dealing with this question is, once again, the passage describing the ordination of Rav and Rabbah bar Ḥanah.[21] In the passage it was Rabbi Judah the Prince (Rebbe) who was the one granting ordination, and in its analysis of Rebbe's actions, the Talmud asks why it was necessary for him to grant permission to Rav and Rabbah bar Ḥanah *lehorot*, since they were clearly knowledgeable in the laws of *issur ve-hetter*. The *prima facie* assumption that underlies the question is that ordination is not a necessary condition *lehorot*. In answer to the query, the *gemara* responds that the necessity for ordination by one's teacher is the result of a particular rabbinic *gezerah* (decree) which resulted from an incident in which a qualified student rendered a decision without taking sufficient care to ensure that his meaning was clearly understood. Indeed, his decision was misunderstood, and re-

---

Of the three possibilities, only the second seems to this author to be reasonable. Regarding the first, it should be noted that nothing seems more reasonable than to turn to the greatest scholars of the age for decisions, as has almost always been the case. The scholar who lacks experience does so, as a rule, because of self-imposed restrictions and could surely gain the requisite experience if he so chose. Regarding the third, the claim may be self-defeating. If the scholar is concerned lest his scholarship be inappropriately applied within the halakhic system, there could be no better safeguard than his own engagement in decision-making, since, by virtue of his stature, his own application of his scholarship would be weighty indeed. Failure to make use of his own conclusions allows others to make use of them (admitting the possibility of their applying his scholarship inappropriately). If, in fact, a scholar believes that there can be no application at all of the results of scholarship (particularly modern scholarship) to *halakhah*, he would perform a much greater service to the halakhic process by stipulating that scholarship is within the realm of "one may not teach so (*ein morim ken*)" and explicating that position. Disguising such a position behind the claim that he is not a *posek* does great harm because it implies that were he one he might indeed consider the application of the results of scholarship to be within the realm of the halakhic process.

20. Horayot 2b. While the statement there is in the name of Abayee, the continuation makes clear that the Talmud itself affirms that there is no difference of opinion between him and Rava regarding the qualifications *lehorot*. See commentary attributed to Rashi, s.v. *tanna mishnah yetera*.

21. Sanhedrin 5a-b.

sulted in the inadvertent violation of the law by the community involved. Consequently, "they decreed at that time that a student should not instruct (*yoreh*) except if he has received permission to do so from his teacher."[22] The act of ordination is not necessary as certification of the academic qualifications of the student;[23] its function, rather, is to attest to the ability of the student to expound clearly and carefully upon that which he knows.[24] The act of ordination constitutes, in other words, an elevation of the student from the class of students to the class of teachers; it certifies pedagogic prowess, not academic accomplishment. Knowledge and the ability to reason cogently remain, of course, prerequisites for teacher status.

If it can be shown that there are, in fact, systemically acceptable indicators of teacher status that can be determinative even if formal ordination is lacking, it would demonstrate that formal permission *lehorot* is not a necessary condition for the right to do so.

In his comments to Sanhedrin, when contrasting ordination *lehorot* and *ladun*, the Me'iri wrote:

> Ordination for instruction cannot be equated with ordination for judging, for the function of the former is to prevent inadvertent violation as a result of instruction (*she-lo lifroẓ geder be-hora'ah*). . . . Anyone who is expert (*baki*) in *issur ve-hetter* has the status of a specialist (*mumḥeh*). . . . For instruction one does not require the permission of the Patriarch; rather it is sufficient that he be granted permission by his teacher. And even that is required only to prevent inadvertent violation as a result of instruction. . . . Thus, anyone who is a specialist is as though he had received permission.[25]

Since the possible obligation to recompense for an error in decision does not apply to *issur ve-hetter*, as the Me'iri makes clear in the

22. *Ibid*. 5b.

23. See the Me'iri's comment in *Beit ha-Beḥirah* to Horayot, ed. A. Sofer, 4th ed. (Jerusalem: Kedem Publishers, 1976 [5736]), p. 247, s.v. *kevar be'arnu:* "Who is meant by the Mishnah's statement 'entitled to instruct *(ra'ui le-hora'ah)*'? One who has learned sufficiently to qualify him to instruct, who is insightful (*ḥarif*) and capable of cogent reasoning (*ba'al sevara*). One who has learned but is not capable of cogent reasoning is not called 'entitled to instruct,' but rather is called 'student (*talmid*).' " The Me'iri is forced to make this distinction because he read in the Mishnah (Horayot 1:1): "A student or one who is entitled to instruct (*talmid o ha-ra'ui le-hora'ah*)." Our reading is: "A student who is entitled to instruct (*talmid ve-hu ra'ui le-hora'ah*)." Thus, according to our reading, even one who is insightful and capable of cogent reasoning is classified as a *talmid*. In any case, though, it is clear that ordination is not among the requirements for being "entitled to instruct."

24. See below, the quotations from Me'iri and Isaac ben Sheshet.

25. *Beit ha-Beḥirah* to Sanhedrin 5b and 33a, Ralbag ed., pp. 12 and 120.

continuation of the above passage, so that permission *lehorot* is not necessary to ensure exemption from such payment, a specialist in *issur ve-hetter* acquires teacher status simply by virtue of his being a specialist—without benefit of formal ordination. Exemplary expertise (best expressed in Hebrew as *beki'ut* or *beki'ut mufleget*), as opposed to simple knowledgeability, is to be considered a sufficient safeguard against inadvertent violation of the law as a result of misunderstood instruction. This being the case, such an expert is entitled to the status of teacher without the need for formal ordination.

In a lengthy responsum dealing with ordination in France and Germany in the fourteenth century, Rabbi Isaac ben Sheshet Perfet (Ribash, 1326–1408) considers both its function and its limitations.[26] He writes:

> The function of ordination as practiced in France and Germany is as follows: That a student has attained the requisites for instruction (*she-higgia lehorot*)[27] . . . and is allowed, by law, *lehorot* . . . and is even obligated *lehorot*.[28]. . . But because of the *gezerah*, he is forbidden to do so unless he has received permission from his teacher, which means that his teacher grants him permission to establish an academy in any location he wishes, to expound and to instruct any who might come to ask. And this is demonstrated by his being called "Rabbi," which is to say that he is no longer to be considered a student, but one who is worthy and entitled to teach others in any place, and to be called a rabbi. And if that be not its function, I find no support for this ordination at all.[29]

The Ribash states clearly that the function of ordination, which entitles one to be called Rabbi, is to affirm the right of the recipient to assume the duties of a teacher. He is no longer to be considered in the category of student.[30]

---

26. *Responsa of Ribash*, no. 271, p. 75b. Cf. Moses Isserles, *Shulḥan Arukh, Yoreh De'ah*, sec. 242, par. 14.

27. I.e., knowledge and age. The Talmud (Avodah Zarah 19b) defines the age of forty as the minimum age *lehorot*. From the passage in Avodah Zarah 5b it is unclear whether that means chronological age or number of years spent in study. On this subject, however, see below, p. 143.

28. Avodah Zarah 19b.

29. There is a play on words in the original which is lost in translation: *eini ro'eh la-semikhah ha-hi semakh kelal.*

30. It is not clear whether the phrase *be-khol makom* ("in any place") means to include, for the Ribash, even the locale of his teacher. It could mean "in any other place" rather than "in any place," although the latter is more likely. See Eruvin 65b. If the Ribash meant the latter, he implies that upon ordination a student attains the status of colleague (*talmid ḥaver*) in relation to his teacher.

There are, however, limitations on the applicability of the *gezerah*. Perfet continues:[31]

> It seems, nonetheless, that after the death of one's teacher,[32] he does not require the grant of permission from any rabbi. For even though the *gezerah* was intended as a safeguard against error, by virtue of the student's being tested regarding the precision of his declaration (*she-yehe medakdek bi-devarav*) and his careful use of language *(ve-shomer piv u-leshono)*, so that one might be inclined to think that it [the *gezerah*] applies both during the life of his teacher and after his death, yet it could also be explained that the actual incident being as it was,[33] i.e., within the lifetime of his teacher, [since, evidently, that student was a student of Rabbi Judah the Prince,] the *gezerah* applies only to circumstances similar to it.[34] . . . And furthermore, [it is unlikely that the *gezerah* applies after the death of one's teacher,] since one's primary teacher (*rabbo muvḥak*), from whom he has derived most of his learning and who saw him regularly (*ve-ragil bo*), would have known him best and been most qualified to judge whether he was qualified to be granted permission and whether he was careful enough in his use of language that people would not be misguided by his words . . . such that if he required a grant of permission from another rabbi, who was not his primary teacher, he would have to become his student, serving him for a long time, before the latter teacher would know him sufficiently well to be able to judge whether he was entitled to be ordained. And if, in fact, that was the case, the student would be restrained from instruction for a long time. And being so restrained would itself border on the forbidden (*ve-yesh ba-meni'ah ẓad issur*).[35]

Isaac ben Sheshet offers two possible interpretations of the restriction imposed by the *gezerah*. According to the first, ordination is a necessary requirement for the authority to instruct; without it there can be no assurance that the student is indeed qualified to assume teacher status. Thus, if one did not receive ordination from his rabbi during the rabbi's lifetime, he must receive it from another after the rabbi's death, even if

---

31. *Responsa of Ribash*, no. 271, p. 75b.
32. I.e., from whom, during his lifetime, he had not yet received ordination.
33. I.e., the incident that was the precise motivation for the *gezerah*. See above, p. 139.
34. I.e., does not apply after the death of one's teacher.
35. Avodah Zarah 19b: *va-aẓumin kol harugeha* ("many are her slain") [Proverbs 7:26]—*zeh talmid she-higgi'a le-hora'ah ve-eino moreh* ("this refers to a student who achieves a level of knowledge which would permit him to rule on legal matters, but who does not rule").

that entails a lengthy delay. According to the second, the *gezerah* applies only during the lifetime of one's rabbi, not after his death. If one belongs to the category of those who have attained the requisites for instruction but lack formal ordination, the negative ramifications of the delay that would be entailed in awaiting ordination from another rabbi would outweigh the requirements of the *gezerah,* which is then interpreted to apply only in circumstances identical to those of the original case. Since the first interpretation imposes restraints on the right of a qualified person *lehorot,* and since such restraints are in conflict with the rabbinic interpretation of the verse in Proverbs 7:26,[36] the Ribash opts for the second interpretation, affirming that ordination is not a necessary condition for instruction.[37]

Ordination *lehorot,* therefore, is the general method for elevating a student to the status of teacher.[38] . . . It is not, however, a necessary condition for the attainment of that status.

Since an age requirement before the satisfaction of which an authority is forbidden to instruct has been alluded to,[39] a slight digression on the subject is called for, although age is neither an academic nor a personality characteristic *per se.* Actually, it is sufficient to point out that the age restriction was not adamantly adhered to, even in talmudic days. The Gemara itself expresses awareness that the age of forty (or the accumulation of forty years of study) is meant more as an indication of maturity (or of a sufficient time in which to acquire the reguisite knowledge) than a definitive statement of law.[40] The Tosafot make very clear that knowledge and wisdom are of greater concern systemically than is age.[41]

Of great interest with regard to this restriction, however, is the fact that Maimonides makes no mention of it anywhere in the *Mishneh Torah.*

---

36. See the preceding note.

37. It ought to be noted that the weight which the Ribash accords an aggadic (homiletical, nonlegal) exegesis of a verse indicates a degree of seriousness regarding the halakhic implications of *aggadah* which is often overlooked by halakhists. The possible halakhic implications of an aggadic statement are among the factors the arbiter must consider before rendering his decision.

38. Since the sole function of ordination *lehorot* is to effect a change of status from student to teacher regarding *issur ve-hetter,* it seems plausible that any recognizable type of such attestation would have systemic validity. Thus, ordination granted by an institution, as opposed to an individual, or granted by means of a document which attests to the qualification of the recipient for the status of teacher but which omits the formula *yoreh yoreh* ("May he rule [in matters of ritual]? He may rule!") should be systemically sufficient.

39. Above, p. 141, and n. 27.

40. Sotah 22b.

41. Tosafot Sotah 22b, s.v. *be-shavin.* Of equal importance is their admonition against haste in donning the mantle of *hora'ah.* See, too, Maimonides, *Mishneh Torah,* Talmud Torah 5:4.

In offering an explanation for this apparent omission, Rabbi Abraham ben Moses Di Boton (ca. 1545–1588) makes the following observation:[42]

> It seems to me that [the omission] can be explained, according to Maimonides, on the grounds that he felt that the statement of the Gemara, "until age forty," implies concern with wisdom, not time . . . and he [Maimonides] would affirm that it applies only to very early periods during which study took place orally, without the benefit of books (*she-lo hayu lomedim ella mi-pi soferim ve-lo mi-sefarim*), . . . but now that the Torah is written and we study from books, surely such an age requirement is not needed. . . . And in a similar vein, I have heard from someone who wrote in the name of a certain scholar that the principle that forbids one to instruct in the presence of his teacher (*moreh halakhah bi-fenei rabbo*)[43] does not apply in modern times (*ba-zeman ha-zeh*), since we study from books, and the books themselves are the teachers.

Clearly, according to Di Boton, the nature of modern study obviates the necessity for a lengthy "studenthood" in order to acquire the necessary knowledge to qualify *lehorot;* consequently, a specific age requirement is no longer to be considered a systemic necessity.

As for the nonacademic qualifications for recognition as a rabbinic authority, the Bible itself lists them: Jethro recommends to Moses that he select "men of valor, God-fearing, men of truth, and haters of unjust gain."[44] And in his first discourse before the people enter the land of Israel, Moses states that he will select "wise men and understanding, known within your tribes," to become judges.[45] The sages combined the statements, proposed their own definitions of the terms used in the Bible, and concluded that there are seven characteristics that the ideal judge should possess. Maimonides codifies the conclusion as follows:[46]

> Each of them must possess seven characteristics, as follows: wisdom, humility, fear of God, hatred of unjust gain (*sinat mamon*),

42. *Leḥem Mishneh* to Maimonides, Talmud Torah 5:4. Cf. also *Responsa of Radbaz* (New York: Otzar Hasefarim, 1967), pt. V, no. 2147. It is noteworthy that Di Boton's own lifespan did not greatly exceed forty years! Radbaz, however, lived almost one hundred years (1479–1573). Di Boton's comment will be of significance in our analysis of the place of nonhalakhic considerations within the halakhic process, below, p. 260.

43. See Berakhot 31b, Eruvin 63a, and Sanhedrin 17a.

44. Exodus 18:21.

45. Deuteronomy 1:15. See also Deuteronomy 1:13.

46. *Mishneh Torah,* Hilkhot Sanhedrin 2:7. Cf. *Sifrei Deuteronomy,* sec. 15, Finkelstein ed., p. 24; *Mekhilta D'Rabbi Ishmael,* Yitro, Mesekhta de-Amalek, *parashah* 2, Horovitz-Rabin ed., p. 198.

> love of truth, respected (*ahavat ha-beriyyot lahen*), upstanding reputation (*ba'alei shem tov*). And all of these characteristics are stated explicitly in the Torah. It states: "Wise and understanding men"[47]—thus stipulating wisdom; "Known within your tribes"—these are those who are respected (*she-ru'aḥ ḥakhamim noḥah me-hen*). And what is the source of their respect? Their concern for the welfare of others (*ba'alei ayin tovah*), their humility (*nefesh shefalah*), the pleasantness of their company (*ḥevratan tovah*), and their gentle speech and dealings with their fellow men. And further it says: "Men of valor"[48]—these are those who are heroic in the *miẓvot*, demanding of themselves, masters of self-control, to the point that no statement of denigration nor of ill reputation could be held against them—of impeccable repute (*vi-he pirkan na'eh*). And included within the meaning of "men of valor" is their fortitude to save the oppressed from his oppressor . . . And just as Moses was humble,[49] so must every judge be humble. "God-fearers"—as the meaning of the words implies. "Haters of unjust gain"—that they do not become anxious (*nivhalim*) even concerning their own money and do not pursue the amassing of money . . . "Men of truth"—who pursue justice because of their own natures (*maḥmat aẓman be-da'atan*), who love the truth and detest violence, who flee from all types of injustice (*avel*).

These are high standards, and the sages themselves point out that the possession of these seven characteristics by any one person constitutes an ideal not easily realized.

> Rabbi Berakhiah said in the name of Rabbi Ḥaninah, "Judges must possess the following seven characteristics. . . . And why were the seven not written in one verse? To indicate that if one cannot find all seven in one person, a judge possessing only four may be appointed. And if judges possessing four cannot be found, a judge possessing only three may be appointed. And if judges possessing three cannot be found, a judge possessing one may be appointed."[50]

Of the nonacademic characteristics listed, there is one that is considered the *sine qua non* of systemic halakhic authority: *Yirat ha-shem* (or its

---

47. Deuteronomy 1:13, for this and the following qualification.
48. Exodus 18:21, for this and the three qualifications following humility.
49. Numbers 12:3.
50. *Deuteronomy Rabbah* 1:10. While no proof-test is offered for the conclusion, it is apparently derived from Exodus 18:25, which lists only "men of valor" as the character of the judges selected by Moses.

synonyms).[51] The term is generally translated as "fear of God," as I have translated it above. I intend to demonstrate however, that the translation is inadequately clear and insufficiently precise to be used without qualification, and will henceforth leave the term untranslated.

The quintessential nature of this characteristic is clearly reflected in halakhic sources. The Talmud itself records that Judah the Prince (Rebbe) attributed a preeminent place to it.[52] Prior to his death, he stipulated that his son Gamli'el should ascend to the Patriarchate, although his son Shimon was more qualified academically. In explanation of Rebbe's statement, "Shimon my son is wise, Gamli'el my son is patriarch," the Talmud says:

> This is what he meant: Even though my son Shimon is wise, my son Gamli'el should become patriarch. . . . And why did Rebbe do so? For although he [Gamli'el] could not replace his ancestors in terms of wisdom, in *Yirat ḥet* [fear of sin] he could indeed replace them.[53]

Thus, the nonacademic qualification of Gamli'el superseded the academic superiority of his younger brother Shimon as the determining factor in his ascendancy to the partriachate. The Talmud implies, further, that Rebbe's decision was not a foregone conclusion, but his considered opinion, and that it clearly indicates the primacy of *yirat ha-shem*.

This view is also codified by Maimonides, in his usual succinct style: "No one who lacks *yirat shamayim* [fear of Heaven] may be appointed to any position of authority among Jews, even though his knowledge may be exceptional."[54]

The Talmud equates the appointment of an unworthy judge with idolatry.[55] In commenting upon that passage, Rabbi Joseph ben Solomon Colon (Maharik, ca. 1420–1480) emphasizes the connotations of "unworthiness."[56]

---

51. Synonyms include, for example, *yirat shamayim* ("fear of Heaven") and *yirat ḥet* ("fear of sin"). Note, as well, that there is some overlap in Maimonides' definitions. Thus, *anshei ḥayil* ("men of valor") includes *gibborim be-miẓvot* ("heroic in the *miẓvot*") and *medakdekin al aẓman* ("demanding of themselves"), which are also implied by *yirat ha-shem*. And, assuming that the proof-text offered in the preceding note is correct, the one absolute requirement for judgeship, even in the Bible, is *anshei ḥayil*.

52. Ketubbot 103b.

53. *Ibid.* The statement requires an explanation because one would ordinarily not be surprised that Gamli'el ascended to the patriarchate, since he was older than Shimon. Thus, the very fact that Judah the Prince mentioned his younger son required an explanation.

54. *Mishneh Torah,* Hilkhot Melakhim 1:7.

55. Sanhedrin 7b. See Deuteronomy 16:18 and 21.

56. *Responsa of Mahari Colon* (= Maharik) (Warsaw, 1884), no. 117.

> The verse "You shall not plant"[57] cautions us against the appointment of a judge who is not worthy on account of his evil . . . and even if he is very brilliant . . . and able to proliferate ideas and originate thoughts in the explication of the *halakhah.* Even so we are warned against the appointment of such a man as a judge, lest he pervert justice . . . since he is not worthy and is not a *yere elohim* [God-fearer].

The lack of *yirat ha-shem* categorizes a potential judge as unworthy, regardless of academic qualifications.

Finally, Rabbi Moses Isserles (Rema, 1525–1572) affirms:[58]

> Whoever has recognized status (*she-huḥzak*) as the rabbi of a city passes on the right of succession to his son and his grandson forever above all others, so long as they replace their fathers in *yirah* [fear] and are somewhat knowledgeable *(ḥakhamim keẓat)*—even though someone greater than him has come.[59]

Interestingly, although the characteristic of *yirat ha-shem* constitutes the ultimate systemic qualification for recognition as a rabbinic authority, [60] the term is generally left undefined—undoubtedly because it is too difficult to define it. Indeed, it can be cogently argued that any definition of *yirat ha-shem* is necessarily so subjective that not only is precise definition impossible, but it is even impossible to draw up a list of externally observable behavior by which its presence might be indicated. It is therefore worthwhile to remember that our discussion concerns the characteristics required of halakhic authorities only. Behavior that would indicate the presence of *yirat ha-shem* in halakhic authorities is not the same behavior that would indicate the presence of *yirat ha-shem* in other kinds of people in other situations. Surely, for example, it is possible for non-Jews to possess *yirat ha-shem,* yet the behavior expected of them would be far different from the behavior of halakhic authorities. Even among Jews, the behavior of halakhic authorities with regard to *yirat ha-shem* might be different from that expected of other Jews in other situations.

---

57. Deuteronomy 16:21.

58. *Yoreh De'ah,* sec. 245, par. 22.

59. A responsum of Rabbi Joseph Ibn Migash (no. 114) (quoted in *Birkei Yosef* to *Shulḥan Arukh, Ḥoshen Mishpat,* sec. 8, s.v. *ve-ra'iti,* and in Elon, *Jewish Law,* 3:978, n. 14) that allows a non-God-fearing judge to serve in a temporary capacity is, to the best knowledge of the author, a unique and singular position.

60. Cf. the succinct statement of Rabbi Samuel bar Naḥmani in the name of Rabbi Jonathan (Yoma 72b): "Woe unto the sages who occupy themselves with Torah but lack the fear of Heaven."

It is also important to note, once again, that the validity of the halakhic system is internal to it.[61] Therefore, if the system requires *yirat ha-shem* of its recognized authorities, any intimation that such a requirement is not, in fact, a necessary one is, by definition, external to the system, and therefore systemically invalid (unless the recognized authorities of the system so redefine the requirements of authorities). And in order for the position that denies that *yirat ha-shem* is a necessary qualification for recognition as a halakhic authority to have potential validity within the system, it must be stated by one who is himself a recognized authority of the system (i.e., one who possesses *yirat ha-shem).* And in order for such a statement, one that as yet only possesses *potential* systemic validity, to attain *actual* systemic validity, he who suggests it must demonstrate cogent and compelling reasons for ignoring the weight of almost universal precedent that affirms that *yirat ha-shem is* a systemic requirement for the exercise of authority. If he could do so, his opinion would then constitute a valid opinion, giving rise to a legitimate *maḥaloket,* and becoming grounds for the legitimate exercise of judicial discretion. Obviously, the likelihood of such an eventuality, theoretically possible, is minimal.

Although the bahavior that would indicate the presence of *yirat ha-shem* in recognized authorities is impossible to describe precisely or in detail, it seems undeniable that such behavior would be that which supports and buttresses the continued viability of the halakhic system. Since, as was demonstrated in the preceding chapter, it was the sages themselves who interpreted the *grundnorm* to mean that they were its sole legitimate interpreters, and did so primarily to ensure their own authority and to guarantee thereby the continued viability of the system as they themselves understood it; and since it was the sages themselves who postulated *yirat ha-shem* as an essential characteristic of the recognized authorities of the system, it follows that the sages considered *yirat ha-shem* to be necessary to the exercise of authority. If that is not the case, *yirat ha-shem* is an absurd systemic requirement. Thus, with regard to systemically recognized authorities, behavior that indicates *yirat ha-shem* must be behavior that reflects commitment, clear and undeniable, to the system the viability of which this exercise of authority is intended to guarantee. Behavior that belies a commitment to the halakhic process belies the presence of *yirat ha-shem* in its recognized authorities.

Although commitment to the system can be affirmed verbally, such verbalization is probably neither necessary nor sufficient for the recognized authorities of the system. It is not necessary, since behavior that

61. See above, pp. 122 f.

indicates *yirat ha-shem* is clearly observable whether or not it is verbally affirmed. Nor is it sufficient, since certain types of behavior belie the commitment, verbal affirmation thereof notwithstanding. In essence the requisite characteristic of *yirat ha-shem* must be reflected in behavior, behavior that is consonant with the system itself and that demonstrates a concrete commitment to it. In traditional terms, such behavior is described as *shemirat mizvot* (i.e., observance of the *mizvot* [both positive and negative] as it is understood by the halakhic process).[62]

Having postulated observance as a prerequisite for systemic recognition as an authority, several warnings are in order. These will demonstrate, once more, the difficulty, if not the impossibility, of defining *yirat ha-shem* precisely, as well as the degree to which even the observance of *mizvot* is not necessarily an indication of a commitment to the halakhic process.

First, it is possible for two potential authorities to engage in identical behavior, the behavior of one of them reflecting a commitment to the halakhic system and that of the other reflecting an absence of such commitment. If both, for example, drive or ride to the synagogue on Shabbat, the one affirming that such behavior is systemically defensible (if not, indeed, required), and the other affirming that, although not systemically defensible, he does so anyway[63]—the former qualifies as an authority of the system, and the latter does not.

Second, it is possible for two potential authorities to engage in contradictory behaviors, and for both kinds of behavior to reflect commitment to the system. If, for example, the weight of precedent favors one behavior, although there also exists a nonprecedented position advocating the contrary behavior, and if one of the potential authorities finds a systemically defensible reason for overturning the precedent, while the other does not, their disagreement concerns only the need to overturn the precedent, but not the halakhic process itself, and both qualify as authorities.[64]

---

62. See above, n. 19, the second possible claim by a scholar for not functioning as a *posek*, viz., that he lacks the nonacademic qualifications, i.e., *yirat ha-shem*.

63. I.e., the former claiming that it is permissible, and the latter claiming, "It is forbidden, but I shall do it nonetheless *[asur ve-af al pin khen e'eseh]*."

64. The potential complexities of such possibilities are infinite. The example given postulates the existence of a nonprecedented contrary opinion. As we shall discuss in a later chapter, however, there may be systemic grounds for overturning precedent even in the absence of a nonprecedented supporting opinion—and the *mahaloket* may be about whether or not a specific case warrants invoking this systemic right. Possibly, in addition, their *mahaloket* may revolve around the validity or acceptability of certain nonhalakhic data vis-à-vis a specific halakhic issue. There are other possibilities, too, that will be discussed in the course of the remainder of this work.

Third, it is possible for the behavior of a potential authority to reflect an ostensible commitment to the halakhic process, while he himself lacks such a commitment. If he affirms, for example, that *halakhah* is not normative and that its observance is dependent entirely on its meaningfulness to the individual, but that he, personally, finds almost all of *halakhah* meaningful, he would not qualify as an authority of the system.[65]

Yet it should be noted that these complexities and difficulties are not only the natural but the necessary result of the system itself. A system that recognizes the legitimacy of *maḥaloket*, even to the point of permitting dispute about the *de-oraita* or *de-rabbanan* status of a given *mizvah*, that permits a broad range of divergent behaviors, that postulates *Ein lo la-dayyan ella mah she-einav ro'ot* as the central systemic principle, that affirms the idea that *Ellu ve-ellu divrei elohim ḥayyim*, and that, at the same time, demands *yirat ha-shem* of its recognized authorities, dictates such complexities and difficulties.

Lest one conclude, however, that the number of possible complexities is so vast that the observable behavior of a potential authority is, in fact, no indication whatsoever of a commitment to the halakhic process, let me stress that the general areas of clarity and agreement are far greater. While a person committed to the system may argue that turning on electric lights on Shabbat is not forbidden, the remainder of his observance will surely reflect an abstention from activities that are universally acknowledged as forbidden. Or while such a person may argue that swordfish is *kasher*, his other eating habits will surely reflect a commitment to the normative nature of the laws of *kashrut*. Or while such a person may argue that women are allowed to receive *aliyyot*, his general behavior will surely reflect a commitment to the legal requirements of prayer. It is precisely *against* the contention that any deviation from accepted or precedented behavior constitutes proof of a lack of commitment to the halakhic process *(yirat ha-shem)* that the system itself argues.

Judging the nonacademic qualifications of a potential authority is

---

65. The disqualification of individuals from acceptance as recognized authorities does not necessarily disqualify the views they may express from objective halakhic legitimacy. If a recognized authority also affirms the systemic rectitude or defensibility of the view, even though the view had not been previously expressed by a recognized authority, it becomes legitimate halakhically. The idea that a view expressed by a nonauthority must be rejected as invalid by recognized authorities is an absurd vitiation of the system, excluding views from legitimacy on the sole grounds that the originator of view was not a recognized authority, irrespective of any other systemic considerations. To assume that one outside the system is, by definition, incapable of defensible systemic insights is to confuse the ultimate internality of the system with the claim that that which must be ultimately internal must also be originally internal.

undoubtedly a difficult matter. Still, it seems plausible to assert that the "testing period" that Rav Sherira Ga'on posited as part and parcel of becoming "recognized" academically[66] can also be used to test the nonacademic qualifications of the potential authority. Not only is it possible for his colleagues to judge his status as *gamir* and *savir,* it is also possible for them to judge his status as one reflecting *yirat ha-shem.* To the extent that his behavior may appear to deviate from the norms implied by a commitment to the halakhic process, the "testing period" will be utilized to ascertain whether those deviations do or do not *in fact* reflect such a lack of commitment.[67]

At the conclusion of the theological digression in the preceding chapter, the question of whether there exists a systemically prescribed theological position for recognized authorities was raised.[68] At this point the answer to that question should be clear. Since *yirat ha-shem,* a commitment to the halakhic process reflected in behavior, is a systemic prerequisite for rabbinic authority, the theological assumptions necessarily implied by such a commitment are the systemic prerequisites for that authority.

There are two theological assumptions entailed in a commitment to the halakhic process, and they are: (1) that the *grundnorm* is the reflection of the word and the will of God; and (2) that the sages of the Torah are the sole legitimate interpreters of the *grundnorm.* The systemic requirement that all those who are recognized as rabbinic authorities accept these two hypotheses results, to begin with, in the exclusion from positions of authority of atheists and all who deny the authority of the oral tradition. Positing the *grundnorm,* however, does not entail any specific theological stance regarding *the manner* in which it reflects the word and the will of God. Neither the acceptance nor the rejection of direct Divine revelation or of Divine revelation mediated through the sources known as J, E, P, and D is necessary in order to posit the *grundnorm* as the reflection of the word and will of God. The legal system requires the acceptance of the assumption, it does not dictate acceptance of any specific circumstances under which the *grundnorm* is supposed to have been produced.

The systemic assumption that only the sages of the Torah are its legitimate interpreters imposes the acceptance of another theological hypothesis on the part of those who are or wish to be recognized authorities, that is, that the sages' interpretations of the *grundnorm*

66. See above, p. 138.

67. The ultimate complexity would be a situation in which two recognized authorities disagree about the qualifications of a potential authority.

68. See above, p. 121 f.

represent the will of God. The major portion of the preceding chapter was devoted to an analysis of this thesis.[69] We saw that it is possible to maintain that the oral tradition reflects the will of God in that He has no actual objectifiable will independent of the sages' interpretation thereof. It is also possible, however, to maintain that He does have a "true" will, the "true" determination of which is guaranteed by His providential supervision of the halakhic process.[70] However, since both positions are based on the assumption that the halakhic process, in one way or another, is engaged in the determination of the will of God, the theological position that maintains that the process is entirely independent of God would appear to disqualify a potential authority from systemic recognition.[71]

69. See the discussion beginning on p. 119.

70. The distinction between these two positions is sometimes quite straightforward. See, for example, Caro's explanation of *Ellu ve-ellu divrei elohim ḥayyim*, above, p. 131. The distinction, however, can also be extremely complex. According to the second position, it is possible to explain the incident involving Rabbi Eli'ezer (above p. 123) only by affirming that the "true" will of God is expressed in the maxim "Follow the majority." Thus although God Himself joins the minority, His true will is that of the majority. This position is very close to that expressed by Algazi in the name of Rabbenu Ḥananel (above, p. 131). But, as noted there, its practical result is no different from the first position.

71. We have mentioned above (p. 119) that failure to make regular or frequent mention of God in no way implies that the system is independent of Him.

Chapter Seven

On Rabbinic Authority vis-à-vis Matters *De-oraita*

In this chapter our attention will be focused primarily on the right of the sages to amend or abrogate the Torah itself, as well as their right to amend or abrogate those norms that have the status of *de-oraita*.

On one level this issue is a nonissue. We have seen in Chapter 5 that although the system posits the Torah as its unassailable *grundnorm*, it also takes the position that the meaning of the Torah is determined by the sages and that their interpretations alone are normative. Consequently, since rabbinic interpretation and exegesis of the Torah constitute its definitive meaning, it is impossible to contend, systemically, that any particular meaning is at variance with the Torah. If, for example, the rabbis understand "and it was evening and it was morning"[1] to imply that the day begins at night, then that is what the verse means, systemically, regardless of any other theoretical possibility.[2] If the sages understand the words "for a sign upon your hand"[3] to refer to phylacteries, then that is what the words refer to, regardless of any other theoretical possibility.[4] As we have also seen, the *peshat* of a verse, to the extent that it is at variance with the rabbinic interpretation of that verse, is, systemically, legally insignificant (p. 117).

1. Genesis 1:5.
2. See the explanation of this phrase offered by the Rashbam (Rabbi Samuel ben Me'ir) in his *Commentary to the Torah*, ed. David Rosin (Breslau, 1881), p. 5.
3. Exodus 13:9.
4. Rashbam, *op. cit.*, p. 98.

Yet, as subtle as the distinction may be, there is a difference between the above examples and the rabbinic affirmation that the maximum number of lashes permissible is thirty-nine[5] or the rabbinic exegesis that effectively cancelled the Torah's provision concerning the rebellious son.[6] The ambiguities of the text of the *grundnorm* in the first two examples are such that, even if not *peshat,* the rabbinic interpretations of them are, at the very least, reasonable and plausible attempts to grapple with the verses. Regarding the examples in this paragraph, however, one has the feeling that even if the texts are slightly ambiguous, the rabbinic interpretations do not represent serious attempts to deal with the supposed ambiguities. Thus, the contention that the *peshat* of the verse is legally insignificant (i.e., that the legal meaning of the Torah is what the sages say it is) seems more defensible with regard to the first pair than to the second pair of examples.[7] Indeed, regarding the latter two one is inclined to affirm that the sages did, in fact, abrogate the intent of the *grundnorm.*[8]

On another level, the issue involves us for the first time with the legislative functions of halakhic authorities, as opposed to their judicial and interpretive functions, upon which our discussion has centered until now. Legislation, according to Elon is concerned primarily with filling in the *lacunae* that exist within the *halakhah* and with instituting corrections and changes in its body of laws, which is accomplished by means of procedures called "decree" (*gezerah*) and "ordinance" (*takkanah*).[9] Since legislation is required, by definition, only when the rabbis are unable, simply by the exercise of their right to interpret, to fill in the *lacunae* or to justify the corrections needed and changes desired,[10] and since rabbinic *interpretation* of the *grundnorm* can never be at variance, systemically, with the *grundnorm* itself, it follows that conflicts between rabbinic authority and the Torah will be most acutely felt in the

5. Mishnah Makkot 3:10, 22a, and above, p. 47. See Deuteronomy 25:3. Cf. Rava's statement in Makkot 22b: "How foolish are those who stand before a Torah scroll but not before a sage. For in the scroll it is written forty, and the sages reduced them by one."

6. Deuteronomy 21:1–22. See Sanhedrin 68b–71a, particularly the contention of the *gemara* (71a): "There has never been [anyone convicted] as a rebellious son, nor will there ever be."

7. It should be noted, however, that since the abrogations of the *grundnorm* in the latter two cases are deduced exegetically in the Talmud, they are, *prima facie,* no less defensible systemically than the former two. All four are interpretive, not legislative. See, however, p. 155, concerning the overlap of judicial and legislative functions.

8. There have been earlier intimations of this problem as well. See above, chap. 2, n. 5; chap. 5, n. 48; chap. 6, n. 7.

9. *Jewish Law,* 2:405. See his thorough treatment of the entire matter of legislation on 2:391–712.

10. *Ibid.,* 2:391.

realm of legislation. Indeed, the very existence of a legislative function would seem to be at variance with the *grundnorm.*[11]

Yet, in the halakhic system, the distinction between legislation and decision-making on the basis of rabbinic interpretation is very narrow indeed. First, because the exercise of these two functions is not assigned to two distinct groups of sages, but, rather, to the selfsame group; and second, because, to the extent that *lacunae* are filled and new needs and demands met through the exercise of the judicial function (i.e., through the interpretation of the Torah or other legal sources), the judicial function is also fulfilling a legislative function. The decision to favor one position over another, or to adopt a nonprecedented position over a precedented one, may well be motivated by considerations similar to those that would have inspired an act of legislation if there had been no possible interpretation of the *grundnorm* that would allow the sages to achieve the same result judicially. A farfetched interpretation of a verse in the Torah that serves as the source of a judicial decision has no less a legislative function for its being attached, however tenuously, to the *grundnorm,* than an act of pure legislation. Third, the distinction between interpretation and legislation is narrow because the exercise of the legislative function is itself not free of interpretive-judicial aspects. While the distinction can be strictly maintained when an act of legislation is intended to fill a *lacuna* in the corpus of the law, it cannot be strictly maintained when an act of legislation is intended to correct or change existent law. The ultimate act that institutionalizes a change or correction may be legislative in nature, but the impetus for the legislative act is likely to be a consideration on the part of some judge-legislator that a particular change or correction is necessary. If the judge-legislator were able to effect the desired change through the exericse of his interpretive-judicial function he would do so; if not, he must effect the change through legislation. As we shall see, some systemic principles that govern acts that are technically legislative are themselves scripturally based. That is, the systemic principles that validate the right to legislate are derived from a rabbinic interpretation of biblical verses. In the final analysis, the decision of an authority to exercise his legislative function is itself judicial, not legislative.

Because the legislative and the judicial functions in the halakhic system are so closely interrelated, we will consider the problem of the authority of the sages vis-à-vis matters *de-oraita* without taking into consideration which specific function the sages are exercising (except, of course, in cases in which the distinction is relevant). Such treatment is

11. See Deuteronomy 4:2, 13:1, and below, p. 156.

not intended to blur the differences between the two functions, but to make it absolutely clear that, systemically, the same types of considerations that give rise to legislative action can also, in certain circumstances, give rise to judicial action.

The source of the problem regarding rabbinic authority vis-à-vis matters *de-oraita* lies in the fact that the Torah itself apparently prohibits anyone from initiating noninterpretive (i.e., legislative) actions with regard to its body of laws. It not only lacks an amendment clause authorizing the sages to add to or take away from the *grundnorm*, it actively prohibits any such actions. Deuteronomy 4:2 reads: "You should not add to the word that I command you, nor should you take away from it, to observe the commandments of the Lord your God that I command you." And Deuteronomy 13:1 reads: "Every matter that I command you, you should observe and do. You should not add to it, nor take away from it."

The prohibition against adding to the Torah is called *Bal tosif;* the prohibition against subtracting from it is called *Bal tigra*. The rabbinic sources treat both prohibitions primarily as legal norms; later commentators treat the systemic implications of the norms.

The following *midrash* illustrates by example the meaning of the prohibitions as legal norms.[12]

> "You should not add to it": Hence they said[13] that if the blood of an offering the blood of which is to be sprinkled once is mixed with blood of an offering the blood of which is to be sprinkled once, the mixed blood should be sprinkled once.[14] Another explanation: "You should not add to it": Whence [do we know] that one may not add to the *lulav*[15] or to the fringes?[16] The Torah says: "You should not add to it." And whence [do we know] that one may not take away from them? The Torah says: "You should not take away from it." Whence [do we know] that [a priest] who has begun to bless the people should not say, "Since I have begun to bless I shall say [i.e., add], 'The Lord, God of your fathers, increase you'?"[17] The Torah

---

12. *Sifrei Deuteronomy*, no. 82, Finkelstein ed., p. 148.
13. Mishnah Zevaḥim 8:10, 80a.
14. Assuming, for example, that the bloods mix with each other, one act of sprinkling is adequate to ensure that the blood of each offering has been included. If one were to sprinkle twice, i.e., once for each offering, the fact that the bloods are mixed would result in a violation of *Bal tosif*, since, in fact, blood from each offering would have been sprinkled twice.
15. I.e., more than the required four species. See below, n. 21.
16. I.e., increase the number of threads or knots.
17. Deuteronomy 1:11.

> says *ha-davar* ["the word"],[18] [implying that] you should not add to it [even if the addition is] merely verbal.

Nevertheless the statement of the *midrash* offers little guidance as to whether the application of the prohibitions is limited in any way, except that it makes abundantly clear that the prohibitions *do not apply to rabbinic interpretations of the grundnorm.* Of the four examples included in the *midrash,* the last one indicates this point most clearly, since it is itself based on a rabbinic exegesis of the word *ha-davar.* The fringes, too, are not described in detail in the Torah; the number of threads and knots are rabbinically derived. Regarding the *lulav,* one can affirm that the four species are stipulated in the Torah,[19] but the meanings of at least two of the terms[20] are known only through rabbinic interpretation.[21]

It remained, then, for the classical commentators to deal with the systemic implications of the prohibitions. There are two major positions among the commentators, that of Rabbi Solomon ben Abraham Adret (Rashba, ca. 1235–1310) and that of Maimonides.

The Rashba offers a brilliant solution that effectively eliminates the entire problem that the prohibitions of *Bal tosif* and *Bal tigra* raise regarding amendment and might be construed to raise regarding the interpretation rights of the sages. He writes:[22]

> Why is the *shofar* sounded when they are seated [i.e., not during the recitation of the *Amidah*] and sounded when they are standing [i.e., during the recitation of the *Amidah*]? In order to confuse the *satan.*[23] [Concerning this matter] the Tosafot raised the objection that [sounding the *shofar* twice] constitutes a violation of *Bal tosif*[24] . . . and they, of blessed memory, explained that *Bal tosif* does not apply to the fulfillment of a *mizvah* twice . . . and they, of blessed memory,

18. Deuteronomy 4:2, 13:1.
19. Leviticus 23:40.
20. I.e., *peri ez hadar* ("the fruit of a lovely tree" or "the lovely fruit of a tree") and *anaf ez avot* ("the bough of a leafy tree").
21. Since *rabbinic interpretations are excluded from the prohibitions,* it is conceivable that this *midrash* refers not only to the specific four species but also to the number of each species used (on which the Torah is silent) as well, i.e., one palm, one *etrog,* three myrtles, and two willows. Thus, using one myrtle would be a violation of *Bal tigra,* and using two *etrogim,* of *Bal tosif.* While this is not the generally accepted opinion, see Lieberman's lengthy commentary to *Tosefta Sukkah* 2:8, in *Tosefta Ki-fshutah* (New York: Jewish Theological Seminary, 1962), IV:859–863.
22. Rashba, Rosh ha-Shanah 16a, ed. H. Z. Dimitrovsky (New York, 1961), s.v. *lamah toke'in,* p. 73.
23. Rosh ha-Shanah 16a.
24. *Ibid.* 16b, s.v. *ve-toke'in.*

> sought diligently to substantiate this position, but were not very successful. Rather, it is reasonable to affirm that there is no problem whatsoever. For they [the sages] never claimed that *Bal tosif* applies except when one adds on his own (*mi-da'at azmo*), as, for example, a priest who adds his own benediction. . . . But concerning anything that the sages ordained for some cause (*tikkenu le-zorekh*), the prohibition of *Bal tosif* does not apply, for the Torah already states: "According to the instruction which they render, etc."[25] And you should know this, since the eighth day of Sukkot is, at present, a rabbinic *mizvah*, and we sleep and eat in the *sukkah* for the sake of the *mizvah*.[26] . . . Therefore, they are empowered to enact an addition (*gozerin u-mosifin*) for some reason. And the same is true of *Bal tigra* for a reason, as, for example, Rosh Hashanah that falls on Shabbat, concerning which they decreed with reason not to sound the *shofar*, even though the Torah requires that it be sounded. Here too [i.e., the sounding of the *shofar* twice] they saw some cause to sound it once and then again, and it is a *mizvah* to obey the words of the sages from the verse "You shall not deviate (*Lo tasur*)."[27]

The Rashba, in other words, seems to have sensed a type of contradiction between the dictum *Lo tasur,* which dictates obedience to the sages, and the prohibitions of *Bal tosif* and *Bal tigra.* He resolved the conflict by offering the broadest possible interpretation of *Lo tasur,* and the narrowest possible interpretation of the other two. Thus, *Lo tasur* is read not only as a guarantee of the right of the sages to interpret the Torah, it is also made to function as the amendment clause of the *grundnorm;* that is, the Torah itself is seen as empowering the sages both to interpret and to amend it. The Rashba is careful to include the words "for reason" or "for cause" each time he refers to rabbinic amendment of the Torah, indicating, minimally, that the use of this power cannot be capricious.[28] It follows, though, that since the *grundnorm* itself includes an amendment clause, no rabbinic amendment of the Torah can be considered a violation of the Torah.

The final step in the elimination of the problem is the restriction of *Bal*

25. Deuteronomy 17:11.

26. I.e., without concern that fulfillment of the rabbinic requirement for an additional day constitutes a violation of *Bal tosif*.

27. Deuteronomy 17:11.

28. It is noteworthy, tangentially, that the Rashba does not define "cause" or "reason." Thus, "confusing the *satan*" was sufficient cause for invoking the power to amend. General categories of "cause" will be discusssed within this chapter and throughout the remainder of the book.

tosif and *Bal tigra* to individuals. The establishment of such a restriction makes the primary concern of the *grundnorm* to have been the prevention of systemically illegitimate amendments or abrogations, not the prevention of systemically legitimate amendments or abrogations. Illegitimate amendments would be amendments introduced by nonrecognized authorities, and legitimate amendments those introduced by systemically recognized authorities.

The Maimonidean position rejects the contention that violation of *Bal tosif* and *Bal tigra* apply only to individuals. His explanation of the prohibitions deals instead with the nature of a rabbinic enactment. He maintains that the prohibited or permitted nature of an enactment depends, even for recognized authorities, upon the intent and manner of its promulgation. In the *Mishneh Torah* Maimonides wrote:[29]

> Since the court may make an enactment that forbids that which is permissible (and its forbidden nature becomes permanent), and may, as well, permit temporarily (*le-fi sha'ah*) matters that are forbidden according to the Torah, what is the meaning of the Torah's warning, "You shall not add to it, nor take away from it"?[30] [It means] that one may neither add to the words of the Torah nor diminish from them, and establish that matter in perpetuity as from the Torah (*ve-likbo'a ha-davar le-olam she-hu min ha-Torah*),[31] either concerning the written or the oral Torah. How? It is written in the Torah: "You should not cook a kid in its mother's milk."[32] On the basis of tradition we have learned that this verse forbids the cooking and eating of meat and milk, both the meat of domesticated animals (*behemah*) and of beasts of chase (*ḥayyah*), but that the meat of poultry with milk is permissible from the Torah.[33] If some court were to declare the meat of beasts of chase with milk permissible, that would be taking away. And if it were to forbid the meat of fowl

---

29. *Mishneh Torah,* Hilkhot Mamrim 2:9.
30. Deuteronomy 13:1.
31. Thus in the Rome manuscript and early printings. Modern printings read ". . . *le-olam be-davar she-hu* . . ." The reading of the earlier printings is superior. The latter reading, however, would make sense if *be-davar* ("in a matter") were *ke-davar* ("as a matter"). See below, p. 163.
32. Exodus 23:19 and 34:26, and Deuteronomy 14:21.
33. See Mishnah Zevaḥim 8:1 and 8:4. For the context of the present discussion, it is sufficient to accept Maimonides' words at face value. It is true, however, that the words *mi-pi ha-shemu'ah,* which imply an undisputed tradition, are probably an overstatement, since Rabbi Akiva apparently disagrees with the claim that the prohibition applies to beasts of chase *de-oraita.* (See Tosafot Yom Tov to Zevaḥim 8:4 for a different explanation.) The accuracy of Maimonides' specific example, however, does not affect his systemic explanation of *Lo tosif* and *Lo tigra.*

> [with milk] by maintaining that it is included in the category of "kid," and is forbidden from the Torah, that would be adding. But if [the court] said, "The meat of fowl is permissible from the Torah, but we forbid it; and we shall inform the people that it is an enactment, in order that the matter not bear negative results (*she-lo yavo min ha-davar ḥurbah*), that people might say that fowl is permissible, since it is not stated explicitly, and someone else will claim that the meat of domesticated animals is also permissible, except for goats; and someone else will claim that even the meat of goats is permissible in the milk of a cow or a ewe, since naught is stated other than "its mother," who is of the same species; and yet another will claim that [even the meat of a goat] is permissible save in its own mother's milk, since only its mother is stated explicitly, therefore, we forbid all meat with milk, even the meat of fowl," this is not adding, but putting up a fence around the Torah. And so anything similar.

Maimonides proposes that the crucial element in determining whether a given rabbinic enactment is a violation of *Bal tosif* or *Bal tigra* is the manner in which it was enacted. If that which is added or subtracted because of the enactment is declared to reflect the intent of the Torah, the enactment is a violation either of *Bal tosif* or *Bal tigra*. If, however, the enactment that adds or subtracts is avowed to have been promulgated as a safeguard for the Torah and is not declared to be the Torah's intent, the enactment does not violate these prohibitions. The Torah, therefore, forbids only such amendments or abrogations that overturn its dictates in theory as well as in practice. So long, however, as its writ remains theoretically sacrosanct, insofar as it reflects the intent of God, the sages are empowered to add to it or subtract from it in practice, provided that the avowed function of that which is added or taken away is to safeguard the very dictate that it actually overturns. To state this idea in legal terminology: When rabbinic enactments are clearly stipulated to be secondary legislation and not primary legislation, they constitute no violation whatsoever of the prohibitions *Bal tosif* and *Bal tigra*.

There are other elements of Maimonides' position that must be stressed as well. First, Maimonides distinguishes between those matters that forbid the permissible and those that permit the forbidden with regard to the length of time he posits that an amendment may remain effective: An enactment that forbids the permissible can remain in effect permanently; an enactment that permits the forbidden cannot remain in effect permanently. It is, after all, conceivable that a precept can be protected only by the addition of a permanent prohibition that forbids that which is theoretically permissible; it is not conceivable that permanently permitting that which is forbidden could possibly be a necessary condition for its ultimate preservation.

Second, Maimonides also imples that both *Bal tosif* and *Bal tigra* can apply both to positive and to negative commandments; that is, it is possible to add to and to take away from both positive and negative commandments. (His example, which includes a clarification of both adding and taking away, is based upon a negative commandment.) In theory, therefore, it is possible to violate the prohibitions in four ways: by adding to a positive commandment and taking away from a positive commandment, and by taking away from a negative commandment and adding to a negative commandment. Examples of the first two possible kinds of violations are included in the midrashic statement quoted above,[34] and the application of the prohibitions to these instances is, therefore, undeniable. All would agree, as well, that the abrogation of any aspect of a negative commandment (i.e., permitting behavior that the commandment forbids) would be a violation of the third category, except if the abrogation was the result of an urgent contemporary need, and applied only for a restricted time span. It is, consequently, in regard to the fourth category, adding to a negative commandment, that Maimonides' comment evoked strong reaction.

Rabbi Abraham ben David (Ravad, ca. 1125–1198) reacted vehemently to Maimonides' statement. He wrote:[35]

> The prohibition does not apply to any matter concerning which the sages made an enactment forbidding [the permissible] as a fence or safeguard to the Torah, even if they established it for ever (*le-dorot*) and made it as the Torah itself (*ve-asa'uhu ke-shel Torah*), and supported it with a verse, as we find in several places, "[Such and such] is *mi-de-rabbanan,* and the verse is a mere support."[36] And if one diminishes according to the need of the hour, as Elijah on Mount Carmel,[37] even that is according to the Torah *(devar Torah),* [i.e.,

34. P. 156. Adding a fifth species to the *lulav* and reducing the number of species to three would be examples of these violations.

35. *Hassagot ha-Ravad, Mishneh Torah,* Hilkhot Mamrim 2:9.

36. See, for example, Berakhot 41b, Yoma 74a and 80b, Sukkah 28b, and many other places. The thrust of the Ravad's comment here is that the phrase "[Such and such] is *mi-de-rabbanan,* and the verse is a mere support" indicates that the sages often instituted enactments and made them as the Torah itself *(asa'um ke-shel Torah),* even though their origin was rabbinic.

37. I Kings 18:14–39. According to rabbinic tradition, Elijah was in violation of the prohibitions against slaughtering and offering sacrifices outside of the central sanctuary. The period of Elijah was *she'at issur ha-bamot* ("a time of prohibition against private altars").

> having *de-oraita* authority], on the basis of the principle "When it is time to act, they may violate Your Torah" (*Et la'asot heferu toratekha*).[38] Thus, one cannot find the prohibition *Lo* [= *Bal*] *tosif* except in positive commandments, such as *lulav*, phylacteries, fringes, and similar things—either temporarily or permanently, established as a *devar torah* or not established so.

At first glance, the disagreement between the Ravad and Maimonides seems quite narrow. Indeed, they appear to disagree only concerning the applicability of *Lo tosif* to negative commandments, Maimonides affirming that it does apply to negative commandments, and Abraham ben David affirming that it does not. None of the Ravad's other statements seem to be in conflict with Maimonides at all. In fact it is the case that both Rabbi Joseph Caro and Rabbi David ben Solomon Ibn Abi Zimra (Radbaz, 1479–1573) understand the disagreement just this way. The Radbaz agrees with the Ravad, affirming that the institution of rabbinic enactments that add to negative commandments constitutes no violation of *Bal tosif*, since the erection of safeguards for the Torah is part and parcel of the Torah itself.[39] Caro, on the other hand, defends Maimonides. He writes:

> It seems that the basic contention of the Ravad against Maimonides is his claim that one cannot find the prohibition of adding [except in positive commandments]. Yet I cannot understand his argument. Would, indeed, one not be adding if he were to claim that the meat of fowl with milk is forbidden from the Torah, since the Torah forbade one species of meat, and that the same holds true to any other species which is called meat? Surely such [a claim] would constitute adding.[40]

While it is possible to view the dispute between Maimonides and the Ravad as a limited one, that view, upon careful analysis, cannot be upheld: Ravad and Maimonides are involved in a much more fundamental argument. Somewhat paradoxically, however, once the fundamental nature of the dispute is recognized, the entire conflict tends to vanish. The Ravad misunderstood Maimonides as claiming that the crucial factor in determining the presence or absence of a violation of *Bal*

38. Psalms 119:126. See below, pp. 169–176, on the entire matter of *Et la'asot*.
39. In all standard printings of Maimonides' *Mishneh Torah*, comments to Hilkhot Mamrim 2:9.
40. See *Kesef Mishneh*, in all standard printings of Maimonides' *Mishneh Torah*, to Hilkhot Mamrim 2:9.

tosif or *Bal tigra* lies in according the behavior resulting from rabbinic enactments adding or taking away the same authority as behavior dictated by the Torah itself. We have intimated above, however, that the crucial factor for Maimonides lies not in the authoritativeness of the behavior resulting from the enactment, but in the intent and manner of its promulgation. It is indeed because of the very fact that Maimonides does *not* deny the authority of the behavior resulting from the rabbinic enactments that Caro cannot understand the vehemence of the Ravad. Maimonides is concerned only to see that rabbinic enactments retain the status of secondary legislation and that they not be accorded *de-oraita* status. He does not deny the fact that the authority of rabbinic enactments can, indeed, be equal to the authority of dictates of the Torah itself; in fact, he does not even address himself to that issue in the selection we have cited.

How then can one account for Rabbi Abraham ben David's vehemence against Maimonides? It seems most plausible to hypothesize that the Ravad's version of Maimonides read, "and establish that matter in perpetuity *as a matter* that is from the Torah *(ve-likbo'a ha-davar le-olam* ke-davar *she-hu min ha-torah*)."[41] He understood this reading to refer to the legal authority of the enactment, not to the intent and manner of its promulgation, and therefore his vehemence reflects concern for the legal authority of the enactment, proof for which he deduces from the fact that in many cases the sages accorded their own safeguards authority equal to that of the Torah: "Such and such is *mi-de-rabbanan,* and the verse is mere support *(mi-de-rabbanan u-kera asmakhta be-alma*)." Even when they take away from the Torah, their subtractions possess the authority of the Torah—"When it is time to act, they may violate Your Torah." Nowhere, however, does the Ravad maintain that rabbinic enactments are themselves *de-oraita.* On the contrary, the verses he quotes clearly indicate that the enactments are *mi-de-rabbanan,* although they possess authority equal to the Torah. Thus, one might well conclude that Abraham ben David's dispute with Maimonides is based solely on the reading in his particular text, and nothing more. Had his reading omitted "as a matter (*ke-davar*)," there would have been no dispute at all.[42]

---

41. See above, n. 31. That his reading was *ke-davar* instead of *be-davar* seems to be substantiated internally from the Ravad, who paraphrases his understanding of Maimonides' intent as follows: *Afillu keva'uhu le-dorot ve-asa'uhu* ke-shel *Torah* ("even if they established it in perpetuity and made it *as [a matter] of* the Torah").

42. One is inclined, as well, to claim not only that Caro did not have the reading *ke-davar* in his Maimonides, but that he was unaware of such a reading. Thus, he failed to see that

There is a second implication of Maimonides' statement that must be considered. He affirms that the prohibitions of *Bal tosif* and *Bal tigra* apply not only to matters stipulated in the Torah itself but also to the Oral Law. Since, by definition, the prohibitions apply only to those matters that add to or take away from the *grundnorm*, it follows that Maimonides is referring to those things in the Oral Law that have the status of *de-oraita*. We have already seen, however, that Maimonides accords *de-oraita* status only to matters in the Oral Law that are undisputed and long-standing traditions and that are so defined by the sages themselves.[43] Thus, in the example Maimonides uses, the prohibition against cooking or eating milk and meat mixed together has *de-oraita* status because it is a long-standing and undisputed tradition, and is so characterized by the sages themselves.

Maimonides summarizes his position regarding *Bal tosif* and *Bal tigra* in his Introduction to the *Mishneh Torah*.[44] He writes:

> Concerning what did the Torah caution: "You shall not add to it nor take away from it"?[45] That no prophet shall be entitled to introduce anything new and say that the Holy One, blessed be He, commanded us concerning this *miẓvah* either to add it to the *miẓvot* of the Torah or to take away one of these 613. But if a court, together with the prophet who might exist at that time, added a *miẓvah* either through an enactment (*takkanah*), a temporary injunction (*hora'ah*),[46] or a decree (*gezerah*), that is not an addition, since they did not claim that the Holy One, blessed be He, commanded to make an *eruv*, or to read the *Megillah* at its appropriate time. Had they said so, they would have been adding to the Torah.[47]

---

the Ravad's comment was based upon a variant reading, and consequently, found the vehemence of his comment incomprehensible.

Since the comment of the Ravad deals with rabbinic enactments, not rabbinic exegesis, it is not possible to claim that he is adopting the Naḥmanidean position regarding the *de-oraita* status of rabbinic exegesis above the Maimonidean contention that such exegesis, by and large, has *de-rabbanan* status (pp. 16–22 above).

43. See above, pp. 16–20 and nn. 17, 18, and 25 to those pages.

44. *Introduction to the Mishneh Torah,* the passage immediately following the enumeration of the commandments.

45. Deuteronomy 13:1.

46. I.e., a *Hora'at sha'ah*.

47. Naḥmanides, in his *Commentary* to Deuteronomy 4:2, Chaval ed. (Jerusalem: Mossad Harav Kook, 1960 [5720], p. 361, agrees with Maimonides' contention that rabbinic enactments must be known to be other than directly from God. He adds, however, on the basis of Yevamot 21a, that the very enactment of safeguards is itself a *miẓvah* from the Torah, based on a variety of possible verses. Although the final verse he quotes (Leviticus 18:30) is called an *asmakhta be-alma* ("mere support") by the Talmud, which should qualify the *miẓvah* deduced therefrom as *de-rabbanan* according to Naḥmanides, the other verses

Third, although the prohibitions of *Bal tosif* and *Bal tigra* reflected in the quotations from the Rashba and Maimonides are widely different, in that for the Rashba the very categories are not applicable to the sages, it is important to emphasize that the disagreement between the two centers almost exclusively on the circumstances that would involve violations of the prohibitions. Since the quotation from Maimonides is not concerned with stipulating the kinds of reasons that would tend to induce the sages to issue decrees or to introduce enactments, one should not be misled into thinking that his silence on the issue here implies any endorsement of the view that the sages were entitled to exercise their rights to abrogate or to amend capriciously and without due cause. There can be no question that both the Rashba and Maimonides would require similar, if not identical, systemic justification for any invocation of the powers of abrogation or amendment, each, of course, requiring that the resultant legislation not constitute a violation of his understanding of the prohibitions of *Bal tosif* or *Bal tigra*.

The discussion thus far has been concerned with the basic systemic right of the sages to amend or abrogate matters *de-oraita*. Throughout, of course, has been the assumption that the sages do, in fact, possess the right to do so *for cause*. But as a prelude to the analysis of what constitutes cause, systemically, it will be useful to consider the relationship between the two prohibitions and the implications of that relationship for the rationale of the prohibitions and for determining and understanding those causes that constitute systemically justifiable grounds for invoking the right to amend or to abrogate. That is, if the purpose of an amendment to or an abrogation of the *grundnorm* is to strengthen or safeguard the very reason for the existence of the prohibitions, such an amendment or abrogation is more likely to be systemically defensible than one whose purpose is not that. Furthermore, since the matter we are concerned with is the halakhic system, the rationale must be a legal one, not a theological one, the latter being of only tangential (historical) relevance to the system.

Rabbi Baruch ha-Levi Epstein (1860–1942) offers the following ideas:[48]

> Indeed it seems surprising why, in fact, it is forbidden [for a priest] to add to the benedictions[49] . . . and it seems [most plausible to explain it on the basis] of the general contention that whoever adds

---

are not so called. Furthermore, even that verse itself is used for a similar purpose in Mo'ed Katan 5a and is not called an *asmakhta* there.

48. *Torah Temimah* (Vilna, 1904) to Deuteronomy 4:2, letter *aleph*.

49. See the end of the quotation from *Sifrei Deuteronomy*, above, p. 156.

takes away.[50] Which means that once a man allows himself to add, he will believe that that which the Torah stipulates explicitly (*she-kaẓuv ba-torah*) is not intended literally (*ein zeh le-ikkuva davka*). As a result, he will, at times, allow himself also to take away, as is known from the matter of the serpent in *parashat Bereshit*.[51] And since the permission to add might result in taking away or subtraction, it is obligatory that the priest not add to the stipulated [benedictions] in order that he not take away [from them].

And thus, it seems to me, the entire matter of *Bal tosif* ought to be understood. Namely, that the primary concern is that an addition should not bring in its wake a taking away, as I have indicated above. But were it not for this [concern], there is no sufficient reason for the prohibition of *Bal tosif*. For what does it matter to us, for example, if one were to use two citrons, two palms, or if one were to wear phylacteries with five compartments, etc. But according to our explanation, the matter is clear. Namely, that when a man would see concerning that which is written in the Torah, i.e., one citron and four sections in the phylacteries, that the number is not meant literally, he would be inclined to deduce permission also to take away, i.e., to fulfill his obligation with a defective citron or with phylacteries of three sections. . . . [And the explanation of the Rashba] makes sense according to our interpretation, according to which the basic reason for the prohibiton [of adding] is that it should not result in taking away, since that concern applies only to additions that an individual makes for himself, by his own decision and based on his own judgment. But it does not apply to the enactments of the sages—general enactments for all Jews, the authenticity of which is uncontested (*she-ein meharharin ba-zeh*)—who will not be inclined to base some other change, resulting in taking away and subtraction, upon it.

Epstein hypothesizes that the crucial prohibition is *Bal tigra*, to which the prohibition of *Bal tosif* is ancillary. The actual function of the latter is

---

50. Sanhedrin 29a.

51. The reference is to the fact that in Genesis 3:3 Eve tells the serpent that she is forbidden not only to eat from the Tree of Knowledge but also to touch it. The original command (Genesis 2:17), however, forbade only eating, not touching. According to rabbinic legend, Eve was convinced that she could eat from the fruit after the serpent pushed her against the tree with no resulting dire consequences. Thus, the addition of the prohibition to touch the tree resulted in the abrogation of the actual command. Ergo, "Whoever adds, takes away (*Kol ha-mosif, gore'a*)."

to ensure the nonviolation of the former.[52] Epstein understands his own theory to support the position of the Rashba over that of Maimonides insofar as only additions by an individual run the risk of resulting in subtractions. That contention, however, may not be conclusive.[53] If it is not conclusive, it follows only that Epstein's theory might be consonant with the Maimonidean position as well as with the Rashba's position. The implications of the theory itself, however, are independent of the rectitude of the claim that it supports the Rashba's theory.

Certain implications follow clearly from Epstein's theory. First, he implies that an enactment subtracting from or abrogating any dictate of the *grundnorm* should be extremely difficult to justify systemically, particularly if such an enactment is intended to remain permanently in force. Since *Bal tigra* is the central prohibition, it should be possible to abrogate or to subtract only on the theoretical grounds that such action is intended to prevent even further abrogation or subtraction. To the extent that such a claim is possible at all, it is so only as a temporary action. As we have already noted, it is difficult to theorize that the *permanent* abrogation of a commandment of the *grundnorm* could be construed as a necessary safeguard of the *grundnorm* itself. This implica-

---

52. It should be noted that Epstein's justification is entirely legal, since it nowhere gives any reason or rationale for *Bal tigra*. That is, the validity of the prohibition is not an issue, being either self-evident or theologically based. While it is theoretically possible that one could hypothesize a counterclaim according to which *Bal tosif* is crucial and *Bal tigra* ancillary—why, after all, is it any worse to wear phylacteries of three sections than phylacteries of five?—such a claim would ignore the fact that Epstein's theory has a sound systemic basis, since it is grounded in the rabbinic contention that *Kol ha-mosif, gore'a*. Had the rabbis claimed, instead, that *Kol ha-gore'a, mosif* ("Whoever takes away, adds"), the countertheory would be systemically based. Epstein posits, therefore, a systemically justified theory, internal to the system. Any argument against it would, in essence, be against the rabbis, not against Epstein. On what grounds the sages felt that diminishing is worse than adding is not a legal question, but a theological one.

53. One could posit that the prohibition applies to the sages as well as to individuals by assuming a real concern that individuals might draw their own conclusions about adding or taking away based upon what they saw the sages doing. Epstein may be correct in asserting that the sages themselves would not be misguided by their own additions, resulting in violations of *Bal tigra*. That, however, does not ensure that individuals may not be misguided by the sages' actions. The safeguard against individual misunderstanding of the actions of the sages is the application of the prohibition to the sages themselves. That, one could posit, is why Maimonides insists that rabbinic enactments be stipulated as rabbinic. Such a stipulation indicates not only that the enactment itself is not God-given but also that the ground of its authority is the authority of the sages. No individual would equate his own authority with that of the sages, and, thus, the stipulation guarantees that individuals will not take similar action on their own. Were there no such stipulation, an individual might conclude that the additions and subtractions reflected not rabbinic authority but the idea that the commandments are guidelines rather than definitive prescriptions and proscriptions. Thus, the prohibitions of *Bal tosif* and *Bal tigra* apply to sages no less than to individuals, except insofar as rabbinic authority allows the sages to add or subtract as secondary legislation.

tion applies equally, furthermore, for the abrogations of positive commandment (three compartments in phylacteries, for example) and negative commandments (permitting the forbidden).

Second, since the prohibition of adding to the *grundnorm* is ancillary to the central prohibition against subtracting from it, additions that run little risk of resulting in future subtractions should be relatively easy to justify systemically. This type of addition would be reflected most clearly in enactments forbidding the permissible, that is, in additions to negative commandments forbidding that which the negative commandment itself permits.[54] Such additions can even be permanent, since it is not easily conceivable that the permanent forbidding of the permissible should result, in the future, in causing a subtraction from that which had been forbidden.[55] Regarding additions to positive commandments, however, the situation is quite different. It is because of the possibly nefarious results of just such additions that the prohibition against adding was promulgated in the first place. Thus, systemic justification for adding to positive commandments should be as difficult to establish as is justification for subtracting from either positive or negative commandments.

The remainder of this chapter will be devoted to an analysis of the systemic principles that govern the rights of the sages vis-à-vis matters *de-oraita*. That is, we will study those types of systemically legitimate grounds that allow the sages to add to or take away from the *grundnorm*, either by virtue of the amendment power granted to them according to the Rashba or, according to Maimonides, by virtue of their right to engage in clear secondary legislation. The digression we have just completed on the underlying rationale behind the prohibitions *Bal tosif* and *Bal tigra* and the relationship between them was intended to aid us in determining and understanding the systemically justifiable grounds for invoking the right to amend or to abrogate. And, though our attention hereafter will be directed primarily to an analysis of the primary sources that deal with actual active rabbinic amendment or abrogation of the *grundnorm*, it should be noted from the outset that

---

54. The ultimate claim, of course, would be that forbidding the permissible should not even be considered within the realm of adding. Cf. the Ravad's position, above, pp. 161 f. The irony is that the proliferation of stringencies that forbid the permissible is, according to this theory, a safeguard against the violation of *mizvot* the prohibition against adding to which is itself a safeguard against detraction. It is, as it were, almost a *Gezerah li-gezerah*—a decree on a decree.

55. See, however, above, n. 51 for an instance in which an additional prohibition of that which had been permissible did, in fact, result in the abrogation of the original command the prohibition was intended to safeguard.

Epstein's thesis concerning the prohibitions will be borne out almost entirely: Enactments that subtract from or abrogate dictates of the *grundnorm* will be most difficult to justify, particularly if the enactment is permanent; enactments that add to the *grundnorm* and run little risk of resulting in future subtractions will be relatively easy to justify; and enactments that add to positive commandments will be as difficult to justify as those that take away from either positive or negative commandments.

The Talmud uses a variety of general dicta to justify the abrogation or the amendment of the norms of the Torah, both by adding to them and by subtracting from them. The drawback to the use of these dicta, of course, is the fact that they are general, not specific: they offer general indications of the types of considerations that warrant the amendment or the abrogation of the *grundnorm,* but they do not offer precise definitions. Yet, what to one may be a drawback may be an advantage to another; a lack of precision has the advantage of allowing the authorities of the system to interpret and apply the dicta broadly or narrowly, as their discretion dictates. The result of this situation is that, even if the specific circumstances giving rise to consideration of the use of one of the dicta in order to justify an amendment are not themselves a matter of contention, the question of whether this dictum should, in fact, be applied to these precise circumstances can be a matter of legitimate argument and thus, ultimately, a matter of judicial discretion.

To begin with, we shall deal with four of the most common of such dicta, analyzing their meanings, the manner in which they are applied in the sources, and finally, their implications for the halakhic process. Following this we shall discuss the two basic methods of implementing an amendment, namely, active abrogation and desuetude. The chapter will conclude with a discussion of the implications of the rights of the sages vis-à-vis matters *de-oraita* in particular with regard to the problem of *ultra vires.*

Et la'asot la-donai heferu toratekha

The final two words of the dictum *Et la'asot la-donai heferu toratekha*[56] are clear. They mean: "They have violated [or, voided] Your Torah." The first half is more problematic, since the words can be translated to mean either "It is time for the Lord to act" or "It is time to act for the Lord." The latter clearly means that others must act for the sake of the Lord,

56. Psalms 119:126. Quoted above, p. 162, by Rabbi Abraham ben David.

and the former, clearly, that the Lord must act for Himself. Reflections of both meanings can be found in rabbinic literature.

Rava offers two interpretations of the dictum that emphasize the difference between the two possible readings of the first clause.[57]

> Rava said, "This verse may be explained both forward and backward. Forward: 'It is time for the Lord to act!' Why? 'Because they have violated Your Torah.'[58] Backward:[59] 'They have violated Your Torah.'[60] Why? 'Because it is time to act for the Lord.' "

Two examples will demonstrate that both these interpretations are utilized in the sources. The first example requires a brief introduction. Apparently, the earliest formulation of the law of inheritance stipulated that only sons were to inherit from their father. If a man had no sons, his property passed to his brothers, even if he had daughters. Such was the case of Zelophehad.[61] His five daughters, however, appealed to Moses. In the course of a midrashic interpretation of the episode,[62] the following is related:

> When did they [i.e., the daughters] stand before Moses? At the time that Israel was saying to him, "Let us appoint a leader and return to Egypt."[63] Moses said to them [i.e., the daughters]: "All of Israel is requesting to return to Egypt, and you are seeking an inheritance in the land?" They said, "We are certain that all of Israel will ultimately possess the land, as it says: 'It is time for the Lord to act, they have

---

57. Berakhot 63a.

58. Rashi, *ibid.*: "There are times when the Lord must execute just punishment against those who transgress His will, because they have violated Your [His] Torah." According to this explanation, "they" refers to sinners who transgress the will of God.

59. See the quotation from Mishnah Berakhot, below, p. 172, for proof that the same meaning can be deduced without reversing the order of the verse. Its reversal simply makes that meaning clearer. Also, see below, n. 74.

60. Rashi, Berakhot 63a: "Those who do His will have violated His Torah, like Elijah on Mount Carmel, who sacrificed on a noncentral altar (*bamah*) during a period when that was forbidden, because it was a time to make a fence and a hedge among the Jews for the sake of the Holy One, blessed be He." According to this explanation, "they" refers to those who serve God faithfully but may be forced at times to violate His will in furtherance of their very service to Him.

61. Numbers 27:1–11.

62. *Sifrei Zuta*, ed. H. S. Horovitz (Jerusalem: Wahrmann Books, 1966), beginning of *parashat Pinḥas*, p. 316.

63. Numbers 14:4. Admittedly, the text of the Torah does not intimate any connection between the two incidents. That fact, however, is irrelevant to the application of *Et la'asot* to the case.

> violated His Torah.' "[64] Do not read [the verse] thus. Rather: "They have violated Your Torah; it is time to act for the Lord."[65]

Thus, the first interpretation of the *midrash* follows Rava's first explanation of the dictum, and the second interpretation, his second. One implication of the second interpretation[66] is that one type of consideration that justifies invoking the power to amend or to abrogate is the contention that the amendment or the abrogation will result in the ultimate strengthening of the Jews' commitment to the will of God; although whether or not the desired result would actually follow from the act of amendment or abrogation might be a matter of *maḥaloket*. Consequently, in the final analysis, whether authorities should invoke the power to amend or to abrogate in a specific case becomes a "matter of opinion."[67]

The second example juxtaposes both possible interpretations of the dictum and reads as follows:

> [Hillel said,] "When you see that the Torah is being forgotten among Jews, and many are paying it no heed, you should keep it inward, as it says, 'It is time for the Lord to act.' " [Erfurt manuscript and other sources add: "Rabbi Me'ir says, 'They have violated Your Torah; it is time to act for the Lord.' "][68]

Hillel, interpreting the verse according to Rava's first explanation, affirms that God must act in His own behalf to ameliorate the situation. Rabbi Me'ir, however, disagrees. His contention is that the circum-

---

64. The thrust of their claim is as follows: Surely Israel will take possession of the land, since the very fact that they now are violating the will of God by refusing to enter it ensures that God will act on His own behalf and bring them into it. Thus, we seek a portion in it.

65. The *midrash* proceeds to offer several examples of this interpretation of *Et la'asot*. It is not clear whether the conclusion of the quoted passage intends to apply this latter understanding of *Et la'asot* to the daughters of Zelophehad. It seems plausible that it does, as follows: The daughters, seeing that the people wished to return to Egypt, thus violating the will of God, felt the hour worthy to seek an abrogation of the law that would have forbidden them to inherit. Such an abrogation would result in the actual strengthening of the word of God insofar as granting an inheritance to the daughters of Zelophehad would demonstrate their commitment and readiness to obey the word of God and enter the land. Else, why be concerned about a portion in it!

66. See preceding note.

67. Meant in the sense defined above, chap. 3, n. 49.

68. Tosefta Berakhot 6:24, Lieberman ed., p. 40. Cf. *Sifrei Zuta*, Horovitz ed., *parashat Pinḥas*. p. 316; Yerushalmi Berakhot 9:8, 14d; Bavli Berakhot 63a; *Midrash Samuel*, chap. 1; *Midrash Mishlei*, S. Buber ed. (Vilna, 1897), p. 52.

stances described warrant positive and affirmative action on the part of those who do pay heed to the Torah, in order to strengthen it and disseminate it among those who are ignoring it. Thus, Rabbi Me'ir favors the second possible interpretation of the first clause.[69]

It is, of course, Rava's second interpretation that becomes the systemic principle providing the grounds of the right of the sages to amend or abrogate. Therefore, it is to the use of this interpretation in the sources that we must turn for guidance with regard to the types of circumstances warranting its employment.

Such an interpretation is found in the Mishnah itself, although only once.[70] It reads:

> In the conclusions to all benedictions in the Temple they used to say, "Forever" (*min ha-olam*).[71] When the sectaries caused corruption (*mi-she-kilkelu ha-minim*) and said that there is only one world,[72] they ordained that "Forever and ever" (*min ha-olam ve-ad ha-olam*) be said.[73] . . . And it says, "It is time to act for the Lord; they have violated Your Torah." Rabbi Nathan says, "They have violated Your Torah; it is time to act for the Lord."[74]

The dictum serves as proof-text for the grounds on the basis of which the sages instituted the change, not as proof of the change itself. Rashi explains the meaning of the dictum as used in this passage as follows: "There are times when we abrogate *(she-mevattelin)* the words of the Torah in order to act for the Lord. . . . It is permissible to violate the Torah and to do that which seems forbidden."[75] Thus, at least according to Rashi, this example indicates that the strengthening and reaffirmation

---

69. This example indicates, as well, the degree to which the meaning of a dictum can vary. Thus, Rabbi Me'ir's employment of Rava's second interpretation does not imply the need for any abrogation of the law in order to fulfill "acting for the Lord." Indeed, it seems plausible to maintain that the meaning of the phrase in Rabbi Me'ir's dictum represents the earlier stage, and the employment of the phrase to imply amendment power reflects a later stage in the understanding of the verse.

70. Mishnah Berakhot 9:5, 54a.

71. For example: *Barukh ha-shem elohei yisra'el min ha-olam go'el yisra'el* ("Blessed is the Lord, God of Israel, forever, Redeemer of Israel"). Cf. Ta'anit 16b.

72. I.e., when the Sadducees denied the existence of the world-to-come.

73. The antidote to the Sadducean contention was the institution of a phrase containing the word *olam* ("world") twice, meaning "this world and the world-to-come."

74. Rabbi Nathan is not disagreeing with the use of *Et la'asot* as a proof-text for the right of the sages to introduce a new formula for the benediction. Nor is he contending that it can be deduced from the verse only when it is explained backward. He is affirming only that that meaning of the verse is clearer when it is explained backward. See Tosafot Yom Tov, Mishnah Berakhot 9:5, and above, n. 59.

75. Rashi, Berakhot 54a, s.v. *ve-omer*.

of a normative Jewish position in the face of a non-normative and contrary opinion constitutes sufficient grounds for the abrogation of the *grundnorm*.[76]

We have already intimated that the same type of considerations that motivate abrogation of the *grundnorm* can also be invoked as grounds for other decisions, when no abrogation of the *grundnorm* is involved.[77] Thus, for example, the Mishnah states that the Ten Commandments were recited daily in the Temple.[78] The Yerushalmi claims: "It would be fitting that the Ten Commandments be recited every day [i.e., even outside the Temple]. And why are they not read? Because of the adamance of the sectarians [i.e., Christians], and so that they should not claim that only these were given to Moses at Sinai."[79] That is, the Jews do not recite the Ten Commandments because they do not wish to encourage the claim of the Christians that they alone constitute the revelation of God.

In the context of a description of an encounter between Shimon the Righteous and Alexander the Great, the Talmud records the following:[80]

> It is forbidden to leave the Temple precincts wearing the priestly garments . . . [Shimon the Righteous] put on his priestly garments . . . and when he arrived at Antipatris.[81] . . . If you want, you may claim that they were garments which were appropriate to be priestly garments [but were not, in actuality]. Alternatively, "It is time to act for the Lord; they have violated Your Torah."

The function of Shimon's visit to Alexander the Great was to seek revocation of Alexander's permission to the Samaritans to destroy the Temple. Thus, this example, too, indicates that a threat to the Jewish people from outside its normative confines constitutes valid grounds for abrogation of the *grundnorm*. This last example indicates, in addition,

---

76. Since the source for the prohibition against answering only amen rather than *min ha-olam ve-ad ha-olam* ("forever and ever") is deduced in Ta'anit 16b from Nehemiah 9:5, i.e., on the basis of *divrei kabbalah* ("words of tradition") rather than *divrei Torah* ("words of Torah"), certain complications follow. Either we must claim that *divrei kabbalah* are themselves considered *de-oraita*, which may be the case (see Elon, *Jewish Law*, 1:195, and n. 91 there) or we may say that *Et la'asot* can be invoked as grounds for abrogation of matters of law in the first sense, even if such matters are not themselves *de-oraita*. The latter seems most plausible.

77. Above, pp. 154–155.

78. Tamid 5:1.

79. Yerushalmi Berakhot 1:8, 3c. Cf. Bavli Berakhot 12a.

80. Yoma 69a.

81. I.e., a city built by Herod and named for his father. Clearly, outside the Temple precincts.

that the grounds for invoking *Et la'asot* are not a foregone conclusion. If it were clear which precise set of circumstances necessarily warrants invoking the dictum, there would be no need for two possible interpretations of Shimon's actions by the Talmud.

On the other hand, it would be erroneous to conclude that only dire threats constitute valid grounds. There are, as well, less calamitous threats which the sources reflect as worthy of warranting the abrogation of the *grundnorm*.

On the basis of a juxtaposition in Scripture of terms referring to the Written Law and the Oral Law,[82] the Talmud deduces that "things intended to be in writing may not be transmitted orally, and things meant to be oral may not be transmitted in writing."[83] Thus, the *grundnorm* itself forbids the commission of the Oral Law to writing. The Talmud deduces, furthermore, that the books of the Bible are to be committed to writing only in scrolls containing complete books, not fragments.[84]

Nonetheless, there is undeniable evidence that Rabbi Yoḥanan and Resh Lakish used to study from written scrolls of *Aggadah*.[85] They apparently justified their actions by invoking *Et la'asot*, adding: "It is better that the Torah be uprooted [violated], so that it not be forgotten among Jews."[86] That is, the ultimate preservation of the Torah itself may sometimes dictate its violation. The grounds for that contention: *Et la'asot*.

Utilizing the actions of Rabbi Yoḥanan and Resh Lakish as precedent, and employing the same rationale, the Talmud expands the circumstances under which *Et la'asot* may be applied.[87]

> It is forbidden to read from a *haftarah* [prophetic portions] scroll[88] on Shabbat. Why? Because it ought not to be written.[89] . . . But it is not so. It is permissible both to carry it and to read from it, as Rabbi Yoḥanan and Rabbi Shimon ben Lakish used to study from written *Aggadah* scrolls on Shabbat. But it, too, should not have been

---

82. Exodus 34:27: Ketov *lekha et ha-devarim ha-elleh ki* al pi *ha-devarim* ha-elleh ("*Write* for yourself these words, for *by the mouth of these* [on the basis of these] words").
83. Gittin 60b.
84. Gittin 60a, on the basis of Deuteronomy 31:26.
85. Gittin 60a, and Temurah 14b.
86. Temurah 14b. See also below, pp. 176–181, concerning all aspects of this principle.
87. Gittin 60a.
88. I.e., one containing only those sections from the Prophets that are recited as *haftarot*, but not completed books of the Prophets.
89. Rashi, Gittin 60a: less than an entire book.

> written.[90] Since, however, it was impossible[91]—*Et la'asot la-shem, heferu toratekha.*[92] Here, too,[93] since it is impossible[94]—*Et la'asot la-shem, heferu toratekha.*

The circumstances that motivated the abrogation of the scriptural norm that forbids the writing of incomplete books of the Prophets was, apparently, the inability of many communities to procure a complete scroll, probably because of its cost. Thus, the possibility that compliance with the law might result in the omission of the *haftarot* constituted sufficient reason to invoke *Et la'asot*.

Rabbi Mordecai ben Hillel (ca. 1240–1298) records a further extension of the use of *Et la'asot*, based on reasoning similar to that of the last two passages.[95]

> One may write a partial scroll of the Torah for a child to use for study.[96] It is also the case that it is permissible to write the sacrificial section of the service and the entire *Shema* because of *Et la'asot la-shem*. For, indeed, it is the case that not everyone knows them by heart, nor do they possess Pentateuchs that they might bring to the synagogue. [And this combination of factors] might result in the abolition of prayer and the recitation of *Shema*, which is itself from the Torah. Therefore, it is permissible to write these things even though they ought not to be written.

It should be noted that these abrogations, which were introduced ostensibly to meet the specific need of a specific time, have never been

---

90. Because things meant to be oral may not be transmitted in writing. See Gittin 60a.

91. Rashi, Gittin 60a: "It was impossible to refrain from writing the scroll, since later ages were incapable of mastering by heart what earlier ages could (*she-nitma'et ha-lev*), and the Torah was being forgotten."

92. Rashi, Gittin 60a: "If the time comes to make an enactment for the sake of Heaven, they [may] violate the words of the Torah for the time which requires it (*la-sha'ah ha-ẓerikhah*)."

93. I.e., the case of the *haftarah* scroll.

94. Rashi, Gittin 60a: "Since not every community is able to write a complete scroll of the Prophets."

95. *Sefer ha-Mordecai* (printed in most standard editions of the Talmud), Gittin, chap. 5, sec. 407.

96. Contrary to the statement of the Talmud, Gittin 60a. The source of the Mordecai's decision is the Alfas. The reason for the Alfas' decision is explained by Rabbi Asher ben Yeḥi'el, *Piskei Rosh*, Gittin 5:20. Rabbi Asher wrote: "[The Alfas] saw fit to rule leniently, since it is impossible for every poor Jew to write a complete Torah scroll for his son." Cf., too, *Responsa of Rema*, Ziv ed., no. 34, p. 194a.

revoked. Their permanence reflects the fact that amendments of the *grundnorm*, even those that permit the forbidden, need not necessarily apply only to a restricted time period. This issue will be addressed toward the end of this chapter, since it seems to conflict with our contention that such enactments could not be permanent.

We shall offer one final example of the employment of *Et la'asot*, in order to indicate that its application is not restricted to instances in which its ameliorative effects apply only to large numbers of individuals. Maimonides was asked to decide what ought to be done in an instance in which a Jew had purchased a beautiful non-Jewish slave and was suspected of having had sexual relations with her.[97] Maimonides states at once that the court must compel him to put her out. But, he continues:

> Or he should free her and take her as his wife, even though that action would be like a transgression, since one who is suspected of having had relations with a slave woman who was later freed is forbidden *a priori* to marry her. For we have already decided several times in similar circumstances that he should free her and marry her. And we did so because of the Enactment for Penitents . . . and have relied on the words of the sages, of blessed memory: *Et la'asot la-shem, heferu toratekha*.

Allowing a reasonable solution to a problem for those who wish to repent encourages repentance. Since repentance is a desirable end, invoking *Et la'asot* in order to encourage repentance is legitimate.

Mutav te'aker ot aḥat min ha-Torah

The second systemic principle that governs the determination of cause vis-à-vis the amendment or abrogation of matters *de-oraita* is, in fact, not even a complete sentence. It is, rather, just the beginning of a sentence, the end of which is completed as warranted. The translation of this beginning clause is: "It is better that one letter of the Torah be uprooted." In the Talmud, three different endings are supplied to the clause. One of the endings has already been cited, coupled with *Et la'asot*.[98] Rabbi Yoḥanan and Resh Lakish justified committing a scroll of *Aggadah* to writing by affirming that it was a time to act for the Lord, it being better to uproot the Torah[99] than to allow the Torah to be forgotten

97. *Teshuvot ha-Rambam*, Blau ed., no. 211 = Freiman ed., no. 154.
98. P. 174, from Temurah 14b.
99. Variant reading: "One letter of the Torah."

(ve-lo tishtakkaḥ Torah mi-yisra'el). Thus, *ve-lo tishtakkaḥ* both explains the need for acting for the Lord and implies what results are to be expected from the uprooting of the Torah.

The other two endings supplied to the phrase in the Talmud do not couple it directly with *Et la'asot.*

In explaining David's behavior in giving over seven descendants of Saul to the Gibeonites for execution,[100] in violation of the dictum of the Torah that fathers should not die for the sins of their sons nor sons for the sins of their fathers,[101] the Talmud says: Rabbi Ḥiyya bar Abba said in the name of Rabbi Yoḥanan, "It is better that one letter of the Torah be uprooted that the name of Heaven not be publicly desecrated (*ve-al yitḥallel shem shamayim be-farhesia*).' "[102]

The passage implies that preventing the desecration of God's name is sufficient cause for the abrogation of the *grundnorm.* What is equally interesting, however, is the nature of the desecration in this specific case. The biblical text gives scant information about the encounter between Saul and the Gibeonites. We know, however, that the Gibeonites were a group that attached itself to the Israelites, but was never admitted formally to the Jewish people.[103] The desecration that David feared would ensue and that warranted uprooting the Torah was, according to Rashi, the fear that other nations would conclude, on the basis of David's dealings with the Gibeonites, that the Jews were not a people to be emulated: They had taken advantage of the Gibeonites by imposing menial labor upon them, yet would not redress their legitimate grievance against Saul. Since such a conclusion would constitute a desecration of the name of God, David allowed himself to abrogate the law in order to prevent it. And since the desecration would not result from any reaction on the part of the Jews themselves to David's behavior, but from the reaction of others to them, here, too, we find a threat to the Jews from outside themselves accepted as a sufficient reason for the abrogation of the Torah.

The third ending provided by the Talmud is a corollary of the second.[104] In the course of explaining the action of Riẓpah bat Aiyah, Saul's concubine,[105] who violated the Torah's dictate that the body of one who has been executed be quickly interred,[106] the Talmud explains:

---

100. II Samuel 21.
101. Deuteronomy 24:16.
102. Yevamot 79a.
103. See Joshua 9:3–27 and below, n. 107.
104. Yevamot 79a.
105. II Samuel 21:10.
106. Deuteronomy 21:23.

Rabbi Yoḥanan said in the name of Rabbi Shimon ben Yehoẓadak, "It is better that one letter of the Torah be uprooted that the name of Heaven be publicly sanctified" (*ve-yitkaddesh shem shamayim be-farhesia*). For passersby would ask, 'Who are these?' 'They are princes.' 'What did they do?' 'They took advantage of self-proclaimed proselytes.'[107] They [the passersby] will say, 'There is no nation more worthy of emulation than this one. If they treat princes thus,[108] surely nonroyalty as well. [And if they execute justice even for an offense against] self-proclaimed proselytes, surely against another Jew as well.' " Immediately, one hundred and fifty thousand were added to Israel.

Thus, as with the preceding example, an action that requires the abrogation of the *grundnorm* in order to sanctify the name of God can stem from the reaction of non-Jews. The positive result that it is presumed will ensue as a result of such an abrogation is deemed sufficiently desirable to warrant the abrogation.

It should be noted that none of the proposed endings to the phrase *Mutav te'aker ot aḥat min ha-Torah* offers precise criteria on the basis of which to decide whether or not the Torah is in danger of being forgotten; nor do they give us any idea of what types of actions will result either in the desecration or the sanctification of God's name. Such judgments must be made by the sages, as they see fit. Furthermore, it seems reasonable to hypothesize that the number of possible endings to *Mutav te'aker ot aḥat min ha-Torah* is not restricted to those specifically mentioned. On the contrary, the fact that as many as three different conclusions are found in the sources seems to indicate that the principle is open-ended and that any number of conclusions are theoretically conceivable, the only condition being that the sages consider them sufficient grounds for the abrogation or amendment of the Torah.

Pe'amim she-bittulah shel Torah zehu yesodah

The systemic principle *Pe'amim she-bittulah shel Torah zehu yesodah* is found only once in the Talmud. It is stated explicitly by Resh Lakish as follows:[109]

---

107. *Gerim gerurim*, i.e., the Gibeonites.
108. Not allowing them to be free from punishment for trespasses.
109. Menaḥot 99a.

> Resh Lakish said, "There are times when the annulment of the Torah is its establishment [foundation], as it is written: "Which you have broken" (*asher shibbarta*).[110] [Implying] that the Holy One, blessed be He, said to Moses, 'Congratulations (*yishar koḥakha*) on having broken them.' "

From a play on the words *asher* and *yishar (koḥakha)*, Resh Lakish deduces that God approved of Moses' breaking the Tablets of the Law when descending from Sinai. The grounds for the approval would seem to be reflected in this systemic principle, which is understood to imply that the firm establishment of the Torah could not take place amidst the apostasy of the Golden Calf episode: Its establishment could be brought about only by its total, although temporary, abrogation. Resh Lakish understands Moses' act not as the mere destruction of the Tablets, but as a symbolic act abrogating the entire Torah.

Even if this was not what Resh Lakish meant, it is clear that this is what he was understood to mean. Thus, the Talmud reads elsewhere:[111]

> Moses did three things on his own and his actions met with God's approval. . . . He broke the Tablets. What exegesis did he employ to reach his conclusion? He said, "If concerning the paschal lamb, which is but one of 613 commandments, the Torah says: 'No foreigner may eat therefrom,'[112] surely the entire Torah[113] [must be withheld from the Jews] when Israel is behaving as apostates." And Moses' position was in accord with that of the Omnipresent, as it is written: "Which you have broken," [concerning which] Resh Lakish said that the Holy One, blessed be He, said to Moses, "Congratulations on having broken them."[114]

---

110. Exodus 34:1.
111. Shabbat 62a. Cf. also Yerushalmi Ta'anit 4:8, 68c.
112. Exodus 12:43.
113. Which is embodied in the Ten Commandments.
114. Rashi, in Menaḥot 99b, offers a totally different explanation of Resh Lakish's statement. He maintains that it refers to *bittul talmud Torah* ("the suspension of the study of Torah"), as it were. Thus, at times the suspension of the study of Torah is itself the establishment of the Torah, as, for example, the burial of the dead or participation in the celebration of a marriage. Resh Lakish, according to Rashi, is not referring to the actual abrogation of commandments. Not only does the *baraita* from Shabbat reflect a different understanding of Resh Lakish's intention from that of Rashi, the language of Resh Lakish himself argues against Rashi's interpretation. It is difficult to maintain that *bittulah shel Torah* ("the annulment of the Torah") means *bittul talmud Torah*.

When the ultimate goals of the Torah would be better served by its abrogation, even in its entirety, it is within the purview of the sages to take that step. The circumstances that might warrant such action are never defined. In the final analysis, the determination of the need for such action lies with the sages themselves. As Moses rendered the decision on his own, so, too, must the sages make the decision on their own. The Talmud's interpretation of Resh Lakish's statement assures the sages that even a radical decision can meet with the approval of God.

We can see from the discussion of each of the principles governing the rights of the sages vis-à-vis matters *de-oraita* that none of them is a clearly defined legal norm, that is, a norm the applicability or nonapplicability of which to specific circumstances can be clearly determined. Rather, each of them allows the maximum discretion to the recognized systemic authorities in determining whether any specific circumstance would dictate its application. Moreover, I would affirm that there is every reason to believe that the lack of precision to be found in these principles is not accidental. Somewhat paradoxically, perhaps, even the area of the legal system that is most crucial systemically—the area involving the rights of the legislator-judge vis-à-vis the *grundnorm* itself—concerning which it would be logical to expect the most precise systemic dicta, is, in fact, not susceptible of precise definition. But paradox should not be confused with lack of reason.

Since the sacrosanct nature of the *grundnorm* is central to the system as a whole, perhaps the greatest danger to the continued viability of the system itself is the very right of the sages to amend or abrogate it. That being the case, exercise of that right is naturally restricted to the most extraordinary circumstances. Precise legal norms can often deal with unusual circumstances, since the unusual, although infrequent, is not necessarily unanticipated. The extraordinary, however, is much less likely to be anticipated, and therefore precision regarding the extraordinary is an unreasonable demand. The very imprecision of the rules governing amendment or abrogation intimates that the employment of these rules must be limited to extraordinary circumstances. Indeed, it seems reasonable to claim that with regard to these rules the degree of precision is inversely related to the extraordinariness of the situation. If the rules governing amendment or abrogation were more precise, their employment would be less extraordinary. Thus, the principle that offers the greatest amount of protection to the sacrosanct *grundnorm* is the one that affirms that its amendment or abrogation is legitimate only in extraordinary circumstances, and the most useful definition of the extraordinary is one that implies that changes of the *grundnorm* be instituted only when action for the Lord is required in His own interest—even if that action involves the uprooting of His own will as reflected in the *grundnorm*. In this sense, the last two systemic principles may be considered subcategories of *Et la'asot*.

Authorities of the system will not mistake the maximal discretionary power they possess in determining which circumstances warrant invoking their right to amend or abrogate for *carte blanche* to exercise that power whimsically or capriciously. They are much more likely to ponder whether any given set of circumstances is sufficiently extraordinary to warrant exercising their legitimate right. The theoretical broadness of their power is as likely as not to be a more moderating influence than precisely defined legal norms would be.

Va-ḥai bahem ve-lo she-yamut bahem

There is another systemic principle governing the abrogation of the Torah that can be much more precisely defined, although there is some difference of opinion about the definition. The principle *Va-ḥai bahem*[115] *ve-lo she-yamut bahem*, which means, "One should live by them, not that he should die by them," posits the suspension of the Torah in almost all cases in which its observance would constitute an endangerment to life. Yet as different in nature as this principle seems to be from those discussed previously, we shall see that its implications, deduced primarily from the exceptions to the principle, support the general framework underlying the abrogation or amendment of the *grundnorm* detailed above.

The clearest statement of both the principle and its exceptions is found in Talmud Sanhedrin.[116] It reads:

> If one be told concerning any transgression in the Torah that he must violate it in order not to be killed (*avor ve-al tehareg*), he should violate it and not be killed, except for idolatry, incest, and murder. . . . Rabbi Ishma'el said, "Whence do we know that if one is told to engage in idolatrous behavior in order not to be killed that he should do so and not be killed? The Torah says: 'And live by them'—not die by them."[117] Does [Rabbi Ishma'el's position apply

115. Leviticus 18:5.

116. Sanhedrin 74a.

117. Rabbi Ishma'el applies *Va-ḥai bahem* to idolatry as well. According to the first statement, however, idolatry is excluded from *Va-ḥai bahem*. Regarding Rabbi Ishma'el's opinion, see *Sifra, Aḥare Mot*, 13:14, Weiss ed. (New York: OM Publishing Co., 1946), p. 86b.

even] to a public act [of idolatry]? The Torah says:[118] "You shall not desecrate My holy Name, so that I might be sanctified."[119] . . . Rabbi Yoḥanan said, "[The statement that one may violate all commandments save three, upon threat of death,] applies only to a time of nonpersecution. During a time of religious persecution, however, one ought to die rather than transgress even a simple commandment (*mizvah kallah*). . . . Rabbi Yoḥanan said, "Even during a time of nonpersecution, the sages [did not intend their dictum] to apply except to violations in private. In public, however, one should die rather than transgress even a simple commandment."

The view of the sages, as explained by Rabbi Yoḥanan, contains the following categories: (1) during a time of nonpersecution, and provided that the threat is private, all commandments are suspended when life is threatened, except for the three cardinal transgressions; (2) under the same circumstances, if the threat is public, one should die for *all* commandments; (3) during a time of religious persecution, one should die for all the commandments, whether the threat is private or public. Common to these instances in which one should give up one's life rather than violate the commandments is the idea that in these instances the ultimate aims of Torah would be better served by one's death than by the continuation of his life. Thus, for example, during a time of persecution, when reinforcement of the commitment to the Torah is most needed, the willingness of a Jew to die for its commands serves that purpose much more than would suspending the Torah in order to live. During a time of nonpersecution, however, a private act of martyrdom is just that and no more; and since the ultimate preservation of the Torah is not enhanced by private martyrdom, in such a situation *Va-ḥai bahem* is invoked.[120]

Nor is the application of *Va-ḥai bahem* restricted to cases in which there is a verbalized threat against a person's life, or to cases in which the danger is only to oneself. Indeed, as the following statement of Rabbi

---

118. Leviticus 22:32.

119. I.e., a public act of idolatry, contrary to a private act, is a desecration of God's name. Since that is forbidden, even the threat of death does not warrant abrogation of the prohibition against idolatry under such circumstances.

120. According to Rabbi Yoḥanan, therefore, we must claim that public martyrdom serves the ultimate goals of the Torah, even during a period of nonpersecution, better than the preservation of life. To the extent that it is conceivable that his interpretation of the sages' position is at variance with their actual intention, it follows only that their disagreement centers around the commitment-reinforcing value of public martyrdom during a period of nonpersecution. Neither denies the criterion of commitment—reinforcement as the primary basis for determining whether or not one should allow himself to be killed.

Akiva makes clear, the principle is invoked even if it is not certain that the abrogation will absolutely ensure the saving of a life. The Tosefta reads:[121]

> Rabbi Aḥa said in the name of Rabbi Akiva, "Scripture says; 'If the thief be caught in the act of intrusion.'[122] What is the status of the homeowner's knowledge of the murderous intention of the intruder, certain or doubtful? One must say it is doubtful.[123] If a man [i.e., the intruder] may be murdered in order to save the life of one whose life is doubtfully endangered [i.e., the homeowner], surely the Sabbath may be superseded in order to save a life in a case of doubt.[124] Indeed, the commandments were given to Israel that they might live by them, as it says: 'That a man should do them, and live by them,'[125] not die by them. [Therefore] nothing takes precedence over the endangerment of life (*pikku'aḥ nefesh*) except idolatry, incest, and murder."

If one bears in mind that the willful violation of the Sabbath was a capital offense, and that fastidious observance of the Sabbath was the norm, he can better understand the far-reaching implications of Rabbi Akiva's contention that the Sabbath is to be superseded for all possible cases of endangerment to life.

While both passages quoted thus far permit the abrogation of the Torah in order to save a life, there is a fundamental difference between them that is more than theoretically significant. The first passage deals with a life-endangering situation imposed by an outside force, presumably a non-Jewish enemy. As such, the endangerment is extraordinary, even if not necessarily uncommon. The second passage deals with more ordinary life-threatening situations, those generally caused by crime, natural calamities, accidents, considerations of health, etc.

It would be reasonable to affirm that one should be allowed to sacrifice

---

121. Tosefta Shabbat 15:17, Lieberman ed., p. 74, Cf. also *Mekhilta,* Mishpatim, *parashah* 13, Horovitz-Rabin ed. (Jerusalem: Bamberger & Wahrman, 1960), p. 242; *Mekhilta,* Ki tissa, *parashah* 1, Horovitz-Rabin ed., p. 340; Yerushalmi Sanhedrin 8:8, 26c.

122. Exodus 22:1. The biblical passage allows a homeowner to kill an intruder, caught in the act of intrusion, without incurring any guilt. The rabbis contend that the intruder is assumed to be willing to murder whoever tries to thwart him, even if he does not actually anticipate doing so at the time he breaks in.

123. I.e., the homeowner is not certain that the intruder is intent upon killing him, even if confronted. Nonetheless, the Torah allows the preemptory murder of the intruder in order to ensure saving the life of the homeowner.

124. The doubt could be of two types: (1) that the life was actually endangered, and (2) that the efforts to save the person would be successful.

125. Leviticus 18:5.

his life in situations of the first type, even if such a sacrifice is not a requirement of the law itself. That is, reinforcement of commitment to the Torah might be effected by an act of martyrdom that is not necessarily required by the law. Indeed, there is a *maḥaloket* on just this point between Maimonides and the Tosafot. Maimonides maintains that one who gives up his life in circumstances in which the law does not require it, even in circumstances of the first type, is himself culpable *(mitḥayyev be-nafsho).*[126] The Tosafot, on the other hand, affirm that one may martyr himself under those circumstances.[127] They wrote:

> And if one wishes to be more strict upon himself [than the law dictates], even concerning other *mizvot* [than the three cardinal sins], he is entitled to do so. As in the case of Rabbi Abba bar Zimra in the Yerushalmi, who was in the company of a pagan who said to him, "Eat carrion. And if you don't, I will kill you."[128] He answered, "If you wish to kill me, do so!" And he [Rabbi Abba] was being more strict upon himself than required, since, evidently, the episode took place in private.

Even the position of the Tosafot, however, cannot be applied to situations of the second, more ordinary type. Although martyrdom in extraordinary conditions might have a beneficial effect, no reasonable argument to the same effect can be made for the sacrifice of life under ordinary situations. In some people, however, piety may cause confusion between the categories; they may be inclined to confuse what is really an unnecessary and foolish loss of life with real martyrdom. It is against just such confusion that the following responsum of Rabbi David ben Solomon Ibn Abi Zimra (Radbaz, 1479–1573) is directed.

> You asked of me that I inform you regarding one for whom the evaluation was made that [saving his life] required the violation of the Sabbath; yet he does not wish that the Sabbath be desecrated on his account, because of piety. Does his wish reflect piety, in which case it should be honored, or should it not be honored?
>
> *Response:* Indeed such a one is a foolish saint *(ḥasid shoteh)*, and the Lord will requite his own blood from him, for the Torah said: "And live by them," not die by them. And not only according to the view

126. *Mishneh Torah,* Hilkhot Yesodei ha-Torah 5:1.
127. Tosafot Avodah Zarah 27b, s.v. *yakhol.*
128. Yerushalmi Shevi'it 4:2, 35a.

> of Maimonides, of blessed memory . . . [that] if one allows himself to be killed rather than transgress he is culpable, but even according to those who claim . . . [that] if he allows himself to be killed rather than transgress he stands in the presence of the righteous and it is a characteristic of piety. . . . Even so, in this case, all would agree that he is culpable . . . [for] there is no element of the sanctification of God present at all.[129]

The situations in which the principle *Va-ḥai bahem ve-lo she-yamut bahem* is applicable can be clearly defined. Only circumstances in which the commitment-reinforcing effects cannot be gainsaid require martyrdom. When no such results can possibly ensue, martyrdom is forbidden. Only when the positive effects of martyrdom are a matter of dispute can there be a legitimate *maḥaloket* about whether one should live or die.[130]

It is noteworthy that none of the selections cited in our examination of the systemic principles governing the abrogation of the *grundnorm* included any instructions about possible methods of implementing such an action. They do, however, include examples of both active and passive abrogation. Passive abrogation is the functional equivalent of desuetude, that is, of the failure to carry out a prescribed action. Thus, Riẓpah bat Aiyah's failure to fulfill the Torah's requirement to bury an executed criminal immediately was an example of passive abrogation.[131] It is evident, moreover, that such passive abrogation can apply only to positive commandments, since only they prescribe an action which one ought to take but can fail to take. Such abrogation is referred to in halakhic language by the precept *Shev ve-al ta'aseh,* that is, "Sit, and do not act."

Most of the other passages cited in our discussion have been examples in which proscriptions of the Torah were abrogated by permitting behavior contrary to that which had been proscribed. The abrogation resulted not from the permission to neglect a positive commandment,

---

129. *Responsa of Radbaz,* pt. 2, no. 1139.

130. The status of Jewish sectaries seems to have been the subject of conflict. Avodah Zarah 27b records an episode in which Rabbi Ishma'el urged his nephew Ben Dama not to allow himself to be treated by a certain Jacob of Sikhania, a disciple of Jesus. Although Ben Dama expired before he could be treated, the Talmud maintains that he would have proved his right to be treated by Jacob through invoking *Va-ḥai bahem.* It is interesting that the very Rabbi Ishma'el who did not insist on martyrdom even for idolatry, on the basis of *Va-ḥai bahem,* evidently felt so strongly about the Christians that he affirmed the position reflected in Avodah Zarah 27b in a *baraita,* that one may have no dealing whatsoever with sectaries nor be treated by them in any way. Ben Dama's position undoubtedly reflected a different attitude concerning the applicability of *Va-ḥai bahem* to treatment by sectaries. Cf. also Yerushalmi Shabbat 14:4, 14d; and Yerushalmi Avodah Zarah 2:2, 40d.

131. Above, p. 177.

but rather from the permission to do that which was forbidden. Clearly, then, active abrogation of the *grundnorm* applies to negative commandments. In talmudic language such abrogations are designated by the precept *Kum va-aseh,* that is, "Arise and do."

Still, even though most of our examples involved active abrogations, passive abrogations are, in theory, considerably less problematic, since, virtually by definition, passively refraining from a prescribed action cannot be equated with actively taking a proscribed action. The rabbinic sources distinguish clearly between the two types of abrogation and indicate that restrictions on the right of sages to institute abrogations of the passive type are far less severe than restrictions on the right of sages to institute abrogations of the active type.

Abrogations of the *Shev ve-al ta'aseh* nature are governed by the systemic principle "A court may make a condition uprooting a matter *de-oraita* through passive abrogation." (*Beit din matnin la'akor davar min ha-Torah be-shev ve-al ta'aseh*). In many instances, the application of this principle goes entirely unstated, indicating that the right of the sages to apply it as they see fit is unquestionable. One passage, however, clearly states the conclusion of the principle and clearly distinguishes between the kind of action the principle is intended to deal with and active abrogation.[132]

> Sacrificial blood that became impure but was inadvertently sprinkled fulfills the sacrificial obligation (*hurẓah*); if it was purposely sprinkled, it does not fulfill the sacrificial obligation. How could the statement be accurate, since even in the latter case the sacrificial obligation is fulfilled *de-oraita,* as is taught in a *baraita:* "For what does the *ẓiẓ* [plate, frontlet][133] affect sacrificial acceptability? For the blood, the meat, and the fat which became impure either inadvertently or purposely, accidentally or willingly, for either individual sacrifices or communal sacrifices."[134] And the rabbis claim that the sacrificial obligation is not fulfilled, resulting in the bringing of nonsacred sacrifice to the Temple precincts?![135] Rabbi Yosé bar

132. Yevamot 90a.

133. Exodus 28:36–38.

134. Thus, the *baraita* means to include in its statement impure blood that was purposely sprinkled, claiming that the presence of the *ẓiẓ* makes it acceptable.

135. I.e., the one who brought the sacrifice the blood of which became impure and was purposely sprinkled on the altar, and who obeyed the rabbinic dictum declaring that it was unacceptable, would offer another sacrifice in lieu of the first. The second sacrifice, in fact, however, would not have sacrificial status, since the former was sufficient *de-oraita*. Thus, the very observance of the rabbinic dictate would result in a violation of the Torah, viz., by offering a nonsanctified sacrifice.

Ḥanina said, "The nonfulfillment of sacrificial obligation to which the statement refers applies only to the right to eat the meat, but atonement has been effected [through the sprinkling of the blood] for him who brought the sacrifice." Nonetheless, in the final analysis, the eating of the meat is abrogated, and the verse says: "And those for whom atonement was made through them should eat them,"[136] teaching that the priests eat and atonement is effected for him who brought the sacrifice. He answered him,[137] "*Shev ve-al ta'aseh* is different."[138]

In attempting to explain why *Shev ve-al ta'aseh* is different, Rashi explains that "it is not uprooting. For example, the eating of the meat is a positive commandment concerning which the sages said, 'Sit, and do not eat.' That is not active uprooting (*akirah be-yadayim*), but rather it is uprooted by itself [i.e., passively *(mi-meila hi mi'akra)*]."[139]

As the conclusion of the talmudic section just quoted indicates, the idea that *Shev ve-al ta'aseh* falls within the legitimate domain of rabbinic authority vis-à-vis matters *de-oraita* serves as the explanation of other passive abrogations of the law. That is, the claim that "*Shev ve-al ta'aseh* is different" is not being made about this case alone, but rather that this case is included among other instances in which *Shev ve-al ta'aseh* is invoked to justify passive abrogation of the *grundnorm*. The most widely known application of the principle will suffice to demonstrate both that it is employed and how it is employed, even in the absence of a clear statement that it is, in fact, serving as the grounds for the passive abrogation of the *grundnorm*.

The Talmud reads:[140]

---

136. Exodus 29:33.

137. Rabbah answered Rav Ḥisda. They are the disputants in an extended controversy of which this selection is one section. We shall deal with other parts of the controversy below, pp. 190 ff.

138. In the final analysis, the original rabbinic statement is interpreted to mean that the sacrificial obligation is not fulfilled only insofar as the sacrificial meat is not eaten. And while, it is true, that also constitutes an abrogation of the Torah, it is only a passive abrogation, leaving a requirement of the law unfulfilled. Were the original statement interpreted to mean that atonement had not been effected, it would have resulted in the active abrogation of the Torah, since the one who brought the sacrifice would have brought a nonsacred sacrifice into the Temple precincts unnecessarily.

The acceptance of the final explanation is predicated on the assumption that the sages have the right to institute a passive abrogation for whatever reason seems appropriate to them.

139. Yevamot 90a, s.v. *shev ve-al ta'aseh*.

140. Rosh ha-Shanah 29b.

> Rava said, "From the Torah it is surely permissible [to blow the *shofar* on the Sabbath], but it was forbidden by the sages in accordance with the position stated by Rabbah. For Rabbah said, 'All are obligated for the blowing of the *shofar*, but not all are expert in the blowing of the *shofar*. [The prohibition] is thus a decree, lest one take it in his hand to go to an expert in order to learn, and carry it four cubits in the public domain.' " And the same is the reason for *lulav*[141] and for *megillah*.[142]

By rabbinic decree, the *mizvot* of *shofar, lulav,* and *megillah* go unfulfilled in circumstances in which the fulfillment would have been permissible *de-oraita*. The only possible legal justification of these acts of passive abrogation is the affirmation of the right of the sages to abrogate the *grundnorm* on the grounds of *Shev ve-al ta'aseh*. In these three instances the motivation for the sages' action was the preservation of the Sabbath from violation. At least three other examples based on the same motivation and presenting the same result can be cited.[143] In one further case, the motivation for the passive abrogation of the *grundnorm* was concern about the requisite purity of one who offers the paschal lamb.[144] In yet another instance, the passive abrogation of the *mizvah* of *zizit* was permitted in order to prevent the inadvertent violation of the laws of *kilayim* (mixing species).[145]

While each of the above passages either states explicitly or clearly implies the motivation behind the abrogation of the *grundnorm*, not one states the grounds upon which the sages decided that the danger was sufficiently great to warrant invoking the right to abrogate in the first place. Only the judgment of the sages can determine whether or not the right should be invoked; and the grounds for those judgments are not discussed in the talmudic sources.[146]

Since the primary sources are so silent, it is not unanticipated to find later commentators and legalists articulating general statements intended to serve as broad guidelines.

---

141. The prohibition against its use on the Sabbath of *ḥol ha-mo'ed sukkot*, even in the Temple. See Sukkah 42b.

142. The prohibition against reading the Scroll of Esther on a Purim that falls on the Sabbath. See Megillah 4b.

143. Pesaḥim 69a, Shabbat 130b, and Beiẓa 20b.

144. Pesaḥim 92a.

145. Menaḥot 40a.

146. It is interesting, for example, that the abrogation of the prescription on the use of the *lulav* in the Temple did not apply when the Sabbath coincided with the first day of Sukkot.

Rabbi Jonah ben Abraham Gerondi (ca. 1200–1263) wrote in his commentary to the Alfasi:[147]

> [Concerning the *terminus ad quem* of the evening recitation of the *Shema*] the sages hold the position that even though its recitation is from the Torah itself, and extends throughout the entire night, one may not recite it after midnight. For the sages are able to exempt one from a positive commandment[148] so long as they do so as a safeguard (*seyag*), or to preserve the observance of the *miẓvah* itself (*mi-shum kiyyum ha-miẓvah aẓmah*).

The Mishnah stipulates that one may not transact business with the produce of the sabbatical year, with firstborn animals, or with *terumah* (consecrated food).[149] In his comment regarding the inclusion of firstborn animals in this prohibition, Rabbi Samson ben Abraham of Sens (late 12th cent.) remarks that the prohibition is not *de-oraita,* but is a preventative measure against the misuse of these animals *(dilma atu beho li-dei takkalah).*[150]

Maimonides explains the rabbinic decree that forbids the kings of Israel (as opposed to the kings of Judah, members of the Davidic line) from judging or being judged, and from witnessing or being witnessed against, on the grounds that they are arrogant *(libban gas bahen).*[151] Their arrogant attitude toward the judicial process and their being subject to it might result in its perversion *(takkalah)* and render a discredit to the entire religious system *(hefsed al ha-dat).* Thus, it is better that the sages abrogate the *grundnorm* in this regard, and prohibit the kings of Israel from engaging in such activities.[152]

Maimonides affirms further that, although it is a positive commandment to lend money at interest to non-Jews,[153] the sages forbade such lending, lest Jews learn non-Jewish ways through frequent contacts.[154] That danger was sufficiently great to warrant a prohibition of a permissible (indeed, commanded) act.

Each of the instances noted above involves an abrogation of the

---

147. Alfasi, Berakhot la, s.v. *ve-yesh le-hakshot*.
148. I.e., the abrogation of a positive commandment is the functional equivalent of exemption from its observance.
149. Shevi'it 7:3.
150. *Commentary to the Mishnah* ad loc., s.v. *ve-lo bi-vekhorot*.
151. Sanhedrin 19a.
152. *Mishneh Torah,* Hilkhot Melakhim 3:7.
153. *Mishneh Torah,* Hilkhot Malveh ve-Loveh 5:1–2.
154. Deuteronomy 23:21. See Bava Meẓi'a 70b.

grundnorm in the form of a prohibition of or permission to neglect actions that the *grundnorm* permits. But as in the case of the examples from the primary sources that we have examined, the guidelines that these passages offer are very broad and leave the determination of the kind of danger that requires such a safeguard, as well as the decision to erect that safeguard in the form of an abrogation of the *grundnorm*, to the ultimate discretion of the sages themselves.[155] The ultimate systemic justification of the decision to abrogate the *grundnorm* is the principle "A court may make a condition uprooting a matter *de-oraita* through passive abrogation" *(Beit din matnin la'akor davar min ha-Torah be-shev ve-al ta'aseh).*

If the rabbis' right to abrogate the Torah passively is uncontested, the same cannot be said of their right to abrogate it actively, through *Kum va-aseh*. To the extent that this right does exist, it is embodied in the principle "A court may make a condition uprooting a matter *de-oraita* through active abrogation" (*Beit din matnin la'akor davar min ha-Torah be-kum va-aseh*).

The subject was a matter of controversy between Rabbah, who affirmed that no such right exists, and Rav Ḥisda, who affirmed that it does. The Talmud reads:[156]

> It is not permissible to offer *terumah* [consecrated food] from the impure for the pure. If one did so inadvertently, the *terumah* that he offered has the status of *terumah*.[157] [If he did so] purposely, he has done nothing.[158] What is the meaning of "he has done nothing"? Rav Ḥisda said that it means he has done absolutely nothing, and even the amount so designated as *terumah* reverts to its original

155. The examples indicate, as well, that there is no apparent restriction on the right of the sages to invoke this right. The sages have the right even to abrogate matters explicitly permitted by the Torah. It should be noted, however, that Rabbi David ben Samuel (Taz, 1586–1667) rejects the contention that the right of the sages is without bounds. He affirms that the right does not include the prohibition of that which the Torah permits explicitly; it is restricted to cases in which the assumption that the act is permissible *de-oraita* derives from the fact that the Torah does not stipulate clearly either a prohibition or a permission. See Taz, *Yoreh De'ah*, sec. 117, par. 1.

156. Yevamot 89a–90b. See Simon Greenberg, "And He Writes Her Bill of Divorcement," *Conservative Judaism* 24, no. 3 (Spring 1970), p. 96 ff.

157. *Terumah* is a small percentage of produce which is separated from it and becomes sanctified for priestly consumption. In addition to separating the percentage from the produce itself, one could separate it from one pile of produce for another. Our passage claims, at this point, that if one separated *terumah* for pure produce from impure produce, and did so inadvertently, the *terumah* is valid, and thus sanctified. Clearly, therefore, separating *terumah* for the pure from the impure is permissible *de-oraita*. Otherwise, *terumah* so separated would not become sanctified.

158. Mishnah Terumot 2:2.

nonsanctified state. . . . For if you would claim that it is *terumah*,[159] there might be times when a man might transgress and not separate again.[160] . . . Rabbah said to Rav Ḥisda: ". . . Could there be anything that is actually *terumah* according to the Torah, which the sages reassign to a nonsacred status because of the fear that a man might transgress? Does a court have the right to uproot a matter from the Torah?!" He said to him [i.e., Rav Ḥisda to Rabbah], "And do you not think so? Have we not learned in a *mishnah* that the offspring of both are *mamzerim* [offspring of incestuous or adulterous unions]?[161] Granted that the offspring of the second are actually *mamzerim*,[162] why are the offspring of the first so considered? She, after all, is his wife; and he is a Jew in good standing (*ve-yisra'el me'alya hu*). [Furthermore, as a result of this ruling] we permit him to marry a *mamzeret*."[163] <He answered him, "Samuel has said that he may not marry a *mamzeret*. And why is he called a *mamzer?* In order to indicate that he is forbidden to marry a Jewish woman of good standing (*le-osero be-vat yisra'el*).[164]>

Rav Ḥisda sent to Rabbah through Rav Aḥa the son of Rav Huna; "And does a court not have the right to uproot a matter from the Torah? Have we not learned in a *baraita:* 'At what point does a man inherit from his minor wife? . . . he inherits from her, and may become ritually impure for her [if he is a priest], and she may eat

159. I.e., if *it* became sanctified, even though there is a requirement for the separation of *additional terumah* in compliance with the rabbinic insistence that *terumah* for that which is pure be separated only from that which is itself pure.

160. Thus, because of the fear that one might transgress and refrain from separating the additional *terumah* from that which is pure, the sages ordained that separation for the pure from the impure is totally invalid, and the supposed *terumah* reverts to a nonsanctified status. Therefore, the abrogation of the *grundnorm* involved in requiring a new separation for one that was legitimate *de-oraita* is of the active type.

161. Mishnah Yevamot 10:1. The case is one in which a man went abroad and people came and told his wife that he had died. After she had remarried on the basis of their statement, her husband returned. The Mishnah stipulates that she may not remain married to either man, and that the offspring of both are legally *mamzerim*.

162. Since she was a married woman at the time of their birth.

163. A *mamzer* may marry only a *mamzeret*. A non-*mamzer* may not marry a *mamzeret*. Thus, the rabbis' declaring the offspring of the first to be a *mamzer* results in the active abrogation of the *grundnorm* by forcing him to marry a woman whom he is forbidden to marry *de-oraita*.

164. I.e., the offspring of the first is not legally a *mamzer*, but, as a penalty imposed by the sages as a safeguard to the Torah, he is, in addtion to being ineligible to marry a *mamzeret*, also ineligible to marry a non-*mamzeret*. Thus, his status does not actively abrogate the *grundnorm*. At most it is passive abrogation, prohibiting him from marrying one whom he would be otherwise entitled to marry, viz., a non-*mamzeret*.

terumah on his account. . . .'[165] Thus, in this case she ought to be inherited, according to the Torah, by her father's relatives, and according to the rabbis [it is] her husband [who] inherits from her!"[166] <That which the court declares ownerless is ownerless.[167]>

If one ate pure *terumah* [inadvertently], he should make restitution from pure nonsacred produce.[168] If he paid from impure nonsacred produce by error, his restitution is valid according to Sumkhus in the name of Rabbi Me'ir, but if such restitution was made on purpose, it is not considered restitution.[169] . . . Thus, this case, in which the restitution is valid according to the Torah, such that if the priest were to betroth a woman with it the betrothal would be valid, and the sages [i.e., Rabbi Me'ir] said that the restitution is invalid, results in our permitting a married woman to marry someone else.[170] <What is the meaning of Rabbi Meir's statement, "It is not considered restitution"? It means that he must make a second restitution from pure nonsacred produce.[171]>

---

165. According to the Torah, only a father has the right to marry off his minor daughter. In order to prevent improper behavior *(minhag hefker)* on the part of others with minor girls whose fathers had died, the rabbis granted the mother and brothers of a minor girl the right to marry her off (Yevamot 112b). According to the Torah, furthermore, a man inherits from his wife, but the father's relatives inherit from an unmarried fatherless daughter. The *baraita* quoted, however, indicates that, nevertheless, a husband *does* inherit from a minor wife who was married to him by her mother and brothers.

166. Thus, the rabbinic decree allowing a minor girl to be married off by her mother and brothers results in the active abrogation of the *grundnorm* by changing her heirs from her father's relatives to her husband.

167. The principle *Hefker beit din hefker* affirms that the court has the right to declare money or articles ownerless. Thus, in this case, the *grundnorm* regulations regarding inheritance are not actually abrogated, because the minor wife's estate has been declared ownerless by the sages and passed by them to the husband. See below, p. 193.

168. Leviticus 22:14.

169. The fact that inadvertent restitution of impure nonsacred produce is valid indicates that *de-oraita* the restitution need not be from pure nonsacred produce. Once the produce passes into the possession of the priest, it acquires *terumah* status and may be used by him to betroth a wife if he wishes. If the restitution were invalid, the produce in the priest's possession would not really belong to him, and his betrothal of a woman therewith would be invalid, since the man must give the woman something of worth that belongs to him.

170. By declaring invalid the purposeful restitution of impure nonsacred produce when, in fact, it is valid according to the Torah, the produce does not belong to the priest by rabbinic decree, whereas it does belong to him according to the Torah. Thus, if he betroths with it, his betrothal is valid according to the Torah and invalid according to the sages. Declaring the marriage invalid results in the automatic granting of permission to the woman to marry someone else when, in fact, she is already married according to the Torah. Thus, it constitutes an active abrogation of the *grundnorm*.

171. Rabbi Me'ir's view is thus interpreted to mean that the restitution was insufficient but not invalid. Thus, if the priest betrothed with the impure produce, his betrothal would be valid. According to this interpretation, therefore, there is no abrogation of the *grundnorm* at all. Rather, the sages impose a penalty for infraction of their decree.

The sections of this selection in angled brackets are the answers which Rabbah gave to the cases raised by Rav Ḥisda. Rav Ḥisda offered three proofs for the position that the sages possess the right to uproot a matter from the Torah, even through *Kum va-aseh*. Rabbah answers all three cases. It should be noted from the outset, however, that Rabbah's answers do not constitute refutations of Rav Ḥisda's views; they are only alternative explanations. Thus, the selection taken as a whole intimates that neither view can be either conclusively proved or rejected. In the Talmud itself, the matter remains a *maḥaloket*.[172]

Of the three alternative answers Rabbah offers, the first and the last are clearly forced, even if theoretically possible, interpretations of the language they purport to explain. The second answer is even weaker than the other two, since the principle "That which the court declares ownerless is ownerless" *(Hefker beit din hefker)* is itself a legal principle whose ultimate source is the sages' right to abrogate a matter *de-oraita* actively, through *Kum va-aseh*.[173] The fact of the widespread acceptance of this principle, even to the point that it becomes an oft-invoked exception to the claim that the sages do not have the right to abrogate through *Kum va-aseh*, in no way mitigates the truth that in this argument it is itself an instance of the very claim it is being used to deny.

When coupled with the fact alluded to above, namely, that most of the passages quoted earlier in this chapter were instances of active abrogation of the *grundnorm*,[174] the relative strength of Rav Ḥisda's position as opposed to Rabbah's position presents a strong case for the affirmation of the sages' right to abrogate matters *de-oraita*, even through *Kum va-aseh*.

None of the above, however, is meant to deny that the weight of precedent greatly favors Rabbah's view, as we shall see presently. That this should be so is eminently reasonable. "Arise and do" offers the probability of more direct conflict with the *grundnorm* than does "Sit and do not act." The former actually mandates an action contrary to a proscription of the *grundnorm;* the latter merely acquiesces to the nonfulfillment of a prescription of the *grundnorm*. To mandate the active violation of the Torah clearly puts one in violation of the prohibition of *Bal tigra*. Allowing a dictate of the *grundnorm* to fall into disuse cannot be

---

172. The same is true of the Yerushalmi. The *sugya* (passage) in Yevamot 15:3, 14d, seems to imply an ultimate decision that the sages do not have the right to actively abrogate the *grundnorm*. The *sugya* in Gittin 4:2, 45c not only affirms a tannaitic dispute on the matter but contains an unrefuted proof for the claim that the sages do possess the right on the basis of Mishnah Terumot 1:4.

173. See Elon, *Jewish Law*, 2:415–21.

174. P. 185 f.

equated with the amendment of the *grundnorm* by means of permitting an action heretofore proscribed.

Yet the exigencies of reality may require the guardians of a tradition to take actions of a kind that may seem *prima facie* to be systemically the most illogical; and require that they do so in order to safeguard the very tradition and *grundnorm* the action itself apparently violates. It is the manifestation of this tension between the real and the ideal in the post-talmudic legalists that we will now consider.

The following statement of Rabbi Solomon ben Abraham Adret (Rashba, ca. 1235–1310) is representative of the general acceptance of Rabbah's position. As do most such statements, this one, too, contains a clause indicating that while generally true, Rabbah's view is not without its exception. The Rashba wrote:[175]

> The court may not stipulate the active uprooting *(la'akor be-yadayim)* of a matter from the Torah. And concerning the view of Rav Ḥisda, who affirms that it may . . . the decision is not in accordance with his view, but rather in accordance with the view of Rabbah, who disagrees with him. . . . For the court may never stipulate the uprooting of a matter from the Torah except under extraordinary circumstances *(le-migdar milleta)*,[176] as Elijah on Mount Carmel[177] and similar situations, but generally not. And this seems clear to me.

The same legalist, however, comments in another responsum that we can find numerous examples in which the sages actively abrogated commandments for cause *(le-ẓorekh)*.[178] Still, the Rashba nowhere defines the particular circumstances that would permit active abrogation of the *grundnorm* with any greater precision than to affirm that they should be *Le-migdar milleta* or *Le-ẓorekh*. As others do, he offers the example of Elijah as a paradigm, not so much because it constitutes definitive guidance, but because the Talmud itself uses this example in a discussion of this very matter.[179] He can do no more than define other cases as similar to that of Elijah. But "similar to" does not necessarily mean

175. *Responsa of Rashba*, pt. 1, no. 1166.

176. *Le-migdar milleta* (lit. "to fence in a matter," "to check a matter"), a commonly used term to indicate the motive for the active abrogation of the *grundnorm*. The extraordinariness of the circumstances can involve the prevention or the reversal of a religious catastrophe. See, for example, Rashi's comment on Yevamot 90b, s.v. *migdar*.

177. I Kings 18:14–39.

178. *Responsa of Rashba*, pt. 1, no. 127.

179. Yevamot 90b.

"identical with": The ultimate determination of similarity to the Elijah paradigm cannot be decided objectively.

Rabbi Menaḥem ben Solomon ha-Me'iri (1249–1316) offers a comprehensive outline of possible legitimate grounds for abrogation of the *grundnorm,* passively and actively. He wrote:

> The court may not stipulate the uprooting of a matter from the Torah except in one of three ways: either through *Shev ve-al ta'aseh* or through the declaration of ownerlessness or through a temporary decision *(hora'at sha'ah)* as a hedge or fence. . . . In any temporary decision as a hedge or fence or for the sanctification of God's name, a matter from the Torah may be uprooted even actively. And that is the basis upon which Elijah slaughtered sacrifices outside the central sanctuary and offered them on a noncentral altar during a period when such was forbidden.[180]

Rabbi Yom Tov ben Abraham Ishbili (Ritba, ca. 1250–1330) proposes the same categories in the following way:

> The law is as follows: The court may uproot through *Shev ve-al ta'aseh* or even a negative commandment [i.e., through *Kum va-aseh*] for the need of the hour *(le-ẓorekh sha'ah),* or through the declaration of ownerlessness permanently. But it may not uproot a matter from the Torah [i.e., through *Kum va-aseh*] in perpetuity.[181]

These two selections refer again to a crucial dimension of the right of the sages to abrogate the *grundnorm* to which we have already alluded on several occasions, namely, that even if the exigencies of reality may require the occasional active abrogation of the Torah, it is difficult to conceive of a set of circumstances in which the permanent mandating of an action forbidden by the *grundnorm* can be required in order to protect it. Both the Me'iri and the Ritba stress the fact that active abrogations can only be temporary. *Le-migdar milleta* and *le-ẓorekh sha'ah* may be appropriate and acceptable motivations for mandating the forbidden, but the mandate can only be a temporary one. When the reason which gave rise to the need ceases to obtain, the mandated behavior reverts to its forbidden status.

---

180. *Beit ha-Beḥirah* to Yevamot 89b, 90b, ed. Samuel Dickman (Jerusalem, 1962 [5722]), pp. 327 and 329.

181. Ritba to Yevamot 90b, s.v. *ve-nigmar minei.*

Maimonides, too, emphasizes the necessarily temporary nature of any active abrogation of the *grundnorm* by the rabbis. He writes:

> Any court may uproot even the words of the Torah as a *Hora'at sha'ah* . . . if they deem it necessary to annul a positive or to transgress a negative commandment temporarily *(le-fi sha'ah)* in order to bring the multitudes back to the religion *(dat)* and to save many Jews from faltering in other matters. In such matters they may do as the hour requires, as a doctor might amputate the arm or the leg of a person in order that he might live. Thus, too, the court may instruct at times *(bi-zeman min ha-zemannim)* to transgress some of the *mizvot* temporarily in order that the rest may be preserved.[182]

There is, however, a more flexible strain within the halakhic tradition on this issue. Although it, too, emphasizes the general rule that the sages may not amend or abrogate the *grundnorm* through *Kum va-aseh,* this strain of the tradition provides a wider latitude in determining what kinds of circumstances might permit the sages to take such action. The clearest and most definitive statement of this position is found in the Tosafot.[183] They wrote:

> Even though the sages do not have the authority to uproot a matter from the Torah through *Kum va-aseh,* when there is sufficient cause and reason involved *(Panim ve-ta'am ba-davar),* surely all agree that they have the authority to uproot. Know, too, that this is so since the entire section[184] does not quote the fact that a woman is believed to say that her husband has died,[185] which is an uprooting of a matter from the Torah through *Kum va-aseh.* Therefore, surely, when there is sufficient cause and reason, the authority to uproot exists.

The specific case of the woman who is believed when she says that her husband has died, which the Tosafot quote as proof of their contention that the authority to uproot actively exists for the sages, also proves that their phrase "sufficient cause and reason" is not to be equated with *Le-migdar milleta.* The death of a husband can hardly be

182. *Mishneh Torah,* Hilkhot Mamrim 2:4. Cf. Hilkhot Mamrim 2:9, quoted above, p. 159.
183. Tosafot Nazir 43b, s.v. *ve-hai.*
184. From Yevamot, above pp. 160 ff.
185. Mishnah Yevamot 15:1. The *mishnah* deals with a couple who has gone abroad. The wife returns and states that her husband has died. If their marriage was a stable one, and it was not a period of war, she may remarry on the basis of her statement alone, even though no witnesses substantiate her claim.

called extraordinary. Nor is there any way to claim that the case of the woman is comparable, in terms of the needs of the Jewish community as a whole, to Elijah's episode on Mount Carmel. Finally, too, the stipulation that the woman is to be believed concerning the death of her husband is clearly intended to apply in every instance that the same situation arises. That is, it is not intended as a temporary abrogation of the *grundnorm*'s dictate but as a permanent one.

Nevertheless, while the grounds for invoking the right to amend actively are broader according to this position, they are no more precise than in the less flexible position: "sufficient cause and reason" *(Panim veta'am ba-davar)* is not more precise than "extraordinary circumstances" *(Le-migdar milleta)*.

There are, in addition, at least four other instances in which the Tosafot either refer directly or allude to this broader interpretation of the sages' rights vis-à-vis matters *de-oraita,* in none of which is the issue of the severity implied by *Le-migdar milleta* raised, and in none of which could the abrogation involved be construed as temporary.[186]

When the position of the Tosafot is combined with the fact that none of the issues raised by Rav Ḥisda are classifiable as *Le-migdar milleta,*[187] that none are temporary in nature, and that this is true of the great majority of the examples of active abrogation of the *grundnorm* cited earlier in this chapter,[188] one must conclude that *Le-migdar milleta* and *Hora'at sha'ah* are not the only criteria that can motivate, or that, indeed, have motivated, active rabbinic abrogation of the *grundnorm*.

Even Maimonides himself, whose statement above seems to leave little room for doubt concerning his view of the subject,[189] was not consistent. Joseph Caro's comment on the following passage in Maimonides has important possible ramifications concerning the entire discussion. Maimonides wrote:

> He who takes an oath to fast every Sunday and Tuesday for his entire life . . . [and one of those days] coincided with Ḥanukkah or Purim, his oath is superseded because of these [festive] days. Since the prohibition against fasting on them is rabbinic *(mi-divrei soferim),* they require strengthening *(ḥizzuk),* and his oath is superseded because of the decree of the sages.[190]

186. Yevamot 24b, s.v. *amar,* and 110a, s.v. *lefikhakh;* Ketubbot 11a, s.v. *matbilin;* Bava Batra 48b, s.v. *teinaḥ*.
187. Above, pp. 190 ff.
188. Above, pp. 169–185.
189. P. 196.
190. *Mishneh Torah,* Hilkhot Nedarim 3:9.

Maimonides is clearly positing the active abrogation of the *grundnorm*'s prohibition against the nonfulfillment of an oath. To insist that a man eat on days on which his oath would require him to fast is clearly an instance of *Kum va-aseh*. Furthermore, the situation cannot fit in the category of *Le-migdar milleta* or even in *Panim ve-ta'am ba-davar*.

In giving what he considers to be a plausible explanation of Maimonides' decision, Joseph Caro says:[191]

> The Talmud affirms that in a case of *Migdar milleta* the sages are empowered to uproot a matter *de-oraita*, even through *Kum va-aseh*. And the strengthening of the words of the sages, in whatever they say, even though not literally *Migdar milleta*, results in the observance of their words through *Migdar milleta*. For if people would treat one of their dicates lightly, they might do so with all of them. Therefore, anything that strengthens their words is like *Migdar milleta*. Furthermore, the Tosafot have written . . . that even though the sages do not have the authority, etc.[192] . . . And in this case [i.e., Maimonides' decision], since the words of the sages require strengthening, it is a legitimate case of *Panim ve-ta'am ba-davar*.

Caro maintains that the Maimonidean decision is defensible according to either interpretation of the sages' right vis-à-vis the active abrogation of the *grundnorm*. If one adopts the position of the Tosafot, the Maimonidean decision affirms that the strengthening of rabbinic legislation is itself sufficient grounds for the abrogation of the *grundnorm*, in whatever case it may seem desirable to the rabbis to do so. Since the Tosafot's position is the more liberal position, this explanation does not demand that the act of strengthening be defined as *Migdar milleta* at all.

According to the stricter explanation of the right of the sages to engage in active abrogation of the *grundnorm*, Caro hypothesizes that the wanton and willful disregard of rabbinic legislation as a whole would constitute a religious catastrophe for the halakhic process and for the Jewish people. The prevention of such a catastrophe, therefore, falls within the category of *Migdar milleta*. If, in any given instance, people would see that a particular act of rabbinic legislation can be easily disregarded, they might deduce that the same is true of all rabbinic

191. *Kesef Mishneh* to Hilkhot Nedarim 3:9, s.v. *u-mah she-katav rabbenu*. See, too, *Responsa of Radbaz*, pt. 5, Leshonot ha-Rambam, par. 1461; also, Caro, *Beit Yosef* to *Tur, Oraḥ Ḥayyim*, sec. 418, s.v. *u-mihu*.

192. Nazir 43b, s.v. *ve-hai*. Above, p. 196.

legislation. Thus, the strengthening of rabbinic legislation in any given situation, even if that situation is not itself in the category of *Migdar milleta*, has the effect of strengthening all rabbinic legislation. Since abrogating the *grundnorm* in order to prevent a general wanton disregard of rabbinic leglislation is justifiable on the grounds of *Migdar milleta*, it is also justifiable in order to prevent the disregard of specific rabbinic legislation, because any disregard of specific legislation may result in the disregard of rabbinic legislation in general.

Caro asserts that safeguarding and protecting the halakhic process may sometimes dictate the active abrogation of the *grundnorm*. In those infrequent instances when the sages feel that such action is necessary, it is justifiable not only on the grounds of *Panim ve-ta'am ba-davar*, but even on the grounds of *Migdar milleta*.

Ultimately, then, it seems incontrovertible that the sages do possess the right to abrogate the Torah both actively and passively, and in both cases both temporarily and permanently. Since the halakhic system posits the *grundnorm* as the ultimate authority and as sacrosanct, invoking the right to amend or abrogate it is done only with the greatest caution, and only when there is sufficient cause to warrant such a step. While the system itself has established principles to help the arbiter decide what constitutes sufficient cause, these principles, as we saw earlier in the chapter, are not definitive. In the final analysis, it is the judge-arbiters of the system who must determine whether or not the cause is sufficient for them to exercise their right to amend or to abrogate the Torah, demonstrating again the absolute centrality of the sages of each generation to the smooth functioning of the halakhic system.

The term *Hora'at sha'ah*, which appears so frequently in the context of abrogations of and amendments to the Torah, possesses two different, though similar, meanings. It is used to designate a decision that because of some extraordinary circumstances abrogates the *grundnorm* temporarily. In this sense it is truly a *Hora'at sha'ah*. The actions of Elijah on Mount Carmel, of Shimon ben Shetaḥ (who executed more than one person on the same day, contrary to the law),[193] and of Shimon the Righteous[194] were instances of *Hora'at sha'ah* of this kind.[195] The same

193. Mishnah Sanhedrin 6:4, 45b.

194. Yoma 69a. See above, p. 173.

195. See Tzvi Hirsch Chajes, *Kol Sifrei Mahariẓ Ḥayyot* (Jerusalem: Divrei Ḥakhamim, 1958), *Torat ha-Nevi'im*, Hora'at Sha'ah, pp. 27–28, for a more extensive list of similar *Hora'ot sha'ah*.

temporary abrogation, however, can be enacted more than once; if a similar set of circumstances should arise, there would be systemic justification for abrogating the Torah again, on the same grounds.[196]

In its second sense, however, *Hora'at sha'ah* operates as a kind of legal fiction. We have already given examples of decisions of this kind.[197] The original impetus in each of these cases was, indeed, a *Hora'at sha'ah,* a single, temporary abrogation of the Torah. However, the circumstances leading to the original abrogation tended to repeat themselves with such frequency and regularity that the effect of the necessarily repeated decision was to make apparently permanent that which was temporary. It follows that the quality of being extraordinary, which is a prerequisite for the abrogation or amendment of the *grundnorm,* is predicated upon factors that may not necessarily be temporary. So, even in its second sense, then, the term *Hora'at sha'ah* is not a misnomer.[198]

The findings of this chapter indicate that the authority of the sages extends far beyond their position as the sole interpreters of the Torah. Indeed, their authority includes the right to amend and to abrogate the prescriptions and proscriptions of the Torah. Moreover, in no case that we have examined have we seen an amendment or abrogation justified on the pretense that it resulted from rabbinic interpretation of the Torah and was, therefore, the true meaning of the Torah. Rather, the position of the rabbis is that their right to amend or to abrogate clearly gives them the right to supersede the Torah.

However, for a legal system that posits a Divine document as its *grundnorm,* the broad scope of the legislative authority of the systemically recognized authorities with regard to the dictates of the *grundnorm* is problematic. In legal terms the problem may be stated as follows: The system accedes to the assumption of legislative authority by the sages

196. Cf. Tosafot Yevamot 90b, s.v. *ve-ligmar:* "Since it is permitted by God's own statement because of the need of the hour, the same is true even in the absence of God's own statement."

197. See above, pp. 174 f.

198. We have already mentioned the systemic institutionalization of the rabbinic right to abrogate matters *de-oraita* through the principle of *Hefker beit din hefker* ("that which the court declares ownerless is ownerless"). There is also another principle which institutionalizes the same right, viz., "the court is empowered to inflict lashes and to execute even in cases not so mandated by the Torah" (*Beit din makkin ve-oneshin* she-lo min ha-Torah). In these instances, too, the grounds for extraordinary punishments are *Migdar milleta, Hora'at sha'ah, La'asot seyag la-Torah* ("to make a fence for the Torah"). See, for example, Sanhedrin 46a (Yevamot 90b, Yerushalmi Ḥagiga 2:2, 78a); *Mishneh Torah,* Hilkhot Sanhedrin 24:4; *Oẓar ha-Ge'onim to Tractate Sanhedrin* (Jerusalem: Mossad Harav Kook, 1966), par. 805, p. 357; *Responsa of Rosh* (New York: Grossman's Publishing House, 1954), *kelal* 18:13; *Responsa of Rashba, Attributed to Ramban* (Tel Aviv: Eshel Publishing, 1959 [5719]), no. 244. See also Elon's treatment of this principle in *Jewish Law,* 2:421–25.

only because the resulting legislation is considered to be secondary legislation; primary legislation being embodied in those matters the ultimate authority for which is the Torah (i.e., norms *de-oraita*). But if the power of the systemically recognized authorities were extended to the amendment or abrogation of matters *de-oraita,* would not the authority of the sages be, in fact, primary, and not secondary? And if, in fact, that was the case, would not the primacy of the *grundnorm* within the legal system have been undermined? This is the problem of *ultra vires* (lit. "beyond the power, authority"). In theological terms the problem may be stated like this: If the power of the sages includes even the right to amend or abrogate the undisputed or accepted will of God, as embodied in those norms designated as *de-oraita,* is it not the case that the system recognizes the sages as God, rather than recognizing God as God? And if this is the case, does it not follow that the God-centered legal system has collapsed because of the sages' usurpation of God's place within it?

It is to this problem that we must now seek a resolution.

Having stated the problem in the strongest possible terms, we ought also to point out that on one level the entire formulation is nothing but the creation of a straw man. The problem of *ultra vires* is real only if the *grundnorm* does *not* grant the power to amend or abrogate. Once it does, however, the use of that power by recognized authorities cannot be considered a usurpation of primary authority by secondary authorities. Rather, even the amendment of the *grundnorm* becomes an act within the realm of secondary legislation, being a right granted by the primary legislator to secondary legislators.

It will be recalled that the apparent lack of an amendment clause within the Torah, indeed the apparent prohibition against amendment, is based on the dictates of *Bal tosif* and *Bal tigra.*[199] Still, these seemingly absolute prohibitions have been systemically defined both by the Rashba and Maimonides in such a way as to exempt from these restrictions either all rabbinic enactments or, at least, those that are properly promulgated.[200] It follows, therefore, that neither the Rashba nor Maimonides understands the Torah to forbid its own amendment. Moreover, according to the Rashba, at least, the phrase *Lo tasur* ("do not deviate") in Deuteronomy 17:11 is itself an amendment clause. Thus, any suspension of the dictates of the Torah is duly authorized by the primary legislation (i.e. the Torah itself); it falls within the realm of secondary legislation and does not involve *ultra vires* in any way.[201]

---

199. Deuteronomy 4:2; 13:1. See above, p. 156.
200. See above, pp. 157–161.
201. Cf. Elon's handling of the problem of *ultra vires* in *Jewish Law,* 2:439–41.

Obviously, this approach to the problem is very appealing, as would be any approach to a problem that demonstrates that the problem does not even exist. Nevertheless, there are shortcomings to this solution.

First, it is difficult to equate *Lo tasur* with an amendment clause, as the Rashba does.[202] The verse, after all, does not clearly stipulate the right to amend, as one might reasonably expect an amendment clause to do.[203] Indeed, one is forced to conclude that the right to amend the Torah is deduced not from the Torah itself but from the interpretation of a sage to that effect. This interpretation is a *deus ex machina.* That is, its claim that the rabbinic right to amend the Torah is mandated by the Torah is itself based upon an interpretation of the Torah. And, basing himself upon this interpretation, the Rashba postulates that any amendments that the sages promulgate fall within the realm of secondary legislation. The fallacy, of course, is that the very interpretation that is supposed to solve the problem of *ultra vires* may itself be an instance of *ultra vires.*

And if one were to counter this objection by asserting that every legal system is ultimately internal and circular, the answer would be that the circle that circumscribes any legal system means only that the system must feed upon itself exclusively and cannot be subject to external intrusions; that what legitimates actions and decisions systemically is the fact that they fall within the circle. The existence of such a circle does not imply that there is nothing that can fall outside of it: An act of *ultra vires* would surely be of such a nature. In less abstract terms, the circle is the *grundnorm* itself. Decisions and actions consonant with the *grundnorm,* the interpretation of which is entrusted to recognized authorities, fall within the circle. But the right of the recognized authorities to interpret the Torah does not extend to an interpretation that is at variance with the *grundnorm,* since such an interpretation would be an external intrusion upon the circle. While the consonance or inconson-

---

202. For Maimonides, the problem is greater, since he does not postulate the existence of an amendment clause at all. Instead, he affirms that *Bal tosif* and *Bal tigra* only apply to amendments of a certain type. Thus, by implication, amendments that are not forbidden are permitted.

203. Lest one argue that the verse does not stipulate the right of the sages to interpret the Torah either, it should be noted that although the claim would be technically correct, the context in which the verse appears clearly implies the right and the need to interpret the Torah. The context refers to uncertainty about correct adjudication. Such uncertainty can only exist because of unclarity in the law itself or because of its failure to deal with the circumstances of the case in question. If the former, the question is one of law in the second sense, which, by definition, implies the need to interpret the law. If the latter, the use of existent law as a source from which to derive new law is implied. That, too, implies the need for interpretation. Thus, in the final analysis, rabbinic reliance upon the verse as the source for the right to interpret the Torah is much more strongly based than is the Rashba's interpretation of the same verse as an amendment clause.

ance of any given interpretation with the *grundnorm* may be a matter of dispute, the plausibility of such a dispute when the interpretation is such that it affirms a rabbinic right on the basis of a passage that ostensibly denies that right, is highly unlikely. On the contrary, such an interpretation is undoubtedly the ultimate act of *ultra vires,* since it disguises the usurpation of the primacy of the *grundnorm* in the cloak of a systemically legitimate act.

We are not contending that the Rashba and Maimonides have misunderstood the halakhic system. On the contrary, their theses provide the systemic justification of the sages' right to amend the Torah. We contend only that their theories are not sufficient, insofar as they do not offer any assurance that the halakhic reality that they explain, the right of the sages to amend the Torah, is not itself an act of *ultra vires.* If it is, then *any* abrogation of the *grundnorm* would be an act of *ultra vires,* since each would have been justifiable only on the grounds that the sages possess a right which, in fact, they do not.

It must be remembered, however, that the problem of *ultra vires* arises only in the context of rabbinic rights vis-à-vis matters *de-oraita.* No matter how broad and extensive the authority of the sages may be, the integrity of the system itself would be challenged only if the scope of that authority included the amendment and abrogation of the Torah itself. Only in that realm would the systemic recognition of the primacy of the Torah be called into question. If the actions of the sages in that realm were acts of *ultra vires,* the sages would become the *grundnorm* of the system rather than the Torah itself, and the halakhic system would be, minimally, other than it purports to be and other than the sages themselves have understood it to be; maximally, it would be a fraud perpetrated by the sages upon the Jewish people in the name of God.

There is, however, a possible solution to the problem. It is possible to assert that the same action, taken by two different people, might in one instance be an act of *ultra vires,* and in the other, not. The factor that would distinguish one such action from the other would be motivation. If an act is carried out by one whose intention is to establish his own systemic primacy over that even of the Torah, the act is one of *ultra vires.* If, however, the action is motivated by a real concern for the preservation of the primacy of the Torah itself within the halakhic system, and if the situation is such that this preservation can be accomplished best through the abrogation of one of its dictates, the very same act of abrogation, which in the first case would be one of *ultra vires,* would not be so in the second case.

We have dealt at length in the preceding chapter with the contention that *yirat shamayim* is a *sine qua non* of halakhic authorities, that it is the characteristic that guarantees, to the extent that anything can, that what motivates halakhic authorities is their commitment to the integrity of the system they govern. *Yirat shamayim* on the part of the systemic authorities assures that their actions are taken *Le-shem shamayim.* An abrogation of the *grundnorm Le-shem shamayim*—even the affirmation that the sages possess the right to amend or abrogate the *grundnorm,* which may itself be an abrogation of the *grundnorm*—is not an act of *ultra vires.* In other words, the assurance that rabbinic legislation abrogating the Torah is secondary, not primary, is dependent upon the personal virtues required of the authorities of the system, which include the characteristic of *yirat shamayim.*

In the final analysis, therefore, this chapter not only demonstrates the broad scope of rabbinic authority vis-à-vis matters *de-oraita,* but it also reaffirms our contention that *yirat shamayim* is an essential characteristic of systemic authorities.

Chapter Eight

On Custom in the Halakhic System

The role, status, and authority within the halakhic system of matters commonly classified as custom is exceptionally complex. The complexity derives both from the nature of custom in general and from the fact that customs are of various types.[1]

Two kinds of customs have the authority of law.[2] The first of these is legal custom, "which is operative *per se* as a binding rule of law, independently of any agreement on the part of those subject to it" (p. 192). Moreover, legal custom is itself divisible into two categories: local custom, with regard to which the force of law is restricted to a specific locality; and general custom, with regard to which the force of law applies to all localities governed by the prevailing legal system. The second kind of custom that has the authority of law is conventional custom, or usage, "whose authority is conditional on its acceptance and incorporation in agreements between the parties to be bound by it" (p. 193).

The acceptance of a conventional custom by the parties to an agreement is predicated either on its having been stipulated in the agreement itself or on the presumption that, even though not specifically stipulated

1. For extensive treatments of the subject of customs, see Tchernovitz (Rav Tzair), *Toledot ha-Halakhah*, 1:144–50, and Elon, *Jewish Law*, 2:713–67.

2. See Fitzgerald, *Salmond on Jurisprudence*, pp. 189–212. Any quotations in this chapter followed by a page number in parenthesis are quotations from that page of *Salmond*. Most of the descriptive portions of the chapter are based upon Salmond's analysis.

by the parties, their intent was to enter into the agreement on the basis of the particular conventional custom. Of course, such a presumption would be invalid if the custom was not widespread, since the presumption is based on the reasonableness of the claim that it was the intent of the parties to abide by it. In the period before such an assumption can be considered reasonable, the applicability of the conventional custom is contingent on the ability of the parties to *prove* that their intention was to behave in accordance with the custom. Thus, the presumption of the acceptance of a conventional custom marks a second stage in its development. A conventional custom might, as well, enter a third stage, namely, the incorporation of its requirements into a legal system as a legal norm. If such a development does take place, the authority of the conventional custom no longer lies in the fact that it is a conventional custom, but in the fact that it has become a requirement of the law. At that point, the fact that the law originated as a conventional custom becomes nothing more than a historical source of the law, and is legally irrelevant. Moreover, implied by the definition of the first two stages of conventional custom is the right of the agreeing parties to stipulate disregard of any or of all the requirements of the custom. If and when the conventional custom enters the third possible stage, this right ceases to exist, except insofar as the legal system itself allows agreeing parties to disregard the requirements of the law by mutual consent.

In the halakhic system, which has long lacked a definitive and recognized body empowered to elevate conventional custom to the status of law, but which, on the other hand, has not ceased to function as a viable legal system, such elevation has come to take place *de facto* than rather *de jure,* thereby engendering a situation in which the grounds for confusion are many. There can, in theory, be a *maḥaloket* concerning the current relevance of the customary status of the conventional custom (i.e., is the customary status still legally relevant or only a historical source of a law now incorporated into the system *de facto?*). Clearly, too, confusion or disagreement on this issue can have ramifications regarding the right of the parties to disregard the custom.

As stated above, legal custom differs from conventional custom primarily in that the former applies independently of the agreement of those subject to it. When one kind of custom is mistaken for the other kind, the extent of its authority is also mistakenly perceived. Thus, for example, if one mistakes a legal custom for a conventional custom, one will erroneously think that either the stipulated or the presumed agreement of the parties is necessary when, in fact, it is not. Conversely, if one mistakes a conventional custom for a legal custom, one will erroneously think that the agreement of the parties is not needed when, in fact, it is.

Although there are, of course, fundamental differences between them, customs have much in common with legal norms: "Custom is to society what law is to the state. Each is the expression and realisation, to the measure of men's insight and ability, of the principles of right and justice. The law embodies those principles as they commend themselves to the incorporate community in the exercise of its sovereign power. Custom embodies them as acknowledged and approved, not by the power of the state, but by the public opinion of the society at large" (p. 191). "Custom is frequently the embodiment of those principles which have commended themselves to the national conscience as principles of justice and public utility" (p. 190).

On the other hand, the fact that customs originate among the people, independent of governmental-legislative action, virtually guarantees that the hold of those customs on the people is very great and that conflicts between customs and the legal system are bound to arise. For example, in the formative stages of the development of a legal system, the degree to which the law conforms to accepted customary behavior can only enhance the entrenchment of the system. If the system is an indigenous outgrowth of the group it is intended to govern, it can be fairly assumed that the law will conform to custom, not only as a means of making the law acceptable to the people, but also because the systemically recognized leaders will necessarily share the principles of right and justice embodied in the customary behavior of their people. And if the legal system is being imposed from the outside, its acceptance will be enhanced if the customary behavior of the people on whom it is imposed is incorporated into it. "Nothing, therefore, is more natural than that, when the state begins to evolve out of the society, the law of the state should in respect of its material contents be in great part modelled upon, and coincident with, the customs of the society" (p. 191).

"This influence of custom upon law, however, is characteristic rather of the beginnings of the legal system than of its mature growth. When the state has grown to its full strength and stature, it acquires more self-confidence, and seeks to conform national usage to the law, rather than the law to national usage. Its ambition is then to be the source not merely of the form, but of the matter of the law also" (p. 191). As the system develops, therefore, the grounds for tension between customary behavior and the law increase. The legal principles and norms of the system may indicate that certain customs are now either inappropriate or contrary to the newly developed ideals of the system. However, since the observance of these customs would have continued to be as firmly entrenched as before, the question is whether, at this stage, the law should continue to conform to custom, or whether custom should be made to conform to the law. If the latter, by what steps may the legal system effect the desired change? How is it to confront the possibility that the populace may continue its customary behavior even though the law may abrogate it? As we shall see, the halakhic system, like other legal systems, has had to confront these problems, as well as others, regarding the role, status, and authority of custom.

In the functioning of the halakhic system, as in other systems, custom, especially legal custom, bears many resemblances to legal norms. Yet it should be noted from the outset that the degree of its authority is not equal within *halakhah* to that of legal norms—a distinction that has many important ramifications. The following selection indicates one of the ramifications of the distinction between custom and legal norms in the *halakhah*.[3] The Talmud reads:

> The morning service, additional service, afternoon service, and concluding service [of Yom Kippur] all contain the benediction of the priests *(birkat kohanim)*, according to Rabbi Me'ir. Rabbi Yehudah says that the morning and additional services contain the benediction, but the afternoon and concluding services do not.[4] Rabbi Yosé says that the concluding service contains the benediction, but the afternoon service does not[5] . . . Rav Yehudah said in the name of Rav that the law is as Rabbi Me'ir, and Rabbi Yoḥanan said that the people act *(nahagu)* as Rabbi Me'ir, and Rava said that the custom *(minhag)* is as Rabbi Me'ir.

All agree that practice follows the view of Rabbi Me'ir. The disagreement revolves around the status of the practice. Implied is the fact that the assignment of the practice to any one of the three different categories mentioned will have different ramifications, although the practice will remain identical. The Talmud itself proceeds to outline the ramifications.

> He who claims that the law is as Rabbi Me'ir [implies thereby] that the view is to be publicly expounded upon *(darshinan lah be-firka)*.

3. Ta'anit 26b. See also Eruvin 62b and 72a.

4. Since *birkat kohanim* is normally recited throughout the remainder of the year only before the priests are likely to have eaten or drunk, allowing them to recite it at *minḥah* and *ne'ilah* on *Yom Kippur* might create confusion regarding the rest of the year. Thus, although the priests would surely not have eaten or drunk on *Yom Kippur,* Rabbi Yehudah forbids their recitation of *birkat kohanim* at *minḥah* and *ne'ilah* on *Yom Kippur,* as well.

5. Recitation of *birkat kohanim* at *ne'ilah* could not result in confusion, since that service does not exist on any other day.

He who claims *minhag* [implies thereby] that the position is not to be expounded, but that one who asks is to be directed so to act *(oroyei morinan)*. And he who says *nahagu* [implies thereby] that even one who asks is not to be directed to act so, but that if he does act so, it is acceptable, and need not be reversed *(ve-i avid avid ve-lo mehadderinan leih)*.

There was a conscious effort on the part of the sages to engage in the active and public instruction of the law.[6] Conventional custom, however, no matter how widespread and how deeply entrenched, was never the subject of public direction, since custom, because its authority derives from the people, can never hold the status of the law itself in the hierarchy of the system. Public direction regarding matters of customary behavior by legal authorites might result in confusion about the grounds for the authority of the custom. When a custom is deeply entrenched, however, it is reasonable to assume that people who know of it would choose to conform to its requirements. Therefore, private direction by the legal authorities in such matters merely reinforces the hold of the custom upon the people, without suggesting that the grounds for the authority of the custom are anything other than custom itself. Such matters constitute the category of *minhag*. Conventional custom in its early stages, however, is not so firmly entrenched as to warrant the assumption that anyone knowing about it would automatically wish to conform to its requirements. Therefore, any private direction at all by the legal authorities, either in favor of the custom or in opposition to it, could be easily misconstrued. If they offered private direction to abide by the requirements of the conventional custom, it would indicate that the custom was sanctioned by the legal system. And if they offered private direction not to abide by the requirements of the custom, it would indicate that there was some systemic objection to the custom. Thus, the systemic authorities must refrain from any private direction concerning such matters. Such matters constitute the category of *nahagu*.

The fact that three sages disagree upon the level of authority inherent in the behavior in question, one calling it law, the second considering it a firmly entrenched conventional custom, and the third regarding it only as a conventional custom in its early stage, also bears another important implication, namely, that the status of a given behavior might be a matter of legitimate *maḥaloket*.

---

6. Even if the law being taught is, in essence, a custom incorporated into law. See Elon's analysis of Rabbi Yoḥanan's decision that the law is according to Rabbi Me'ir, in *Jewish Law*, 2:729.

Just as custom lacks the ultimate status of law, both in the halakhic system and in other systems, with regard to its ultimate authority in the area of non-religious matters, so, too, does it lack the status of law in the halakhic system with regard to its ultimate authority in religious and ritual matters.[7] Rabbinic legal enactments regarding ritual matters acquire the status of *miẓvot*, that is, of religious law, and therefore qualify for the recitation of the usual blessing, which includes the word *ve-ẓivvanu*. This formula for the blessing praises God, who has sanctified us through His *miẓvot* and commanded us *(ve-ẓivvanu)* to do such-and-such. Thus, for example, the kindling of Ḥanukkah lights and the reading of the Scroll of Esther are rabbinic enactments and are accompanied by the usual blessing. Indeed, since rabbinic enactments acquire their status by virtue of the authority of the scriptural verse *Lo tasur* (Deuteronomy 17:11), compliance with their enactments is itself a *miẓvah*, and the recitation of *ve-ẓivvanu* in the blessing formula is legitimate. This is not the case, however, with customary behavior. While a custom may be binding, especially a general legal custom,[8] acting in almost all regards as a legal norm, the ultimate source of its authority is not law, and the inclusion of *ve-ẓivvanu* in the blessing formula would be inappropriate and erroneous.[9] Only the actual incorporation of the custom into the legal system *per se* could effect a change in its religious status.

The following talmudic selection, which deals with the use of a willow branch as part of the ritual of Sukkot,[10] discusses this matter.[11]

> It has been said that Rabbi Yoḥanan and Rabbi Yehoshu'a ben Levi [disagree concerning the willow], one claiming that it is an enactment of the latter prophets *(yesod nevi'im)*[12] and the other that it is a custom of the prophets.[13] . . . Aiybo said, "I was once in the presence of Rabbi Elazar ben Ẓadok when a man brought a willow to him. He took it and shook it vigorously, but did not say a benediction." He [i.e., Rabbi Elazar] held that it was a custom of the prophets.

---

7. Cf. the statements of both the Bavli (Yevamot 13b, Niddah 66a), *amina lakh ana issura, ve-at amrat minhaga* ("I tell you it is forbidden, and you say it is a custom"), and the Yerushalmi (Shevi'it 5:1, 35d), *ana amar minhag ve-at amar halakhah* ("I say custom, and you say law").

8. See above, p. 207.

9. See Rashi, Sukkah 44a, s.v. *minhag*.

10. The reference is not to the willow used as part of the *lulav* assemblage. Rather, it is to the willow used today only on the seventh day of *Sukkot* at the conclusion of the *hoshanot* service.

11. Sukkah 44a–b.

12. I.e., acting in their formal legislative capacity. See Rashi *ad loc.*

13. I.e., a custom dating from that period, even perhaps instituted by them, but never formally enacted by them as law. See Rashi *ad loc.*

The obvious implication of the passage is that a blessing would have been recited over the use of the willow had this particular behavior been legislated by the Prophets. Tangentially, the passage indicates, as we have already seen, that the actual status of a given behavior—whether it is enjoined by a legal norm or by custom—can be a matter of dispute.

As we turn the discussion to other aspects of customary behavior within the halakhic system, particularly to the question of the limitations of its power to compel obedience, the tension between it and the law, the possibility of abrogating it, and the various functions it serves, it should be carefully noted that the basic assumption throughout the discussion is the idea we have just examined, namely, that in the halakhic system custom has the status of law neither in the sphere of general behavior (secular) nor in the sphere of religious behavior (ritual). Although custom functions in many ways in a manner similar to that of binding rules of law, and although, therefore, the language of the discussion will be similar to that of a discussion of legal norms, this similarity should not obscure the fact that there is a fundamental difference between them.

The strongest expression of the authority of custom *per se,* as well as of its authority in relation to law, is found in the principle *Minhag mevattel halakhah* ("custom supersedes [abrogates] the law"). While the wording itself does not occur in the Babylonian Talmud, the idea does. The wording does, however, appear twice in the Yerushalmi. In one place, the context is purely and clearly monetary.[14] That this principle should be operative in monetary matters is logical, if one bears in mind that even in matters *de-oraita* there is general agreement that a person may make a valid stipulation contrary to the Torah—*Matneh adam al mah she-katuv ba-Torah be-daver she-bemamon.* That being the case, the existence, with regard to a monetary matter, of a conventional custom in the presumptive stage or of a legal custom that is at variance with the dictates of a legal norm is sufficient to validate the customary behavior and supersede the norm. Thus, we can deduce, the principle *Minhag mevattel halakhah* applies to and is determinative in monetary matters.

The second occurrence in the Yerushalmi deals, however, with *ḥaliẓah* (a ritual which permits a childless widow to marry someone other than a brother of her deceased husband) and implies ostensibly that the principle of *Minhag mevattel halakhah* applies equally well to the realm of *issur ve-hetter* (ritual matters) as to monetary matters.[15] This is the broadest

14. Yerushalmi Bava Meẓi'a 7:1, 11b.

15. Yerushalmi Yevamot 12:1, 12c. See, however, Elon's explanation of this passage, *Jewish Law,* 2:736 and n. 45 there. See also below, n. 16, and quotation from Rabbi Joseph Colon, p. 226.

possible interpretation of the principle, and, indeed, some authorities have adopted it. Rabbi Israel ben Ḥayyim Bruna offers a concise statement of this position: "Custom overturns *(oker)* law in matters of divorce and *ḥalizah,* for *issur ve-hetter,* and for monetary matters."[16]

Nonetheless, there is a marked tendency to restrict this broad interpretation. The earliest such restriction can be found in the minor tractate Soferim, and it limits the applicability of the principle *Minhag mevattel halakhah* to ancient customs *(Minhag vetikin).*[17] Customs that are of hoary antiquity can be presumed to have originated with or to have been approved by the earliest formulators of the legal system itself. Since, in theory, those primeval greats could not, by definition, as it were, have approved a custom inimical to the system, the custom retains its validity even if it is in conflict with a later legal norm. The contention verges on the claim that ancient custom, guided by the unassailable spirit of the very formulators of the system, stands in a class by itself; it is almost meta-legal. To question the validity or authenticity of such custom borders on sacrilege.

The succinct statement of Soferim implies that being a *Minhag vetikin* is a sufficient condition for superseding the law. It does not clarify whether it is also a necessary condition. Are there, in other words, any customs that supersede the law even though they are not in the category of *Minhag vetikin?* The continuation of the statement, although ambiguous, as we shall see, sheds some light on the question. It reads: "But a custom that cannot be proved from the Torah is as an error in judgment *(Eino ella ke-to'eh bi-shikkul ha-da'at).*"

Before exploring what value this sentence has for the issue at hand, it is necessary to attempt an explication of its meaning, independent of that issue. Whatever the category of custom it is that lacks proof from

---

16. *Responsa of Rabbi Israel Bruna* (Jerusalem: Tiferet ha-Torah Publishing, 1960 [5720]), no. 23.

Evidently, he extrapolates from *ḥalizah* to all matters of *issur ve-hetter,* there being no grounds for restricting the principle to *ḥalizah* alone. Clearly, too, his sources for this inclusion are the passages in the Yerushalmi. It follows, therefore, that Bruna understod the Yevamot passage to mean that even if it were clear that the law prohibited *ḥalizah* with a *sandal,* that law would be uprooted by the people's custom. Furthermore, even if Elon's explanation of the passage is its *peshat,* the systemic legitimacy of Bruna's position is not denied thereby. The actual *peshat* of a talmudic section is no more (nor any less) relevant to the development of the legal system than is the actual *peshat* of the Bible to the rabbinic interpretations thereof.

17. Soferim 14:16, M. Higger ed. (New York: De-vei Rabbanan, 1937 [5697]), p. 271.

Cf. Salmond's treatment of the requirement of "immemorial antiquity" as a prerequisite for legal customs (p. 201). In halakhic literature there is a variety of expressions that reflect the same requirement: *Minhag vetikin* ("custom of the ancients"), *Minhag rishonim* ("custom of the early ones"), *Minhag avot ha-kedumim* ("custom of the ancient fathers"), *Minhag nevi'im* ("custom of the prophets"), and others.

the Torah, it is at least clear that the observance of these customs is not an outright error, but, rather, an error of *Shikkul ha-da'at*. (We have seen in Chapter 4 that an *error* of *Shikkul ha-da'at* involves the adoption of a position that is not supported by the weight of evidence and/or precedent.) Furthermore, the stipulation of a category of custom that cannot be proven from the Torah implies (although not necessarily) the existence of a class of custom that *can* be proven from the Torah. The kinds of customs intended with regard to either of these classes is difficult to fathom. It is theoretically possible that the reference is to customs the authenticity of which can be traced to the nonlegal sections of the Bible. That, however, is unlikely on two grounds. First, such customs were generally incorporated into the system as legal norms and did not remain in the realm of customary behavior. Second, why should the observance of any custom that cannot be so traced be considered an error of *Shikkul ha-da'at?* It seems more probable, therefore, to explain "proved from the Torah" to mean that the customary behavior can be proved to be consonant with the spirit of the Torah. That which "cannot be proved from the Torah" would mean, accordingly, a particular customary behavior that cannot be *shown* to be consonant with the spirit of the Torah, but which would not necessarily imply that the behavior is *not* consonant with the spirit of the Torah. And finally, it seems evident both contextually and logically that what is under consideration is the authority of the customary behavior to supersede the law in the event that it is at variance with it. Contextually, because the language that precedes it, namely, *Minhag vetikin,* refers to that eventuality; logically, because it is illogical to suppose that the statement means to imply that the observance of a custom not at variance with the law is, nevertheless, an error of *Shikkul ha-da'at* if it cannot be *demonstrated* to be consonant with the spirit of the Torah.

The continuation of the statement from Soferim therefore means that the observance of any customary behavior that cannot be demonstrated to be consonant with the spirit of the Torah, and that is contrary to a legal norm, is considered to be an error of *Shikkul ha-da'at.* It cannot be considered an outright error, since the behavior has the practice of the people to support it, and since, in addition, it cannot be demonstrated to be contrary to the spirit of the Torah. However, since it cannot be demonstrated to be *consonant* with the spirit of the Torah either, that lack constitutes evidence favoring the law above the custom, and observance of the custom is considered an error of *Shikkul ha-da'at.*

We can now return to the original question, namely, whether or not being a *Minhag vetikin* is a necessary condition for custom to supersede law. If a customary act that "cannot be proved from the Torah" and that violates a legal norm is an error of *Shikkul ha-da'at,* it follows that one that can be "proved from the Torah," even though it violates a legal norm, is not an error of *Shikkul ha-da'at*. That is, its observance, though in conflict with a legal norm, is not even an error of *Shikkul ha-da'at* but, rather, incontrovertibly legitimate. Thus, it is not necessary for a custom to be *Minhag vetikin* in order to supersede the law; customs that can be "proved from the Torah" also supersede the law, even if they are not *Minhag vetikin.*

It should be noted, too, that while the statements from Soferim restrict the application of the principle *Minhag mivattel halakhah* to two categories of custom (those that are *Minhag vetikin* and those that can be "proved from the Torah"), they intimate no restriction at all on the areas of Jewish law to which the categories can apply, namely, monetary matters and *issur ve-hetter.* Indeed, the broader context in which the passage appears is one that concerns ritual; it deals with the appropriate time for the recitation of the various *megillot* (scrolls) on the various holidays.

As restrictive as the passage from Soferim may be, it does ultimately recognize instances in which customary behavior, never incorporated into the system as legal norms, supersedes existent law. Naḥmanides, however, is even more restrictive in his conception of the limits of the principle.[18] He writes:

> The claim that custom supersedes law *(Minhaga milleta hi)* applies only if the residents of the city or the seven elders of the city in their presence[19] stipulate its acceptance. For any other custom we do not abrogate the law, except in the case of an unclear legal decision *(ba-halakah rofefet).*[20] And the law is according to this explanation.[21]

In essence Naḥmanides nullifies entirely the authority of customary behavior to supersede the law. Stipulation of the acceptance of the custom by the residents of the city or their appointed representatives is the equivalent of its incorporation into the legal system through an act of legislation. Moreover, while it is clear that Naḥmanides is speaking of

18. Ramban to Bava Batra 144b, s.v. *ha de-amrinan.*

19. See *Responsa of Rashba,* pt. 1, no. 617, for clarification of the concept of *shivah tuvei ha-ir* ("seven elders of the city"). Also, Rabbi Israel Isserlein, in *Terumat ha-Deshen,* Wolf ed., *Ketavim u-fesakim,* no. 214, wrote concering their judicial and legislative function: *ve-tuvei ha-kahal ke-yoshevin le-fake'aḥ al iskei rabbim vi-ḥidim, bi-mekom beit din kayyamei* ("the elders of the community are as those who supervise the affairs of the many and of individuals, they stand in the place of the court").

20. This concept is discussed below, p. 217.

21. Naḥmanides offers the quoted explanation as a second interpretation. Thus, the final sentence indicates his own decision in favor of that explanation.

local custom, it seems reasonable to extrapolate from his words that he would make the same claim concerning general custom. The question was an academic one for him, however, since in his day there was no central body that was empowered to legislate for the entire Jewish people. Thirdly, it should be noted that Naḥmanides, too, does not distinguish between monetary matters and *issur ve-hetter,* implying that the nullification of the principle *Minhag mevattel halakhah* applies to both areas of Jewish law.

While one is inclined to deduce both from Soferim and from Naḥmanides that their restrictions apply both to customs that forbid the permissible as well as to those that permit the forbidden, this may not necessarily be the case. It is possible that both Soferim and Naḥmanides would agree with this distinction, notwithstanding our inclination to view their restrictions on the principle *Minhag mevattel halakhah* as all-encompassing. That is to say, it is possible that Soferim might deny that *Minhag vetikim* or custom that "can be proved from the Torah" supersedes the law if it permits the forbidden. And it is possible that Naḥmanides might agree that a custom that forbids the permissible does supersede the law (since forbidding the permissible can be considered to be a protective fence around the law rather than a contradiction of it). Similarly, it is possible that Rabbi Bruna, whose interpretation of *Minhag mevattel halakhah* was most liberal, would also agree with the more restrictive theory to which we now turn. Since none of the three comments directly on the subject, however, we must leave their agreement to the realm of possibility alone.

In two of his responsa, Rabbi Solomon ben Simon Duran (Rashbash, ca. 1400–1467) gives us his theory of how the distinction between forbidding the permissible and permitting the forbidden relates to the principle that custom supersedes the law. In one of them he writes:[22]

> The principle that a custom supersedes the law applies only to one that does not involve a forbidden act *(issur).* But [a custom may not supersede law if it involves] the abrogation of a prohibition. Know, for the Talmud says in the first chapter of Rosh ha-Shanah: "In the face of a prohibition do we permit people to persist in their customary behavior?"[23] . . . And the matter is self-evident, for if we would abrogate a prohibition because of a custom, all prohibitions would be abrogated one by one, and the Torah would become null and void, God forbid.

---

22. *Responsa of Rashbash,* no. 419, p. 83c.
23. Rosh ha-Shanah 15b.

In the other he writes:

> Know, people say regularly that *Minhag mevattel halakhah.* That statement is partially true and partially false. . . . It is true that custom supersedes law in monetary matters, and false in any matter that involves a prohibition regarding which the custom is permissive. For a custom may only forbid the permissible, but not permit the forbidden.[24]

From these responsa of the Rashbash we may deduce the following about his view of the applicability of the principle: (1) It applies most broadly to monetary matters, in which custom may supersede law both in forbidding the permissible and permitting the forbidden. (2) In matters of *issur ve-hetter,* custom may supersede law only in forbidding the permissible. (3) In matters of *issur ve-hetter,* custom may in no way supersede the law by permitting the forbidden.

As we shall see later in this chapter, these distinctions are widely accepted. For the present, however, one example of a decision codified by Maimonides demonstrates his own acceptance of the second and third of these propositions.[25] Maimonides wrote:

> At this time, one who had a nocturnal emission on the Day of Atonement . . . may not wash his entire body nor immerse himself. For one who immerses himself at this time does not become ritually pure, because of impurity through contact with the dead.[26] Thus, washing after an emission before engaging in prayer is only a custom at this time,[27] and no custom may abrogate that which is forbidden. It may only forbid the permissible.

What are the ramifications that follow from the application of this distinction? For while the quotations from the Rashbash establish the distinction, they say nothing about how to deal with the many questions that arise because of it. Are firmly entrenched customs that permit the forbidden to be abrogated? Should customs that do not permit the forbidden but that might lead to permitting the forbidden be treated as those that actually permit the forbidden? What action should be taken if the populace refuses to abide by a decision to abrogate a custom? Are

---

24. *Responsa of Rashbash,* no. 562, p. 111b.
25. *Mishneh Torah,* Shevitat Asor 3:3.
26. From which purification is no longer possible because of the unavailability of the ashes of the red heifer. See Numbers 19.
27. Since it does not, in fact, result in ritual purity.

there any circumstances or grounds that would warrant the abrogation of a custom forbidding the permissible? What is the status of customary behavior that forbids the permissible but that is observed by most as law rather than custom?

The variety of possible answers to these questions brings into sharper focus the possible conflict between custom and law in general, and especially insofar as custom originates in and receives its ultimate authority from the people and not from the systemic authorities.

Rabbi Asher ben Yeḥi'el (Rosh, ca. 1250–1327) proposes answers to several of these questions.[28] He writes:

> All of the customs concerning which the sages affirmed that they ought to be observed are such that they originated as a preservative or protective fence *(la'asot seyag ve-harḥakah)*. . . . But if the customary behavior in any locale involves a transgression,[29] the custom should be changed, even if it was instituted by masters. For no court may make a condition to uproot a matter from the Torah. Even the Great Sanhedrin that meets in the Chamber of Hewn Stone does not have the authority to uproot a matter from the Torah except passively, but not actively. . . .
>
> While it goes without saying that a custom the observance of which itself contains an infraction ought to be changed, it is also the case that a custom that originated as a preservative or protective fence but that might result in some mishap *(kilkul)* ought to be annulled. . . .[30]
>
> And thus does the Yerushalmi claim: When the law is unclear *(rofefet be-yadekha)*, follow the custom.[31] Which means that if there is some unclarity in the law, i.e., that it is not clear according to whom the law has been determined, and you see that there is a customary

28. *Responsa of Rosh*, 55:10.

29. The immediate context implies a transgression of a prohibition *de-oraita*. The conclusion of the passage, however, clearly indicates that the Rosh is referring also to prohibitions *de-rabbanan*.

30. The Rosh quotes an example of such a custom from Pesaḥim 50b. The inhabitants of a certain place observed as a custom the separation of *ḥallah* (Numbers 15:17–21) from rice. The custom had to be stopped lest it result in confusion between grains that legally require *ḥallah* and those that do not. Such confusion, in turn, might result in an actual infraction.

31. Yerushalmi Pe'ah 7:6, 20c. The precise wording of the Yerushalmi is: "Concerning any law that is unclear to the court, and you do not know what behavior to follow *(ve-ein at yode'a mah tivah)*, go and see how the community behaves *(noheg)*, and act similarly *(u-nehog)*."

> behavior, follow the custom, for one could surmise *(de-yesh litlot)* that the masters who instituted the custom did so because it seemed to them that the law was thus. This is the law concerning customs in matters of *issur ve-hetter.* But concerning monetary matters, the court has the authority to make ordinances according to the time and the need, even in violation of the rule of the Torah.

Rabbenu Asher asserts that compliance with customary behavior in violation of the law is legitimate only in the case of customs that forbid the permissible (i.e., that originate as a preserving or protecting fence), but not in the case of customs that permit the forbidden. Compliance with the latter category of customs, in violation of the law, is contraindicated by the very nature of the system, which cannot easily brook any active abrogation of its legal norms. His statement, however, is more than a mere reiteration of a distinction we are already familiar with. He also maintains that any custom that actively violates a norm (by permitting the forbidden) must be actively *abrogated.* Moreover, he maintains that there is a category of customs that must be abrogated even though they do not actively violate norms, i.e., those customs that although legitimately forbidding the permissible, nevertheless result in permitting the forbidden. For even a custom that does not itself actively violate a norm, but that might result in such a violation as a result of mistaken inferences drawn from compliance with it, must be abolished.[32]

Rabbenu Asher also discusses that area in which the strength of custom is greatest, namely, the area in which the behavior in question is not actually considered to be customary at all, in the sense we have been discussing, but rather, is considered to be behavior that is in compliance with a resolution of a question of law in the second sense.[33] In this situation, behavior may be called *minhag* but is, nevertheless, assumed to have been dictated by an actual legal decision made by earlier masters, even though that legal decision itself cannot be found.

There are also several implications inherent in the Rosh's comment that should be noted. First, any of the possible considerations that could induce the sages to exercise their rights vis-à-vis matters *de-oraita* could also induce them to prefer a permissive custom over a restrictive requirement of the law. Rabbenu Asher's point is that any such preference, the practical result of which would mean an abrogation of the law, must be the result of this kind of consideration, not the result of any intrinsic right of custom to serve as grounds for the abrogation of legal norms.

---

32. See above, n. 30.
33. See Elon, *Jewish Law,* 2:728 ff.

Second, the Rosh's contention that even customs that forbid the permissible must be abrogated if compliance with them results in the active violation of a norm (i.e., results in permitting the forbidden) clearly implies that a nonscholar might confuse firmly entrenched customary behavior with law. If he were not confusing custom with law, the nonscholar would have known that no customary behavior could ever result in permitting what a law forbids. Only because he misperceives the custom as law does he allow himself to draw the conclusions that follow from the misperception and consider a forbidden act permissible.

Misperceiving custom for law could happen, of course, even if the customary behavior were not one that might lead to these undesirable consequences. This possibility, in turn, raises again the question of the status of customs that are popularly, although mistakenly, thought to be law rather than custom. The Rosh addresses this question too.[34] He writes:

> Matters concerning which it is known that they are permitted, yet are observed customarily as forbidden because the people wish to be more strict with themselves, you may not declare permitted before them. But if their customary behavior is based upon an error, namely, that they believe that the behavior is actually forbidden when, in fact, it is permitted, you may permit it before them. . . . Similarly, too, a man whose customary behavior forbids something that is permitted, as a fence or a self-imposed restriction *(perishut),* no sage ought to declare the act permitted to him. But a sage may permit it to him if he expresses regret *(lehattir lahem ha-ḥaratah).*[35]

The thrust of the comments of Rabbenu Asher here is that customary behavior is not easily abolished. The strength of its ability to compel obedience, however, is predicated upon the assumption that the fact that it is a custom is known and understood. If the nature of a behavior pattern is misperceived as legal rather than as customary, then the fact that it is misperceived reduces the ability of that custom to continue to compel obedience. Once it is publicly announced that an entrenched behavior pattern that is perceived as being a norm is really only a custom, the status of that custom is reduced to the level of its first stage of development. One can no longer presume that it is the intent of those ostensibly bound by the custom to be bound by it. Such intent can only

34. *Piskei Rosh,* Pesaḥim 4:3.

35. I.e., declares that he regrets having accepted the custom upon himself, and wishes to be released from its observance.

be demonstrated through continued observance of the behavior pattern on the part of the people after they have been made aware that it is based on custom rather than law. In the absence of such a demonstration, there is no basis for the authority of the custom other than the will and desire of the people to be bound by it. One who hears a sage declare what he thought a law to be a custom is entitled to modify his accustomed behavior.[36]

The concluding lines in the Rosh's comment are also significant. While he refers to the abrogation of a custom followed by only one individual (such a custom would be similar in nature to a vow), he leaves the way open to the possibility that even widespread customs may be abrogated on the basis of demonstrable expressions of regret by those bound by these customs. It does not seem unreasonable to hypothesize that the same types of considerations that would induce scholars to adopt nonprecedented positions or to invoke their rights to institute changes in the law itself would also lead them to expressions of regret concerning some customary behaviors.

Conclusions similar to those of Rabbi Asher ben Yeḥi'el will be quoted below in the course of the discussion of related issues, making it clear that there is widespread agreement that any custom that permits the forbidden, in violation of the law, is to be abrogated. Yet it must be recalled that the ultimate authority of a custom lies in the fact that it originates among the people themselves and that consequently its hold upon them is strong. This being the case, the possibility of conflict between the people and a sage who attempts to abrogate a popular custom is great. What if the people persist in the observance of a forbidden custom?

Rabbi Isaac ben Sheshet Perfet (Ribash, 1326–1408) addresses himself to this question in at least two places. In one, he cautions his questioner to choose carefully those customs he will attempt to abrogate, primarily because they are firmly entrenched and not likely to be easily abandoned by the people.[37] He writes:

> I have already requested of you several times that you not be overly zealous *(le-val tedakdek)* in changing customs regarding matters such as these.[38] And furthermore, the people will not accept this [the

36. Obviously, then, the Rosh means that the custom was not universally (i.e., even by the sages) misperceived as law. Else, there would be no one to declare it permissible.

37. *Responsa of Ribash,* no. 158, p. 34c.

38. He refers to the custom of mourners to visit the cemetery even during the first week. Perfet contends that although the practice is not desirable, it is not strictly forbidden, since it is done out of honor to the deceased *(kevod ha-met).* Thus, though it should not be encouraged, it should not be forbidden, since it is not an actual violation of a prohibition.

> abrogation of the custom] from anyone. And even a matter which is absolutely forbidden *(issur gamur)*, if it is the case that the people will not accept a change, our sages have said: "Better that they should act inadvertently than in willful violation of the law."[39]

The sage must protect his authority to abrogate customs that, by permitting the forbidden, violate the law. He must, therefore, exercise the greatest discretion in choosing those issues on which to confront the community. And even then he may fail to persuade the community to forgo its customary behavior. When it is clear to him that this is the case, a systemic prinicple comes into play. According to this principle, in such a situation the custom must be permitted to prevail even if it is in blatant violation of the law. It is better that the sages give silent sanction to a custom than that they should fail in their attempt to uproot it. The result of persistent attempts to abrogate the custom would be the willful violation by the people of a clear rabbinic statement outlawing the custom.[40]

In a second reference to this problem, the Ribash reiterates the above contention while making most of the same points made by Rabbi Asher ben Yeḥi'el more than one hundred years before.[41] He writes:

> There are matters that are permissible according to law but concerning which Jews have a customary prohibition of their own, without an enactment of the sages, the purpose of which is preventative or self-sanctification *(lehitkaddesh)* even in matters that are permissible. Such customs are as inviolate as the Torah itself *(gufei Torah)*. . . . However, a matter that is universally recognized as permissible but

---

39. Shabbat 148b. *Mutav she-yehu shogegin ve-al yehu mezidin* ("it is better that they act inadvertently than purposely"). This is an extremely important systemic principle that requires extensive treatment in its own right. It is the hope of the author to publish a series of monographs dealing with such crucial systemic principles.

40. Two points ought to be emphasized. First, the more frequently the people ignore the dictates of systemic authorities, the less authoritative the status of the authorities becomes. Furthermore, the diminution of their authority forebodes the destruction of the orderly functioning of the system. Thus, the greatest judiciousness on the part of the authorities is demanded in putting their own ultimate authority on the line. Cf. the statement of Rabbi Elazar ben Shimon: "As it is incumbent *(mizvah)* upon one to state that which will be heeded, so is it incumbent upon him to refrain from stating that which will not be heeded" (Yevamot 65b).

Second, there could easily be a *maḥaloket* between authorities concerning the likelihood of their being ignored by the people were they to attempt the abrogation of a custom. Their *maḥaloket*, in turn, could result in an attempt by one of them to abrogate and in a decision by the other to refrain from such an attempt. The *maḥaloket*, however, would not indicate any fundamental disagreement between them concerning the way the system works regarding rabbinic rights vis-à- vis customary behavior.

41. *Responsa of Ribash*, no. 44.

> concerning which one practices a customary prohibition, not as a preventative measure but because he erroneously thinks that it is forbidden by law—such a matter, if he seeks absolution from it as one seeks absolution from an oath, it may be allowed to him. . . . And in an instance in which a customary behavior permits that which is universally recognized as completely forbidden [i.e., by law], they ought not to be allowed to persist in the customary behavior under any circumstances. . . . But if they would not accept rebuke, and pay no heed to the dictates of their teachers, nor listen to their instructors, they may be allowed, since it is better that they should act inadvertently than in willful violation of the law.

Throughout this chapter we have noted one type of custom concerning which there is nearly unanimous agreement as to its binding nature; that is, a custom that is intended to establish a preventative or protective fence around the law by forbidding the permissible. The statements we have quoted consider such customs as almost unassailable. It ought, however, to be noted that the underlying assumption of all these assertions is that such a custom can be seen as a reasonable one, that is, that it can be seen to serve the function for which it was intended. Nonetheless, it is not difficult to conceive of a custom that has come into being for the correct reasons, but that, since it originated among the people, that is, without rabbinic input, forbids the permissible beyond the reasonable limits of prevention and preservation. What shall be the status of such customary behavior?

Rabbi Ḥezekiah ben David Da Silva (1659–1695) addresses this question succinctly.[42] He writes:

> Know that any custom, be it an individual one or a communal one, which is made as a fence or a hedge must have some basis and reason. [But if,] for example, the people of a given locale customarily refrain from work on the entire day of Sabbath eve as a protective fence around the rabbinic prohibition to work from *minḥah* time on,[43] and similar cases, such is a custom of ignorance *(minhag borut)*, and does not require even absolution.

A custom that stretches the idea of prevention or preservation beyond reasonable limits has no status whatsoever; it is self-abrogating, requir-

42. *Peri Ḥadash* (printed in most standard editions of the *Shulḥan Arukh*), *Oraḥ Ḥayyim*, sec. 496, Minhagei Issur, par. 15.

43. See Pesaḥim 50b.

ing no further action than the recognition of its being beyond reasonable limits.[44]

There is still one more type of behavior that is referred to as custom that we must consider. We say "referred to as custom" because it is, in fact, not technically custom at all. We refer to a set of circumstances in which a question of law is a matter of dispute between groups of sages (or individual sages), some allowing an act and others forbidding it. However, both those who permit and those who forbid view their decision as a decision of law, not of custom. To the extent that the *maḥaloket* is known and acknowledged by later authorities, they may refer to both the behavior of community X that is consonant with the view of the permitting sages and the behavior of community Y that is consonant with the view of the forbidding sages as *minhag*. Concerning such disputed behavior the Ribash wrote:[45]

> If a certain issue was a matter of *maḥaloket* between sages, of blessed memory, one forbidding and the other permitting, and [the people of a given community] acted according to the lenient position because their rabbi or the local sages inclined toward that position, they should be allowed to persist in their customary behavior even though there might be many places in which the customary behavior forbids the action. . . . But matters that are undisputedly forbidden, yet several places behave customarily as if it were permitted because they do not know that it is forbidden, such a case constitutes an erroneous custom *(minhag ta'ut)*[46] and is of no import *(ve-eino kelum)*. For even if they behaved customarily, forbidding that which is permissible, because they did not know that it was permissible, and afterwards it became known to them in truth [that it was permissible], it is not necessary for them to persist in the behavior pattern which forbids. . . . And it goes without saying that those whose customary behavior permits matters which then become known to them as forbidden—that this is not a binding custom.

The Ribash deals in this selection with three different types of behavior. Two of them involve kinds of erroneous customary behavior that we have already considered: (1) a custom that, because of ignorance,

44. For additional examples, see Elon, *Jewish Law*, 2:763.
45. *Responsa of Ribash*, no. 256, p. 69a.
46. See Elon, *Jewish Law*, 2:761.

permits a certain behavior that is actually forbidden, and (2) a custom that, because of ignorance, forbids a certain behavior that is actually permissible.[47] In both these cases, the custom has no binding authority and compels no obedience. However, divergent behaviors based, not upon error, but upon the divergent decisions of different authorities in a matter of dispute, may be allowed to persist, since the behaviors do not reflect custom at all, but, rather, differing legal decisions. In this sense, then, we again find that divergent behaviors are legitimate within the halakhic system.

Da Silva adds some other points, too, with regard to this last category of customary behavior.[48] He writes:

> A matter concerning which there is a *maḥaloket* between sages, and the custom of one locale follows the opinion of those who forbid, their custom does not establish a new [customary] prohibition [of that which is permissible][49] . . . for the prohibition is a legal one *(asur ve-omed)* according to the opinion of that sage. . . . And if the community has an outstanding sage [within it], he may issue a decision *(yakhol lehorot)* favoring leniency concerning the matter. For they do not act as they do [i.e., forbidding the behavior] except on the basis of the prior decision forbidding, thinking that the law is thus. And since the rabbi [who is deciding in favor of the lenient position] has proofs to rebut the position of the other authority, they are duty-bound to follow the dictates only of the judge of their own time. . . . Thus, [as a result of the decision of the later authority,] the earlier custom, based upon the decision of the former authority, is an erroneous custom. . . . And an erroneous custom may be summarily permitted [i.e., terminated, abrogated] *(yesh lehattir ha-peshitut af be-lo hattarah).*

The contention Da Silva rejects is the claim that a prohibition of the permissible retains its obedience-compelling status *as customary behavior* even if it did not originate as a custom, but rather as one of the opinions in a legal disagreement between sages. According to this thesis, if a later sage finds sufficient reason to adopt an opinion other than the one that is the basis of the community's behavior, as is his systemic right, the entrenched behavior of the community can yet be considered binding

47. See above, pp. 218 f.
48. *Peri Ḥadash, Oraḥ Ḥayyim,* sec. 496, Minhagei Issur, par. 2.
49. If it did, of course, it would be as obedience-compelling as customs that forbid the permissible in general.

customarily, the lenient decision of the later sage notwithstanding. The contention is that once a prohibition is established, it retains its status as a prohibition even if the grounds of its authority shift from the strictly legal to the customary. This thesis Da Silva rejects completely. For him, matters that originate as customary prohibitions may later be incorporated into the legal system as legal prohibitions, but matters that originate as legal prohibitions compel obedience only so long as they remain legal prohibitions; their status cannot be changed to that of customary prohibition.

Da Silva implies, in truth, even more than that. Were a community to persist in forbidding that which a later authority has declared permissible, the status of their behavior becomes that of erroneous custom. And erroneous custom not only does not compel obedience, obedience to it is unthinkable.

We have discussed above the possibility that customs stemming from time immemorial may have a special status.[50] If, indeed, they do have such a status, it should follow that they would retain their power to compel obedience even against a unanimous later opinion that the custom is in violation of the law. Rabbi David ben Solomon Ibn Abi Zimra (Radbaz, 1479–1573), quoting Rabbi Yom Tov Ibn Abraham Ishbili (Ritba, ca. 1250–1330), rejects not only this second claim, but even the lesser claim that a custom from time immemorial supersedes nonunanimous later opinion that it is in violation of the law.[51] He writes:

> . . . but a custom advocating leniency [i.e., in opposition to the law] is never to be considered binding *(ein ḥosheshin lo)* even if it is from time immemorial *(al pi gedolim she-ba-olam).* Rather, if there appears to some authoritative sage *(ḥakham ba'al hora'ah)* of a later time some indication that the custom is in violation of a legal norm [it should be abrogated]. For we have none but the judge who exists in our own time. Nonetheless, in an instance in which the prohibition is not absolutely certain, and the custom is firmly entrenched such that it is impossible for him to abrogate it . . . he should act for himself in such a way as not to evoke controversy, until he might bring the people back to the appropriate behavior little by little. But if the error is incontrovertible *(mukhra),* "there is no wisdom nor understanding nor counsel against the Lord."[52]

---

50. See pp. 212 ff.
51. *Responsa of Radbaz,* pt. 4, no. 1145.
52. Proverbs 21:30.

The Radbaz in the name of the Ritba affirms the right of a later authority to abrogate an ancient custom that permits the forbidden when it is clearly in violation of the law. The system vouchsafes to all authorities, in their own time, prerogatives equal to those of the earliest authorities. Failure to exercise their systemically guaranteed authority when necessary is itself acting "against the Lord."

Yet on careful reading, the Ritba says even more than that. Even when an ancient custom is not *incontrovertibly* in violation of the law, but in the opinion of a later authority it seems to be in violation of the law, the later authority is obligated to move his community—slowly, judiciously, and with discretion—toward the opinion he holds, even though the matter may not be absolutely certain. Although he must be aware of the difference between circumstances that demand immediate and unquestionable action and those that do not warrant such definitive action, he ought not to abdicate his legitimate authority even in the latter circumstance. His obligation to move his community in the direction he deems appropriate remains. The nature of the circumstance dictates only the method and the tactics by which he fulfills his obligation to his community.

Though the Radbaz and the Ritba clearly subordinate even custom from time immemorial to the legal system, it is not unanticipated to find other authorities who disagree. We have already quoted the succinct statement of Rabbi Israel Bruna, even though he does not mention ancient custom explicitly.[53] Probably the strongest advocate for the far-reaching authority of ancient custom is Rabbi Joseph ben Solomon Colon (Maharik, ca. 1420–1480). The following quotation indicates the extent of his claim.[54]

> Ancient custom is as law itself *(minhag avot Torah hi)*, as we read in the final chapter of Ta'anit:[55] "Rav came to Babylonia and noted that they would read the *Hallel* on *Rosh Ḥodesh*. He thought to stop them. When he heard that they recited it with omissions,[56] he said, 'One can deduce from this that they possess an ancient custom *(minhag avoteihem bi-deihem)*.' " Since he originally wished to stop them, one can deduce that they were not accustomed to recite it in Rav's locale, even with omissions.[57] But [i.e., indeed] it is obvious that he

53. See above, p. 212.

54. *Responsa of Mahari Colon, shoresh* 9.

55. Ta'anit 28b.

56. I.e., that they did not include Psalms 115:1–11 and Psalms 116:1–11, although these verses are part of *Hallel*.

57. Had they been so accustomed, Rav would obviously not have considered stopping the residents of this locale from a similar recitation.

also disagreed wtih the recitation.[58] And even so, once he saw that they possessed an ancient custom he did not wish to prevent them [from complying with it]. And even though it is clear that they would recite a benediction prior to its recitation, as is our custom,[59] . . . and according to the position of Rav that custom entailed the recitation of an unnecessary benedition, and we affirm in the first chapter of Berakhot[60] that such is a transgression of "Thou shall not take the name of the Lord your God in vain"[61]—he relied nonetheless on their ancient custom, and did not wish to annul it.[62] . . . And it is obvious that he could have prevented them from reciting it, as was his original proclivity, yet did not want to change their ancient custom.[63] And most assuredly there is nobody in the present generation who could change any customs of any locale that were instituted in time immemorial *(al pi avot ha-kedumim),* it being obvious that they [i.e., the institutors of the custom] were sages *(benei Torah)* who established their customs in accordance with the Torah and the commandments.[64] And we follow the custom even though it might be in violation of the law, whenever it was instituted by the sages of the place. . . . And one could bring further

58. I.e., had he not disagreed with the legitimacy of the recitation, there would be no reason for him to consider stopping it merely because it was not so recited in his own locale.

59. I.e., as we do today.

60. Berakhot 33a.

61. Exodus 20:7.

62. Q.E.D. Since Rav allowed them to continue their accustomed behavior, even though that behavior entailed the recitation of an unnecessary benediction in violation of a law, it follows that an ancient custom has the status of law. Thus, just as there is no violation of the law entailed by the recitation of the benediction on those days when the reading of *Hallel* is legally mandated, there is also no violation of the law entailed by the recitation of the benediction prior to the reading of *Hallel* on a day on which an ancient custom—having the status of law—prescribes its recitation.

63. In this sentence Colon defends his own analysis of the incident with Rav by rebutting the possible claim that Rav allowed them to persist in their behavior because he could not have stopped them even if he had so desired. Were that, in fact, the case, Rav would have been adopting the principle *Mutav she-yehu shogegin ve-al yehu mezidin,* which has already been discussed above, p. 221. And were that the case, Rav's action would indicate nothing about the obedience-compelling nature of the custom, but would indicate, rather, his inability to take the necessary action against the custom effectively. Colon's refutation of that possible argument is based upon his assumption that Rav would never have even considered stopping them were he not certain that it would have been in his power to do so.

64. The thrust of Colon's argument in this last passage is as follows: Rav, the most powerful authority of his time, accorded obedience-compelling status to ancient customs. In out day, when nobody compares with Rav in stature or authority, customs from time immemorial can surely not be abrogated. Particularly is this so in light of the fact that such ancient customs cannot be in actual conflict with the legal system, since they originate with those who constructed the system. See above, p. 212.

> proof that we follow custom even in violation of law, and even in matters of *issur*, from what we read in chapter *Hakometz Rabbah:* Rav said, "If Elijah will come and say, etc., one may not perform *ḥaliẓah* with a *sandal*, we would pay him no heed, for the people are already accustomed to do so with a *sandal*."[65] . . . And one cannot say that these customs are different . . . since they are general *(de-khulei alma nahug hakhi)*, but a local custom *(minhag she-ein ella bi-medinah aḥat)* . . . one might contend, is not obeyed when in violation of the law. . . . For the statement of Rav is in support of the claim of the Yerushalmi that *Minhag mevattel halakhah*,[66] and that claim of the Yerushalmi was made in the context of chapter *ha-Po'alim*, in which we learn in the Mishnah, "Everything follows local custom."[67] And there we are clearly dealing with local customs, i.e., which are not customary with all, since the Mishnah states, "Everything follows local custom," which implies [that we abide by the local custom] even though it may not be the custom of other places. From which we must surely deduce that Rav's statement applies even to custom that is not general *(she-ein shaveh be-khol makom)*.

Upon analysis it seems that, for two reasons, Colon's position reflects the strongest defense of the authority of ancient custom. First, the tone of the responsum is very strong, allowing no doubt whatsoever that he considers that such customs are indeed authoritative. Second, Colon goes to great lengths to demonstrate that the authority of customs is not restricted to monetary matters but includes, as well, permitting the forbidden in ritual matters. Furthermore, he proposes and rejects a thesis that would place general custom in a different class from local custom. The thesis he rejects would recognize that *Minhag mivattel halakhah* in general custom, on the grounds that it is universally observed among Jews. Yet, on the basis of the Talmud, he cannot accept the distinction. Local custom from time immemorial supersedes law in its locale.

Yet, since Colon refers repeatedly to the antiquity of the custom and to its origin in time immemorial, and since we have already noted that even Soferim and Naḥmanides, who impose far-reaching restrictions on the applicability of the principle *Minhag mivattel halakhah*, recognize ancient custom as superseding law,[68] we cannot deduce from Colon's

---

65. Menaḥot 32a. See above, p. 211, the passage from Yerushalmi Yevamot.
66. Yevamot 12:1, 12c.
67. Bava Meẓi'a, chap 7. See *ibid.*, the first *mishnah*, and the Yerushalmi, Bava Meẓi'a 11b. See above, p. 211 and n. 14 to that page.
68. See above, pp. 212 f.

words any similar far-reaching conclusions regarding customary behavior that cannot be categorized as *Minhag vetikin.* And custom that cannot be categorized as *Minhag vetikin* has, in the final analysis, been the subject matter of most of this chapter.

The chapter ends as it began, with a reaffirmation that the status, role, and authority of custom within the halakhic system is a complex subject. Despite that complexity, however, it is clear that in its development the halakhic system has usually subordinated customary behavior to the law itself. Indeed, the areas in which custom is not subordinated to the law are comparable to areas in which legal norms themselves are also not strictly subordinate to the legal system. Just as there is a systemic principle that allows one to make a stipulation contrary to the law in monetary matters *(matneh adam al mah she-katuv ba-Torah be-davar she-bemamon)*, so, too, a custom may be in violation of the law when it affects a legal norm regulating monetary matters. Just as the sages could legislate new prohibitive norms as a preventative measure against the violation of other norms, so, too, could custom that originated as a preventative or preservative measure violate the law by prohibiting the permissible. But as a general rule, custom that permits the forbidden, or custom that is mistakenly assumed to be law, or custom that can be cogently demonstrated to be not consonant with the spirit of the Torah, or custom that forbids the permissible beyond the reasonable limits of prevention or preservation can be abrogated and made subordinate to the law.

The three most important factors that contribute to the complexity of the role of custom in the halakhic system are: First, the fact that the status of *Minhag vetikin,* custom from time immemorial, is a matter of considerable controversy among halakhic authorities. Some put it in a class by itself, virtually above the law, while others, like the Radbaz and the Ritba, subordinate it, too, to the legal system. Second, the fact that since custom originates among the people, its hold upon the people may prevent its abrogation even when it seems to scholars that it ought to be abrogated. As a result, authorities have allowed erroneous custom to be retained when it seems that the scholars are likely to fail in their attempt to abrogate it—although the judgment of how likely the scholars are to fail is hardly an objective one.

And third, the fact that although custom in the halakhic system can no longer be elevated to the level of legal norms *de jure,* it is elevated *de facto,* can result in misunderstanding and confusion. Clearly, no authority can maintain that a custom has been elevated to the status of a legal norm, because such a statement would imply *de jure* elevation, which is impossible. Indeed, it seems plausible to assert that a major dispute between today's sages regarding custom would tend to revolve around the *tacit* contention of some that a great deal of customary behavior has attained the *de facto* status of legal norms and the denial of that contention by others. Both positions are tenable, and the resultant dispute is a legitimate *maḥaloket*.

Chapter Nine

Extralegal Sources within *Halakhah*

Up until this point we have been concerned with examining the various legal procedures that lead to the determination of the law in the halakhic system: the resolution of questions of fact or law in the second sense, the exercise of judicial discretion, and the continued adherence to, or the rejection or modification of, precedented behavior or custom. We have noted frequently, however, that the system does not present us with objective criteria on the basis of which to apply to these procedures systemic principles like *Et la'asot ladonai heferu toratekha, Mutav te'aker ot aḥat min ha-Torah,* or *Le-migdar milleta.* Furthermore, while we have demonstrated the legitimacy of the exercise of judicial discretion, we have not considered the kinds of factors which might incline an arbiter to adopt one position over another or to reject a precedent or abrogate a norm or a custom. Regarding these factors, too, we shall see that the system does not provide objective criteria for determining their use.

In other words, we have thus far been dealing with the systemic machinery of the decision-making process and must now proceed to examine the factors that may legitimately be taken into account by *posekim* as they utilize the machinery. These factors constitute the extralegal sources of the halakhic system, which, although not themselves legal norms, nevertheless bear greatly on the determination of the law.[1] Among these factors are some that are stated explicitly in the literature as well as others that are implicit.[2]

Before we proceed, however, a crucial caveat is necessary. The fact that these factors are admissible as data in the decision-making process might lead to the idea that they are also, by themselves, capable of determining the law rather than merely affecting it. However, in truth, extralegal sources constitute only one among many kinds of information available for and subject to the arbiter's evaluation: It is *he* alone who determines the law. For example, icthyologists may offer data concerning the nature of the fins and scales of swordfish, but the *posek* alone can determine whether or not they fulfill the requirements of *senappir* (fins) and *kaskeset* (scales) required by Leviticus 11:9. Sociologists, demographers, and ecologists may offer data concerning the ability of the earth to sustain increasing numbers of humans in the next thousand years, but only *posekim* can determine whether those data warrant overturning the precedent that advocates large families for Jews. Chemists may provide analyses of the changes in chemical composition resulting from various steps in the processing of foods, but only *posekim* can determine whether these chemical changes affect the status of the finished foodstuff in relation to the laws of *kashrut*.

Moreover, since extralegal sources, although admissible, are not determinative, it follows that two arbiters can disagree concerning the actual significance of specific extralegal data. But it must be stressed, what they would *not* be in disagreement about is the potential significance (i.e., the admissibility) of extralegal sources in general.

The Talmud itself provides a clear case that reflects the fact that the law is determined by the sages, not predetermined by the data provided by extralegal sources.[3] The passage reads:

> Rav Yehudah said in the name of Rav, "It happened once that a certain man lusted for a certain woman to the point that he became ill *(he'elah libbo tina)*. They came and asked of the doctors, who responded that there was no cure for him other than intercourse with the woman. Said the sages, 'Let him die rather than have intercourse with her.'

---

1. We shall see that some of these factors reoccur with such regularity that they *appear* to assume the status of legal norms. For example, the economic consideration of *Hefsed*. See, however, n. 7 below.

2. It should be noted again that implicit principles are considerably more problematic than explicit ones, insofar as it is possible for some to deny that they are operative within the system at all, while others assert that their existence is "irrefutably" proven from the sources. See above, pp. 2 f.

3. Sanhedrin 75a.

" '[Let her] stand before him nude.' [Said the sages,] 'Let him die, but let her not stand before him nude.'

" '[Let her] speak with him from behind a partition.' [Said the sages,] 'Let him die, but let her not speak with him from behind a partition.' "

Concerning this episode there was a difference of opinion between Rabbi Ya'akov bar Idi and Rabbi Samuel bar Naḥmani, one asserting that she was a married woman, and the other that she was unattached *(penuyah)*.

The stringency of the sages can be easily understood according to the view that she was married, but what justifies the stringency according to the view that she was unattached? Rav Papa said that [the stringency was motivated by concern] for the ignominy of the family *(pegam mishpaḥah)*.[4] Rav Aḥa the son of Rav Ika said that [the stringency was motivated by concern] lest Jewish girls become licentious with forbidden relations.[5]

One would have expected the sages to pay heed to the treatments prescribed by the doctors in order to save the life of the man. Yet in this case those prescriptions, the extralegal sources, were insufficient to warrant the abrogation of a norm, no matter how dire the consequences to the man. Having considered them, the sages concluded, legally, that they were outweighed by other factors that favored adherence to the accepted norm. The doctors provided the extralegal sources, but the sages determined the law.[6]

Extralegal sources can be divided into four basic categories, and this chapter will be devoted to the analysis of the systemic functioning of

4. I.e., who would be embarrassed by the episode (cf. Rashi, ad loc.), since the episode would become a negative mark against them.

5. I.e., that inconsequential acts can lead to more drastic, and forbidden, results.

6. It should be noted tangentially that the factors that outweighed the advice of the doctors were also extralegal. According to the position that the woman was married, even a tinge of adulterous behavior outweighed the acceptability of non-normative, and easily misunderstood, behavior. According to the view that the woman was unattached, the possible social-psychological ramifications of compliance with the doctors' advice were judged more detrimental than the consequences of noncompliance. In theory, though, there could have been sages who disagreed with the ruling on the grounds that the tinge of adultery would *not* likely be misunderstood, or that the possible social-psychological ramifications of compliance *were* worth the risk in order to save a life—the latter being itself worth taking risks for.

these categories of data in the resolution of questions of fact in the second sense, in the exercise of judicial discretion, in the adherence to or rejection of precedent, and in the abrogation or modification of norms.[7] While there are instances of overlap between the categories, the division into categories serves, nonetheless, as an indication of the types of concerns the sources reflect. We shall call these categories: (1) medical/scientific; (2) sociological/*realia;* (3) economic; (4) ethical/psychological.

Medical/Scientific Data

The admissibility of medical/scientific evidence in the halakhic system is most clearly and explicitly attested in the sources. Maimonides offers an eloquent rationale for the acceptability of such evidence. Since, as we have already seen, extralegal sources do not determine the law itself, the personal character or the legal qualifications of the doctor or scientist are insignificant factors; what is salient is the specialist's expertise, and nothing else.

After delineating the complex laws that regulate the Jewish calendar, Maimonides writes:[8]

> And the proof for each of these matters is the astronomical and geometric knowledge concerning which the Greek scholars have written many books. . . . And since all of these matters [were substantiated] by clear proofs, which are beyond doubt and incontrovertible, one need not be concerned with the authors—whether they were composed by prophets or by non-Jews *(ha-umot).* For

7. However, see below, pp. 279 ff. The following point, too, bears emphasis: that extralegal sources are admissible as considerations in the decision-making process is a *systemic principle,* i.e., a principle that *governs the process* by which the system works. No extralegal factor, however, can be a *legal principle,* since none is sufficient in and of itself to determine the law in any given case. Caution is urged against confusing *explicit systemic principles* regarding the use of extralegal sources, i.e., principles which can be called by a specific name, such as *Hefsed* or *Nishtannu ha-ittim,* with *legal norms.* The principle of *Hefsed,* for example, can never determine the law. When a sage decides a given case on the basis of the principle of *Hefsed,* he is claiming that in that case the systemic principle that allows the consideration of monetary loss as an extralegal datum is sufficient to warrant the apparent abrogation of a legal norm. The potential confusion arises primarily because the wording of the decision may contain a well-known phrase like *Mi-shum hefsed,* which can lead to mistaking the principle for a legal norm, the applicability of which to the specific case can be objectively determinable. *Implicit systemic principles* regarding extralegal sources are much less likely to be confused with *legal norms* precisely because they are implicit and are not expressed in specified words or phrases that identify them as systemic principles.

8. *Mishneh Torah,* Kiddush ha-Ḥodesh 17:24, quoted by Elon, *Jewish Law,* 3:984 f. See n. 28 there. See, too, Maimonides' *Guide for the Perplexed,* pt. 2, chap. 8, as well as Pesaḥim 94b.

> concerning any matter whose reason has been demonstrated and whose truth has been substantiated by proofs that are beyond doubt, we may rely upon the man who noted them.[9]

What Maimonides is saying is that since the medical/scientific data offered by an expert in the subject are objectively verifiable, the personal character or the legal qualifications of the testifying expert are not significant. Moreover, since neither the expert nor his data determine the law, the sages are clearly entitled to consider the data in the decision-making process, finding it, in the end, either legally germane and relevant or the opposite.

It is the nature of expert opinion that it will function most often in either one of two ways within the halakhic system. It will often be used to answer questions of fact of the second sense (i.e., "any question except a question as to what the law is"),[10] or else it will be used to justify the abrogation or modification of a norm or a matter of precedent when the evidence proves that the norm or precedent had been erroneously decided on the basis of an inaccurate answer to a question of fact. Two talmudic examples will demonstrate these uses of medical/scientific data.

The Talmud records the following:[11]

> Rabbi Elazar the son of Rabbi Ẓadok said: "There were two cases which father brought from Tibin to Yavneh [for adjudication]. One concerned a woman who used to have discharges which appeared like red-colored rinds. And they came and asked father.[12] Father asked the sages, and the sages asked the doctors, who said to them: 'This woman has an internal disorder which causes her to discharge the rindlike discharges. Let her put them in water, and if they [i.e., the clotlike discharges] dissolve, she is ritually unclean.' "[13]

---

9. This translation follows the version of the later printings, which read: *Anu somekhin al zeh ha-ish she-amaro o she-limmedo al ha-re'ayah.* Earlier printings read: *ein somekhin al zeh ha-ish she-amaro o limmedo ella al ha-re'ayah.* The two versions are identical in meaning, viz., that the objective nature of the proof, not the authority of the man himself, accounts for the acceptability of the data.

10. Fitzgerald, *Salmond,* p. 68; and see above p. 52.

11. Niddah 22b. Cf. Tosefta Niddah 4:3 and Yerushalmi Niddah 50c.

12. I.e., whether the blood is to be considered menstrual blood or not. If it is, it induces a state of ritual impurity.

13. If the clots dissolve, it proves that they are congealed menstrual blood. If they do not dissolve, it proves that they are not congealed blood, but some other discharged substance.

The last sentence of this passage is missing in both the Tosefta and the Yerushalmi. Indeed, it seems most plausible that it is not part of the *baraita.* Were it, in fact, part of the

The sages sought clarification from experts on a question of fact in the second sense; that is, they sought data that would help them determine a matter of law: the purity or impurity of the woman in question. In order to reach a legal determination, they sought expert counsel on a question of fact. Without this expert opinion, they could not have determined the matter of law.

The Talmud also records an example of the use of expert opinion that results in the abrogation of a norm. The Mishnah states:[14]

> There was a case concerning a cow whose womb had been removed which Rabbi Tarfon fed to the dogs.[15] The matter came before the sages,[16] and they permitted it, for[17] Todos the doctor had said that no cow or sow is exported from Alexandria unless its womb has been removed, so that it not give birth.[18] Rabbi Tarfon said, "You have forfeited your ass, Tarfon."[19]

Rabbi Tarfon had obviously concluded on the basis of expert opinion that he had made a judicial error, even though his decision must have been based upon something he considered to be a matter of law in the first sense, or else upon a precedent that he followed in the exercise of his judicial discretion.[20] Thus, the extralegal source convinced him

---

baraita, the doctors would, indeed, seem to have made the legal determination in the case, a right they did not possess. It is more reasonable to assume that the last sentence of the passage is a later addition based on the law that the sages ordained on the basis of the doctors' recommendation. That is, the sages observed that the medical test involved soaking the discharges in water to see if they dissolved and deducing from the results whether or not they were menstrual blood. The legal principle based upon this extralegal source is included in Mishnah Niddah 3:1 and may have been transposed from there to the passage in Bavli Niddah.

14. Bekhorot 4:4. See also Sanhedrin 33a.

15. I.e., declared it *terefah* (an animal afflicted with an organic disease and, therefore, unfit for consumption), and disposed of it.

16. The Mishnah in the Bavli Bekhorot and as quoted in Sanhedrin adds, "at Yavneh."

17. Following the reading of Sanhedrin: *she-amar*. The version of the Bavli Bekhorot reads *ve-amar*, which may mean substantially the same thing or else may indicate that the sages had made the legal decision, which was later reaffirmed by the expert opinion of Todos. If the latter is the case, there is no indication of the basis for the sages' decision prior to Todos' statement of fact. The printed editions of the Mishnah read simply *amar*, which leaves the question totally unresolved.

18. A practice instituted by Alexandria to protect its monopoly on a superior species. The fact that animals with their wombs removed lived after the operation indicated that they could not be considered *terefah*, about which the general rule is *terefah einah ḥayyah* ("an animal which is *terefah* cannot live").

19. I.e., he would have to sell his own ass in order to make restitution to the party against whom he had erroneously judged.

20. There exists a third theoretical possibility, namely, that the matter was a question of law in the second sense (i.e., a question as to what the law was), and that Rabbi Tarfon was guided in his decision by what he assumed to be the obvious answer to a question of fact in

beyond all doubt either that the matter of law in the first sense had been erroneously decided on the basis of an inaccurate answer to the question of fact, and that this warranted its abrogation, or that the nonprecedented position (the position he had at first rejected) had to be reconsidered on the basis of the new data and elevated to a matter of law in the first sense on that basis. Indeed, the Mishnah later records as a matter of law in the first sense that the absence of a womb does not make an animal *terefah* (i.e., inedible according to the dietary laws).[21]

In essense, then, an extralegal scientific source allowed a matter of law in the first sense, or a matter of precedent, to revert to a question of law in the second sense, the resolution of which was contingent upon a matter of fact in the second sense.

The use of medical/scientific sources continued throughout the Middle Ages and into the modern period. It is a matter of record that the number of matters of law in the first sense stipulated in the talmudic sources and contradicted either by the expert scientific opinion of later ages or by the personal observation of later sages has produced many problems. How could it be that the talmudic sages had been mistaken? Surely it was not reasonable to suppose that the talmudic sages had misperceived their own reality. It was much more reasonable to surmise that the reality had changed, and once it became acceptable to make such a claim, medical/scientific sources that might result in the abrogation of previously held legal norms could be introduced without impugning the reliability or integrity of the talmudic sages. A new systemic principle, referred to as *Shinnui ha-ittim* ("a changed reality"), became the vehicle that enabled later sages to make use of new medical/scientific knowledge without vitiating the smooth functioning of the halakhic system.[22]

The principle is invoked by the Tosafot.[23] In reference to the *mishnah*

---

the second sense, viz., the potential for such an animal to live. This possibility gains credibility only if we assume that this was the first such case he had ever seen. If, on the other hand, he had seen such cases before and had observed that the animal did not live, he undoubtedly considered the matter as one of law in the first sense.

21. Mishnah Ḥulin 3:2. Note, too, that Rabbi Akiva's response to Rabbi Tarfon (Mishnah Bekhorot 4:4 and Sanhedrin 33a) in no way disputes the admissibility of the extralegal sources or their power to overturn an earlier norm or precedent.

22. In the sociological/*realia* section of this chapter we shall see a similar turn of events. To the modern mind, a claim of *Shinnui ha-ittim* is much less problematic regarding sociological reality than regarding scientific reality. Yet, as we shall see, in certain instances, though not in all, the claim of *Shinnui ha-ittim* can be readily understood as an unsophisticated way of indicating advance in scientific knowledge, or an increased ability to recognize variables probably not noted in earlier eras. To the extent that a reasonable explanation of the recource to *Shinnui ha-ittim* can be made regarding the examples soon to be addressed, we shall attempt to do so.

23. Tosafot Avodah Zarah 24b, s.v. *parah*. Also, cf. Tosafot Ḥulin 47a, s.v. *kol*.

that states that if one buys either a cow or an ass under three years of age from a non-Jew he may be assured that its firstborn under his ownership is also, in truth, the animal's firstborn,[24] and therefore consecrated,[25] the Tosafot wrote:

> The meaning of the *mishnah* is that prior to three years of age the animal could not have given birth. But the claim is surprising, since it is an everyday occurrence that a two-year-old cow gives birth. And one might answer that surely the times have now changed *(attah nishtannah ha-et)* from what they were in earlier generations, as is the case with the little rose-lobe of the lung *(aninuta de-varda),* concerning which it says in chapter *Ellu Terefot,* that all prairie animals have it,[26] implying that nonprairie animals do not have it, and now it is present in all our animals.

The Tosafot affirm on the basis of simple observation that two statements of the Talmud are no longer correct, since times have changed the reality. These changes could, theoretically, result in changes in the application of the laws regarding the sacred nature of firstborn animals, as well as of the *kashrut* (dietary) laws. With regard to the former, the status of an animal as consecrated because it is firstborn becomes doubtful, even though its status is clear according to the Talmud. With regard to *kashrut,* a specific rule that affects the *kashrut* of an animal becomes operative for a class of animals to which, by talmudic implication, it had not been applicable.[27]

Rabbi Moses Isserles makes a similar comment regarding the decision of Rabbi Joseph Caro, recorded in his code,[28] that a pregnant woman whose husband has died is exempt from the law of levirate marriage[29] if she has a live birth, even if the infant dies immediately. Yet, Caro adds, the sages imposed a stringency upon her, exempting her from the levirate law in case of the child's death only if she carried to full term. Regarding this stringency Isserles wrote:[30]

> Some say that in modern times the child is considered viable *(velad kayyama)* even if the woman has carried but one day into the ninth

24. Bekhorot 3:1.
25. Exodus 13:11–13.
26. Ḥulin 47a.
27. Might the Tosafot be referring to the results of a slow evolutionary change and a gradually sensed earlier maturation in animals?
28. *Shulḥan Arukh, Even ha-Ezer* 156:4.
29. Deuteronomy 25:5–10.
30. Rema, *Shulḥan Arukh, Even ha-Ezer* 156:4.

> month, exclusive of the day of impregnation. And though we say in the *gemara* that viable births are possible in the ninth month only when carried to full term *(yoledot le-tishah einah yuledet li-mekuttain)*,[31] many have already expressed wonder at that claim, since experience contradicts it. Rather, we must say that the matter has now changed *(she-akhshav nishtannah ha-inyan)*. And that is the case in several matters.

Isserles utilizes empirical evidence of a medical/scientific nature as grounds for invoking the claim of "a changed reality," which, in turn, results in his abrogation of an earlier legal norm.[32]

Rabbi Abraham ben Ḥayyim ha-Levi Gumbiner (Magen Avraham, 1637–ca. 1683) invokes the same claim regarding a different issue. Caro codifies as a norm that one should wash between eating meat and fish, because eating them together is dangerous *(kasheh)*, causing leprosy *(le-davar aḥer)*.[33] On this passage Gumbiner wrote:

> It is possible that nowadays there is not great danger, for we have seen several things mentioned in the *gemara* as dangerous for an evil spirit and other things, and now they do not harm, for nature has changed *(nishtannu ha-tiviyyot)*. Furthermore, much depends upon the nature of the countries.[34]

Gumbiner reaffirms the applicability of the principle *Shinnui ha-ittim* to a variety of circumstances in which experience has taught that the related medical assumptions of the Talmud are no longer valid. Equally important is his additional comment that because of natural factors like climate and geography, "scientific" realities may vary from locale to locale. Gumbiner's affirmation that objective reality is not necessarily absolute, but dependent upon variables that differ with time and place, further facilitates the use of medical/scientific sources: It allows later

---

31. Rosh ha-Shanah 11a, Yevamot 42a, Niddah 38b.

32. Might there have been greater precision in the ability to calculate the onset of pregnancy in the sixteenth century, or a greater pool of raw data from which to draw conclusions than in talmudic days? Note, too, that the principle that viable births are possible in the ninth month only when carried to term was not universally held even in the Talmud. In each of the passages in n.31 above the Talmud states, "Mar Zutra said, 'Even according to the one who holds that viable births . . .,' " obviously implying that there was another position that denied the principle. Is this a "scientific" *maḥaloket* in which more complete data incline the arbiter to overturn the precedented position?

33. *Shulḥan Arukh, Oraḥ Ḥayyim* 173:2. We have followed Rashi (Pesaḥim 76b) in our translation of *davar aḥer*.

34. *Shulḥan Arukh*, loc. cit.; *Magen Avraham*, par. 1.

sages to assert that a talmudic claim and its contradiction are *both* correct, each for its own locale. In such cases, the integrity of the talmudic source is not impugned, and the radical claim of a universal change in nature is unnecessary.

Of the four categories of extralegal sources, the medical/scientific is the one most likely to cause observers (and, on occasion, even some legalists) to forget that these sources do not determine the law. Since this type of data appears to be more objective than sociological, psychological, or even economic data, there might well be a tendency to overlook the fact that the truth of a scientific fact is also often a matter of *maḥaloket*, as well as a tendency to ignore the fact that scientific evidence may sometimes offer an alternative to precedented legal behavior without at the same time denying the potential of the precedented behavior to lead to the same ultimate result.

An excellent example of legal reasoning that reflects awareness of the limitations of medical/scientific extralegal sources can be found in a passage by Rabbi Israel Lifshitz (Tiferet Yisra'el, 1782–1861).[35] Regarding the affirmation of the Mishnah that one may perform even the sucking of the blood *(meẓiẓah)* during a circumcision on the Sabbath, he wrote:

> He may suck the blood from the wound even though that act causes the blood to flow and creates a new wound.[36] Nonetheless, if he does not suck there is a possible danger that because of the wound, the blood in the flesh of the organ may become hot and congeal, causing a possible swelling of the penis. Yet according to what the doctors say now, the contrary may be true, namely, that there is possible danger because of the *meẓiẓah*. And one should not be astonished by the fact that this is contrary to the *gemara*, for in several matters nature has changed *(nishtannah ha-teva)*.
>
> On the surface, it would seem appropriate to follow their advice in all such matters, for even in matters punishable by *karet* [death by the hand of God] and execution we heed the doctors,[37] even to behave more leniently. How much more so when our concern is only one of possible danger, and they are expert in matters of danger much more than we. Thus, we should be lenient also

35. *Tiferet Yisra'el* (printed in most standard editions of the Mishnah) to Shabbat 19:2, *Yakhin*, no. 15 and *Bo'az*, no. 1.

36. And making a wound is forbidden on the Sabbath.

37. See Shabbat 129a for leniencies on the basis of medical advice in matters of execution, and Yoma 82a and Niddah 22b for matters of *karet* (death by the hand of God). See above, p. 235, and below, p. 257, concerning the reliability of doctors.

concerning the desecration of the Sabbath regarding the need to suck the blood.[38]

> Nonetheless, it seems to me that we should not budge from the words of the sages. . . . Do not the doctors admit that the sucking might prevent the swelling of the organ, except that in the northern lands the danger [of swelling] is not as great as in the warmer climates of the lands of the Fertile Crescent *(arẓot Bavel ha-ḥammim)?* Even so, it is possible that there might be endangerment through swelling. And even though the swelling can be prevented by placing a compress soaked every half-hour in extract or cold water upon the organ, according to the doctors, nonetheless, since they admit that sucking the blood is also effective, we should abide by the words of the sages, of blessed memory. For even concerning matters from the Torah, the early ones *(rishonim)* were careful to do as their teachers had done, even if it made no difference whether they did it that way or another.[39]

The argument of Lifshitz presents a careful blend of the recognition that expert opinion is admissible as a datum in the decision-making process *and* the recognition of the danger that exists in allowing such opinion to determine the law independently of other considerations. He claims, ultimately, that the weight of precedent outweighs the weight of the extralegal sources, since, while they offer an alternative to the precedented position, they do not deny the efficacy of that position. From a legal point of view, therefore, he does not consider the data derived from the extralegal sources sufficiently compelling to overturn the precedent upon which they bore. It might well have been equally tenable to affirm that the advice of the doctors should have been followed, on the legal grounds that doing so would have obviated the necessity of violating the Sabbath unnecessarily.[40]

---

38. That is, we should accept the opinion of the doctors which indicates that sucking the blood could itself be dangerous and adopt a lenient ruling regarding it such that that leniency would allow us to refrain from sucking the circumcision blood on the Sabbath. The result would prevent a desecration of the Sabbath which is allowed by the legal norm, but which is unnecessary in light of the data available from the extralegal medical sources.

39. Cf. the behavior of Rava vis-à-vis the statement of Rav Huna concerning the *shenei tavshilin* (two foodstuffs) on Pesaḥ, in Pesaḥim 114b.

40. Of course, if the soaking or application of the compress is also considered a violation of the Sabbath, and of equal severity as the sucking of the blood, the legal process would favor the precedent over the alternative, since both involve a violation. Clearly, then, the grounds for a systemically legitimate *maḥaloket* here are many. Lifshitz reaffirms the precedent, even though it mandates a violation of the Sabbath. But one could reaffirm the precedent on the grounds that both it and the alternative require a violation of the

The use of medical/scientific data as extralegal sources for the resolution of questions of fact or as grounds for the abrogation or modification of norms or the overturning of precedent presents little systemic difficulty so long as the norms they affect are not systemically considered part of the *grundnorm* itself (i.e., *de-oraita*) or are not systemically incontrovertible, like *Halakhah le-Mosheh mi-Sinai.* A claim of *Shinnui ha-ittim* is defensible provided only that the source of the contested data is not God Himself.[41] When a claim of *Shinnui ha-ittim* affects a norm that is *de-oraita* or that is *Halakhah le-Mosheh mi-Sinai,* it becomes a very great problem.

There is another problem that arises from the admissibility of the claim of *Shinnui ha-ittim.* Legal norms grounded in medical/scientific facts are presumably based upon the observation that the relevant facts apply in the vast majority of cases, but not necessarily in all. Thus, for example, it would be patently absurd to contend that *meẓiẓah* always prevented infections after circumcision. The most that could be reasonably claimed is that it often did so. If new medical/scientific evidence indicated that *meẓiẓah* was no longer to be considered a reasonably effective preventive, at what point would that evidence be likely to be considered sufficient to overturn the precedent requiring it? Would it have to be demonstrated to be totally ineffective, ineffective in a majority of cases, ineffective in a significant number of cases? There are, after all, many laws designed to protect a small number of people from *potential* danger. In a majority of circumcisions no infection would result even without *meẓiẓah;* it is performed in order to prevent infection in a minority of cases. If medical/scientific extralegal sources indicated that it was ineffective as a preventative in a majority of the minority, but remained effective in a minority of the minority, would we say that the legal norm requiring it is contraindicated by the new evidence? Might it not be equally plausible to claim that the norm remains, since it was instituted to protect a minority, and still does so?

Rabbi Moses Schick (Maharam Schick, 1807–1879) attempts to grapple

---

Sabbath; or one could overturn the precedent on the grounds that the alternative does not violate the Sabbath and the precedent does; or one could overturn the precedent on the grounds that the alternative, while violating the Sabbath, need be employed only if swelling actually occurs, while the precedent mandates a violation of the Sabbath as a preventative measure, not dependent on actual swelling of the organ.

41. This comment is made in its theologically simplest form, attributing the *grundnorm* to God. It is almost as difficult to make the claim, however, even if human authorship of the *grundnorm* is affirmed. The restrictions on amending or abrogating the *grundnorm* (see above, chap. 7) would have to apply, as well, to abrogations motivated by scientific/medical sources.

with both of the aforementioned problems in one of his responsa.[42] He writes:

> The principle is that the claim of *Shinnui ha-ittim* is inapplicable in two circumstances: (1) One cannot claim *Shinnui ha-ittim* in a matter which is *Halakhah le-Mosheh mi-Sinai,* for the words of our Lord are forever valid. . . . And if it is the case that God would know if there were destined to be a time at which the nature of a thing would change, how could He have handed that matter over as a *Halakhah le-Mosheh mi-Sinai?* Perforce it must be the case either that its nature has not changed or that, even if it has, the prohibition stands. For example, it is impossible for the eighteen indicators of *terefah,* which are *Halakhah le-Mosheh mi-Sinai,*[43] to have changed. And even if we perceive a change, namely, that the animal does continue to live, even though our sages, of blessed memory, have said that a *terefah* animal cannot live, it proves only that the indicators of *terefah* are not contingent upon the ability of the animal to continue to live. Thus, even if it does live, the absence of one of these organs or the presence of one of these defects renders it *terefah.* And the proof of this fact is that there were sages, of blessed memory, who affirmed that a *terefah* animal might live.

Schick's resolution to the first problem is very clever. Our perception of change in the nature of things that are *Halakhah le-Mosheh mi-Sinai* is predicated on the assumption that we have correctly grasped the underlying commonality among the members of the class covered by it. For example, we assume that the indicators of *terefah* all share the characteristic that they prevent the animal from prolonged life. Our perception that that fact is inaccurate, says Schick, proves only that we have misidentified the common characteristic, and does not prove that the nature of anything has changed. Thus, the law remains unchanged, because it was undoubtedly based on something other than our first presumption. Schick clearly stresses, by recalling that the ability of a *terefah* animal to live is a matter of *maḥaloket,* that the definition of the common factor of the members of the class is not itself *Halakhah le-Mosheh mi-Sinai,* but the result of human understanding. Thus, since God could surely not have commanded something the nature of which He knew would change, it must be the case that human understanding is erroneous—the command eternally valid.

42. *Responsa of Maharam Schick* (Munkács, 1881), *Yoreh De'ah,* no. 244.

43. Ḥulin 42a.

Regarding the second issue, Rabbi Schick continues:

> (2) Regarding the law of the Torah we follow the presumption.[44] And all the laws of the Torah are based *(meyussadim)* upon majority and presumption.[45] Therefore, since we know that a fact was thus-and-so at the time that it was transmitted to us, the law remains as it was by virtue of the presumption;—i.e., the presumption that it [i.e., the fact] did not change—except if it is clear to us that it has changed. . . .
>
> Therefore, this principle [of *Shinnui ha-ittim*] applies to a matter for which the majority is sufficient and which is not a *Halakhah le-Mosheh mi-Sinai.* Thus, the principle applies if experience *(ha-nissayon)* certifies *(me'id)* that the matter has changed in a majority of cases, and the matter is neither a *Halakhah le-Mosheh mi-Sinai* nor a doubtful case of *Halakhah le-Mosheh mi-Sinai,* nor a matter that is not governed by majority *(davar she-ẓerikhin laḥush affilu le-mi'uta).* In the final circumstance it is impossible to decide that the matter has changed, since, perhaps, for the minority it has not changed. In that case, the presumption stands.

If new medical/scientific evidence indicates that a norm no longer applies to a majority of cases, and the norm itself was grounded in earlier medical/scientific evidence that it did apply to a majority of cases, the extralegal sources allow the reopening of the question of the factual basis upon which the norm was predicated. In such a case, the extralegal sources allow the norm to be overturned by the claim of *Shinnui ha-ittim* if the evidence is strong enough. If, however, the norm was not based upon its applicability to the majority, the medical/scientific sources do not warrant its abrogation, provided it may still apply to some minority, no matter how small.

Consistent with his own theory, Maharam Schick takes exception to the view of Gumbiner quoted above[46] on the grounds that since the issue there was one of the prevention of possible endangerment (i.e., *Pikku'aḥ nefesh*), and since such regulations are not contingent upon the majority, the presumptive applicability of the norm ought to remain.

There are several possible conclusions to be deduced from the ap-

---

44. The *prima facie* presumption is that the law remains valid and unchanged.

45. I.e., most laws, particularly of a scientific nature, are based on their applicability to the majority, and that applicability continues to be *presumed* as applicable to the majority.

46. P. 239.

parently opposing views of Schick and Gumbiner. First, of course, is the possibility that Schick's contention is a matter of *maḥaloket*. It is also possible that Gumbiner understood the danger involved in eating meat followed by fish to be applicable to a majority of cases, and that fact, therefore, was the salient consideration for him. Finally, it is conceivable that the Magen Avraham understood the extralegal sources to indicate that the danger no longer existed at all, not even for a minority. Thus, even according to Schick, the weight of extralegal sources would permit a decision to abrogate the norm.

Before proceeding to an analysis of the next category of extralegal sources, we must backtrack for a moment in order to introduce a new and important element to the theme of this chapter. At the beginning of this book we drew the distinction between the legal and the historical sources of norms. The basic claim was that legal sources are those recognized by the system itself and that historical sources lack such recognition. That is, we asserted that historical sources may influence the promulgation of norms but have no real legal authority except if they are actually incorporated into the legal system through its norms. Moreover, once incorporated, a historical source becomes legally insignificant to the legal authority of the very norm the promulgation of which it so influenced. At the same time, we saw that the distinction between historical and legal sources is not as neat and precise as the definitions we offered would seem to indicate. Indeed, we noted then that it would be necessary at one point to analyze the question of the nexus between the historical and legal sources of the law.[47] We have now begun to touch upon that question.

It is clear that medical/scientific data provided by extralegal sources constituted the historical sources of the norms that we have discussed thus far in this chapter. In other words, these data influenced the promulgation into the halakhic system as legal norms of the very norms which we have seen abrogated in the examples we have dealt with thus far. Now, were the distinction between the historical and legal sources neat and precise—that is, if the historical sources did, indeed, fade into complete legal insignificance after the norms whose promulgation they influenced were actually incorporated into the legal system—we should be forced to claim that the scientific reality that gave rise to any norm would be totally irrelevant to any future question that might arise regarding the application of the norm. Yet clearly, in virtually all of the examples we have considered thus far, the abrogation of the norms in

47. See above, p. 11.

question was justified on grounds of denying the factualness of the historical sources that gave rise to them in the first place. That is, in the examples in this chapter it was assumed that some kind of nexus continues to exist between historical and legal sources, and that historical sources can and sometimes do remain legally relevant even after the norms whose promulgation they influenced were actually incorporated into the legal system.

A preliminary observation with regard to the issue of nexus: It seems reasonable to posit that the historical sources of a norm remain legally significant only when these sources are not simply the specific historical impetus behind the promulgation of the norm, but also continue to be the entire *raison d'être* of the norm. For example, the norm requiring washing between the eating of meat and fish arose solely as a result of the perception that eating them together was dangerous. Moreover, that danger continued to be the only justification for the existence of the norm; that is, the norm seemed incapable of cogent reinterpretation on any other grounds, at least according to Gumbiner. Similarly, the legal norms that trace their origin to the perception that *Yoledet le-tishah einah yoledet li-mekutta'in* ("viable births are possible in the ninth month only when carried to term") continue to be justifiable only if the scientific data, their historical source, continue to be true. Should the historical source become demonstrably inaccurate, no other justification for the derivate norms seems either possible or cogent.

This idea finds support in the words of the Palestinian *amora,* Rabbi Abba bar Memel, who said:[48]

> If I had someone who would join with me *(she-yimmaneh immi)*[49] I would permit the flesh of [maimed] firstborn animals to be sold in small quantities *(lehishakel be-litra)*[50] and I would permit work to be done on *ḥol ha-mo'ed.*[51] Did they [i.e., the sages] not forbid the meat of firstborn animals to be sold in small quantities in order that it be sold cheaply?[52] Yet they [i.e., the priests] deal deceitfully *(ma'arimin alav)* and sell it at expensive prices. Did they [i.e., the sages] not

48. Yerushalmi Mo'ed Katan 2:3, 81b.

49. The hesitancy of Rabbi Abba to take the actions he advocates should be attributed to the natural reticence of a sage to take radical steps unilaterally, and not to any feeling on his part that the principle implied by his statement is systemically invalid. See below, n. 55.

50. Mishnah Bekhorot 5:1. Rabbi Abba stipulates the reason for the prohibition immediately.

51. That is, all manner of work, not only work necessitated by irretrievable loss.

52. So that undue profit not accrue to the priests. Therefore, they allowed the private sale of the animal in bulk, and forbade the sale of smaller, but more costly, quantities.

> forbid work on *ḥol ha-mo'ed* in order that people might have leisure to eat, drink, and study the Torah? Yet they [i.e., the people] eat, drink, and make merry.

Surely Rabbi Abba is contending that the historical sources of the prohibitive norms have remained the sole *raison d'être* for their continued observance. Since these historical reasons have ceased to be operative, the ground is set for the possible elevation of the historical sources of these norms to legal significance.

Nevertheless, even if one were to assume as demonstrable, for example, that the historical sources of *kashrut* lay in considerations of health, fundamental changes in the norms of *kashrut* on the basis of changed scientific reality would involve an unwarranted confusion of historical and legal sources. Since *kashrut* regulations have received regular and cogent reinterpretations and justification,[53] advocating their abrogation on the basis that the reality that originally dictated their promulgation no longer obtained would indicate a failure to recognize that the original reality, the historical source of the norms, has *not* remained the sole justification for their observance.[54] Reasoning based on such a failure to distinguish between the original rationale and present interpretations is referred to as the "genetic fallacy." In other words, an argument based on the genetic fallacy entails the unwarranted intrusion of historical sources into the legal decision-making process.[55]

In the end, it is clear that we must reaffirm the centrality of the principle *Ein la-dayyan ella mah she-einav ro'ot* in the halakhic system.[56] An

---

53. Such as (1) self-discipline, (2) the recognition of God's concern for even the mundane acts of man, and (3) sensitivity to man's exercise of human control over animals for his own needs.

54. This contention should not be misconstrued as indicating that specific norms of *kashrut* might not be subject to a claim of changed reality. For example, only the continued absence of the little-rose lobe of the lung in certain animals justifies the nonapplication of a specific norm of *kashrut* to that class. Thus, advocating a change in the law on that basis does not represent an unwarranted intrusion of historical sources into the legal system, those historical sources have remained the sole justification for the specific norm.

55. It is possible that Rabbi Abba (above, p. 246) found no support for his position for one or more of a variety of reasons. Perhaps his colleagues understood the historical sources of the norms differently. Perhaps, for example, they understood that the prohibition against selling the meat of firstborn animals was based on the idea of disrespect for sacred objects (see Zevaḥim 75b and the comment of Israel Eisenstein in his commentary, *Ammudei Yerushalayim* [printed in standard editions of the Yerushalmi], to Mo'ed Katan *ad loc.*). Perhaps, though, they might have agreed with his interpretation of the historical sources, yet felt that they were not the sole ongoing justification for the norms, that is, that Rabbi Abba's contention was an instance of the genetic fallacy.

56. See above, pp. 85 ff.

arbiter can be guided, ultimately, only by his own perceptions in attempting to determine whether an accepted reinterpretation of the justification for a legal norm is cogent enough to make the abrogation of the norm on the grounds of a changed reality an instance of the genetic fallacy. Should he find the reinterpretation totally lacking in cogency, he would affirm that the original reason still remains the sole systemic justification of the norm, and his advocacy of its abrogation would not be an instance of the genetic fallacy. Ultimately, therefore, the presence or absence of the genetic fallacy could itself be a matter of legitimate *maḥaloket*.

Another preliminary observation: The nexus between extralegal and legal sources that we have been describing necessarily proceeds from the present to the past, not from the past to the present. When an arbiter is confronted with a question of law in the second sense, he may correctly perceive that a given legal norm appears applicable to the situation. Yet he may perceive, too, that the scientific reality of his period does not seem to correspond with the scientific reality on which the norm was based. If he does perceive this, he would then be compelled to analyze the original historical sources of the norm in order to determine whether they have remained the norm's sole justification and, depending on the answer, whether the norm is or is not applicable to the question of law in the second sense.

In actual practice, legal norms are presumed to be applicable. As Maharam Schick states in the second selection quoted, it is those who want to change the norm who must prove its inapplicability: ". . . the law remains as it was by virtue of the presumption, i.e., the presumption that it [i.e., the fact] did not change, except if it is clear to us that it has changed."[57] Such a presumption is overturned only by a real confrontation between present reality and the reality on which the norm was based.

Sociological/Realia Data

Extralegal sources of a sociological/*realia* nature that are judged legally significant share one fundamental characteristic with those of a medical/scientific nature. Both are predicated upon a changed reality. As we have noted (above, p. 237), however, in the sociological/*realia* realm, the nature, measurement, and possible legal implications of the change are not nearly as objectifiable as in the medical/scientific realm. By virtue of this fact alone it follows that the grounds for the existence of a *maḥaloket*,

57. Above, pp. 244 f.

resulting, quite probably, in the legitimate exercise of judicial discretion, are far greater when dealing with the extralegal sources of this nature than when dealing with more objective medical/scientific data.

Yet for all of its complexities, the use of sociological/*realia* data as an extralegal source of law is clearly demonstrable in the halakhic sources. An example from the Talmud and several from later sources will attest to this, while at the same time also demonstrating the complexities involved in the consideration of such data, caused by their relative nonobjectifiability.

The Talmud records the following:[58]

> At first, when the intention of those who performed levirate marriage *(yibbum)* was the fulfillment of the *miẓvah,* levirate marriage was preferable to *ḥaliẓah.*[59] But now that their intention is not the fulfillment of the *miẓvah, ḥaliẓah* is preferable to levirate marriage.
>
> Rami bar Ḥama said in the name of Rabbi Yiẓḥak, "They reversed themselves and claimed *(ḥazeru lomar)* that levirate marriage takes precedence over *ḥaliẓah.*" Rav Naḥman bar Yiẓḥak said to him, "Have the generations improved *(akhshorei darei)?*" Originally[60] they [i.e., the sages] held the view of Abba Saul, and ultimately[61] they affirmed the position of the sages.[62] As we have learned:[63] "Abba Saul said, 'He who weds his sister-in-law *(yevimto)* because of her beauty *(le-shem noi),* or because he would have liked to have her as a wife *(le-shem ishut),* or because of sexual attraction *(le-shum davar aḥer)*[64] is as one who has had an illicit relationship *(poge'a be-ervah),* and I would be inclined to consider the offspring a *mamzer* [illegitimate].' But the sages said, ' "Her brother-in-law should have relations with her"[65] implies having relations, regardless of the motivation *(mi-kol makom).*' "

58. Yevamot 39b, based on Mishnah Bekhorot 1:7.

59. Deuteronomy 25:5–10. *Yibbum* refers to the actual marriage, and *ḥaliẓah* to the shoe-removal ceremony that dissolves the relationship between the woman and her brother-in-law.

60. I.e., when they advocated *ḥaliẓah* above *yibbum.*

61. I.e., when they reaffirmed the preference for *yibbum.*

62. I.e., those who dispute Abba Saul in the *baraita* to be quoted immediately.

63. Tosefta Yevamot 6:9.

64. Such a meaning would be consistent with the meaning of *davar aḥer* in the Talmud in general. The wording of the Tosefta (6:9), however, *le-shem nekhasim* ("for the sake of possessions"), and a parallel in the Yerushalmi (Yevamot 1:1, 2b), *le-shem devarim aḥerim* ("for the sake of other things"), indicated that its meaning here might be "for other [presumably economic] reasons." See Saul Lieberman, *Tosefta Kifshuta,* ad loc.

65. Deuteronomy 25:5.

This passage has several elements of importance. First, the original norm, which preferred levirate marriage to *ḥaliẓah,* was predicated on the observation that such marriages were usually contracted in order to comply with the intent of the *miẓvah.*[66] When the sages perceived that there had been a change in the sociological reality, that is, that the marriages could no longer be assumed to have been contracted with the intent of complying with the *miẓvah,* they changed the norm, giving preference to *ḥaliẓah* over actual levirate marriage. Rami bar Ḥama, without denying that the sages had, in fact, changed the norm, affirmed that they had later reversed themselves, reinstituting the original norm. Rav Naḥman apparently understood that the reversal was predicated on yet another sociological change, but his own perception of the sociological reality was at variance with the reality implied by the reversal. Thus, he asked: Has there been a sociological change that would warrant reinstituting the original norm?

Clearly, then, the *mishnah,* Rami bar Ḥama, and Rav Naḥman all recognize the legitimacy of overturning a previously accepted norm and of accepting in its place a previously rejected or nonprecedented position, on the basis of a changed sociological reality.[67] Indeed, they even recognize that there can be a succession of changes on that basis. Rav Naḥman simply contests the apparent perception that there had, in fact, been such a change in the sociological reality.

The final statement of the Talmud affirms the perception of Rav Naḥman and explains the ultimate reversal of the sages' position on legal-technical grounds. In other words, having first affirmed the position of Abba Saul, they later rejected his position and, in the exercise of their judicial discretion, affirmed the position of those who disagreed with Abba Saul.

Since the Talmud is itself silent regarding the reason for the change of position on the part of the sages, from the view of Abba Saul to the view of those who disputed him, this question can be answered only on the basis of reasonable conjecture. One possibility, of course, is that the sages found some legal flaw in Abba Saul's position, a flaw that had previously gone unnoticed. While it is theoretically possible, this thesis is not very strong.[68]

---

66. To perpetuate the name of the deceased husband. See Deuteronomy 25:6–7.

67. For examples of a similar nature see Avodah Zarah 31a, Sanhedrin 25b, and Ḥulin 93b.

68. First of all, the possible legal flaw is, clearly, not immediately discernible. Indeed, were it so, it would be difficult to comprehend why it had not been noted earlier. Secondly, if the flaw were present, even if not self-evident, it is most probable that the sages would have indicated what the flaw was, if only in order to elevate the position of the sages in the

Much more probable (although admittedly still conjectural) is the likelihood that the same sociological change that resulted in the decrease in the number of those who performed levirate marriage with the intention of fulfilling the *mizvah* also resulted in the decision of the sages to opt for a previously rejected legal position. When the number of levirate marriages that verged on the illicit was small, it was possible to castigate those who entered into such relationships without calling into question the legitimacy of the vast majority of levirate marriages. When the numbers were reversed, however, a legal position was affirmed that recognized the majority of the marriages as valid. Since they could not prevent those marriages from taking place, they felt it was better to recognize them than to cast aspersions on the marriages and on their resultant offspring.[69]

The type of sociological change we see in this example is one in which behavior is perceived to be different now from what it had been previously. In this specific case the change in the nature of the behavior is indicated by a change in the nature of the intention of those concerned when entering upon a levirate marriage. Recourse to such sociological considerations persists throughout the development of the *halakhah*, and further examples will not only verify that fact, but will also indicate the wide range of halakhic concerns on which these data have been brought to bear.

Rabbi Solomon ben Abraham Adret (Rashba, ca. 1235–1310) wrote the following:[70]

> Concerning your surprise at having heard in the name of Rashi, of blessed memory, that *Aneinu* is not recited at the evening service prior to the onset of the fast, lest something unavoidable happen and one eat, making the prayer [i.e., *Aneinu*] a lie,[71] and you claim that it says in the Yerushalmi: "It [i.e., *Aneinu*] is said as on Sabbath

---

Abba Saul *baraita* to a matter of law in the first sense. The Talmud's silence on the subject allows Abba Saul's position to remain legitimately within the realm of judicial discretion.

69. It is further likely that the phrase "they reversed themselves and claimed that levirate marriage takes precedence over *halizah*" is so stated in order to present it as a literary parallel to the original norm, since the sages surely would not have *favored* levirate marriage that was "*not* for the sake of the *mizvah*." Or, alternatively, it is possible that the "they reversed themselves" statement reflects a second stage of development. That is to say, after adopting the position of the sages in the Abba Saul *baraita*, it was only natural, after a while, to reaffirm the primacy of *yibbum* over *halizah*, since that is the clear indication of the Torah itself.

70. *Responsa of Rashba*, pt. 1, no. 142.

71. Since the paragraph begins: "Answer us on this day of our fasting."

eves and Sabbath day."[72] And if the concern is for unavoidable circumstances, the Merciful One has exonerated him.[73]

What you have stated in the name of Rashi, of blessed memory, is correct. Indeed, he made that claim not only concerning the evening service, but concerning the evening and the morning service—until the afternoon service. Yet it was not his intention to disagree with the Yerushalmi or with the *baraita* which is quoted in the second chapter of Shabbat:[74] "Days on which no additional sacrifice is brought, like the Monday-Thursday-Monday fasts[75] and the *ma'amadot*,[76] an appropriate addition *(me-ein ha-me'ora)*[77] is inserted into the *shome'a tefillah* benediction of the *Amidah* in the evening, morning, and afternoon." Rather, he [i.e., Rashi], of blessed memory, gave a reason for his view, namely, that weakness *(ḥulsha)* has become more prevalent, and it has become more likely that one would have to eat. Therefore, one should not have sufficient trust in himself[78] to mention the special occasion[79] in his recitation of the *Amidah*.

At any rate, we do not act according to Rashi vis-à-vis the morning and afternoon services. But all act according to his statement concerning the evening service, the *baraita* and the Yerushalmi notwithstanding. . . . In all such matters, see how the people act, and do accordingly *(puk ḥazei mah ẓibbur noheg u-nehog ken)*.

Rashi, based upon the *ge'onim*, and followed in part by the Rashba, advocates a ritual practice at apparent variance with the Talmud. The

---

72. Yerushalmi Berakhot 4:3, 8a. Rabbi Jonah said in the name of Rav that even an individual who decreed a fast upon himself is obligated to recite *Aneinu*. The Talmud, apparently, then asks at what point in the *Amidah* it is to be recited, to which R. Ze'ira answers in the name of Rav Huna, "As on Sabbath eves and Sabbath day." (The answer seems to imply that *Aneinu* is recited in the fourth benediction, as are the specially inserted prayers [e.g., *Ya'aleh ve-yavo*] on the Sabbath. The answer is problematic, since it implies that *Aneinu* is recited during the *attah ḥonen* benediction. See Louis Ginzberg, *A Commentary on the Palestinian Talmud* [New York: Jewish Theological Seminary, 1941], 3:298–302, on the entire passage.)

At any rate, the passage implies that *Aneinu* is to be recited on the eve of the fast as well as during the day.

73. Thus, why should not *Aneinu* be recited on fast-days even at the evening service?

74. Shabbat 24a. See Rashi *ad loc.*, s.v. *arvit*, in the name of the *ge'onim*.

75. Mishnah Ta'anit 1:4, and Bavli Ta'anit 10a.

76. Mishnah Ta'anit 4:2–3. The men of the *ma'amad* (singular of *ma'amadot*) fasted from Monday through Thursday.

77. I.e., the *Aneinu* prayer.

78. That he will be able to complete the fast.

79. I.e., to recite *Aneinu*.

grounds for the change rest on the changed nature of human beings, that is, their inability to fast as easily or for as prolonged a period as they had previously been able to do. The assumptions and the legal logic of Rashi's argument can be summarized as follows: (1) Prayers that probably incorporate lies ought not to be recited; (2) the statement that unavoidable circumstances that might result in belying a prayer do not warrant its nonrecitation assumes that such unavoidable circumstances will arise only rarely; (3) if the sociological reality is such that these unavoidable circumstances are likely to arise frequently, then the recitation of a "false" prayer is to be avoided, even if such avoidance necessitates the abrogation of a norm. Therefore, (4) since the present reality is such that the recitation of *Aneinu* at the evening and the morning service is likely to be belied before the legal end of the fast, it should be recited only in those circumstances in which its becoming "false" is unlikely to occur, namely, at the afternoon service alone.

The original sociological reality that gave rise to the original norm, and on which basis alone the norm continued to be justifiable, became the underlying assumption of the norm. When a changed sociological reality vitiated this assumption, the new sociological reality permitted the historical sources of the original norm to become legally relevant and to influence the determination of the law.

Although our concern with the Rashba has been primarily with regard to his explanation of Rashi's view on sociological grounds, his conclusion is also interesting insofar as it highlights one element of the complexity of determining the legal significance of sociological data. The Rashba affirms that Rashi's logic is cogent and defensible; yet he also is aware that people in general do not restrict their recitation of *Aneinu* to the afternoon service, but recite it in the morning as well. The question confronting him is whether to attempt to force total compliance with Rashi's position or not. He concludes that it is not necessary to attempt to force such total compliance, since the behavior of the people already reflects the changed sociological reality by virtue of its having eliminated the recitation of *Aneinu* at the evening service. If the Rashba's conclusion were to be expressed as a *maḥaloket* between himself and Rashi, it could be expressed thus: It is clear that the changed sociological reality makes the recitation of *Aneinu* at the evening service unwarranted. It is also clear that it should be recited at the afternoon service, since the likelihood of its becoming "false" is minimal. Regarding the morning service, there is a chance that *Aneinu* will become "false," but that chance is not so great as to dictate attempting to force a change in the people's behavior.

We have referred earlier, in a different context, to a statement of Rabbi

Me'ir ben Baruch of Rothenburg that also reflects the use of sociological data as an extralegal source of law in the decision-making process.[80] Regarding the acceptability of a woman's claim that her husband could not achieve an erection, he wrote:

> Concerning any matter about which he would know for certain, she would not lie, as, for example, the presumption that a woman would not be audacious enough to claim that he had divorced her.[81] Thus, in this case, too, she should be believed. But in these times, when there are lewd women, she should not be believed.

Although an explanation of this passage has already been offered, we can now refine it further. Because Rabbi Me'ir of Rothenburg perceived the sociological reality of his own time to be different from that reflected in the underlying assumption of the law, he was moved to reopen the question of the factualness of the original assumption (illustrating, incidentally, how the nexus between historical and legal sources of the law proceeds from the present to the past). Moreover, when he concluded that the continuing factualness of the original assumption had remained the sole justification for the norm, the nexus between the extralegal and legal sources of the law was created, and the extralegal sociological sources were permitted to become legally relevant. Ultimately, therefore, he overturned a norm that had been based upon an assumption now found to be no longer capable of being assumed and, therefore, no longer applicable.

Rabbi Moses Isserles (Rema, 1525–1572) invoked a change in the nature of human beings as a salient consideration in the resolution of a question of law.[82] He wrote:

> When the early authorities *(rishonim)* wrote that an oath made in jest *(neder shel ẓeḥok)* cannot be annulled, it applied only to their own time, when they had self-restraint and self-control. But if they [i.e., the earlier generation] were as people, we are as asses.[83] And in such cases the judge can be guided only by his perception regarding the man who took the oath *(ve-ein la-dayyan ba-zeh ella mah she-einav ro'ot be-ish ha-noder)*. . . . If it seems to the sages of your locale or to you that the matter is likely to involve undesirable results *(she-karov*

80. *Responsa of Rabbi Me'ir of Rothenburg,* Crimona ed. (1557), no. 271. See above, p. 65.
81. See above, chap. 3, n. 34.
82. *Responsa of Rema,* Ziv ed., no. 103, p. 440.
83. Shabbat 112b.

> *ha-davar le-vi'at mikhshol)*, that the one who took the oath is likely to violate it without hesitation, surely that reason justifies annulling it for him.

The developments reflected in this passage can be summarized in the following way: Both earlier and later authorities agree that legal norms about oaths should reflect the seriousness with which oaths should be considered. In order to ensure that oaths should be neither made nor violated lightly, earlier authorities refused to allow the simple annulment of oaths taken in jest. The idea was that when those who had taken such oaths saw that they could not be exempted from complying with them, they would come to recognize the seriousness of oaths, and in the future would exercise self-control and restraint; that is, they would not make such oaths. The logic of this claim is cogent provided one can be reasonably certain of two factors: (1) that those who had been refused annulment of oaths taken in jest would, in fact, then comply with them rather than disregard them; and (2) that after having been forced to comply with oaths they had not seriously intended, they would be able to exercise the self-restraint necessary to refrain from making such oaths in the future.

Were either, or both, of these factors demonstrably false, an order to comply with an oath taken in jest would surely fail to engender the desired attitude, the engenderment of which alone justifies the refusal to annul. That is, one who took an oath in jest and disregarded it, or who could not exercise the necessary self-control to refrain from taking another and disregarding it, too, would surely not find a serious attitude toward oaths reinforced by his behavior. The ultimate aim of emphasizing the seriousness of oaths would be better served by annulling the oath taken in jest; at least the one who took the oath might begin to understand the significance of serious oaths. Were he not exempted from compliance with the oath taken in jest, but instead forced to disregard it, the attitude of disregard would carry over to all oaths.

Isserles, clearly, perceived that the sociological reality of his day demanded that the norm forbidding the annulment of oaths made in jest be abrogated. Since the sole reasonable justification for the norm no longer obtained, the extralegal sources of a sociological nature were permitted to become legally significant, creating again the nexus between the historical and the legal sources of the law.

A passage from the writings of Rabbi Israel Lifshitz (Tiferet Yisra'el, 1782–1861) makes a particularly instructive conclusion to our demonstration of the use of this kind of sociological data. First, it demonstrates the continued use of such data even into the modern period. Second, it marks a transition to the next category of sociological data to be discussed. Third, and perhaps most important of all, it demonstrates that extralegal sources can be used not only to make the law more lenient, but also to make it more restrictive.

Referring to the statement of the Mishnah that an ill person can be fed on Yom Kippur if a specialist (i.e., a doctor) states that fasting would be dangerous for him,[84] and after quoting from the *Shulḥan Arukh* to the effect that the specialist can even be a non-Jew,[85] Lifshitz wrote:

> It seems to me that now we must rethink *(lehityashev)* the matter. For I have seen with my own eyes that they [i.e., the doctors] have lost their reliability, for they say about every nonserious illness that if one fasts he will endanger himself.[86]

Lifshitz had perceived what he took to be a sociological change in the behavior of doctors, namely, that they now deemed that every illness constituted a possible danger to life should the ill person fast. The purpose of the original norm—to safeguard the fast against all but cases of real and probable danger to the one who was fasting—was perverted. Whether the doctors began to define "danger" as "possible danger" rather than "probable danger," or whether they began to view any fasting as resulting in "probable danger," Lifshitz could no longer accept their opinions as sufficient to waive the obligation to fast on Yom Kippur. Only the existence of the earlier sociological reality, in which doctors distinguished between serious and nonserious illnesses, justified the acceptance of their statements as grounds for waiving the legal requirement to fast. The new sociological reality, on the other hand, demanded the abrogation of the norm that relied on the evidence of doctors, an abrogation that resulted not in greater leniency but, rather, in greater restriction, in order to reinforce the intention of the original norm.

Equally interesting is the comment added by his son:

> We see today that Jewish doctors, the majority of whom, because of our great sins, deny our holy Torah, wantonly advise flagrant disregard regarding prohibited foods and fast-days, even more than non-Jews.[87]

---

84. Yoma 8:5.
85. Caro, *Shulḥan Arukh, Oraḥ Ḥayyim* 618:1.
86. *Tiferet Yisra'el* to Yoma 8:5, *Yakhin*, letter *kaf-vav.*
87. Barukh Lifshitz in *Hilkheta Gevirta* (printed in standard editions of the Mishnah), Yoma, end of chap. 8.

Lifshitz's son points to yet another new sociological reality of potential legal significance. The acceptance of the testimony of Jewish doctors had been predicated on the assumption that even if they themselves were not committed to *halakhah*, neither were they determined to undermine it. When the nature of their statements began to indicate that they were abusing their systemically recognized right to offer expert testimony, this new sociological reality allowed the nexus of historical and legal sources to become legally significant, resulting in the adoption of a stricter norm than before.

The selections from both Lifshitz and his son reaffirm the fact that expert testimony, although systemically recognized as admissible, is not determinative. Only *posekim* can determine the law.

Thus far in this chapter we have demonstrated the use, within the halakhic system, of sociological data that reflect a change in the nature of man and/or his behavior. Sociological change, however, is not limited to changes of this type. There are data that reflect changes in the nature of the *realia* of a society, the physical, social, and political conditions under which it operates. These data, too, have been consistently invoked as legally significant by halakhists from the post-talmudic to the modern period.

The Talmud records that a man ought not to betroth his minor daughter until she grows old enough to indicate the man whom she would prefer.[88] Commenting on the fact that the custom during the Middle Ages was at variance with the Talmud's dictate, the Tosafot wrote:

> And now that we regularly betroth even our minor daughters, the reason is that each and every day the onus of the Diaspora becomes more and more burdensome *(ha-galut mitgabber aleinu)*, and if a man is able to provide a dowry for his daughter now, he may not be able to do so later, and his daughter will remain unmarried *(teshev agunah)* forever.[89]

The passage from the Tosafot employs three different types of extralegal considerations, namely, sociological, economic, and ethical (the second and third have not yet been addressed). The Tosafot are claiming that the sociopolitical conditions under which the Jews lived at the time of the promulgation of the norm were such that compliance with the

88. Kiddushin 41a.
89. Tosafot *ad loc.*, s.v. *asur.*

norm was both reasonable and beneficial to them. Indeed, only the continued presence of such beneficial results could justify continued compliance with the norm. If conditions were such that compliance proved harmful, then compliance was no longer justified; better that a girl should be betrothed as a minor than that she suffer the possibility of remaining unmarried. In other words, when the reality of their sociopolitical situation made compliance with the norm result in a situation that was the very opposite of the norm's original intention (and which had remained its sole justification), the grounds for the nexus between the historical and the legal sources of the law were again prepared, the historical sources assumed legal significance and created a situation that permitted the abrogation of the precedented norm.[90]

The Talmud records[91] a list of "offenses" for which Rav had the offenders flogged.[92] The list included, according to one version, one who betrothed by intercourse,[93] one who betrothed without prior arrangement between the two families *(shiddukhin)*, and a son-in-law who lived in his mother-in-law's house. According to another version, quoted in the name of the scholars of Neharde'a, only one who betrothed through intercourse *and* without prior arrangement between the families (i.e., one offense consisting of two parts) was flogged. On this passage, the Tosafot say:[94]

> Sons-in-law in our times who live in the homes of their mothers-in-law rely on this [i.e., the position of the Nehardeans]. But even according to one who might hold the other position, the fact that they live in the homes of their mothers-in-law now is for the benefits which accrue to them by virtue of the fact that they live rent-free, for there is clear indication *(hokhahah)* that they do not live there for their mothers-in-law,[95] but for the other favors *(tovot)* which are done for them.

The present behavior of sons-in-law who live in the homes of their mothers-in-law can be justified in one of two ways: on the basis of the exercise of legitimate judicial discretion in favor of the position of the

---

90. This example clearly reflects a change in sociological reality. However, it fits even more appropriately into the second nexus pattern between historical and legal sources. That pattern is treated in greater detail below, pp. 277 ff.

91. Kiddushin 12b.

92. Thus indicating clearly that such behavior was forbidden, even though no norm had so decreed.

93. See Mishnah Kiddushin 1:1.

94. Tosafot Kiddushin 12b, s.v. *be-khulho*.

95. I.e., with any designs on their mothers-in-law.

Nehardeans, according to whom such an arrangement was not forbidden by Rav; or by abrogating the norm on the grounds of the existence of a nexus between the historical and the legal sources of the law created by extralegal factors demonstrating a change of sociological reality.

The apparent historical source for the original norm was a desire to prevent indiscretion between a son-in-law and his mother-in-law,[96] and only the continued suspicion that such behavior would be likely to occur would justify the continued application of the norm. The Tosafot perceived as clear that grounds for this suspicion no longer existed. Rather, the sociological reality that, in the period of the Tosafot, motivated sons-in-law to live in the homes of their mothers-in-law indicated economic as well as other benefits as the reason for the arrangement. Therefore, in light of the new sociological reality, the historical sources that gave rise to the original norm became legally significant and permitted the abrogation of the norm.

The Tosafot also provide an example of changed *realia* of a very different sort. The Mishnah[97] prohibits the clapping of hands, the slapping of hands upon thighs, and dancing (foot stomping) on the Sabbath as instances of *shevut*.[98] The Talmud justifies these prohibitions on the basis of *shema yitakken keli shir* ("[a safeguard] lest they construct a [simple percussion] instrument");[99] such a construction would involve, basically, the clapping of one object upon another, and thus it would be similar to the forbidden actions. Regarding this enactment, the Tosafot claim:[100]

> Nonetheless, for us it is permissible,[101] for the enactment applied only to their days, when they were knowledgeable *(beki'in)* in the construction of instruments. But the enactment does not apply to us, who are not so qualified to construct instruments.

Whether human capabilities had diminished or instruments had become more complex, the *realia* in the days of the Tosafot was such that the fear that one might be led to construct a percussion instrument as a

96. See Pesaḥim 113a, and Rashi, Kiddushin 12b, s.v. *ve-al ḥatana*.
97. Beiẓa 5:2.
98. A rabbinic enactment prohibiting certain acts on the Sabbath which, though not technically forbidden, might lead one to engage in forbidden behavior, either because the particular acts are commonly linked to a forbidden behavior (e.g., transacting business, which is commonly linked to writing) or because they resemble a forbidden behavior (as in this case).
99. Beiẓa 36b.
100. *Ibid*. 30a, s.v. *tenan*.
101. I.e., to clap and stomp.

result of clapping one's hands seemed extremely remote, perhaps even nonexistent. Since that fear alone justified not only the promulgation of the prohibition but also its continued observance, the Tosafot found it warranted to elevate the original historical sources to legal significance and to declare the norm no longer applicable.[102]

In our discussion on the qualifications of halakhic authorities, we referred to a statement of Rabbi Abraham ben Moses Di Boton (ca. 1545–1588) in which he interpreted a passage from Maimonides on the basis of changed *realia*.[103] He wrote:[104]

> The statement of the Gemara, [that a man ought not to render decisions] until age forty,[105] implies concern with wisdom, not time. . . . And he [i.e., Maimonides] would affirm that it applied only to very early periods during which study took place orally, without the benefit of books. . . . But now that the Torah is written and we study from books, surely such an age requirement is not needed.

Di Boton obviously felt that the age requirement stipulated in the Talmud was calculated to allow a sufficient amount of time to master the knowledge required for making decisions—a time-consuming task when that knowledge had to be memorized and could not be easily recalled from books. Since that rationale alone justified the continued observance of the norm, at least according to Di Boton, the new sociological conditions of Maimonides' time allowed the historical sources of the original norm to assume legal significance.[106] Ultimately, therefore, it is the systemically justified nexus between the historical and the legal sources of the law that makes Di Boton's theory of Maimonides' apparent abrogation of it legally defensible.

---

102. It is interesting to note that the prohibition was apparently widely ignored even in talmudic days, and noncompliance could not be prevented. Although the norm was not abrogated, the principle "Better that they should transgress in error than willfully [*Mutav she-yehu shogegin ve-al yehu mezidin*]" was applied to it. See Beiẓa 30a.

103. Above, p. 144.

104. *Leḥem Mishneh* to Maimonides, Talmud Torah 5:4.

105. Avodah Zarah 19b.

106. This passage serves as an excellent example as the source of a possible legitimate *maḥaloket*. We have persistently affirmed that historical sources can assume legal significance only when those sources also serve as the sole rationale for the continued observance of the norm. If, however, the rationale for continued observance can be reasonably redefined or reinterpreted, allowing the historical sources to assume legal significance falls under the rubric of the "genetic fallacy." In this case it is certainly possible to reinterpret the age requirement as guaranteeing the maturity, insight, and sensitivity necessary for rendering legal decisions. Thus, Di Boton's thesis clearly leaves room for a legitimate controversy even concerning so important a fact as whether or not the historical sources can become legally significant.

We will conclude this section of our discussion with four passages from the modern period that reflect the legitimacy of recourse to sociological/*realia* data in the determination of law.

In two different responsa Rabbi Moses Sofer (Ḥatam Sofer, 1762–1839) takes cognizance of modern communications and their possible influence on legal norms.

The verification of a signature on a written document was generally effected, beginning in the talmudic era, by the testimony of the signator or of other witnesses. Such testimony was justified as the only guarantee against the falsification of documents. Were an equally reliable method of verification available, there would have been little reason for these particular testimonial requirements.

Recognizing this, the Ḥatam Sofer wrote:

> If a letter [or document] has been sent through the mail to a specific addressee *(li-ve'alim yedu'im),* and an answer has been received from him through return mail, it is clear that the latter is from the original addressee, and contains no forgery, as is clear to all *(ka-muvan le-khol mevin),* and needs no further verification.[107]

In a responsum dealing with the difficult problem of *Mayim she-ein lahem sof* (a body of water all of whose shores cannot be seen from any one point),[108] Sofer invoked sociological data attesting both the changed nature of human behavior and the changed *realia.*[109] He wrote:

> It seems to me that this entire matter [i.e., *Mayim she-ein lahem sof*] was applicable in their days, during which two concerns were relevant. Either that the current carried him very far away, and it was impossible for him to let his family know (as, for example, in Yevamot 121a) . . . or that as a result of his injuries he lost a limb and was embarrassed to return home (as, for example, in Yevamot 115a) . . . Yet it is clear that times have changed *(nishtannu ha-zemannim)* regarding this matter from what was true in their time. For now there are established postal services in all significant countries, and we receive mail even from the Balkan states within a very short time. And if he had come out of the water at any spot whatsoever he would notify his family by letter or he would let it be known

107. *Responsa of Ḥatam Sofer* (Pressburg, 1865), *Even ha-Ezer,* pt. 1, no. 43.

108. See Yevamot 121a. In brief, the wife of a man who fell into *Mayim she-ein lahem sof* and was not seen to come out is not allowed to remarry. That is, we do not assume that he drowned but rather suspect that he might have left the water alive but out of sight.

109. *Responsa of Ḥatam Sofer, Even ha-Ezer,* pt. 1, no. 58. Cf. also no. 65.

even through the newspaper. Indeed, in Yevamot 121a Rav Ashi wished to claim that the wife of a scholar *(ẓurba),* whose whereabouts would surely become known if he had surfaced anywhere, is allowed to remarry without hesitation *(le-khatteḥilah)* in a case of *Mayim she-ein lahem sof.* And even though the law is not according to his position in this matter, that [i.e., the rejection of Rav Ashi's position] refers only to remarriage without hesitation. Furthermore, it is possible that the news of his surfacing might not have spread all over. But now, in our times, it is impossible that the news not have spread by means of the established postal service. Therefore, at least after the fact *(be-dei'avad),* if she married, she need not be divorced. And even before the fact *(le-khatteḥilah)* the prohibition would be only *de-rabbanan.*

So, too, regarding the second concern, that he might have fled because of shame, times have changed. For it is clear *(bari)* to us that even if all of his limbs have been broken he would either come or inform his family, and his injuries would not be the cause for any shame.

The Ḥatam Sofer, in this most far-reaching responsum, effectively advocates the abrogation of an entire range of legal norms that fall within the category of *Mayim she-ein lahem sof.* Prohibiting the wives of men who have fallen into such waters from remarrying is justified solely and exclusively on the basis of the two concerns that served as the historical sources of the norms. Neither of those concerns is applicable any longer, one because of changed *realia,* and the other because of a demonstrable change in human behavior. Thus, the original historical sources of the law assume legal significance, allowing Sofer to advocate the abolition of the entire category of norms based on *Mayim she-ein lahem sof.*

The third example also deals with the remarriage of an *agunah* (a woman concerning the death of whose husband there is no testimony). Although the law is very liberal regarding acceptable testimony for establishing the death of a husband, the Mishnah lists five women whose testimony on the subject is not acceptable.[110] Included in the list is *bat ḥammotah,* the daughter of the *agunah*'s mother-in-law, that is, the sister of the *agunah*'s husband. Regarding a situation in which this fact is relevant, Rabbi Isaac Herzog (1888–1959), Chief Rabbi of Israel, wrote:[111]

110. Mishnah Yevamot 15:4.

111. *Heichal Yitzchak* (Jerusalem: Chief Rabbi Herzog Publication Society, 1967 [5727]), *Even ha-Ezer,* vol. 2, no. 12.

[Concerning an *agunah* about whom there is strong reason to believe that her husband has died, and the sister of whose husband has now informed her by letter that her husband has died.]

It should be noted *(yesh lehitbonen)* that the very reason for the hatred of *bat ḥammotah* [toward her brother's wife][112] does not apply in our time *(be-dorenu)* in those countries in which the laws of inheritance are governed by secular law *(le-fi dineihem)*, and one's mother-in-law inherits from her [own] husband, upon his death, just as does her son. And that[113] is the reason for the hatred of *bat ḥammotah* according to Rashi.[114] Indeed, there are those who explain (the Me'iri, of blessed memory, etc.); [that the hatred is based upon] the niggardliness which she [i.e., the husband's sister] feels toward this "stranger" who now enjoys the fruits of her labors.[115] And that explanation, too, could apply only to those places in which the couple eats [lives] for a number of years in the parents' house, that is, the son continues to live with his parents, and his wife with him. And that, too, was in an earlier age (and in Jerusalem even today to a small degree), but is not true in other lands in our time, as everyone knows.

Herzog recognizes that *bat ḥammotah* is prohibited from testifying on her sister-in-law's behalf only because of her hatred for her; and therefore that only the continued likelihood of her hatred of her sister-in-law would justify her continued disqualification as a witness. He introduces the two possible explanations for her hatred, Rashi's and the Me'iri's, and finds that the sociological realities of the modern age make it very

112. Because of which she is disqualified as a witness regarding the death of her brother, and on the basis of which her sister-in-law would otherwise be allowed to remarry. The suspicion that disqualifies her as a witness is that her hatred of her brother's wife would induce her to lie about her brother's death, purposely making her sister-in-law subject to the norms governing adultery.

113. According to Jewish law, wives never inherit from their husbands, and daughters inherit only when there are no sons. Thus, mothers and daughters would harbor resentment against the wife of their son/brother because the son/brother would inherit the deceased father, and his wife would reap the benefits of their familial efforts, while they would be excluded.

114. Yevamot 117a, s.v. *vi-vimtah.* Rashi wrote: The mother-in-law hates her son's wife because she says to herself: "She will benefit from all of my work and efforts." And similarly, the daughter of the mother-in-law says: "She [i.e., the brother's wife] will derive all the benefit from my father's estate, and my mother and I will be shunted aside."

115. According to the Me'iri, the husband's sister hates his wife, not because of her future loss of inheritance, but because of the present intrusion of a new woman into the household who will immediately begin reaping the benefits of an established household to which she has contributed nothing.

unlikely that either still applies. Thus, he is willing to accept the testimony of the sister-in-law, abrogating the prior norm.

The final example in this section comes from the writings of the well-known and influential legalist and moralist Rabbi Israel Meir Kagan (Ḥafeẓ Ḥayyim, 1838–1933). Commenting on Maimonides' claim that one may not teach his daughter the Oral Law and ought not to teach her even the Written Torah,[116] the Ḥafeẓ Ḥayyim wrote:[117]

> It seems that all of this applies only to earlier eras when everyone lived where his family lived *(mekom avotav)*,[118] and family tradition *(kabbalat ha-avot)* had a great influence on each and every one, so that they acted in the same manner as their relatives did. . . . Under such circumstances they were able to state that a daughter should not study Torah, since she would take her behavioral guidance from the upright behavior of her family. But now, through our great sins, when family tradition is very weak, and it even happens that one no longer lives where his family does, and especially for those who accustom themselves to learn the writing and language of foreigners,[119] it is surely a great *miẓvah* to teach the Pentateuch, as well as the Prophets and Writings, and the ethical treatises of the Sages, such as *Avot*, *Menorat ha-Ma'or*,[120] and similar works, in order that they may learn the truth of our holy faith. For if not so, it is plausible that they may stray completely from the path of God, and transgress all of the very foundations of the faith, God forbid.

The claim of the Ḥafeẓ Ḥayyim is absolutely clear. Observance of the norm is mandated only if and insofar as the sociological reality in which it arose, and which alone justifies its continued observance, continues to obtain. Given a changed reality—so changed, in fact that it undermines the historical justification of the law's observance to the detriment of the Jewish people—observance of the law is no longer either mandated or even desirable. Indeed, the Ḥafeẓ Ḥayyim goes to the opposite extreme. Abrogation of the norm in favor of a previously nonprecedented position becomes a "great *miẓvah*."[121]

---

116. *Mishneh Torah*, Talmud Torah 1:13, based upon Rabbi Eli'ezer's comment in Mishnah Sotah 3:4.

117. *Likkutei Halakhot* (Piotrkow, 1918) to Sotah 21b, p. 11a.

118. As will soon become clear, he refers both to the prohibition of teaching the Oral Law and to the nondesirability of teaching the Written Law.

119. I.e., secular study, which opens them to detrimental non-Jewish influences.

120. An ethical religious work by Rabbi Isaac Aboab, first published in 1514.

121. The Ḥafeẓ Ḥayyim does not indicate that he is exercising judicial discretion in favor either of the position of Ben Azzai in Mishnah Sotah 3:4 or of the position implied by Mishnah Nedarim 4:3 (according to those versions which read "and his daughters"), both

Thus, the systemically justifiable employment in the *halakhah* of extralegal sources of a sociological/*realia* nature is clearly demonstrable. As in the medical/scientific section of this chapter, here, too, our concern has been exclusively with the use of these factors in the resolution of questions of law, resulting in the abrogation either of earlier norms or of precedent. In each case we examined we saw that there is a potential nexus between the historical and the legal sources of the law that can become actual if, and only if, the historical source is affirmed to be the sole rationale for the continued observance of the norm. Yet we also saw how that very affirmation can itself be the subject of a legitimate difference of opinion, one *posek* insisting that the nexus is systemically justified, and the other insisting that allowing the elevation of historical source to legal significance is, in that instance, an example of the unwarranted intrusion of historical sources into the legal decision-making process. In the final analysis, it is clear, such a *maḥaloket* is possible because extralegal sources are not determinative. Factors judged legally significant by one *posek* need not be judged legally significant by another, a fact demonstrating once again that, ultimately, *Ein la-dayyan ella mah she-einav ro'ot*.

It should be noted finally, both as a conclusion to these first two sections of the chapter and as a prelude to the third section, that in no instance quoted thus far have the legal norms examined contained any indication in themselves that their applicability was contingent upon either time, circumstance, or the quirks of medical/scientific or sociological/*realia* data. Norms do not generally record the grounds upon which they are based. It is, rather, the *posek* who elucidates the justification of the norms in such a way as to make the potential nexus between the historical and the legal sources actual or not.

Economic Data

The third clearly identifiable category of extralegal sources is economic. Of the passages to be analyzed in this section, some will be similar to

---

of which advocate teaching girls Torah. In fact, the strength of his language leads one to believe that his decision is independent of such considerations; that is, that he is advocating the abrogation of the norm even if there were no other view on which to base himself.

It is interesting that the Ḥafeẓ Ḥayyim could, theoretically, have abrogated Maimonides' codified position on the basis of a sociological change in the nature of people, for Maimonides explains the reason for the prohibition on the grounds that the intellectual proclivities of most women would turn the words of Torah into trivialities (*divrei havai*) because of their inferior intelligence (*le-fi aniyyut ha-da'at*). Had the Ḥafeẓ Ḥayyim made a claim of *Shinnui ha-ittim* vis-à-vis this contention of Maimonides, he could have abrogated the norm even if familial traditions were still influential.

those in the preceding sections in that (1) they will reflect the same type of nexus between historical and legal sources, that is, one which moves from the present to the past, and (2) they will continue to demonstrate that it is the *posek* who construes the justification of the norms in such a way as to activate the nexus between the historical and the legal sources of the norms. Others will be similar to this type in that it is the *posek* who will create the nexus, but also different in that the kind of nexus involved will be different. Still others will appear *on the surface* to be totally different from anything we have seen thus far, in that we will meet what *seem* to be legal norms of an economic nature whose applicability will *seem* to be contingent, not upon the will of the individual *posek,* but upon some impersonal economic circumstance. That is, they will seem to indicate that the extralegal economic consideration that they reflect is an integral part of the original norm, and that the application of this economic consideration to specific circumstances is predetermined, rather than a matter to be left to the determination of the *posek.*

It is our thesis, however, that this last kind of legal passage only *seems* to be different but is, *in fact,* identical to the passages we have already seen in the first two sections of this chapter.[122] Moreover, we shall begin by demonstrating that this is so.

The basis for the confusion lies in the fact that because the conscious and verbalized recourse to economic considerations is so well established, and so old, explicit systemic principles like *Mi-shum hefsed, Mi-shum peseida,* and *Bi-mekom peseida* have been formulated, in the course of time, in order to indicate in a shorthand manner when and how such economic considerations should be employed.[123] The result of this development has been, unfortunately, that when the Talmud itself quotes any of these systemic principles as the grounds for a decision, it is easy to think that the Talmud is using it as a *legal principle* (i.e., as a principle that absolutely governs the determination of the law in a case), instead of recognizing that the Talmud is merely quoting it as a statement by the *posek* of the grounds upon which he has chosen to activate the nexus between the historical and the legal sources of the law. This error is critical, in our opinion, because failure to *recognize* it as an error can lead one to assert that extralegal sources of *any* kind remain legally insignificant except and unless they are explicitly articulated by the Talmud as legal principles.

---

122. See n. 7 above.

123. The term *Nishtannu ha-ittim* is also used with reference to both medical/scientific and sociological/*realia* factors, but its actual verbalization can be traced only to the Middle Ages. Its absence from talmudic sources prevented any subsequent possibility of confusing this systemic principle with a legal principle.

In reality, however, it is very likely that the existence of this type of legal passage, in which extralegal considerations seem to operate as legal principles, is the result of a specific evolution, which, once understood, will substantiate my thesis. The following example should clarify this evolution: The Talmud records a *baraita* in the name of Naḥum of Galia to the effect that if rubble is blocking the flow of water through a drainpipe and causing the water to overflow onto a flat roof, when it either begins to seep into the house or begins to cause damage to the roof, a man may stamp on it with his foot, in private *(be-ẓina)*, on the Sabbath.[124] The Talmud explains the reason for this statement as follows: Stamping with one's foot falls into the legal category of doing something in an unusual way to clear the drainpipe *(metakken ki-le-aḥar yad)*, a kind of activity forbidden on the Sabbath merely by rabbinic decree, as an instance of *shevut*.[125] But in a matter involving financial loss *(makom peseida)*, "the sages did not make [i.e., impose] their decree."

On the surface, this passage seems to imply that the idea that the rabbinic decree was not applicable in cases of financial loss was itself part of the decree *ab initio;* that is, that the principle relating to financial loss was as much a legal principle as the prohibition against engaging in such activities carried out in an unusual way. Upon more careful analysis, however, the following seems to have happened: The sages decreed a *shevut* prohibiting activities carried out in an unusual way lest they be mistaken for an actually forbidden activity. Only the likelihood that such confusion would actually arise could justify the continued applicability of the *shevut*. In the circumstances described above, the convergence of two factors mitigated the possibility of such confusion. First, the person involved took the action in a manner forbidden only *de-rabbanan* (as opposed to the usual manner, forbidden *de-oraita*), thereby clearly indicating his recognition that doing so in the usual forbidden manner would have been in actual violation of the Sabbath. Second, the act was done in private, eliminating the possibility that it could become the source of confusion for another person. Since these factors eliminated totally the sole justification for the observance of the *shevut*, the present circumstances, viz., the financial loss that would surely ensue if the blockage was not eliminated, allowed the historical sources of the law to assume legal significance and resulted in the abrogation of the norm under these circumstances. It is in this sense, and only in this sense, that one can say "The sages did not make their decree" in a matter involving financial loss. The sentence is a shorthand formula,

124. Ketubbot 60a.
125. See n. 98 above. This *shevut* is of the second type described in the note.

meant to simplify a complex idea; in no way is it meant to imply that the *original* promulgation of the norm included an explicit provision of its nonapplicability in cases of financial loss.[126]

Thus, whenever the Talmud uses such shorthand formulae we should recognize them simply as statements indicating the grounds for activating the nexus between the historical and the legal sources of the norm. It is only because the possibility of financial loss is such a common occurrence, and because, as a result, this kind of nexus is created with relative regularity, that these formulae became explicit systemic principles in the first place. But it is the *posekim* alone who determine whether the nexus is or is not legally significant in a given set of circumstances and, therefore, whether the principle does or does not apply. In our case, it was Naḥum of Galia, as *posek,* who decided that the nexus was legally significant, and who, on that basis, allowed the abrogation of the norm.[127]

We have now shown that the extralegal considerations of an economic nature that *seemed* to be totally different from the other kinds of considerations we have been examining are, in fact, not different at all. We can turn our attention, therefore, to examples of the conscious use of economic data within the halakhic system that both *are* like and also *appear* to be like the medical/scientific and sociological/*realia* factors we have already studied. That is, we will turn to examples in which it is quite clear that it is the *posek* who construes the justification of the norms in such a way as to make the nexus between the historical and the legal sources of the norms applicable. Using extralegal factors of an economic

126. It is worth noting, however, that this example is significantly different from others we have considered in that the extralegal considerations that supply the impetus for the abrogation of the norm are clearly transitory. The claim here is one of financial loss, not of a permanent change in reality. Whenever the claim ceases to apply, so does the abrogation.

This type of nexus, leading to temporary abrogation of the norm, is not restricted to extralegal considerations of an economic nature. The claim that *shevut* prohibitions do not apply within the Temple (*Ein shevut ba-mikdash*), for example, is subject to a similar analysis. That claim, in essence, is that the conditions of the Temple surroundings obviate completely the possibility that the *performance* of a *shevut* prohibition can result in an actual violation of Shabbat, since the hordes of people always present in the Temple would include some who would stop any actual violation from occurring. Thus, the nexus between the historical and legal sources of the norm becomes legally significant and permits the temporary abrogation of the *shevut* norm. Once outside the Temple precincts, however, the temporary suspension ends, and the *shevut* prohibition is reinstated.

127. The decision of Naḥum of Galia then can serve as a precedent for a future *posek* to decide that the same set of circumstances warrant judging the nexus legally significant. Thus, in the final analysis, one can find legally significant nexuses codified in the halakhic literature as though they were actual norms. In fact, however, each succeeding *posek* is deciding that the circumstances he is considering allow the nexus to become legally significant, just as Naḥum of Galia did.

nature in order to resolve questions of law in the second sense, he either abrogates the norms in question or adopts previously nonprecedented positions, sometimes permanently and sometimes temporarily.

The Mishnah lists "merchants of the sabbatical produce"[128] among those who are disqualified as witnesses.[129] Rabbi Simon adds to this passage the historical note that this group of witnesses was at first called "gatherers of the sabbatical produce."[130] The Talmud explains:

> At first they claimed that both groups were disqualified. When the "oppressions" *(ha-annasim)* increased, namely, the *anona* [tax], . . . they reversed themselves and claimed that "gatherers" were qualified as witnesses and "merchants" were disqualified.[131]

The sole justification for the retention of the norm disqualifying "gatherers" from serving as witnesses is the likelihood that those who engage in such activity are suspected of a willingness to accept bribes for false testimony. When the economic reality (i.e., the obligation to pay specific amounts of produce in taxes) necessitated the gathering of such produce by everyone, the very fact of gathering could no longer be considered to be grounds for suspicion. The nexus between the historical and the legal sources of the law, moving from present to past, allowed the permanent abrogation of the prevailing norm on the basis of extralegal factors of an economic nature.[132]

A fascinating responsum of Rabbi Menaḥem Mendel Krochmal (Ẓemaḥ Ẓedek, ca. 1600–1661) again illustrates the conscious use of extralegal economic factors.[133] He writes:

---

128. Sanhedrin 3:3. Cf. Rosh ha-Shanah 1:5.

129. The sages interpreted the verse in Leviticus 25:6, "The land at rest shall yield your food," as limiting the use of sabbatical produce exclusively to personal consumption. Commercial use of the produce is, therefore, forbidden, and one who uses it in this way is disqualified as a witness on the grounds that his love of wealth, as reflected in his willingness to violate the law for his own material gain, might also predispose him to accept bribes to testify falsely.

130. Since it is prohibited to store significant amounts of sabbatical produce.

131. Sanhedrin 26a.

132. The Tosafot *ad loc.*, s.v. *mi-she-rabbu*, are concerned with another issue, as well. Payment of the tax required plowing and sowing the fields during the sabbatical year, activities specifically prohibited by the *grundnorm* itself in Leviticus 25:4. How could the obligation to pay a Roman tax supersede the prohibition *de-oraita?* Their answer, based upon the Yerushalmi, reaffirms the rights of the sages vis-à-vis matters *de-oraita* (see above, chap. 7 and, in particular, pp. 181–185), allowing even active abrogation of the *grundnorm* for reasons of *pikku'aḥ nefesh*—here as a result of economic factors.

133. *Responsa of Ẓemaḥ Ẓedek*, no. 28. Cf. *Magen Avraham, Oraḥ Ḥayyim* 242:1.

Once the non-Jewish fish merchants inflated the price of fish because they noted that the Jews continued to buy in honor of the Sabbath, and were not deterred by the expensive price. The community agreed that no one should buy any fish for two months. And the students asked me if they were entitled to do so, since it involved the honor of the Sabbath. And furthermore, it says in the second chapter of Beiẓa, page 16a, that the amount of money a man is destined to earn for his livelihood is predetermined from Rosh ha-Shanah,[134] excluding his expenses for the Sabbath and yom tov, for which, if he overspends, money will be added to his total account. Therefore, he incurs no loss *(ein peseida)* by virtue of his paying exorbitant prices in honor of the Sabbath, for the Holy One, blessed be He, repays him.

Response: It appears that it is perfectly legitimate to do as they do [i.e., declare the embargo on fish buying] on the basis of the following statement of the Mishnah, at the end of the first chapter of Keritot:[135] "It happened once that the price of *kinnim*[136] in Jerusalem stood at a golden *dinar* apiece. Rabban Shimon ben Gamli'el[137] said, 'I swear *(ha-ma'on ha-zeh)*, I will not rest tonight until the price drops to a silver *dinar!*'[138] He entered the court and taught: 'A woman who owes for five definite childbirths and five definite *zivot* [severe hemorrhaging][139] must bring one sacrifice[140] . . . and the rest are not obligatory.'[141] On that very day the price of a "nest" dropped to one-quarter of a silver *dinar.*"

---

134. Thus, he should be cautious not to overspend, lest he end up short of funds, which cannot be replaced.

135. Keritot 1:7, 8a.

136. Literally, "birds' nests" (singular, *ken*). The reference is to the two pigeons or doves that had to be sacrificed, one as a burnt offering and the other as a sin offering, by a *zav* (Leviticus 15:14–15), a *zavah* (Leviticus 15:29–30), and a woman after childbirth (Leviticus 12:6–8).

137. The elder, who lived before the destruction of the Temple, when the matter of sacrifices was still of practical import.

138. Of which there are twenty-five in a golden *dinar.*

139. As opposed to doubtful *zivot.* A doubtful childbirth occurs when a woman has a miscarriage, but it is unclear whether the miscarriage involved a fetus that requires a sacrifice or not. See Mishnah Keritot 1:3–4. A doubtful *zivah* occurs when a woman has seen blood on three days but does not know whether it was during her menstrual period or on the days between one period and another.

140. I.e., one pair of birds (one *ken).*

141. Rabban Shimon ben Gamli'el contradicted the accepted legal requirement, for the Mishnah states clearly that a "nest" must be offered for every definite childbirth or *zivah.* He, however, equated definite childbirths or *zivot* with doubtful childbirths or *zivot,* for which one "nest" suffices for all as an obligatory offering.

Rashi explained (s.v., *nikhnas*): "Even though he was lenient in a matter *de-oraita*, it was an instance of *Et la'asot la-donai*.[142] For if they were unable to find [at a reasonable price] they would desist from bringing even one sacrifice, and would eat sanctified food in a state of impurity."[143]

Thus, if he was lenient in a matter *de-oraita* because of the exorbitant price, surely one can be so regarding the purchase of fish, which is only for the honor of the Sabbath. . . . Therefore if the price of fish becomes exorbitant as a result of the fact that they continue to buy it in honor of the Sabbath, it is legitimate to declare an embargo on the purchase of fish for several weeks in order to force down the price.

And one cannot claim that the case of the *kinnim* is different on the grounds that they will desist from offering even one sacrifice, and that will result in eating sacred food in a state of impurity, thus constituting an instance of *Et la'asot la-donai*, as Rashi explained; whereas the matter of the honor of the Sabbath is not an instance of *Et la'asot la-donai*, since one's livelihood for Sabbath expenditures is not predetermined, and the Holy One, blessed be He, repays it all, thus the expense will not deter one from buying. This argument is not valid. For, just as we suspect concerning *kinnim* that they will refrain from buying even one because of the expense, thus, too, the same suspicion exists concerning the Sabbath. For the poor will never be able to buy fish because of the exorbitant price. For, though it is surely true that one who has available cash can increase his expenditures for the honor of the Sabbath, and be repaid by the Holy One, blessed be He; how can the poor ever buy, since they have no available cash reserve to expend for the honor of the Sabbath? . . . Therefore, it is appropriate to impose a ban on the purchase of fish for several weeks in order to reduce the price and to be able thereafter to honor the Sabbath, even the poor, with fish—and it is an instance of *Et la'asot la-donai*. . . . Indeed, it is similar to the claim "Better that one should desecrate one Sabbath in order to be able to fulfill many."[144]

To Krochmal's responsum his son added the following gloss:

142. See above, pp. 169–172.
143. I.e., would not consider themselves as still ritually impure, and would behave as if pure, even to the point of eating from sacred food, which may not be eaten in a state of impurity.
144. Shabbat 151b, Yoma 85b.

. . . even without all of these proofs it is clear that they are entitled. For any court may institute passive abrogations *(be-shev ve-al ta'aseh)*[145] even to uproot a matter which is from the Torah, as is clear in several places.

Krochmal's responsum has several distinct parts. He begins by rephrasing the question, wondering, in essence, whether extralegal factors of an economic nature are admissible considerations in determining the applicability of norms governing the honor of the Sabbath. The issue, he says, is complicated by the statement from Beiẓa 16a, which can be seen to imply that the economic factor may not be significant, since the ostensible loss will not be ultimately realized. Nonetheless, his answer to the question of whether the economic factors are admissible as considerations is a resounding yes, based on no less an authority than the Patriarch Rabban Shimon ben Gamli'el. Accepting the reading of the *mishnah* as it appears in the standard printed versions,[146] the *mishnah* affirms that Rabban Shimon took a decisive step abrogating the prior norm that dictated that a "nest" must be offered for every definite childbirth and *zivah*. He apparently felt that continued application of the norm was predicated on the assumption that its fulfillment would remain within the realm of a reasonable religious demand. This excluded the possibility that its fulfillment would entail severe financial hardship, as it surely would if the price of each "nest" was a golden *dinar*. When the price-gouging tactics of the *kinnim* salesmen made this impossible, the Patriarch invoked the right of the sages, even vis-à-vis matters *de-oraita*, to abrogate the norm that had made the price-gouging possible.[147] As Rashi explained, the Patriarch exercised his right because it was an instance of *Et la'asot la-donai*.

Furthermore, Krochmal continues, even the talmudic promise that God recompenses for Sabbath and festival expenses does not invalidate the imposition of the embargo on the purchase of fish. Repayment, after all, is possible only when an actual expenditure has taken place. The

145. See above, pp. 186–194.

146. See, however, Tosafot Bava Batra 166a, s.v. *nikhnas*. In our terms, the Tosafot prefer to see Rabban Shimon's action as an exercise of judicial discretion in favor of a nonprecedented position rather than as the abrogation of a matter of law in the first sense because of extralegal factors. See n. 147.

147. The same principle is operative in Pesaḥim 30a, with one variation. There, Samuel threatens pot salesmen to invoke his right of judicial discretion in favor of a previously nonprecedented position unless they lower the prices of their wares to a reasonable sum. Indeed, Samuel was evidently willing to use that threat as the need arose. In Sukkah 34b, he threatened the salesmen of myrtle branches with the adoption of a position requiring fewer than three branches if they refused to moderate their prices.

poor masses have nothing to expend, and, therefore, if the price remained too high, they would never be able to afford fish. Ultimately, the case of the fish is no different from the case of the *kinnim*, both being instances of *Et la'asot la-donai*.

Indeed, he concludes, the temporary abrogation of the norm concerning the honor of the Sabbath is likely to be the very act that, when the prices do come down to reasonable levels, will enable its future fulfillment.

Krochmal's son adds a further consideration that, in his opinion, justifies the action without reservation: There is, after all, a systemic principle that allows the abrogation of norms through *Shev ve-al ta'aseh*, when the sages of the time see such a need.[148]

As we continue our discussion of extralegal factors of an economic nature, and before proceeding to a passage that will introduce a second kind of nexus pattern between historical and legal sources, we offer an excellent example of the nexus pattern we have been already discussing, one in which the recourse to extralegal sources will be conscious and will result in the abrogation of a norm. In one respect, however, this example differs from those we have discussed thus far, in that the specific category of extralegal factors that was instrumental in activating the nexus in this case cannot be definitively identified. This kind of ambiguity can occur when an early norm has been changed and replaced by a new norm whose formulation does not specify the grounds upon which the nexus was created between the historical and the legal sources of the old norm.

The Mishnah stipulates that captives are not to be redeemed for more than their worth, *Mi-penei tikkun ha-olam* ("for reasons of societal stability").[149] While this Mishnah is surely very old,[150] it is most unlikely that

---

148. Krochmal's responsum also serves as an excellent example of the fact that the systemic principle that admits extralegal factors is often used in conjunction with other systemic principles, like *Et la'asot la-donai* and *Shev ve-al ta'aseh*. The extralegal factor may serve as the impetus for the decision of the *posek* to abrogate a norm or to overturn a precedent, but it must often be combined with other systemic principles before it can be elevated to legal significance. In the Krochmal example, the economic factors would not have been sufficient to abrogate the *de-oraita* norm were it not for the fact that there is precedent for overturning *de-oraita* norms on grounds such as *Et la'asot la-donai*.

In chap. 7 we dealt with the rights of sages vis-à-vis matters *de-oraita*. A perusal of the sources we quoted there will show that in many instances the impetus to exercise these rights was to be found in extralegal factors. Furthermore, the extralegal factors in chap. 7 were of the sociologica/*realia* and ethical/psychological kinds.

149. Gittin 4:6.

150. Coming, as it does, from a series of statements connected only externally (i.e., they are examples of *Tikkun ha-olam)* rather than by an internal thematic connection (i.e., they do not deal with the same subject matter, e.g., Shabbat, divorce, sacrifices, etc.). *Mishnayot* of the former type are almost universally recognized as reflecting the earliest compilations.

the original formulation of the norm mandating the ransom of captives included this provision *ab initio*.[151] It is much more likely that its original formulation presented an unequivocal statement which then had to be reconsidered in light of extralegal considerations that arose only later. It is about these possible extralegal considerations that the Talmud speculates as follows: "Is the *Tikkun ha-olam* because of the communal burden *(duḥka de-ẓibbura)* or as a preventative against the proliferation of captives who might be presented for ransom?"[152]

In essence, the Talmud is trying to determine what the factors were that resulted in adding to the original norm mandating the ransoming of captives the stipulation that they may not be ransomed for more than their worth in order that *Tikkun ha-olam* might be ensured. The Talmud offers two possible answers. The first is economic. The continued observance of the original norm could have been justified only if compliance with it continued to allow the community as a whole to fulfill its obligations toward its members without destroying itself. Compliance could not have been justified if ransom demands had been allowed to become so great as to result in the gross impoverishment of the community, to the point where it could no longer have functioned as a viable unit. Since acceding to exorbitant ransom demands would have vitiated the original and sole continuing justification of the norm, the modification of the norm was introduced in order to prevent this from happening.[153]

The second possible reason reflects the ethical/psychological realm of extralegal considerations (which we will be discussing later). Payment of exorbitant ransoms would have debilitated the community psychologi-

151. This *mishnah* is strikingly similar to the *baraita* of Naḥum of Galia and the Talmud's explanation of its (above, pp. 267–268) in that the extralegal factor *appears* to be a legal norm. As there, so here, too, the clause *Mi-penei tikkun ha-olam* is a shorthand formula for expressing the nexus between the historical and the legal sources of a norm. Here, too, it is applied by *posekim* (but see above, n. 127), who alone determine whether the nexus is legally significant in a given set of circumstances.

In truth, though, *Mi-penei tikkun ha-olam* is less likely to be mistaken for a legal principle than *Mi-shum peseida*. Financial loss sounds much more objective and quantifiable than concerns for societal stability. This fact alone virtually ensures that it will be recognized that *posekim* decide what constitutes *Tikkun ha-olam*.

152. Gittin 45a.

153. One might assert that the modification does not support this claim. The stipulation that the community not ransom a captive for more than his value fails to recognize the possibility that payment of even an exorbitant ransom may not, in fact, impoverish a community; or, on the other hand, that payment of even a ransom price not greater than the value of the captive might, in fact, impoverish the community. The accuracy of the claim, however, is not relevant to our discussion. All that is important is the fact that the Talmud here reflects the admissibility of economic factors vis-à-vis consideration of the original norm.

cally because it would have undoubtedly resulted in the proliferation of kidnappings. Thus the stability of the community would be more certain if its willingness to pay were severely restricted, making capture for ransom less lucrative and less worth the risk.[154]

Although the Talmud cannot determine definitively the factors that motivated the modification of the original norm, it is clear that the factors it considers the most likely candidates are extralegal in nature, either economic or psychological/ethical, or a combination of both.

A passage from Rabbi Yom Tov ben Abraham Ishbili (Ritba, ca. 1250–1330) not only reaffirms the conscious use of extralegal sources of an economic nature, but also adds a new dimension to the possible nexus between historical and legal sources.

The Mishnah prohibits business dealings of various kinds between Jews and non-Jews during the three days preceding pagan holidays.[155] Later, the Talmud records that Rabbi Judah II received a gift from a non-Jew on a pagan holiday and pondered, in the presence of Resh Lakish, what action to take: To accept the gift might give the non-Jew joy, and he would then give thanks to his god.[156] This, indeed, is the grounds for the Mishnah's original prohibition. On the other hand, Rabbi Judah wondered whether failure to accept the gift might cause animosity. The Mishnah, however, makes no mention of animosity as constituting a factor of significance in determining the applicability of the prohibition against dealings between Jews and non-Jews. Why, then, was it even a consideration on the part of Rabbi Judah? To this, among other things, the Ritba addresses himself. . . .[157]

> [The meaning of his concern lest animosity ensue from his failure to accept the gift] is that our *mishnah* does not imply a prohibition, even on the holiday itself, when animosity would result. For the prohibition is only *mi-de-rabbanan,* grounded on the suspicion [that the non-Jew might go and give thanks]. The prohibition, therefore, is not unequivocal and all-pervasive *(lo heḥelitu bo issuran ve-lo hishvu middoteihem).* In this regard it is different from other rabbinic prohibitions, which are unequivocal and all-pervasive. But this one is not

154. This assertion, too, may not be supported by the modification. It may be that even a few captives, whom the community ransomed only according to their worth, would have an adverse effect on the psychological well-being of the community. It is probable that the Talmud here is positing two sufficient conditions for the introduction of the modification, but that only together do they constitute a necessary condition.

155. Avodah Zarah 1:1.

156. Ibid. 6b.

157. *Ḥiddushei Ritba ad loc.,* s.v. *ha-hu.*

so. Rather, it is contingent upon the place and the time, as Samuel says, "In the Diaspora transactions are forbidden only on the holiday itself."[158] And how could Samuel have said such a thing if it had been an unequivocal enactment of the sages? Surely, therefore, the intention of the sages from the start must have been that the applicability of the norm was contingent upon place and time. . . . And on the basis of this contention, our rabbis declared that it is permissible to have dealings with non-Jews in modern times, even on the holiday itself. First of all, because of the claim of potential animosity. Furthermore, we are certain that no non-Jew will go to give thanks anymore, since these dealings [with us] are not so important to them. And, finally, that we must have dealings with them for reasons of livelihood *(mi-shum ḥayyei nefesh).*

In this instance it seems fair to say that the claim of the Ritba that the sages intended the prohibition to be contingent on time and place *ab initio* is exaggerated. We have noted above that even when a proviso like *Mi-penei tikkun ha-olam* is actually part of the norm, it is likely that it represents a modification of the earlier norm to which it has been added.[159] Surely it is even more likely that a proviso like "because of potential animosity," which is not part of the norm recorded in the *mishnah,* represents a modification of the *mishnah*'s earlier norm and cannot be considered the intention of that norm *ab initio.* Consequently, it seems reasonable to attempt a reformulation of the Ritba's contention that leaves its basic thrust untouched but expresses it in more circumspect terms.

Since the legal system allows the possibility of a nexus between the historical and the legal sources of norms, it is in the nature of norms that they may be modified on the basis of extralegal sources as warranted. It can be said that inherent in any norm is the idea of its possible modification on the basis of extralegal sources.[160] Indeed, according to the Ritba, it is that aspect of the nature of norms that Samuel recognizes. The modification Samuel introduces vis-à-vis the applicability of the norm to the Diaspora reflects his thinking that the three-day prohibition of the *mishnah* was justifiable only on the assumption that non-Jews would retain their pleasure at having been needed by Jews for that period of time. If this were no longer the case, if non-Jews were to retain

158. Avodah Zarah 7b.

159. See p. 273.

160. The Ritba's claim that this norm is different from other rabbinic enactments because the latter are unequivocal must be considered a hyperbole. The rereading of almost any of the passages cited in this chapter will demonstrate that other rabbinic enactments are, in fact, capable of modification on the basis of extralegal considerations.

their pleasure for only one day, the continued application of the three-day prohibition would be unreasonable. Since the prohibition is based upon the fear that non-Jews might give thanks to their gods, in the new situation that suspicion is judged to exist only on the day of the festival itself. Thus, he acts upon the idea that inherent in the norm was the possibility of its own modification when the changed nature of pagan society warranted the conclusion that the sole continuing justification of the norm no longer obtained. And that is what the Ritba meant by interpreting Samuel's modification of the prohibition as reflecting the idea that the applicability of the norm was contingent on time and place.

More important, however, than the reformulation of the Ritba's statement is the fact that this passage describes a new kind of possible nexus between the historical and the legal sources of a norm. Until now we have seen the nexus between the historical and the legal sources of a norm become legally significant only in those cases in which the original rationale, the sole continuing justification of the norm, no longer obtained. Now, however, we see what happens when a negative result, unforeseen by those who drafted the original norm, results from compliance with it.

The quandary in which Rabbi Judah II finds himself can be described as follows: Accepting the gift might result in the pagan's giving thanks to his god. Rejecting the gift might result in the pagan's animosity. While the animosity could surely be prevented by accepting the gift, accepting the gift could still result in the pagan's giving thanks to his god. Expressed in our terms, since the original rationale and sole justification for the norm continues to be valid (it is still undesirable that the Jew cause the pagan to give thanks to his gods), it seems impossible to create the nexus between the historical and the legal sources of the norm that alone would permit its modification.

In the Ritba's interpretation of the talmudic passage, however, he implies that Rabbi Judah II, in order to deal with the situation in which he found himself, was willing to consider the possibly negative results of compliance with the norm to stand as valid grounds for the norm's modification. In other words, when the present historical reality made compliance with the norm more detrimental than the possible result of noncompliance, the Patriarch permitted the reality to become legally significant and to constitute the possible grounds for the abrogation or modification of the original norm (even though its original justification continued to apply).[161] In this situation, it was the present historical reality that was potentially relevant.

---

161. One example of this nexus pattern has already been introduced—see above p. 258 and n. 90 there. The way in which the nexus pattern was described there ("When the

While the Talmud does not reveal the final decision of Rabbi Judah II, the conclusion of the passage from the Ritba indicates that he himself does reach a decision. Of the three justifications he offers for the total abrogation of the norm, only one fits the first nexus pattern that we have become familiar with; this, of course, is the second justification. It affirms that the sociological reality has changed to such an extent that the original rationale and sole justification of the norm no longer obtains; that is, that business dealings between Jews and non-Jews are no longer so important to the non-Jews that there can exist any suspicion whatsoever that they will go and give thanks to their gods.

The first and the third justifications offered by the Ritba, however, reflect the new nexus pattern we have described. The first asserts that the negative results of animosity that will ensue when the Jews refuse to do business with the non-Jews will be more detrimental to their well-being than the negative results of non-Jews giving thanks to their gods. Thus, the present historical reality assumes legal significance and allows the abrogation of the norm on sociological grounds.

The third explanation is similar to the first. The present historical reality is such that the livelihood of the Jews depends upon their doing business with non-Jews. The negative ramifications of compliance with the norm are far beyond anything the original norm could have envisioned, and far more detrimental to the economic and psychological well-being of the Jewish community than the negative results that would follow upon noncompliance with the norm. Thus, here, too, the present reality assumes legal significance and allows the abrogation of the norm, even though its original rationale continues to obtain.[162]

It should be clear that if the first nexus pattern provides grounds for a legitimate *maḥaloket* (e.g., about whether or not a particular sociological reality really constitutes a change from an earlier sociological reality, or whether or not a changed sociological reality reflects a desirable change), the second nexus pattern provides even more fertile ground for legitimate disagreement. It, after all, requires a value judgment based upon the consideration of two different negative results. Two different observers might surely come to opposite conclusions about

---

reality of their sociopolitical situation made compliance with the norm result in a situation that was the very opposite of the norm's original intention [and which had remained its sole justification]") demonstrates that the second pattern is closely related to the first pattern, and is treated as an independent pattern to obviate the need for circumlocutions.

162. See Tosafot Avodah Zarah 2a, s.v. *asur,* for a fourth justification, similar to the second, namely, that modern-day non-Jews can no longer be considered pagans. See, too, Tosafot Sanhedrin 63b, s.v. *asur* for a similar explanation of the abrogation of a different, but related, norm.

such a matter, one advocating the abrogation of the norm, and the other, its retention.

Until now, we have been primarily concerned in this chapter with the conscious use of extralegal sources in the resolution of questions of law in the second sense that result in the abrogation or modification of norms or the adoption of previously nonprecedented positions. We shall return to this subject when we consider extralegal factors of an ethical/psychological nature. At this point, however, I would like to examine the part that the conscious use of extralegal sources of an economic nature plays *ab initio* in the resolution of questions of law in the second sense (i.e., questions as to what the law is). It is important that this subject be dealt with in order to demonstrate that extralegal considerations influence not only the abrogation or modification of norms but their original promulgation as well. In point of fact, what we shall demonstrate from texts can also be deduced on the basis of logic alone, and the texts will merely indicate that the logical deduction is an accurate reflection of the reality of the halakhic system.

The conscious use of extralegal sources *ab initio* in the resolution of questions of law is but a logical extension of their conscious use in the resolution of questions of law that result in the abrogation or modification of norms, in that to abrogate or to modify an existing norm is, in essence, to promulgate a *new* norm. The basic difference between the two actions is that abrogation and modification begin with existing norms, whereas in an original promulgation, one is concerned by definition, with the creation of an entirely new norm.

We have positioned the discussion of the explicit and conscious use of extralegal factors in the promulgation of norms in the context of the examination of extralegal factors of an economic nature, first, because their use in the medical/scientific realm is self-evident,[163] and second, because proof of their conscious use in the sociological/*realia* realm is very difficult. When medical/scientific data are used as the grounds for abrogation or modification of a norm, the basic claim is one of a change in nature. Obviously, a norm upon which extralegal medical/scientific sources are brought to bear in order to demonstrate a change in nature must itself have been consciously promulgated on the basis of what had been accepted medical/scientific fact at the time. Thus, for example, the claim that *Yoledet le-tisha einah yoledet li-mekutta'in* was obviously based on the promulgators' perception of the scientific reality of their time.[164]

---

163. Though see above, p. 234, for an example of the use of medical/scientific data in the resolution of a question of law *ab initio*.

164. See above, p. 238.

In the sociological/*realia* realm, while the basic claim is also one of the changed nature of people or of the conditions under which they live, proof that the promulgation of the original norm itself was based upon the explicit and conscious use of sociological/*realia* data is difficult, if not impossible, to establish. Surely, the idea that oaths taken in jest cannot be annulled reflects a sociological reality,[165] just as does the norm prohibiting one from rendering decisions until the age of forty,[166] yet it is highly unlikely that those norms were consciously predicated on the sociological reality they reflect. The lack, at the times the norms were drafted, of a science called sociology, possessing its own methodology and vocabulary, makes it most unlikely that those who promulgated the norms were consciously motivated by what we now call sociological reality.

That economic factors and the sociological realities that are determined by economic factors have served *unconsciously* in the promulgation of norms and in the interpretation of biblical norms has long been acknowledged.[167] But it is also true, and can be clearly demonstrated that economic factors have been consciously and explicitly used in the promulgation of norms *ab initio.* We shall proceed with several examples.

The Talmud records:[168]

> According to the Torah *(devar Torah)* a non-Jew inherits from his father. . . . [But the right of a] convert [to inherit from] his gentile father is not from the Torah, but from the rabbis *(mi-divrei soferim)*.[169] For we have learnt in a *mishnah:*[170] "When a convert and a gentile inherit from their gentile father, the convert may say to the gentile, 'you take the idols, and I shall take the money; you take the wine of libations, and I shall take the fruit.' But if they [i.e., the idols or wine] have actually come into his possession, it is forbidden."[171]

---

165. Above, p. 254.

166. Above, p. 260.

167. See as but two classical examples of a large literature the essays of Louis Ginzberg, "On the Significance of the Halacha," in *On Jewish Law and Lore* (Philadelphia: Jewish Publication Society, 1955), and Louis Finkelstein, *The Pharisees* (Philadelphia: Jewish Publication Society, 1962).

168. Kiddushin 17b.

169. That is, the Torah itself is silent on the subject. The rabbis decided that the legal status of converts was that of a fatherless person *(ger ein lo ḥayyis),* that is, a person having no bloodline. Thus, theoretically, a convert should not be allowed to inherit from his biological father, since inheritance follows bloodlines. Obviously, too, a convert is under the same obligation as a natural-born Jew to refrain from deriving any benefit from idolatrous gods.

170. Demai 6:10.

171. I.e., for the convert to arrange the same exchange after the fact that is stipulated by the *mishnah* as permitted before the fact.

> And if it were the case [that the right of the convert to inherit from his gentile father were] *de-oraita,* he would be taking [forbidden] exchanges for idolatrous goods even if the idolatrous goods had not come into his actual possession.[172] Rather, [his right to inherit] is *mi-de-rabbanan,* an enactment that the sages rendered lest he revert to his former state *(shemma yaḥzor le-suro).*

It must be stressed that this rabbinic enactment is nothing other than the promulgation of a new norm. No other norm is abrogated, nor is the modification of any other norm implied. The *prima facie* case against the right of the converted son to inherit is based upon the absence of a legal bloodline connecting him with his father, not upon any prohibition against Jews acquiring nonidolatrous goods owned by gentiles. Thus, the sages promulgated a new norm that allowed the convert to "inherit" his father's goods. Moreover, since the enactment is entirely *mi-de-rabbanan,* the rabbis employed the acceptable legalities of the halakhic system in order to maximize the amount the converted son could acquire. That is, since his acquisition was not technically by virtue of inheritance at all, they decreed that his ownership of the goods would become effective, not from the moment of his father's death, but only from the moment he actually took possession of them. As the Tosafot put it:[173] "The sages ordained a permissible inheritance for him, for it is they who said *(hem ameru)* that he should inherit, and they who said *(ve-hem ameru)* that he does not acquire them until they come into his actual possession."[174]

Economic factors were operative in this instance on two levels. First, the very promulgation of the norm allowing the converted son to "inherit" from his father was based on factors of economics. If no way

---

172. Bearing in mind two facts will make the Talmud's claim comprehensible. First, no Jew may derive any benefit from idolatrous goods. Even the exchange of idolatrous goods one owns for nonidolatrous goods falls under the category of "benefit," and is forbidden. Second, if one acquires an inheritance, his acquisition is counted, not from the moment he actually takes his inheritance into his own possession, but from the moment of the death of the person from whom he inherits. Thus, if the right of a converted son to inherit from his gentile father were *de-oraita,* he would acquire his percentage even of the forbidden idolatrous goods at the moment of his father's death, and exchanging them for permissible substances would be forbidden, on the grounds that he would benefit from the exchange and, therefore, from idolatry. Since the *mishnah* allows him to exchange forbidden articles for permissible ones, so long as he does so before taking actual possession, it follows that he did not acquire the goods by virtue of inheriting them from his father. Therefore, it must be the case that his right to inherit is not *de-oraita,* and that he is entitled to the goods by virtue of some other kind of enactment.

173. Tosafot Kiddushin 17b, s.v. *ella.*

174. Thus reflecting one of the three possible relationships between matters *de-oraita* and matters *de-rabbanan,* namely, the greater the leniency of the latter over the former. See above, pp. 25–31, and pp. 28–31, in particular.

could be found to legalize his "inheritance," the negative economic impact upon the converted son might result in his leaving the Jewish fold in order to gain the inheritance to which he, no doubt, felt entitled. Moreover, having found a method to legalize his "inheritance," the sages, motivated by the desire to maximize his economic gain, chose to make this case one in which rabbinic enactments were less strict than norms *de-oraita*. For it should be noted that even it they had applied the principle *Kol de-takkun rabbanan ke-ein de-oraita takkun*,[175] substantial amounts of inheritance would still have been guaranteed, since only the inheritance or exchange of actual idolatrous goods would have been forbidden.

An example of the conscious and explicit use of economic factors in the formulation of a norm is also reflected in the following talmudic passage.[176]

> It has been taught concerning one who bakes on *yom tov* [festival] for use during the week that Rav Ḥisda said he is flogged,[177] and Rabbah said that he is not flogged. Rav Ḥisda said he is flogged because we do not claim, "Since he might get unexpected guests, he intends it for use."[178] Rabbah said he is not flogged because we do accept the claim "Since . . ." . . . [Rabbah] raised an objection to [Rav Ḥisda] on the basis of the following *mishnah*:[179] "An animal which is in danger of dying *(mesukkenet)*[180] should not be slaughtered [on *yom tov*] except if the owner would be able to eat a minimum amount from it *(ke-zayit)*, roasted,[181] before the end of the day."[182] "Able to

175. See above, pp. 35–40.

176. Pesaḥim 46b.

177. Since baking is a forbidden *melakhah* ("labor"), and is allowed on *yom tov* only for *yom tov* use.

178. If one accepts the claim, it becomes permissible to bake on *yom tov* for weekday use on the grounds that its actual use on *yom tov* has not been precluded by the original intention. That is, the baker would be more than willing to use it for unexpected guests.

179. Beiẓa 3:3.

180. This would render it carrion, and forbidden as food. Thus, the owner is inclined to slaughter it on *yom tov* in order to prevent its loss to himself. Were it clearly for *yom tov* use, its slaughter would be permissible without question.

181. Roasting is taken to be the fastest method of preparation of food. Surely, if there were time to prepare it in any other way it would also be permissible.

182. The version of the *mishnah* itself, as opposed to Rabbah's quotation of it, is somewhat different in form. It reads: ". . . should not be slaughtered except if there is sufficient time left to the day to eat a minimal amount of it, roasted." Whether the Talmud's version reflects a variant reading of the *mishnah*, a paraphrase, or a *baraita* (see *Massoret ha-Shas* [on the printed page of the Gemara], Pesaḥim 46b), the substance remains the same. Even the *mishnah*'s version requires only that sufficient time remain during the day, and does not imply that the owner necessarily eat from the prepared animal.

> eat," which implies "even though he doesn't want to eat," is applicable to me, who claims "Since . . . ,"—[for I could claim,] "Since if he wanted to eat it he could," he may slaughter it. But according to you, who affirm that we do not claim "Since . . . ," on what grounds may he slaughter it? He [i.e., Rav Ḥisda] answered, "Because of his fincancial loss *(hefsed mamono)*." And do we permit a matter forbidden *de-oraita* because of his financial loss? He answered, "Indeed, because of his financial loss he decided to eat a minimum amount of the meat, and that is impossible without slaughtering."

Two different, although seemingly identical, matters are of concern in this passage. The issues are the baking of goods on *yom tov* that are not baked specifically for *yom tov* use and the slaughtering of an animal on *yom tov* when, again, the animal slaughtered was not specifically intended for *yom tov* use. For Rabbah the issues are, in fact, identical, in that for him both reflect the legal principle that forbids the preparation of food on *yom tov* only if it cannot possibly be used until after *yom tov* has ended. If there is a possibility that it might be used on *yom tov*, its preparation is permissible, even if the intention at the time of preparation was not specifically to use it on *yom tov*. Applying strictly legal categories to both cases led Rabbah to conclude that the *mishnah* contradicted Rav Ḥisda's view concerning the preparation of baked goods on *yom tov*, namely, that it is a punishable offense. Rav Ḥisda's response illustrates the influence of economic factors on the promulgation of norms. He declares that there is a salient difference between baked goods and an animal, in that the loss of bread would not cause financial hardship, while the loss of a total animal would. Any Jew facing the imminent loss of such a significant amount of money would, in response, revise his intention in such a way as to make the slaughter of the animal legal. That is, he would salvage his investment in the animal, without at the same time violating the *yom tov*, by deciding to eat at least the minimum amount of meat from the animal before the end of the day. And, since any meat that is to be eaten must be slaughtered, slaughtering the animal becomes permissible on *yom tov*. The case involving the bread, however, is not the same. Since no significant financial loss would be incurred, it would be untenable to presume that its preparation on *yom tov* for use after *yom tov* was, in reality, any other than that which it appeared to be. Thus, its preparation on *yom tov* is in violation of the law and is a punishable offense. Clearly, at least according to Rav Ḥisda, what justifies the *mishnah*'s norm (that permits the slaughter on *yom tov* of an animal in danger of dying) is the probable change in intention on the part of the owner of the animal resulting from his perception that he stands to incur a significant financial loss. Thus, if the intention to eat at least the minimum amount of the animal on *yom tov* can be fulfilled, namely, if there is sufficient time left on *yom tov* to prepare the animal to the point of edibility, its slaughter on *yom tov* is permissible.

The final passage we will consider in this section of this chapter reflects what might well be the ultimate conscious and explicit employment of extralegal sources (in this case, again, economic) within the halakhic system. It deals with the circumvention of the legal system itself. The Talmud records:[183]

> There was an irrigation well that belonged to two people, and from which each would draw on alternating days. One came and drew from it on the wrong day. The other said to him: "It is my day." When the former paid no heed to the latter, he took the handle [or blade] of a hoe and hit him with it.
>
> [Concerning this case Rav Naḥman said to Rav Ḥisda], "He deserved to be hit a hundred times with the handle.[184] Even according to him who holds that one may not make a judgment by himself,[185] he may do so in a case of financial loss."

In certain types of cases, such as the one under discussion, irrevocable financial loss can result if the usual legal processes are followed. In this situation, the one who persisted in drawing water from the well on the wrong day could empty the well during the time it would take the other to procure a judgment against him.[186] Still, it is less likely that the passage we are examining promotes the promulgation of a new norm than that it modifies an apparently unequivocal norm. While theoretically possible, it is not probable that the original formulation of the norm included a provision calling for the circumvention of the entire judicial process on financial grounds. That provision was probably added to the norm as a result of the nexus reflected here between the historical and the legal sources of the law. This nexus, of the kind we introduced only

183. Bava Kama 27b.

184. In the original there is a play on words which cannot be captured in translation: *me'ah pandei be-panda le-maḥyei.*

185. That is, one may not take the law into his own hands. Rav Yehudah held this view, while Rav Naḥman affirmed that one can take the law into his own hands, provided his action is appropriate: *kevan di-be-din avid* ("since he acted appropriately").

186. Rashi, Bava Kama 27b, s.v. *be-makom.*

a few pages ago,[187] was created when the negative results of compliance with the norm were seen to be more detrimental to the one wronged than the negative results of noncompliance were to the legal system. At that point, the present economic reality assumed legal significance and permitted the temporary modification of the original norm.

Ethical/Psychological Data

The fourth category of extralegal considerations is the ethical/psychological. As we shall see, this category is similar to the others we have discussed in that it can apply both to the original promulgation of norms as a result of the resolution of questions of law in the second sense, and to the abrogation or modification of earlier norms as a result of the resolution of questions of law in the second sense. However, we shall see that the nexus between the historical and the legal sources of norms that we find in this category is always of the second type. While the absence of the first nexus pattern from this category of extralegal factors may seem unusual at first glance, it can be readily explained. If modern ethical/psychological data render the original rationale and sole continuing justification of a norm totally inapplicable, resulting in the permanent abrogation or modification of the norm, we would consider such a set of circumstances as reflecting a change in the nature or behavior of people, and would categorize it under the sociological/*realia* heading. In other words, when the extralegal factors of the ethical/psychological category lead to the first nexus pattern between the historical and the legal sources of a norm, we consider the set of circumstances involved to constitute a new sociological reality.[188]

---

187. Above, pp. 277 f.

188. For example, the considerations in the case about *ḥaliẓah* (above, pp. 249–251), and the considerations of "self-restraint" and "self-control" in the case of the oath made in jest (above, pp. 254–255) might both be instances of all-pervasive psychological changes that resulted in a new sociological reality. And we have already noted (above, pp. 273 f.) that ethical/psychological considerations were posited as a reason for the norm prohibiting the ransom of captives at exorbitant prices.

It would, however, be erroneous to conclude that the second nexus type, where compliance with the norm is deemed to have greater detrimental effects than noncompliance would, could not result in permanent abrogation of the norm under all circumstances. Indeed, the very passage on the basis of which we introduced the second nexus type (above, p. 277) posits "animosity" as one of the reasons for abrogating of the norm. That claim, clearly, is ethical in nature, yet results in the total abrogation of the norm. Regarding it, too, we would claim that it reflects a change in the nature of the people. It should be noted, though, that its application in the Talmud was to a specific case, and did not abrogate the norm in other cases. It is the Ritba who extended it to the relationship between all Jews and all non-Jews.

We shall see below how the extralegal considerations of an ethical/psychological nature differ from those which we would categorize as sociological/*realia* factors.

In certain cases, the conscious ethical impetus behind the promulgation of the original norm is made exceptionally clear by the scriptural verse that is quoted by the Talmud as its rationale. For example, the verse "You should do what is proper and good *(ve-asita ha-yashar ve-ha-tov)* in the sight of the Lord"[189] is quoted by the Talmud as the underlying reason for the norm requiring a man to give the first option on the purchase of his land to his neighbor *(dina de-bar meẓra)*[190] No matter how technically detailed the norms governing this right might become, it is clear that the primary factor motivating its promulgation was a concern for the ethical behavior that it is desirable for neighbors to demonstrate toward one another.

There are, of course, instances in which the ethical/psychological factors are not immediately reflected in the actual formulation of the norm, but do become quite clear in the talmudic analysis of the norm. The following example is illustrative:[191]

> [*Mishnah:*] A man [about to be stoned] has his genitals covered, and a woman is covered front and back,[192] according to Rabbi Yehudah. But the sages say that a man is stoned nude,[193] but not a woman.[194]
>
> [*Gemara:*] . . . Rav Naḥman said in the name of Rabbah the son of Abuha, "Scripture says: 'Love your fellowman as yourself'[195] [which means,] 'Choose a nice death *(mitah yafah)* for him.' "[196] Shall we claim that Rav Naḥman's thesis is a matter of disagreement between *tanna'im?*[197] No! All agree with Rav Naḥman. And the disagreement

189. Deuteronomy 6:18.
190. Bava Meẓi'a 108a.
191. Sanhedrin 44b–45a.
192. I.e., wears a small apronlike cloth that covers her genital area both front and back.
193. That is, as described by Rabbi Yehudah, with his genitals covered.
194. Rather, she wears a smock which covers her entirely.
195. Leviticus 19:18.
196. As will become immediately clear, the *gemara*'s assumption is that "nice" means "as fast as possible." Furthermore, the following argument also supposes that the presence of clothing slows the advent of death. The accuracy of that assumption, incidentally, is irrelevant to the present discussion. In theory, though, were the accuracy of the assumption the sole continuing justification for the norms derived from it, and were it demonstrated by medical/scientific evidence to be inaccurate, the grounds for a nexus between historical and legal sources would have been created and would have allowed for the abrogation or modification of the norm, or the adoption of a previously nonprecedented position. If this, in fact, were the case, we would then see extralegal considerations of one category become the grounds for overriding a decision based upon the extralegal considerations of another category.
197. That is, Rabbi Yehudah would agree with Rav Naḥman, as reflected in his view that women, too, are to be stoned basically nude; whereas the sages, who affirm that women are stoned clothed, would disagree with Rav Naḥman's claim that the verse implies choosing a "nice death," i.e., "as fast as possible."

> between the disputants is that one party [i.e., the sages] feels that the prevention of personal embarrassment is more important to people than bodily comfort, and the other [i.e., Rabbi Yehudah] feels that bodily comfort is more important to people than the prevention of embarrassment.

The Talmud's assumption is that "nice" means "as quickly as possible," and that the presence of clothing slows the advent of death. Its solution, in essence, denies only that Rav Naḥman's explanation of the verse need necessarily imply the quickest possible death; a "nice death" means, rather, "as ethically desirable as possible." Rabbi Yehudah, indeed, does equate the "most ethically desirable" with "as quickly as possible." The sages, however, understand "nice death" to imply "least embarrassing." Thus, for a man, who does not suffer unusual shame in being seen nude, so long as his privy parts are covered, the "least embarrassing" ("nice") is also "the quickest possible" death. For a woman, however, the "least embarrassing" death is not the "quickest possible" death, since she feels shame at appearing naked, even if minimally covered.

Ultimately the Talmud reaffirms that both for the sages and for Rabbi Yehudah, the norms that govern the manner in which a person is stoned to death are conscious embodiments of the ethical dictum to love one's fellow as oneself. About that there is no dispute. On the translation of that dictum into ethical behavior there can be, and often is, considerable difference of opinion—a legitimate *maḥaloket,* as this example and the next both indicate.

The Torah specifically prohibits a man from wearing women's clothing.[198] This prohibition was extended by the sages to include all manner of things they considered "womanlike." Now, the Talmud records[199] a statement by Rav Sheshet that *barda*[200] could be used on the Sabbath.[201] Once some *barda* was brought to Ameimar, Mar Zutra, and Rav Ashi, who were sitting together. Of the three, Mar Zutra refused to use it. In explaining his action, the Talmud affirms that his refusal was based not on specific disagreement with the use of *barda* on the Sabbath, but on his more general disagreement with the propriety of its use by men at all, considering the use of *barda* in the category of "womanlike" behavior. A *baraita* is quoted that sustains the thesis that the use of all such soaps by men for the express purpose of "beautifying" themselves is forbidden.

198. Deuteronomy 22:5.
199. Shabbat 50b.
200. A soap made of aloe, myrtle, and violet.
201. Since it doesn't cause the hair of the beard to come out when washing with it.

Preceding that section of the *baraita,* however, is a statement indicating the circumstances in which their use would be permissible. The *baraita* reads: "A man may scrape off the hardened filth or the scabs of wounds that are on his skin, because of the discomfort they cause him. But if his intention in so doing is beautification, it is forbidden." Thus, Mar Zutra, in refusing to use the *barda* offered him, was abiding by the ruling of this *baraita.*

The *baraita* itself, though, reflects the use of ethical/psychological factors in the promulgation of norms. When the psychological mind-set that accompanies a given act is in compliance with what is considered to be legitimate, the act is permissible; the very same act, however, performed with a different psychological mind-set is forbidden.

The Tosafot add another psychological dimension to the norm of the *baraita.*[202] They wrote: "Even if he has no other discomfort than his embarrassment to be seen *(leilekh)* among people, it is permissible. For there is no greater discomfort than that." In essence, the Tosafot see their claim as a simple extension of the thesis of the *baraita* itself. They understand the "discomfort" of the *baraita* to refer to psychological discomfort as well as to physical discomfort. Ultimately, the validity of their claim is based upon extralegal sources of a psychological nature, upon their perception that mental discomfort can cause more unhappiness than physical discomfort.

No less reflective of the use of psychological/ethical considerations in the formulation of norms than the *baraita* we have just examined is the *baraita* quoted by the Talmud as support for the position of Ameimar and Rav Ashi, who *did* use the *barda* that was offered.[203] It reads: "A man may wash his face, hands, and feet each day in honor of his Creator *(bi-shevil kono),*[204] since it is written: 'God made everything for His own honor.' "[205]

The glorification of God is both an ethical and a psychological *desideratum.* Actions that enhance that glorification and that can be performed with the mind-set that glorification is, in fact, the religious function intended, cannot fall into the category of "womanlike" actions.

Actually, there does not seem to be any technical disagreement between the two *baraitot.* Were it possible for the two authors to meet, they might well discover that their basic *maḥaloket* revolves around the theoretical possibility that the average man can engage in a given action

202. Tosafot Shabbat 50b, s.v. *bi-shevil.*
203. Shabbat 50b.
204. In Whose image man is fashioned. Therefore, that which reflects honor for man is also honor for God. Cf. Rashi, Shabbat 50b, s.v. *bi-shevil.*
205. Proverbs 16:4.

with the conscious mind-set that his action is intended for the glorification of God, particularly when the action is as mundane as washing.[206]

Since psychological factors are considered with regularity in the promulgation of norms, it is not surprising that, as happened with extralegal economic factors, there have developed in this category, too, a number of phrases that have been explicitly formulated in order to indicate, in a shorthand manner, when extralegal psychological factors have been considered legally significant.[207] One such formula that appears regularly is *Samkha da'ata* ("The mind relies"), or variations of it. It indicates the presence or absence (if in the negative) of a mind-set that is legally relevant. Several examples will clarify its application.

The Talmud records the following:[208]

> One whose ass drivers and workmen were laden with pure goods[209] [may assume that the goods remain] pure, even if he becomes separated from them by more than a *mil*.[210] But if he said to them, "You go ahead, and I will follow," his goods are considered impure from the moment they are out of his sight. Why is the first case different from the second case? Rava said, "The first case is one in which he [i.e., the owner] could come upon them indirectly."[211] If that be the case, why not make the same claim about the second case? [The same claim would not apply, for] since he said to them,

---

206. It should be noted in passing that the talmudic passage reflects the fact that no precedented position existed during the time of Ameimar, Mar Zutra, and Rav Ashi—otherwise the actions of one of them in ignoring the precedent would have needed explaining. The two positions reflected in the two *baraitot* were, therefore, within the realm of judicial discretion, and the ultimate factor governing the decision of each must have been his own perception of the psychological mind-set likely to prevail. In other words, they acted on the principle *Ein lo la-dayyan ella mah she-einav ro'ot*, and the result of this exercise of judicial discretion by diverse individuals was the establishment of two divergent behaviors, each legitimate.

207. Regarding the explicit shorthand phrases of a psychological nature, the same caveat against mistaking them for legal norms that we stressed regarding shorthand formulae for economic considerations applies.

208. Ḥagigah 20b, quoting Tosefta Tohorot 6:16. Cf. also Avodah Zarah 69a.

209. The workmen were *ammei ha-areẓ*, that is, not careful about matters of ritual purity. If they touched the goods they were transporting, the goods would become ritually impure. In the case under discussion, the goods were enclosed in earthenware containers, which are not susceptible to ritually impurity when touched from the outside by those who are themselves impure. Thus, even though the workmen are assumed to be impure, they do not render the goods within the earthenware containers impure through their contact with the containers. Only if they directly touched the goods within the containers would they render them impure.

210. That is, he may assume that the workmen did not touch the goods, even when he, the owner, was separated from them.

211. Thus in Avodah Zarah 69a.

"You go ahead, and I will follow," they are assured *(mismakh samkha da'ataihu)*.

There is no overt action that distinguishes the former case from the latter. In point of fact, the owner could come upon the workmen in an identical manner in both of these cases. What does distinguish the two cases, rather, is the psychological mind-set of the workmen. In the former, the workmen fear to touch the goods lest they be caught in the act by the owner, who might come upon them by surprise. Since the owner had given no indication of his intention to follow only at a distance, the workmen suspect that, even though he is not visible to them at the moment, he might arrive at any time. In the latter, however, the stated intention of the owner to follow at a distance assures the workmen that the likelihood of his catching them in the act is nonexistent. That psychological difference results in different norms that govern otherwise identical cases.

The Mishnah records in the name of Rabbi Me'ir that any sexual relations that follow a marriage are illicit *(be'ilat zenut)* if the amount of the marriage contract is lower than 200 *zuz* for a virgin or 100 *zuz* for a widow.[212] The Talmud understands Rabbi Me'ir's view to imply that the relationship is illicit even if there had been a clear prior stipulation (*afillu bi-tena'ah*) that the amount of the contract would be less.[213] Since Rabbi Me'ir calls the relationship illicit even when such a stipulation exists, it is clear that he considers the stipulation to be invalid and the woman entitled to the full amount the law demands. But this deduction presents us with a quandary. If, in the final analysis, the woman is legally entitled to the full 200 or 100 *zuz*, as she is according to Rabbi Me'ir, why does he call the relationship illicit? The Talmud answers that since the man stipulated an amount lower than the legal minimum, *La samkha da'ata*, the woman has no psychological assurance that she will, in fact, receive the entire amount to which she is legally entitled. Therefore, it is her mind-set that determines that the nature of the relationship is illicit, not the legal reality (i.e, the fact that she could collect the full amount of the marriage contract dictated by the law). As Rashi puts it: "Even though she would collect in the final analysis, since his stipulation is invalid, nonetheless, since he made a prior stipulation, he [i.e., Rabbi Me'ir] calls it illicit, for she has no assurance concerning the marriage contract from the moment of intercourse."[214]

212. Ketubbot 5:1.
213. Ibid. 56b.
214. Ibid. s.v. *kol*. Cf. the comments of Rabbi Judan ben Nathan (Rivan, 11th–12th cent.) and Rabbi Isaac ben Samuel of Dampierre (Ri, d. ca. 1185) in Tosafot Ketubbot 51a, s.v. *mani*.

Our final example of the general use of psychological factors in the formulation of norms and, as well, of the use of the shorthand principle *Samkha da'ata* comes from a section of the Talmud that asks whether norms regulating unfair dealing are to be applied to verbal commitments. The Talmud reads:[215]

> We have learned in a *mishnah* that it happened once that Rabbi Yoḥanan ben Mati'a said to his son, "Go hire workmen for us."[216] He went and stipulated an agreement to feed them.[217] When he came and reported to his father, the latter said to him, "My son, even if you prepare for them a feast as sumptuous as that of King Solomon,[218] you will not have fulfilled your obligation toward them, for they are the sons of Abraham, Isaac, and Jacob.[219] Rather, before they begin to work, go and tell them that [the agreement to work is valid only] on the condition that their food claim is restricted to bread and pulse."
>
> Now if the norms governing unfair dealing apply to verbal agreements, how could he say "Go and retract"? [No! The rules of unfair dealing can apply to verbal agreements] but this case is different, since the workers themselves were not assured.[220] Why? They know that the matter depends on the father. If so, he should be able to retract even if they had already begun to work.[221] [No!] If they had begun their work, they were certainly assured. For they would think, "Surely he [i.e., the son] reported the agreement to his father, and he accepted it."

One of the factors that determines the presence or absence of unfair dealing is the psychological mind-set of the workers. Before there is any psychological certitude that the father had actually accepted the terms stipulated by his son, and the workers still have the option of rejecting

215. Bava Meẓi'a 49a.
216. Ibid. 7:1.
217. That is, the son agreed that meals would be provided. The Talmud (Bava Meẓi'a 86b) understands that such a stipulation indicates an agreement to feed the workers above and beyond the customary levels, since even without the clear stipulation, feeding at the customary levels would be incumbent upon the employer.
218. I Kings 5:2–3.
219. Whose feast was even more sumptuous, as explained by the sages (Bava Meẓi'a 86b) on the basis of Genesis 18:7, since Abraham prepared three oxen for three guests, and Solomon's feast was for the entire people.
220. That is, they did not assume that the stipulation was, in fact, binding.
221. And if Rabbi Yoḥanan ben Mati'a could have retracted even after the workers had begun their labor, why did he insist that his son retract the agreement with the workers before they began their labor?

whatever offer the father might actually make or of working on the basis of the local custom, there is no unfair dealing involved. However, once the psychological mind-set of the workers is such that they are convinced that the employer intends to abide by the agreement of his son-agent, retraction of that agreement would constitute unfair dealing, and would be forbidden.

In addition to the explicit reference to psychological factors indicated by the use of the term *Samkha da'ata,* the passage also reflects the possible conscious use of extralegal sources that can, in theory, be categorized either as economic or as psychological/ethical. Rabbi Yoḥanan's defense of his intention to retract his son's agreement could be read as an economic one; he might be claiming that compliance with his son's agreement would be too costly for him. More likely, considering his choice of words, "You will not have fulfilled your obligation to them," his claim was psychological/ethical. Stipulating an agreement to feed workers above and beyond the customary levels is likely to induce in them a psychological mind-set that would make actual compliance with the agreement nearly impossible. If the employer has already agreed to provide more food than the customary levels, he will be understood by the employees to have intended a significant amount of additional food, for they might reason that if he had intended only a minimal increase, why would he have bothered to mention any increase at all? Consequently, when the meal is actually served, the perceptions of employer and employees regarding the degree to which the meal complies with what each side understands to be the agreement will be very different. Thus, the most ethical resolution to the problem would be to retract the agreement in order to prevent the ultimate disillusionment of the employees. For, were the misunderstanding to come to pass, the employer would be guilty of an ethical trespass.[222]

Having demonstrated the use of extralegal factors of a psychological/ethical nature in the original formulation of norms, we now turn our

---

222. We should stress again that the enumeration of one possible psychological reaction to a given action does not preclude another. That is, the situation could surely give rise to a legitimate *maḥaloket*. One could also claim, for example, that the workmen would look upon any increase in food beyond the customary level as a kindness to be appreciated rather than as grounds for disillusionment. In the final analysis, the origin of the *maḥaloket* would be traced to varying perceptions of the possible psychological reactions of the workers. Were scientific studies available which either supported or contradicted one of the positions, they would constitute medical/scientific data that might sway a *posek* to adopt one view over the other, even if the adopted view were the nonprecedented position. Or, in the absence of any legal source contrary to the rejected view, such medical/scientific evidence might lead a *posek* to abrogate the norm entirely, on the basis of the first nexus type governing the relationship between historical and legal sources.

attention to their use in the resolution of questions of law in the second sense when the result is the modification or abrogation of already existing norms.

The Sabbath domain called *karmelit* is rabbinically created;[223] *mi-de-oraita* no such domain exists. *Mi-de-rabbanan,* however, the same restrictions apply to it with regard to carrying on the Sabbath as to the public domain. Just as it is forbidden to transfer an object on the Sabbath from the public domain to a private domain, or vice versa, so it is forbidden to transfer an object on the Sabbath from a *karmelit* to a private domain, or vice versa. Thus, if a stream of water were to flow into a courtyard, and the wall surrounding the courtyard (which serves as a necessary indicator of the boundary between the public domain or the *karmelit* and a private domain) were completely absent at the point of entry of the water, it would be forbidden *mi-de-rabbanan* to draw from the water, which itself is legally a *karmelit,* into the private domain. Furthermore, since under normal circumstances, an incomplete wall *(meḥiẓah teluyah)*[224] does not have the legal status of a wall, if there were an incomplete wall at the point of the water's entry into the private domain, its presence would make no difference regarding the right to draw the water on the Sabbath, which would still be forbidden. Yet the Talmud clearly states that an incomplete wall is counted as a wall in cases where doing so would enable the people to draw water on the Sabbath.[225] The stipulated grounds are: *Kal hu she-hekellu ḥakhamim be-mayim* ("it is a leniency which the sages enacted for water"). Since the legal function of the wall is to serve as a necessary indicator of the line of demarcation *(hekker)* between the domains, *any* indicator is considered sufficient when the drawing of water is at stake.[226]

What we have here, clearly, is a situation of *Hem ameru ve-hem ameru.*[227] That is, the sages decreed the status of *karmelit* which made the drawing of water there forbidden in the first place, and they decreed that even an incomplete wall should be considered sufficient to mark the boundary of the private domain in such cases, so as to permit the drawing of water.

What might have motivated the sages to apply the systemic principle *Hem ameru ve-hem ameru* in instances such as these? It seems most plausible that the considerations were basically extralegal, and ethical. The undue hardship that a prohibition against drawing the water would

---

223. See above, chap. 2, n. 47.
224. That is, one that does not extend to the ground.
225. Eruvin 12a.
226. Other talmudic sections that reflect other leniencies regarding water can be found in Eruvin 16b, 48a, 86b, and Ketubbot 101b.
227. See above, pp. 28–31.

impose on the inhabitants of the courtyard into which it flowed prompted them to seek a systemically legitimate means to alleviate it. This was possible if they limited the degree to which the demarcation function of the wall had to be fulfilled, by considering even an incomplete wall sufficient.[228]

Moreover, the leniencies regarding water probably represent modifications of the original norms regarding *karmelit* and incomplete walls. Furthermore, since both the reasons that led the sages to ordain the *karmelit* status in the first place, as well as the reasons that led them to refuse to ascribe to incomplete walls the same legal status as complete walls, continue to apply, the relationship between the historical and the legal sources reflected here cannot be of the first nexus type. Rather, this is a case in which it seemed reasonable to the sages to posit that the negative results (ethical in nature, in this instance) of compliance with the original norm outweighed the negative results of noncompliance; particularly so, since the modification continued to maintain that the stream of water retains its status as a *karmelit* if there was no incomplete wall at its point of entry into the courtyard, and drawing from it into the courtyard remained forbidden. The modification, in the final analysis, involved the recognition of a minimal fulfillment of the demarcation function of walls, instead of a maximal fulfillment, as sufficient.

In certain other instances the sages also legislated changes in order to effect leniencies. They were lenient, for example, with regard to accepting claims made by women on their own behalf when there were no other witnesses to the events, and lenient on accepting other generally unacceptable testimony. These leniencies affected two categories of cases: One consisted of cases involving priests' wives who had been taken captive and then released, and the second, of cases involving wives who had no proof of the death of their husbands.

With regard to the first category, it was suspected in the talmudic era that a woman who had been taken captive had probably been raped. If a priest's wife had been captured and then released, the law prohibited her priest-husband from taking her back, on the suspicion that she had been raped, and had therefore become legally a *zonah* (lit., "a whore").[229] The sages, under certain circumstances, however, permitted her to be reunited with her husband on the basis of her own statement that she

---

228. It should be equally noted and stressed that they did not issue blanket permission to draw water from a *karmelit* to a private domain on the Sabbath. If neither an incomplete wall nor any other of the leniencies they ordained for water was present, the drawing of the water would have remained forbidden.

229. Leviticus 21:7.

had not been raped,[230] or on the basis of what in other circumstances would constitute unacceptable testimony.[231] These leniencies were ultimately justified by the formula *Bi-shevuyah hekellu* ("they were lenient concerning a captive woman").[232] The sages decided that whenever possible, they would not insist on the separation of a priest from his wife on grounds of suspicion alone;[233] only when the fact of the rape was either certain or highly probable would they impose the separation.[234]

The problem with regard to the wife who had no proof of her husband's death was that without such proof she could not remarry, and was called an *agunah* (lit., "bound" or "anchored"). If she did remarry, and if her first husband reappeared, the children of the second marriage became *mamzerim* (i.e., offspring of an illegal or incestuous union). The sages were very lenient, therefore, and accepted testimony about the husband's death that would have been unacceptable in other kinds of cases. The Talmud claims in these cases both *Mi-shum igguna akkillu ba rabbanan* ("because of the problem of the *agunah*, the sages were lenient about her")[235] and *Shane edut ishah de-akkillu ba rabbanan* ("the testimony regarding the right of women to remarry is different, for the sages were lenient regarding it").[236]

In a passage that outlines these leniencies, justifies them, and reflects the ultimate motivation for seeking them, Maimonides wrote:

> Let it not seem difficult in your sight that the sages allowed [the remarriage] of even strict cases of illegal marriages *(ha-ervah ha-ḥamurah)* on the basis of women's testimony, or that of a slave or a maidservant, or that of a non-Jew speaking incidentally *(mesi'aḥ le-fi tumo)* or second hand *(ed mi-pi ed)*, or written and without extensive cross-examination, as we have explained. For the Torah is not punctilious in requiring the testimony of two witnesses and all of the other requirements of testimony, except concerning a matter that could not be substantiated except by the witnesses and their testimony. . . . But a matter that could be substantiated without the

230. Mishnah Ketubbot 2:5.
231. Ibid. 2:9.
232. See, for example, Ketubbot 23a and 27b, Bava Kama 114b.
233. See Rashi on Ketubbot 23a and 27b, s.v. *bi-shevuyah*.
234. Since the prohibition against a priest living with a woman who has been raped is *de-oraita*, these leniencies are not instances of *Hem ameru ve-hem ameru*. Nor, it should be noted, did they invoke their rights to abrogate matters *de-oraita* (in this instance *be-kum va-aseh*). They chose, rather, to ignore suspicion and apply the norm only when there was certain or highly probable proof.
235. Yevamot 88a and 94a, and Gittin 3a.
236. Yevamot 25a–b.

> witness, and concerning which the witness could not escape detection if the matter were not as he said, as, for example, one who testifies that so-and-so has died, the Torah is not punctilious concerning the witness, since it is unlikely that a witness should testify falsely about such a matter. Therefore the sages were lenient concerning such a matter, and accounted as reliable one witness, or a maidservant, from written testimony, and without extensive cross-examination, so that the women of Israel should not remain *agunot* [plural of *agunah*].[237]

The leniencies invoked by the sages were legally defensible on the grounds that the testimony in such matters was supportive, not determinative; the likelihood that a witness would lie, knowing that time might well prove that he had lied, is seen to be minimal. Therefore, the negative results of compliance with the norms of testimony, namely, refusing to allow the women in question to remarry, were permitted to outweigh the negative results of noncompliance, namely, the farfetched likelihood that a witness would lie (resulting in the woman becoming an adulteress and her offspring *mamzerim*), and modifications in the norms governing testimony were introduced.[238] Still, it is clear, despite the legal grounds adduced, that the underlying impetus for the quest for necessary legal justification was the ethical extralegal consideration "that the women of Israel should not remain *agunot*."

We shall now turn our attention to a passage we will examine at length, for several reasons. First, it reaffirms the legitimacy of recourse to extralegal psychological factors, and serves as an example of the second type of possible nexus between historical and legal sources. Moreover, with its multiple interpretations, the passage demonstrates again how complex and ultimately subjective the use and interpretation of extralegal considerations can become. Finally, we see once again how interrelated are the workings of legal and extralegal sources, both of which play significant parts in the determination of the law.

The Mishnah records[239] that a man may carry his son on the Sabbath within the house or courtyard (where carrying is permitted except for

---

237. *Mishneh Torah,* Hilkhot Gerushin 13:29.

238. Recall that Mishnah Yevamot 15:4 specifically excludes several categories of women from the leniency regarding such testimony. Obviously, the sages felt that in the case of those women, the likelihood of a purposeful lie was not farfetched at all. Thus, the negative results of compliance with the usual norm did not outweigh the negative results of noncompliance, and the usual norm remained unmodified vis-à-vis those categories of suspect witnesses. But see above, pp. 262 f.

239. Shabbat 21:1.

items that are *mukẓeh*)[240], even though the child is holding a stone. Since a stone is *mukẓeh,* it would seem to follow that the *mishnah* does not consider the father to be carrying the stone; if it did, the father would be forbidden to carry the son. Rava claims[241] that one who carries a live child who is wearing a pocketbook around his neck from one domain to another on the Sabbath (which is always forbidden whether or not the items are *mukẓeh*) incurs no liability for the child,[242] but is liable for carrying the pocketbook. It would seem, therefore, that Rava must consider the father to be carrying the pocketbook, even though it is around the neck of the child, and his statement is in clear contradiction to the *mishnah,* which does not consider an object held by the child to be carried by the father. The Talmud records that in the school of Rabbi Yannai the apparent contradiction between Rava and the *mishnah* was resolved by affirming that the *mishnah* refers to a child "who yearns" *(she-yesh lo ga'agu'in)* for his father. Rashi explains: "['Who yearns' means] that if his father does not pick him up, he will become sick. And the sages abrogated *(lo he'emidu)* the norm according to which even indirect carrying *(tiltul she-lo be-yadayim)* is considered carrying whenever there is some danger, even if the danger is not really life-endangering, but only the danger of illness."[243] While Rashi couches his explanation in the strongest possible terms, those of "illness," it is clear that *ga'agu'in* ("yearnings") expresses a psychological need more than a real physical one, although a psychological need of this sort, if frustrated, may result in physical manifestations, such as uncontrollable crying or depression.

Surely, the original promulgation of the norms prohibiting indirect carrying did not contain an explicit provision for its abrogation for *mukẓeh* items on the grounds of psychological distress. More likely, the impetus behind the modification of the original norm was the perception of the sages that the psychological harm that might accrue to the child as a result of compliance with the norm was more detrimental than the potential negative results of noncompliance with the norm.

The conclusion of the talmudic section is equally illustrative. It reads:

> If it is so [that the case in the *mishnah* refers to a child who yearns for his father], why is it restricted to the child's carrying a stone? It

---

240. I.e., forbidden by the rabbis to be handled at all on the Sabbath.

241. Shabbat 141b.

242. On the grounds that he is not really carrying the child, since *ha-ḥai nose et aẓmo* ("a live body carries itself"). Compare the difference between carrying a child who is asleep and one who is awake. The former is "dead weight," and feels much heavier than the latter.

243. Shabbat 141b, s.v. *be-tinok.*

> should be permissible even if the child is carrying a coin [i.e., which is also *mukẓeh*]. Why, then, had Rava said about the *mishnah* that it applies only to the case of a stone, but not to the case of a coin? [The resolution is] that if the stone should fall the father would not himself pick it up, whereas if the coin fell the father would pick it up.

Rashi understands the Talmud's resolution of the last problem to offer a totally new explanation of the *mishnah*,[244] very different from the explanation of the school of Rabbi Yannai (which had to be rejected because it could not account for a distinction between indirect carrying of a stone and a coin, while Rava had clearly stated that the *mishnah* allows only the indirect carrying of a stone, but not a coin). The wording of the *mishnah*, "a man may carry his son who is holding a stone," misled us to believe that the primary concern was whether or not the father would be guilty of indirectly carrying the *mukẓeh* object by virtue of the fact that he was carrying his son. But, as Rashi sees it, the Talmud's resolution to the question of the distinction between a stone and a coin (which allows us to understand how Rava could agree with the *mishnah* but forbid the same action if the son was holding a coin) forces us to reconsider the primary concern of the *mishnah* and to see that the concern is not with indirect carrying, but with the father's actually picking up the object (stone or coin) if it fell, and carrying it directly. Furthermore, if this is the primary concern of the *mishnah*, the words "carry his son" are only one example of what the father may be doing with his son, and do not exclude other possibilities of what the father may be doing with his son. Indeed, if the father was merely holding the son's arms for support, aiding him in walking, and the son was holding a stone, the concern of the *mishnah*, as Rashi has now explained it, would apply (even though there is no indirect carrying at all, since neither the child nor the stone is being carried by the father). And under normal circumstances Rava would forbid the father to aid his son in walking if the son was holding a stone, for fear that the father might pick up the stone if it fell. Only if the son has *ga'agu'in* would Rava, according to Rashi, ignore the suspicion—on psychological grounds—that the father would pick up the stone if it fell. And if the object in the child's hand was a coin, Rava would forbid the father to aid his son in walking (or to carry him), for in that case the likelihood that the father would end up carrying the coin if it fell is great, even if the child has *ga'agu'in*. In Rava's judgment, according to Rashi, the psycho-

---

244. Ibid. 142a, s.v. *attei*.

logical needs of the child who is carrying a coin do not outweigh the negative results of the psychological mind-set of the father, which would most likely lead him to pick up the coin and violate the norms of *mukẓeh*. Thus, though the primary grounds of concern have changed from those of Rabbi Yannai's school, according to Rashi, the psychological factor remains the grounds for ignoring the suspicion with regard to the stone and for refusing to ignore the suspicion with regard to the coin.

The Tosafot make two attempts to reconcile the Talmud's resolution to the question of the distinction between a stone and a coin with our original understanding of the *mishnah*, namely, that its primary concern was whether the father's action constituted indirect carrying.[245] The essential difference between the two attempts lies in the attitude of the father to the object while it is in the hand of the child. According to the first explanation, if the father considers the object insignificant *(mevattel leih)*, the object loses its status as *mukẓeh* from the start, and carrying it within the house or the courtyard is not forbidden at all. How would this attitude be reflected in action? The father would ignore the object completely if it were to fall from the child's hand. According to this explanation, it is the loss of *mukẓeh* status from the start which allows the father to carry the object indirectly. If this, indeed, were seen to be the *prima facie* assumption of the *mishnah*, the distinction between a stone and a coin could be easily understood. Since the father is eager to meet the psychological needs of his son, the stone loses all significance for him and loses its status as *mukẓeh*. The father's mind-set regarding the coin, however, is such that it cannot become insignificant to him, no matter how sincerely he may wish to alleviate the child's yearning. Thus, the coin retains its *mukẓeh* status. How would this mind-set be reflected in action? The father would pick up the coin if it were to fall from the child's hand. Thus, if he were to carry the child while the child was holding the coin, he would be in violation of the norm prohibiting indirect carrying. Ultimately, therefore, it is the mind-set of the father vis-à-vis the object held by the child that determines its *mukẓeh* status, and implies either a prohibition against or permission to carry it indirectly.

The second attempt of the Tosafot accords better with the simple meaning of the *mishnah* and with Rava's claim that the *mishnah* allows the father to carry only a son who is holding a stone and not a son who is holding a coin, even if the son holding the coin has *ga'agu'in*, as the school of Rabbi Yannai interpreted the *mishnah*. According to this

245. Tosafot Shabbat 141b, s.v. *i hakhi*.

explanation, the *prima facie* assumption of the *mishnah* is that the stone retains its status as *mukẓeh*. The prohibition of *mukẓeh* is, however, superseded by the psychological yearning of the child. That is, the sages allow the father to carry the stone indirectly even though it is *mukẓeh*. But, the Tosafot ask, if this is true, should any distinction be made between a stone and a coin, since in both cases the object remains *mukẓeh*, and in both cases the same psychological needs of the child obtain? Furthermore, since the sages have already allowed a *mukẓeh* object to be carried, albeit indirectly, no greater violation of the norms of *mukẓeh* would be entailed if the father were to lift the object if it fell. Then, too, he would be doing no more than carrying a *mukẓeh* object directly that he had been carrying indirectly, but with permission. And since permission to carry it had already been granted, the difference between direct and indirect carrying seems insignificant. From the questions of the Tosafot it seems to follow that the same considerations ought to apply even if the *mukẓeh* object in the child's hand is a coin. Its *mukẓeh* status should also be superseded by the child's yearning, since, at worst, the result might be only that the father carries directly the *mukẓeh* object he had been carrying indirectly, with permission. The answer of the Tosafot is that the final step is unwarranted. That is, that the difference between direct and indirect carrying of a *mukẓeh* object *is* significant. Therefore, while the norms prohibiting indirect carrying might be superseded by psychological considerations, when it is unlikely that direct carrying might result (i.e., in the case of the stone), the same psychological considerations would be insufficient to supersede the prohibition against indirect carrying of a *mukẓeh* object when direct carrying might be the likely result (i.e., in the case of the coin).[246]

For the final example of this section we jump again to the nineteenth century and the responsa of Rabbi Moses Sofer (Ḥatam Sofer, 1762–1839). At the end of a long discussion on the admissibility of official non-Jewish documents in establishing the death of a Jew for the purpose of permitting his wife to remarry,[247] the Ḥatam Sofer considers one final problem, namely:

> . . . That the document reflects a purposeful lie *(nikhtav be-sheker)*, having been written because of a bribe offered by someone who wished ill *(lehakhshil)* for the woman. Now we have found this

246. Were it possible to reconstruct this talmudic section, ferreting out exactly what the relation of Rava's original comment was to the *mishnah*, and reconciling his final comment definitively, that reconstruction might have halakhic significance. This kind of problem is one of the subjects to be dealt with in chap. 11.

247. *Responsa of Ḥatam Sofer, Even ha-Ezer*, pt. 1, no. 43.

suspicion applicable only to the five categories of women who hate her.[248] Yet we say at the end of Yevamot:[249] "Perhaps it was a cowife?"[250] And we answer in the name of the school of Rabbi Ishma'el that when it is a time of danger we write the divorce and accept the testimony *(kotevin u-me'idim)*,[251] and do not worry about the five categories of women, since it would be impossible otherwise.[252] Thus it is in our case, too.

The ultimate claim of the Ḥatam Sofer is that we have no ethical choice but to ignore the possibility that the document was written as the result of a bribe, for were we to act on the basis of that suspicion, the woman in question would have to remain an *agunah*. He deduces support for his position from the talmudic section at the end of Yevamot. There, too, the sages allowed a suspicion to go unheeded. There, too, the final justification for the decision seems to be in the realm of the ethical/psychological. There, too, since it was highly improbable that someone would wish to harm the woman, the negative results of compliance with the norm that forbids accepting suspicious evidence were considered more detrimental than the possible negative results of noncompliance with the norm.

We have chosen to end our discussion of ethical/psychological factors with a passage from the Ḥatam Sofer in order to indicate that these factors have been invoked even in the modern era by one whose credentials as a halakhic authority are impeccable. Although many may feel that consideration of ethical/psychological data is most precarious because such data are of a kind least amenable to objective analysis, its use from the talmudic era through the modern period cannot be gainsaid.

---

248. Mishnah Yevamot 15:4.

249. Yevamot 122a. The *mishnah* there states that a woman can be allowed to remarry on the basis of an echo (*bat kol*). It quotes an example of a case in which someone stood on a mountain top and screamed that Mr. So-and-so, the son of So-and-so, from city X, has died. When they went to find him, they could find no one. Yet they allowed his wife to remarry.

250. I.e., the cowife, one of the categories of suspect women, may have screamed and then fled.

251. The reading in the Ḥatam Sofer should undoubtedly be *kotevin ve-notenin* ("we write and deliver [the divorce]"), as it is in Yevamot.

252. Rashi, in Yevamot, explains the passage: When a man is in danger, as, for example, when he cries from a pit and says that whoever hears his voice should write a divorce for his wife, we write and deliver the divorce. We rely on him regarding everything he said, namely: "I am So-and-so the son of So-and-so." And here, too (i.e., in the *mishnah* about the echo), it is like a time of danger, for if we do not heed the echo, the woman will find no other witness, and will remain an *agunah*.

This chapter has been devoted to a demonstration of the legitimacy of extralegal sources within the halakhic system. We have established that extralegal factors are used, on a conscious level, both in the promulgation of new norms and in the resolution of questions of law in the second sense that result in the modification or abrogation of norms or in the adoption of previously nonprecedented positions. We divided extralegal material into four categories—medical/scientific, sociological/*realia*, economic, and psychological/ethical—and saw that the categories frequently overlap. In addition, we discerned two possible kinds of nexus between extralegal and legal sources that allow us to determine when extralegal factors are legally significant and when they are not.

Before closing this discussion, however, several points need to be made.

First, our emphasis on the widespread use of extralegal factors in the halakhic system is in no way meant to imply that they play a part in every legal decision; there are many decisions reached on the basis of legal sources alone. Even more, it is frequently the case that legal sources that were themselves formulated on the basis of extralegal considerations are cited again and again without any reconsideration of those extralegal sources; the possibility of a nexus between the extralegal and the legal sources in these cases remain precisely that, a possibility, no more. If there is no impetus motivating the *posek* to elevate the historical sources to legal significance, they remain legally insignificant.

Secondly, since the question of whether or not the impetus motivating a *posek* to take any one of these actions is compelling can itself be a matter of legitimate *maḥaloket*, we have recognized the role that subjectivity plays in the halakhic system. But subjectivity, we have seen, need be neither capricious nor whimsical. While ultimately *Ein lo la-dayyan ella mah she-einav ro'ot*, no *posek* who is committed to the preservation of the legal system and to guaranteeing its continued viability, and who reflects both the academic qualification of *gamir ve-savir* and the personal characteristic of *yirat ha-shem*,[253] would allow himself the luxury of capricious or whimsical actions.,

Thirdly, rabbinic exegesis of scriptural passages is very similar to the promulgation of norms, the clear difference between them being that rabbinic exegesis purports to be the *direct* interpretation of the *grundnorm* rather than the establishment of new norms consonant with its spirit. But given the similarity between these activities, we can surely expect the categories of extralegal factors we have found to be operative in the promulgation of new norms also to be reflected in the rabbinic

253. See above, chap. 6.

interpretation of Scripture. And, indeed, this is the case. Can it be denied, for example, that the rabbinic explanations of the biblical verses detailing the case of the rebellious son[254]—which in the final analysis, seem to transform this matter into something purely theoretical[255]—were, in all probability, motivated by concerns we have called ethical/psychological? Is it not also probable that the forced interpretations of the biblical verses that form the basis for the institution of "warning,"[256] without which a person cannot be executed, were also motivated by ethical concerns?

And surely the laws of borrowing and lending at interest, as postulated by the sages,[257] reflect the probability that these interpretations were motivated by concerns of economic reality. Indeed, it seems more than probable that the words Rabbi Shimon puts into the mouths of usurers,[258] "Moses was a wise man[259] and his Torah is true[260] . . . and if he had known how much money one could make from interest, he would not have issued the prohibition," reflected more than the thoughts of sinners alone.

Borrowings from other legal systems, whether consciously or unconsciously, also reflect the influence of extralegal considerations. Such borrowings often incorporate the sociological reality into the Jewish legal system, sometimes intact and sometimes modified.[261]

Finally, it should be stressed that recourse to extralegal considerations is not restricted to any one kind of legal procedure. Their applicability, for example, is not restricted to a situation requiring the exercise of judicial discretion when there is no precedented position, or to one that requires overturning a precedented position in favor of a previously nonprecedented position, or one that requires the abrogation or modifi-

254. Deuteronomy 21:18–21. Mishnah and Talmud Sanhedrin, chap. 8.

255. See the *baraita* on Sanhedrin 71a: "The case of a rebellious son never happened and never will. Why, therefore, is it written in the Torah? So that it should be expounded upon, and a reward be received for doing so."

256. Sanhedrin 40b–41a.

257. Bava Meẓi'a, chap. 5.

258. Ibid. 75b. Cf. Yerushalmi Bava Meẓi'a 5:13, 10d.

259. A euphemism for "a fool."

260. A euphemism for "nonsense."

261. On the pervasive Greek influence on Jewish law, see the writings of Prof. Saul Lieberman, including *Hellenism in Jewish Palestine* (New York: Jewish Theological Seminary, 1962) and *Greek in Jewish Palestine*, 2d ed. (New York: Philipp Feldman, 1965). On Roman influences, see Boaz Cohen, *Jewish and Roman Law* (New York: Jewish Theological Seminary, 1966). These volumes are merely examples of a vast literature. Much fertile ground remains for research into the borrowing process in every stage of halakhic development—both the borrowing of actual norms and the borrowing of methods of study, analysis, and exegesis.

cation of norms, or the reconsideration of the ostensible factual basis of a legal presumption. Nevertheless, it would seem to be true that the more systemically severe the legal procedure, the more reticent *posekim* are (and should be) to make use of extralegal material. That is, it is easier for them to invoke extralegal considerations in order to justify choosing one position over another if neither of the positions constitutes a precedent. They are more cautious about invoking them when the rejected position is a precedented one, and even more cautious in invoking them in order to abrogate or modify a matter of law in the first sense.

Indeed, the conclusion is inescapable that recognized systemic authorities can invoke these same categories of extralegal sources even in the exercise of their ultimate rights vis-à-vis matters *de-oraita*. In fact, a rereading of the sources quoted in Chapter 7 will demonstrate the accuracy of this contention (and also the fact that those sources reflect the same two nexus patterns between historical and legal sources that we have described in this chapter). Naturally, the greatest degree of caution would be exercised in the application of extralegal considerations to matters *de-oraita*, since they are part of the *grundnorm*, and abrogation or modification of them bears on the problem of *ultra vires*.[262]

In the final analysis, however, we must continue to keep in mind that terms like *easier to invoke*, *more cautious*, *even more cautious*, and *the greatest degree of caution* are not objectifiable. What may seem to one to reflect the utmost caution may seem to another to reflect insufficient caution, yet the dictum *Ellu ve-ellu divrei elohim ḥayyim* would apply to both. Ultimately, the only guarantee of the integrity of the halakhic system is the integrity of its recognized authorities.

262. See above, pp. 201–204.

Chapter Ten

The Language of *Pesak*: An Excursus

This chapter constitutes a digression from the rest of the volume. It is motivated, as will become clear, by the subject matter of the previous chapter, and serves as an appropriate prelude to the subject matter of the next chapter.

Pesak, short for *pesak halakhah*, is the term used to denote both an actual halakhic decision and the argument that leads a *posek* to that decision. The legal sections of the Pentateuch, vast sections of the literary sources of the talmudic period,[1] the commentaries on the talmudic literature, from the *ge'onim* through the modern period, all of the responsa literature, and, most certainly, all of the codes fall within the broad category of *pesak* literature.[2] Indeed, most genres of classical Jewish literature contain elements of *pesak*, even when *pesak* is not their primary purpose.

No two of the genres listed above are composed in the same literary style, and no two are identical linguistically. This, of course, is not to

1. Halakhic Midrash, Mishnah, Tosefta, and both the Babylonian and Palestinian Talmuds. It seems most plausible that even Albeck, who denies that Rabbi Judah the Prince was himself at all interested in *pesak* in the Mishnah (see Hanock Albech, *Introduction to the Mishna* [Hebrew] [Jerusalem: Bialik Institute, 1959], chap. 6), would agree that the Mishnah is *pesak*. For even if Judah the Prince was not himself rendering decisions, the sources he quotes were rendering decisions.

2. There are even significant elements of *pesak* in genres of literature not often thought of as containing *pesak*, such as religious poetry (*piyyut*). See, for example, Tosafot Makkot 3b, s.v. *ikka*.

deny that later genres appropriated, to a certain degree, some of the vocabulary and style of the earlier ones, but to emphasize that each genre also added its own distinctively individual elements to the vocabulary and style of halakhic literature. Moreover, at each of its stages halakhic literature appropriated—again to a certain degree only—elements of the vocabulary, style, and method of analysis of the contemporary non-Jewish legal literature.[3] The introduction of foreign words, phrases, and idioms capable of expressing new ideas with greater precision than would have been possible in the primary languages of *pesak,* Hebrew and Aramaic, was never considered inimical to *halakhah.* Indeed, although Hebrew (itself containing significant amounts of Aramaic) has remained the most common medium of formal halakhic composition, it is not unusual to find halakhic discussions and decisions in languages other than Hebrew.

Halakhah is religious law and has always been so recognized by both its adherents and its authorities. Thus, since all of the genres listed above *are* part of halakhic literature, it follows that there is no particular literary style, no unique vocabulary, nor any specific method of analysis that qualifies as the *sine qua non* of halakhic literature. The responsa are religious even though their style is different from that of the Tosafot; the Tosafot are religious even though their method of analysis is not identical with that of the Talmud; and the Talmud is religious even though its vocabulary is very different from that of the Bible.

In the final analysis, the only prerequisite for qualification of a halakhic statement as legitimate *pesak* is that the vocabulary, style, and method of analysis used be capable of expressing legitimate *pesak.* There is no intrinsic or objective reason, therefore, that the terminology of the social sciences, for example, should not be introduced into the *pesak* literature being written today. To introduce such language would be to do no differently than the talmudic masters who introduced Greek and Latin terminology and methods into their halakhic deliberations. For even if it is true that later generations did not always recognize that particular terms or analytical methods in talmudic *halakhah* were originally Greek, the same can certainly not be said of those who actually lived in the Hellenistic world and who themselves introduced these terms and methods. The point is that it was clearly inconceivable to any *tanna* or *amora* that any terminology or any method of analysis was, by

3. For the biblical period, see James Pritchard, *Ancient Near Eastern Texts* (Princeton, N.J.: Princeton University Press, 1955). For the early talmudic period, see above, chap. 9, n. 261. For the style and method of the Tosafot, see José Faur, "The Legal Thinking of Tosafot: An Historical Approach," *Dine Israel* 6 (1975).

definition, unsuited to the elucidation of the law. So long as religion and religious law are perceived as encompassing all aspects of life without exception, any tool that enhances the ability of *posekim* to grapple more adequately with any aspect of life cannot be ignored. Indeed, any *posek* who willfully ignores such a useful tool is being remiss in the fulfillment of his religious duty. There can be no discipline, science, or analytical method (or any vocabulary and style that express them) that is, by definition, irrelevant to an all-pervasive religious system.

The discussion of the role of extralegal sources within the *halakhah* in Chapter 9 should have made it abundantly clear that consideration of data derived from the social sciences, for example, is systemically valid in halakhic decision-making. Such data have always been taken into account, even when the social sciences lacked all but the barest rudiments of precise terminology and definable method. Now, therefore, that a vocabulary and a methodology have been fully developed by the social sciences, it is altogether proper that they be consciously used in the elucidation of the law.[4]

Nevertheless, two very different groups viewing *halakhah* from radically different perspectives, have come to the conclusion that the introduction of the vocabulary, style, and methodology of the social sciences into halakhic discourse would be somehow nonreligious in nature and, therefore, unacceptable. The first group views itself as highly committed to *halakhah,* while the second perceives itself as totally uncommitted to the system.

Those who view themselves as highly committed to *halakhah* think of it, with some justification, as a religious legal system that is unique in the modern world. In an age, they argue, when people were more religious and viewed all their decisions and actions in the light of religious values and religious law, the halakhic system was not unique; only the fact that it was Jewish distinguished it from other religious legal systems of the time. Today, however, when people do not view themselves as religious and committed to religious legal systems, *halakhah* stands virtually alone. So much is, indeed, accurate; it is the next step taken by this group that produces the difficulty. For they claim, albeit tacitly, that since the halakhic system is now *sui generis,* its uniqueness as a religious legal system would be seriously undermined if it were to accept the same terminology and methodology that has been accepted by and incorporated into modern secular legal systems. In essence, it is their view that any mode of legal expression and analysis that is utilized

---

4. We stress the social sciences because there has never been real objection to the use of the vocabulary and method of the physical sciences. However, see n. 5 below.

in nonreligious legal systems is, by definition, unacceptable in a religious system. It is, of course, with this tacit premise that we disagree, for its posits that the religious nature of a legal system is contingent upon the terminology it invokes and the methods it employs; the implication being that terminology and methodology, in and of themselves, are either religious or nonreligious.

Those uncommitted to *halakhah,* on the other hand, tend to claim that religious law is totally different in nature from nonreligious law, that the two realms are totally discrete and concerned with totally different subject matter. Religious law, they say, should be restricted to matters of ritual dealing only with a prayer, holidays, *kashrut,* and with those aspects of personal status that relate to religion; but damages, torts, property, contracts, etc., should be the concern of secular law alone. Indeed, they conclude, the types of considerations that are the hallmark of secular legal systems are, by definition, inappropriate to religious systems. Moreover, the employment of secular legal terminology and methodology in a religious system would result in its secularization. So the uncommitted, too, reach the conclusion that secular language and methodology weaken the religious nature of a religious legal system. Our disagreement with this group, of course, stems from our rejection of its major premise, that is, that religious law and nonreligious law are completely distinct realms of discourse.

A direct result of the argument of the committed is a theory we would call the "naiveté theory." This theory proposes that the best *posek* is the one who has no knowledge whatsoever of contemporary sociology, economics, psychology, history, or anthropology.[5] As a result of his

5. This list does not include the physical sciences. As we have seen in the medical/scientific section of chap. 9 (above, pp. 234–248), the physical sciences function primarily in the resolution of questions of fact, not of questions of law. In such a situation, there would be no objection to ascertaining the makeup of a new substance in order to determine whether it is *kasher* or not.

Yet even within the medical/scientific realm one can see ramifications of the "naiveté theory." For once a scientific source has been used to resolve a question of fact, one often detects a hesitancy to allow that resolution to be examined on the basis of *new* scientific evidence. As a theoretical example, suppose that "death" were defined as the "the cessation of a heartbeat and of breathing." Further, suppose this legal definition to have been arrived at on the basis of medical/scientific sources. If future scientific studies were to demonstrate that the moment of death is determined otherwise, one would suppose that to be sufficient grounds for reopening the question of fact (subject to the restriction, however, of not allowing the testifying scientific expert to determine the law). Yet the hesitancy we noted is reflected in statements like "The legal definition of death is different from the scientific definition," which could be true if it meant that the *posekim* had determined that other considerations favored the older position, even against the weight of new scientific evidence. If, however, such a statement intimates hesitancy on the part of the *posekim* to reopen the question simply because it has once been decided, it reflects

noninvolvement in such matters, he is supposedly protected from the possibility of being influenced by them. It is assumed that as a result of his noninvolvement, his halakhic decisions will not consciously reflect any of the knowledge uncovered by these disciplines, and that he will, consequently, be free of the pressure to decide in a particular way that such knowledge might bring to bear. Since such knowledge falls within the domain of nonreligious legal systems, and since the unique legal system called *halakhah*, which is entirely religious, ought to be as free as possible from them, its authoritative *posekim* are, therefore, best confined to the "four cubits of *halakhah*." Only the decisions of such men can be truly religious, the theory proposes. Only the selfless commitment to the preservation of *halakhah* in its "purest" form will ensure its survival as a religious legal system.

There is, however, yet a third group of contemporary Jews (a small one, to be sure) who are committed both to the halakhic system and to the affirmation not only of the acceptability of extralegal data within that system, but also of the acceptability of the terminology and methodology that those data imply. Such a Jew often finds himself on the horns of a dilemma because of the two prevailing views on *pesak* that we have described. If, for example, he encounters a *pesak* on some matter other than ritual, and the matter is one with regard to which extralegal data should certainly have been taken into consideration, yet the *pesak* is written in a way that clearly indicates that the *posek* has either ignored such data completely or has taken it into account without consciousness of its extralegal nature, this member of the third group is disquieted because the *posek* seems to have been uninfluenced by possibly relevant extralegal concerns. If, on the other hand, he encounters a *pesak* that consciously utilizes the terminology and methodology that the extralegal data imply, this third-group Jew, continually bombarded by the image of the *posek* prevalent among the class we have called committed, is also disquieted. This time, however, he is disquieted because this type of *pesak*, which he can accept, is rejected by the large class of the committed on the grounds that the *posek* seems aware of and influenced by extralegal concerns. The image of the *posek* held by this third-group Jew, of an individual committed both to the halakhic process and to the admissibility within it not only of extralegal data, but of the terminology

---

acceptance on the "naiveté theory." The situation would be one in which a legal definition assumes the status of a legal fiction (i.e., a knowing and conscious pervasion of the actual facts of the matter). While there is surely a place for legal fictions within the system (see above, p. 55), they are always consciously fictional. Only a hesitancy to invoke the rights guaranteed to *posekim*, however, could convince someone to elevate what is ostensibly a reflection of actual fact to the level of legal fiction.

and methodology that those data imply, finds scant reinforcement in reality. The ultimate problem, of course, lies in the assumption, of both the committed class and the uncommitted class, that there is such a thing as religious language, which, by definition, excludes certain modes of discourse.

For a Jew who holds the third view to disregard the opinions of those who find the entire halakhic system irrelevant will not be difficult, since he does not even share a universe of discourse with them. To disregard those who claim to be committed to the same legal system as he is, is not as easy, for, although the system to which both affirm loyalty allows wide latitude for legitimate difference of opinion, the differences between them on this point cannot be called a legitimate *maḥaloket:* The disagreement is about the very nature and systemic functioning of the halakhic system. While disputants from within the same system may conclude A and not-A regarding a given issue (e.g., one concluding that swordfish is *kasher* and the other concluding that it is not *kasher*), they are not concluding both A and not-A about the system itself. Regarding disagreements of the first kind, we have long ago affirmed that both may be "right," for *Ellu ve-ellu divrei elohim ḥayyim.* But a dispute of the second kind reflects a fundamental difference of opinion regarding the systemic functioning of the halakhic process itself; it is not a case of *Ellu ve-ellu divrei elohim ḥayyim.* In this situation, one position must be the correct one and the other the incorrect; either the system functions in manner X or it does not.

Thus, the Jew holding the third view must react to the class of the committed in the same way as he reacts to those who find the system irrelevant. He must disregard their opinions.[6] Unfortunately, since the majority of those who affirm commitment to *halakhah* are not members of the third group, this Jew, in the final analysis, has no viable choice but to persevere as a member of a minority. To retract would be to acquiesce to what he knows to be false.

In essence, the position of the contemporary Jew who is a member of the third group is based upon four premises.

1. That the authorities *he* recognizes as legitimate are seriously engaged in *pesak halakhah;* that is, that the decisions of these authorities are

---

6. I.e., regarding the way the system functions *qua* system. Nevertheless, he is duty bound to study their decisions in order to determine whether or not some, in fact, reflect decisions he can find compelling. There can, after all, be cases in which such a Jew would find the argument of his theoretical disputant germane and cogent even from his own perspective of the way the system functions, and even if his disputant bases his argument upon a systemic premise which the "modernist" denies. Not every issue is one which *must* involve a dispute about the systemic functioning of the halakhic process.

legitimate halakhic decisions, made for the benefit of Jews who are committed to the halakhic system. In his view, these authorities are as prepared to be strict as they are to be lenient, and they are confident that their constituency will abide by their decisions, whether based solely upon legal sources or based also upon extralegal sources, whether the decisions reaffirm traditional precedent or invoke the ultimate right of recognized authorities to uproot a matter *be-kum va-aseh* (i.e., actively) from the *grundnorm* itself. No matter how small their constituency may be, their decisions are addressed only to it. If, because they are serious in their approach to *halakhah,* the number of their constituents should increase, so much the better. But even if their constituency does not increase, this will not cause them to compromise either their seriousness or their commitment.

2. That the halakhic system is an all-encompassing system and that there is no subject that is, by definition, outside the theoretical purview of *halakhah.* That social, ethical, and moral issues are as proper subjects for halakhic analysis as ritual matters; indeed, that it is possible to take *halakhah* into account even in some political matters. This is not to say, of course, that there will not be issues about which *halakhah* may, in fact, have nothing to say. One of the considerations to which a *posek* must attend before deciding on the relevance or lack of relevance of extralegal sources of a sociological nature, for example, is whether the sociological reality that may become legally significant reflects a desirable reality—a question about which, in the end, *halakhah* may have nothing to say.[7] Or,

7. The complexity of the problem is indicated by the possibility that existing norms may influence a *posek*'s view on the desirability of instituting a new sociological reality. Thus, while judgments about the desirability of a regularized and dependable postal service will undoubtedly be made completely independent of halakhic influences, the same might not be said about an issue such as male and female coeducation. The latter issue is chosen purposely, because it is not a burning issue at present, already having been resolved by various groups one way or the other. It is surely probable that some *posekim* who decided that coeducation would be an undesirable sociological innovation were influenced, consciously or otherwise, by the fact that traditional halakhic norms do not reflect coeducation as a *desideratum.* Other *posekim,* on the other hand, may have decided that coeducation was desirable, no matter what existing halakhic norms indicated. That is, they assumed, consciously or otherwise, that although the traditional norms reflect a particular sociological reality, that did not preclude the possibility that some other sociological reality might be equally desirable.

It seems reasonable to posit that the influence of halakhic norms in such judgments will be stronger the less firmly entrenched the reality is in the world. As a particular reality becomes more and more entrenched, the likelihood of dispassionate consideration (i.e., consideration independent of existing halakhic norms) becomes greater and greater. Thus, for example, public nudity is likely to be forbidden by almost all *posekim* at present because they feel, consciously or otherwise, that the halakhic norms that apparently forbid it reflect not only *a* sociological reality, but *the* desirable sociological reality. If acceptance of public nudity persists for an extended period, the *posekim* of a later age may be more able to view

for example, before reaching a decision about whether or not to overturn the precedent favoring large families, a *posek* will have to consider the question of whether the earth can sustain more than a certain number of inhabitants, and whether the world's population is likely to reach that level. Although the answers to these questions may achieve legal significance, it is possible that the *halakhah* itself will have nothing to say about these subjects. They are, by definition, extralegal sources.[8]

3. That there is nothing inherently religious or nonreligious about any language or literary style or method of analysis. Any language is acceptable if it reflects religious thought; it is the intent of the person who uses the language that determines whether or not the language reflects religious thought. Since modern language is capable of expressing religious thought, no *posek* need shy away from employing it in *pesak*.

4. That just as the use of modern language is no deterrent to the expression of religious thought, so the use of modern analytic methods and modes of expression is in no way inimical to religious thought; that, on the contrary, the use of modern analytic methods allows for greater precision in defining and understanding the factors that impinge upon the religious decision-making process. For example, there is no question that the phrase *Ha-galut mitgabber aleinu* means "the socioeconomic-political reality in which the Jewish community finds itself";[9] nor is there any question that this English rendering of the Hebrew is far more precise and far more comprehensible to the modern mind than the

---

the issue in terms of sociological desirability, independent of existing halakhic norms. Lest this seem farfetched, suffice it to say that it would be easy to demonstrate that the type of feminine clothing considered acceptable in almost all traditional circles today was decried as immodest and unacceptable by *posekim* who lived in an earlier age.

8. Here, too, we must reemphasize both the complexity of the problem and the fact that extralegal sources, while admissible, are not necessarily determinative. In addition to the extralegal questions mentioned here (which are not addressed unambiguously by the experts, and which therefore require the *posek* to choose the position he finds most convincing), the question of family size involves other extralegal questions as well, and a *posek* must weigh all of the answers before reaching a decision. For instance, there are sociological-ethical questions: Should Jews have large families, even if the earth could not support life if all groups did the same, because they are obligated to recoup the losses of the Holocaust? Should American Jews have large families in order to perpetuate their influence on American politics, not only for their own benefit, but also for the benefit of the State of Israel? And there are economic questions: Might large Jewish families be contraindicated by the parents' potential ability to support and educate their children appropriately, even if the earth can clearly support them physically, and even if there is enough food? How complex the halakhic issues are, and how fertile the grounds for legitimate *maḥaloket*. While the answers to the above quandaries may well be issues about which *halakhah* itself has nothing to say, any *posek* will find the answers to them exceedingly significant, when he finally renders his decision.

9. See Tosafot Kiddushin 41a, s.v. *asur*, and above, pp. 257 f.

original Hebrew. It makes clear what the Hebrew leaves ambiguous, namely, which factors of contemporary Jewish existence might be relevant to a halakhic position advocating the overturning of established precedent.

Indeed, the third-group Jew holds that it is positively desirable to analyze older material in terms of modern concepts, in order to understand it more accurately. The legal opinions of the schools of Hillel and Shammai, he maintains, are no less religious because they may be seen, in part, to reflect the different socioeconomic strata of the constituents of these schools. Whatever insights modern social science can contribute to a more precise and complete understanding of the development of Jewish law should be welcomed. Nor, even if the future brings new insights that contradict our present understanding, will this impugn the religious integrity of our earlier interpretation. It is self-evident that no generation can understand the past in greater depth than the state of its knowledge makes possible. Yet it is absurd for any generation to refrain from attempting to add its own contribution to the understanding of the past because it cannot be certain that its understanding will stand uncontested forever; the understanding of one generation is the starting point for the next. No responsible generation dare to think that it has nothing to offer in terms of increased understanding and depth. To do so is not only irresponsible, it is detrimental to the continued viability of the halakhic system itself.

And, finally, that since the insights of the present generation of social scientists are best understood when they are transmitted in their vocabulary and reflect their methodology, their vocabulary and their methodology must be co-opted for halakhic use.

Indeed, there is at least one sense in which the use of what is generally considered nonreligious language in modern *pesak* is a greater guarantee of the religious orientation of that *pesak* than the continued use of that which is generally considered to be religious language. The factors that influence decision-makers in the decision-making process influence them whether or not they are aware of it. Can it be denied that the rich man's perception of the world influenced the School of Shammai even though the members of that school were not consciously aware of it? Surely not. Similarly, a *posek* of the modern age also carries with him attitudes and biases of which he is not consciously aware. The "naive" *posek* is no less influenced by social currents and world upheavals simply because he pretends to be unaware that he is so influenced. Modern communications technology renders it impossible for him to be uninfluenced, no matter how strong his denial. It is surely no greater evidence of the religious dedication of a *posek* to allow himself to be influenced unconsciously by his cultural environment than to consciously acknowledge its influence and to subject as much of it as he is aware of to the same careful scrutiny and analysis as the legal sources he utilizes.

Indeed, it is possible to imagine that the schools of Shammai and Hillel would have exercised even greater care in reaching their decisions if they had been able to ask themselves whether a decision they were about to render genuinely reflected the "will of God," or whether it merely reflected the "will of God" as seen through the tinted glasses of greater or lesser wealth. They, of course, cannot be faulted for having failed to understand how the unconscious attitudes resulting from wealth or poverty can distort one's outlook, but a modern *posek* who deliberately refuses to make use of such knowledge and such insights as are available to him can, indeed, be faulted. He can no more dismiss as irrelevant the analysis of data available to him as a result of the advancement of human knowledge than he can dismiss as irrelevant the analysis of data available to him from the legal sources of the *halakhah* itself. Both can be rejected after they have been analyzed, but neither can be prejudged as irrelevant and requiring no analysis whatsoever.

Obviously, much terminology considered to be "religious" will continue to be used even in modern *pesak*. The ability to define with greater precision what elements a *posek* considers crucial in the determination of "justice," "righteousness," "uprightness," "morality" and "propriety" in no way undermines the religious values these concepts embody. These words I have just listed, and many others that are similar, will not disappear from the literature of *pesak*. The concepts they express will remain the religious bases of the decision-making process; all that will change is the misimpression that these concepts have a precise and objective meaning and application which transcend all elements of place and time, social and economic reality, and psychological and scientific knowledge.

Finally, the type of *literary style* demanded by modern *pesak* is one that reveals not only what the *posek* decides, but also the issues he has considered in reaching that decision. This, in turn, requires clarification not only of the options adopted, but also of the options rejected, and of the reasons for both. The more thorough, extensive, and detailed the exposition, the easier it will be to determine possible grounds for adopting a position other than the one advocated by the *posek*. Indeed, if such a style of *pesak* became widespread, the halakhic defensibility of most *pesak* would be enhanced. In the final analysis, such a style would result in the proliferation of legitimate *maḥaloket,* but all *Le-shem shamayim,* and all reflecting the idea that *Ellu ve-ellu divrei elohim ḥayyim.*

As modern *posekim* pursue their work they should not be discouraged by the knowledge that later generations will find in their writings evidence that they, too, were influenced by factors of which they were unaware. No generation can be expected to be aware of matters which the knowledge of that generation does not allow. Each generation should be satisfied to bring to its halakhic literature all the knowledge available to it, and should be confident in the knowledge that, just as each past generation has, each future generation will do the same.

Chapter Eleven

On New Legal Sources within *Halakhah*

Halakhic decisions derive primarily from the multitude of texts that comprise the legal sources of the system and from the interpretation of these texts by generations of *posekim*. The early rabbinic sages interpreted the Bible, the *amora'im* interpreted the Mishnah of Judah the Prince (ca. 220 C.E.), the early commentators interpreted the Talmud, the later legalists interpreted the commentaries, codes, and responsa of the earlier,[1] and all of them base their legal decisions upon their interpretations of the legal sources. Since each legal decision became (and still becomes) a legal source for subsequent *posekim*, it is no wonder that the legal sources of the *halakhah* have been (and are still being) subjected to the most careful scrutiny and analysis. Sometimes the analysis takes the form of a philological exposition of the meaning of a word or phrase; sometimes it is contextual; sometimes it attempts to explain or to reconcile two apparently contradictory legal sources. Sometimes, as we saw in Chapter 9, the investigator is interested in analyzing whether the author of a legal source arrived at his interpretation because of extralegal

1. This is not to say, of course, that later *posekim* did not also engage in interpretation of Talmud or Mishnah, or even of Bible. The rule of precedent being what it is, however, the *posek* usually beings his legal analysis with earlier contemporary sources or with the sources of the previous legal era and works in reverse chronological order to the primary sources. His analysis depends most on the primary sources when the more contemporary legal sources do not establish precedent sufficiently. Given the legal principle that *Hilkheta ke-vatra'ei* ("the law follows the latest authorities"), this approach is eminently reasonable.

factors, and if so, whether those factors were medical/scientific, sociological/*realia*, economic, or ethical/psychological.

Now, anyone setting out to interpret a particular text must proceed either on the assumption that the text in question is accurate—a *textus receptus*, as it were—or else on the assumption that it is inaccurate, in which case the interpreter must first proceed to establish the correct version (*girsa*). The very possibility that different versions of a particular text might exist raises a plethora of questions, and it is to the discussion of these questions that this chapter is devoted. For example: Can variant readings have legal significance? If they *can* have legal significance, *must* they have? If they can but need not have legal significance, what criteria are used to establish whether a specific variant reading does or does not have legal significance? What is the status of a legal norm based upon a text for which no variant was known until relatively recent times? Are potentially significant legal sources to be found only in variant *readings?* In other words, what is the status of a variant *interpretation* of a text unknown to a *posek* whose own interpretation has attained the force of precedent? What is the legal significance, if any, of the *peshat* of a text misunderstood until modern times?[2] What is or might be the status of a legal source whose existence is the result of a literary, source-critical, or form-critical analysis of an extant legal text? In what way, if any, does the potential legal significance of a critical textual analysis of the Pentateuch differ from the potential legal significance of a critical textual analysis of postbiblical literature?

To begin with, the passages quoted in this chapter will demonstrate incontrovertibly that the halakhic system has always dealt with new legal sources—variant readings, previously unknown interpretations, etc.—as valid data of potential legal significance for decision-making. The systemic principles that analysis of these passages will yield, however, will be found to be primarily implicit, and only rarely verbalized.

No greater testimony to the potential legal significance of new or previously unknown legal sources is necessary than the clear statement of Rabbi Solomon b. Yeḥi'el Luria (Maharshal, 1510–1573). In explaining

2. The *peshat* of a text is the meaning intended by the author, assuming that his use of language is in accord with the general usage of his time and place. Admittedly, one who wishes to affirm that the meaning of a word in the Mishnah is what *the Gemara claims it to be,* irrespective of any evidence to the contrary derived from contemporary knowledge about mishnaic language, can do so by denying the assumption stipulated above regarding the meaning of the *peshat.* Although theoretically possible, such a hypothesis seems unreasonable, at least regarding those legal sources that are admitted to have been spoken and written by men rather than by God Himself.

the methodology of his work, *Yam Shel Sh'lomo,* the Maharshal asserts that he attempted to be as exhaustive as possible, quoting all the relevant views of both early and later authorities, codifiers, and commentators.

> . . . in order that no disputant might come along and claim, "Note how this author wrote his judgments and decisions *(dinav u-fesakav)* according to the machinations of his own mind, with doubtful proof. Had this author only seen the words of such-and-such a book, or the responsum of such-and-such a rabbi, he would not have had the audacity (*lo nakat libbo*) to disagree, and surely would have retracted his own view."[3]

Luria justifies his lengthy and exhaustive method on the grounds that only such an approach could ensure that his words would be taken seriously. Were his comments less extensive, he would leave himself open to the accusation that he had ignored or been totally unaware of sources in the writings of others which, had he but known them, would have forced him to retract the position he chose to affirm. Indeed we can assume from his statement that by the middle of the sixteenth century, recourse to arguments against the view of a *posek* on the basis of legal sources assumed to have been unknown to him was so widespread as to dictate to Luria a methodology that would free him from such contention. Furthermore, he also makes it clear that such arguments against the view of a *posek* might be considered sufficient to warrant the *assumption* that the *posek* would have retracted had he but known the sources. Luria was concerned that his failure to deal with any of the conceivably relevant sources might lead his detractors to assume that had he known of them, he would have reversed himself, even in the absence of any such intimation from Luria himself. So long as the original *posek* is alive, one supposes that a disputant convinced that the *posek* would retract if he knew of a particular source might apprise him of the apparently unknown source and see whether he wished to retract or not. Once dead, however, the original *posek* has no such protection against a disputant's claim.[4]

3. Luria, *Yam Shel Shelomo* (New York: Abraham Isaac Friedman, 1968 [5728]), Introduction to Bava Kama and Ḥulin.

4. Somewhat paradoxically, the more exhaustive the analysis of a *posek,* the more open he becomes to such a claim. Surely one who has dealt with forty-nine potentially relevant sources would not have failed to deal with the fiftieth had he known it. The less exhaustive the treatment of the subject, the less open to such an argument the *posek* becomes, for in all likelihood his detractors would be more inclined to assume that he ignored so many

The concern of the Maharshal was well founded. There is a long history of the use of new legal sources assumed to have been unknown to the original *posek* as grounds for the abrogation of his view. (By the term *new* we mean either existing and known to others but not to the *posek* or newly discovered [or interpreted] and therefore impossible for anyone to have known at the time of decision.) Several examples from the Talmud itself will demonstrate this.

The Talmud records the following:[5]

> Rava said, "If one ate the Purim festive meal at night,[6] he has not fulfilled his religious obligation." Why? Because it is written: "*Days* of festivity and joy."[7] Rav Ashi was once sitting before Rav Kahana [on Purim day]. It was getting dark, and the sages had not yet come. He said to him [i.e., Rav Kahana to Rav Ashi], "Why have the sages not come?" [He answered.] "Perhaps they are occupied with the festive Purim meal!" He responded, "Would it not have been possible for them to eat it last night?" He replied, "Has the master never heard[8] that which Rava said, 'If one ate the Purim festive meal at night he has not fulfilled his religious obligation'?" He [i.e., Rav Kahana] said to him, "Did Rava say that?" He answered, "Yes."[9] He [i.e., Rav Kahana] repeated it [i.e., Rava's statement] forty times and etched it into his mind as a norm.

It is clear from this passage that Rav Kahana considered eating the Purim meal on the night of the reading of the *megillah* permissible, and was unaware of Rava's statement prohibiting it. When he was apprised of Rava's statement, a legal source heretofore unknown to him, he

---

potentially salient sources because he found them to be irrelevant. In such a circumstance one might well find a potential disputant himself explaining why, in his opinion, the original *posek* ignored those very sources which, had the original treatment been more extensive, the disputant might have claimed that the original *posek* did not know.

5. Megillah 7b.
6. I.e., on the night that the *megillah* is read.
7. Esther 9:22.
8. *La shami'a leih le-mar,* thus in our editions of the Talmud. The Munich manuscript reads: *La sevar lah mar* ("Does the master not agree [with Rava]?"). Though, ostensibly, the Munich manuscript's version implies that Rav Ashi assumed that Rav Kahana knew Rava's statement, Rav Kahana's answer clearly indicates that he did not, even according to the Munich manuscript. The *She'iltot,* no. 67, reads: *La madkar lah mar* ("Does the master not recall?"). See the following note.
9. The *She'iltot* version reads *la shami'a li* ("I hadn't heard it") in place of the words "Did Rava . . . ? Yes." The *She'iltot,* therefore, also assumes that Rav Kahana had known Rava's statement, as indicated in the preceding note, though he might have forgotten it. Yet it, too, clearly indicates in this, his answer, that he, in fact, did not know of Rava's statement.

deemed it sufficient grounds to abrogate his own position in favor of Rava's more stringent view *(le-ḥumera).* Although the passage itself gives no indication of Rav Kahana's reason for accepting Rava's view, three possibilities come to mind: first, that Rav Kahana recognized, after hearing Rava's position, that it was scripturally ordained (as indicated toward the beginning of the passage);[10] second, that Rav Kahana accepted the view of Rava because of Rava's stature; third (and perhaps in conjunction with the second), that he perceived that Rava's position had the weight of precedent, as indicated by the fact that the sages of his academy adhered to it.

Another example of the valid use of previously unknown legal sources (and again resulting in the abrogation of a norm *le-ḥumera*) can be found a few pages later in the Talmud. Immediately following a *mishnah* that lists the differences between the sanctuary at Shiloh and the Temple of Jerusalem, and that includes the statement that sacrifices on altars other than at the central sanctuary became permissible again after the destruction of Shiloh, but not after the destruction of the central altar of Jerusalem, the Talmud records:[11]

> Rabbi Yiẓḥak said, "I have heard that sacrifices may be brought at the Onias temple."[12] . . . They asked him, "Did you say that?" He answered, "No!" Rava said, "By God, he did say it, and I learned it from him." And why did he retract? Because of the objection raised by Rav Mari, "The sanctity of Shiloh was followed by a period in which sacrifice on altars other than at the central sanctuary was permissible; the sanctity of Jerusalem is not so followed."[13] And furthermore we have learned in a *mishnah:* "Once they came to Jerusalem all other altars became forbidden and were never again permitted."[14]

Taken at face value, this passage claims that Rabbi Yiẓḥak was unaware of two legal sources, each of which argued against his view that sacrifices could be offered at the Onias temple. When they were brought

---

10. Since the Talmud quotes Rav Ashi as quoting Rava without the explanatory scriptural proof, it is unlikely that Rav Kahana learned of its scriptural basis from Rav Ashi.

11. Megillah 10a.

12. An Alexandrian temple built, according to tradition, by Onias, the son of the High Priest Shimon the Just. See Mishnah Menaḥot 13:10 and the Gemara, loc. cit., 109b. In any case, it was constructed after the centralization of worship in Jerusalem.

13. From Mishnah Megillah 1:11.

14. Zevaḥim 14:8.

to his attention, he considered them sufficient legal evidence to effect a reversal of his position. He abrogated the lenient position he had taken in favor of the more strict position indicated by the previously unknown (to him) legal sources. Again, the passage itself gives no clear reason for his acceptance of these new legal sources, although one would probably not be far off in surmising that their status as *mishnayot* may have been an important factor.[15]

While these two passages demonstrate that new legal sources constitute valid data,[16] capable of effecting the abrogation of previously held norms, limiting our examples to these two alone might induce one to conclude that the legal significance of new legal sources is restricted to instances resulting in *ḥumera*. This conclusion would be erroneous, as several other examples from the Talmud will prove.

The Talmud records:[17]

---

15. It is interesting to note that Tosafot Megillah 10a, s.v. *u-mai,* raises a number of issues similar to those we will be addressing later in this chapter. Rabbi Ḥayyim ben Ḥananel Katz, a student of Rabbenu Tam, is amazed at the apparent contention that Rabbi Yiẓḥak did not know these legal sources, since they are *mishnayot* which, as he puts it, *ha-lo hen shegurot be-fi kol* ("are well known to everybody"). Rabbi Ḥayyim does not deny the potential validity of new sources, rather he questions the likelihood that these sources could have been unknown to Rabbi Yiẓḥak. Furthermore, since the status of worship at other than the central altar after the destruction of Jerusalem is demonstrated by the Gemara to be a matter of dispute, Rabbi Ḥayyim wonders why Rabbi Yiẓḥak found it necessary to reverse himself. He could, after all, have exercised his right of judicial discretion in favor of the view that noncentralized worship was permissible after the destruction of Jerusalem. Had he done so, he could have reaffirmed his original contention on that basis. In the end, this puzzle forces Rabbi Ḥayyim to interpret the dispute in the Talmud concerning the status of noncentralized-altar worship after the destruction of Jerusalem in a way that eliminates the possibility that anyone could affirm that sacrifices could be rendered at the Oniad temple. Therefore, there is no view on the basis of which Rabbi Yiẓḥak could have exercised judicial discretion in favor of his original position. And, although the Tosafot do not state so explicitly, the first problem is also resolved, for the contention now could be that Rabbi Yiẓḥak had indeed known the *mishnayot* but had misinterpreted them. Once apprised of his misunderstanding, he retracted in favor of the norm implied by the new interpretation of the *mishnayot,* which he had not known.

16. There is a passage in Eruvin 14b that is stylistically similar to the second passage cited here. In that instance, though, Rav retracted his original position not because of some new legal source that came to his attention, but because he had reconsidered his opinion on the basis of the systemic principle *Rabbi Yosé nimmuko immo* ("the view of Rabbi Yosé is always well reasoned"). Theoretically, one might ask why Rav had ignored this systemic principle when rendering his original view. A plausible answer to this question is that *Rabbi Yosé nimmuko immo* became a systemic principle only slightly before Rav's time, since it is recorded as being transmitted by Isi ben Yehudah, one of the last generation of *tanna'im.* Rav, a first-generation *amora,* may not have known of such a systemic principle. When, however, he became apprised of it, he deemed it of sufficient legal significance to warrant retracting his own original position.

17. Ḥagigah 3b–4a. Cf. also Tosefta Terumot 1:3, Yerushalmi Terumot 1:1, 40b, and below, p. 371, for treatment of this passage from another perspective.

Our rabbis have taught, "Who is to be considered an imbecile?[18] One who goes out alone at night and who spends the night in a cemetery and who rips his clothing."[19] It has been said, "Rav Huna said [that he is not considered an imbecile] until he does all of them *(ad she-yehu kullan be-vat aḥat)*." . . .Rav Papa said, "Had Rav Huna known that which we have learned in a *baraita*, 'Who is to be considered an imbecile? One who destroys [or loses] whatever he is given,' he would have retracted."[20]

Rav Papa asserts that the second *baraita* allows him to abrogate the norm suggested by Rav Huna and to adopt a more lenient *(kulla)* position.[21] What is more, he asserts that Rav Huna himself would have understood the *vavs* in the first *baraita* as disjunctive had he but known the second *baraita*. In the final analysis, Rav Papa does not perceive himself as disagreeing with Rav Huna, but, rather, as expressing the view that Rav Huna would himself have expressed if he had known the legal source of which he was ignorant.[22]

The Talmud records another example of an abrogation *le-kulla* on the basis of a new legal source.[23]

---

18. I.e., one who is so mentally inept as to be exempt from legal obligations and culpabilities, and whose purchases and sales have no legal standing. See Rashi, Ḥagigah 3b, s.v. *eizehu*.

19. The second and third clauses are each preceded by the letter *vav*, which has been translated "and," although it could have been translated "or." Cf. the view of R. Yoḥanan in Ḥagigah 3b. The translation reflects the manner in which Rav Huna obviously understood the baraita.

20. The thrust of Rav Papa's comment is that Rav Huna would surely have interpreted the *vavs* of the first *baraita* disjunctively had he known the second *baraita*, which lists only one characteristic as sufficient to establish imbecility.

21. I.e., less strict vis-à-vis the number of characteristics a person must possess before being considered an imbecile. Clearly, though, from the perspective of the person so judged, Rav Huna's position is for *ḥumera*. Legally, though, it is for *kulla*, since classification as an imbecile exempts one from legal obligations. See above, n. 18.

22. One might wonder why Rav Papa was so convinced that Rav Huna would have retracted. Why wasn't it possible for him to assert that the two *baraitot* reflect a *maḥaloket*, the former requiring a combination of characteristics and the latter sufficing with one? Were he to make that assertion he would have no way of knowing whether Rav Huna would have retracted. A reasonable hypothesis would be that Rav Papa was certain that Rav Huna, like all other *amora'im*, would be eager to minimize the disputes between tannaitic sources whenever possible. Thus, since the first *baraita* lends itself so easily and legitimately to reconciliation with the second by understanding the *vavs* as disjunctive, Rav Papa was certain that Rav Huna would have seen it the same way as he did. This point anticipates a claim that will receive more thorough treatment later, viz., that there is a subjective element involved in the claim of any *posek* that a new legal source dictates the abrogation of the decision of another *posek*.

23. Berakhot 53b.

> Rav Yehudah said in the name of Rav, "One need not go searching for a candle[24] as he does for other implements necessary for the fulfillment of *mizvot.*" Rabbi Zeira said, "At first I used to go searching. But once I heard what Rav Yehudah said in the name of Rav, I also ceased looking for a candle. Rather, if one was handy I would recite the benediction."

Rabbi Zeira clearly thought the norm required the use of a light for the fulfillment of the *havdalah* ("separation," ending the Sabbath) ceremony. By his own admission, though, he had not known the legal source embodied in the statement of Rav. Having heard it, he deemed it of sufficient legal significance to warrant a change in his own behavior pattern *le-kulla*.

A final example of the use of new legal sources for the purpose of abrogating norms requires a brief introduction. There are instances in the Torah where negative commandments are juxtaposed to positive commandments. In the majority of such cases it is quite clear that the function of the positive commandment is to provide a remedy for the violation of the negative commandment *(lav ha-nittak la-aseh)*. The classical example is the verse from Exodus 12:10. The first half of the verse dictates that one must not leave any of the paschal sacrifice uneaten until the morning, while the second half ordains that any meat left until the morning must be burned. Under normal circumstances, the remedy for the violation of a negative commandment is lashing. In cases like this, however, the implication is that the remedy for violation of the negative commandment is compliance with the juxtaposed positive commandment, and no lashes are required. In this case, and in most instances of juxtaposed negative and positive commandments, the positive commandment can never be carried out unless and until the negative one has been violated.

Nonetheless, in a minority of cases involving such juxtaposition, compliance with the positive commandment *is* possible prior to violation of the negative. A verse in Numbers 5:3 directs that anyone ritually unclean be sent out of the camp (later understood to mean the Temple precincts) so that he does not contaminate the camp. The verse is in the form of a positive commandment, "They should send [the unclean] from the camp," and a negative commandment, "And let them not defile their camp." In this instance, compliance with the positive com-

24. I.e., a light for the *havdalah* ceremony. Rav implies, therefore, that failure to recite the benediction over the lights does not invalidate the recitation of the remainder of the *havdalah* (*eino me'akkev*).

mandment is not contingent upon prior violation of the negative commandment. It is possible, after all, to refuse impure people entry into the Temple precincts. The following question then arises: If one violates the negative commandment and enters the Temple precincts, does being sent out constitute the entire remedy for the violation, or does the offender incur the punishment of lashes as well?

It is to just such a case that Rabbi Yoḥanan responded with a systemic principle that is also a legal norm.

> Rabbi Yoḥanan said, "Any negative commandment whose juxtaposed positive commandment is applicable without prior violation of the negative *(lav she-kedamo aseh)* is punished by lashes." They said to him, "Did you say that?" He answered, "No!" Rabbah said, "By God, he did say it . . ." But why did he retract? Because the case of the rapist posed a difficulty for him. For we learned in a *baraita:* "A rapist who divorced his wife [i.e. the woman he had raped], if he is a nonpriest, he should remarry her, and he is not lashed; if he is a priest, he should be lashed, and may not remarry her." Why should the nonpriest clause be correct, since it is a negative commandment whose juxtaposed positive commandment is applicable without prior violation of the negative commandment, and [according to Rabbi Yoḥanan] he should receive lashes.[25]

Several points need to be clarified in order to follow the argument in this passage. The Torah commands that a man who rapes an unattached girl must marry her and may never divorce her.[26] The wording of the verse takes the form of a positive commandment, "He must marry her," and a negative commandment, "He may never divorce her." We have here, then, another case of juxtaposed positive and negative commandments in which compliance with the positive is not contingent upon prior violation of the negative, that is, he can marry the woman without first having divorced her. According to what he is quoted as saying, if Rabbi Yoḥanan were confronted with a case in which, after having married the woman, the rapist divorced her, we would expect him to insist that remarrying her would not be a sufficient remedy for the violation of the prohibition of divorcing her; we would expect him to demand lashes in addition. The *baraita* (a legal source) that posed the difficulty for Rabbi Yoḥanan states clearly, however, that remarrying the

25. Makkot 14b–15a.
26. Deuteronomy 22:29.

woman is sufficient remedy for the violation of the negative commandment, and that no lashes are to be inflicted.[27]

The application of the passage to the point we are discussing can now be appreciated. Rabbi Yoḥanan retracted his own position in favor of a more lenient view on the basis of the *baraita* either because its existence had not been known to him or because its importance had not been appreciated by him.[28] For whichever reason, he considered the source of sufficient legal significance to warrant the abrogation of his own view.[29]

Thus far we have demonstrated that a new legal source can constitute valid data sufficient to warrant the abrogation of a norm (a) if the original *posek* had been unaware of the existence of the source, or (b) if he had been unaware of all its implications, and that the resultant abrogation can be either *le-kulla* or *le-ḥumera*. The following passage will serve as a transition to another possibility, namely, that the new legal source may be *rejected* as legally significant and, therefore, may not result in the abrogation of the original norm.[30] It may be rejected, not because it is considered inadmissible or irrelevant, but because it might ultimately be deemed insufficient to warrant the abrogation of the original view of the *posek*. The passage is transitional, because the new source is actually accepted as legally significant, although its significance is first questioned.

The Talmud records the following:[31]

> It has been said: Regarding a *shittuf mavoi*,[32] Rav said that no transfer of ownership to those included in the *shittuf* need be made, and Samuel said that it had to be made. Regarding an *eruv teḥumin*,[33] Rav said that a transfer of ownership to those included in the *eruv* must be made, and Samuel said that it need not. . . . Rav Naḥman said,

---

27. The "if he is a priest" clause is not relevant to the present discussion. Even if remarrying were sufficient, it would be inapplicable to a priest, who is forbidden to marry a divorcée (Leviticus 21:7). Thus, for him no other remedy would be available but the normal remedy for the violation of a negative commandment, viz., lashes. The "if he is a priest" clause, therefore, presents no problem to Rabbi Yoḥanan.

28. It should be stressed that becoming aware of the *implications* of a legal source of which one was previously unaware, even if one actually knew the source itself, is the functional equivalent of becoming aware of a new legal source.

29. Interestingly, the Gemara proceeds to offer an explanation of the *baraita* that would allow Rabbi Yoḥanan to continue to affirm his own position without contradicting the *baraita*. This reflects the fact, which will be discussed at length, that a new legal source can, but need not, result in the abrogation of a norm.

30. See above, pp. 97–99.

31. Eruvin 80a.

32. For a definition of *mavoi*, see above, chap. 2, n. 63. For a definition of *shittuf*, see above, chap 2., n. 84.

33. See above, chap. 2, n. 35.

"We have a tradition that both *eruvei*[34] *teḥumin* and *eruvei haẓeirot*[35] and *shittufei mevo'ot*[36] require a transfer of ownership to those covered by them." Rav Naḥman asked, "Do *eruvei tavshilin* require a transfer of ownership to those included in them or do they not?"[37] Said Rav Yosef, "Why is it a problem for him? Had he not heard that which Rav Naḥman the son of Rav Ada said in the name of Samuel, that *eruvei tavshilin* require such a transfer?" Abayee said to him, "Obviously he had not heard. For had he heard, why would the question have been a problem for him?" He said to him [i.e., Rav Yosef to Abayee], "Did not Samuel say that *eruvei teḥumin* do not require transfer of ownership, yet he [i.e., Rav Naḥman] said that they do?"[38] Really now! Granted that in that case Rav and Samuel disagree, and he [i.e., Rav Naḥman] indicates that the law follows the stringency of the one and the stringency of the other,[39] but here [in the case of *eruv tavshilin*], if, in fact, he had heard it [i.e., Samuel's view], is there anyone who disagrees?

In one regard this passage is different from those considered thus far: It deals with the potential legal significance of a new legal source for the resolution of a question of law in the second sense (a question as to what the law is) rather than with the abrogation of an earlier norm. In

34. Plural construct of *eruv*.

35. The sages forbade carrying on Shabbat in a private domain possessed by several people. Thus, in a courtyard onto which several houses faced, it was forbidden to carry from house to house, or from house to courtyard, or from courtyard to house except if the inhabitants of the courtyard all participated in an *eruv*, called *eruv haẓeirot* ("an *eruv* for courtyards"). The *eruv* was effected by the deposit of food in one of the houses prior to the onset of Shabbat by each of the owners in the entire courtyard. Thus, the legal fiction was created that all the houses and the courtyard were one domain, thus allowing carrying as though it were a single domain. In fact, though, many delete the words "and *eruvei haẓeirot*" on the grounds that each home had to contribute its food in actuality, that just the symbolic transfer of ownership of one's food to another was insufficient to constitute a valid *eruv*.

36. Plural of *shittuf mavoi*.

37. While it is permissible to prepare food on *yom tov*, it is forbidden to prepare food on *yom tov* for the Shabbat that immediately follows it. The institution of the *eruv tavshilin*, by which a small amount of food prepared before *yom tov* is designated for Shabbat, allows the preparation of food for Shabbat on *yom tov*. See Mishnah Beiẓa 2:1.

38. That is, since there is one case, *eruv teḥumin*, where Rav Naḥman disagreed with Samuel, it is possible that he might have disagreed with him regarding *eruv tavshilin*, even if he had heard the source.

39. I.e., granted that Rav Naḥman clarifies his own exercise of judicial discretion in two disputes between Rav and Samuel, adopting the *ḥumera* position in each dispute. But, the Gemara continues, it cannot be said of the *eruv tavshilin* example that Rav Naḥman is exercising his judicial discretion in a *maḥaloket* between Samuel and someone else, because the source indicates no disagreement with Samuel's view.

essence, though, the new legal source is handled in almost exactly the same way as it is in the other examples.

In his statement, Rav Naḥman reflects the *ḥumera* position of Rav regarding an *eruv teḥumin* and the *ḥumera* position of Samuel regarding a *shittuf mavoi*. He then raises a question of law in the second sense about an *eruv* of a third kind, an *eruv tavshilin*. Rav Yosef quotes a source (in the name of Samuel), apparently unknown to Rav Naḥman, that ought to have resolved the question of law in the second sense quite clearly. Abayee agrees wholeheartedly that the new legal source is of sufficient significance to enable it to serve as the basis of the claim that had Rav Naḥman known it he would, without question, have resolved the question of law in accordance with it. Rav Yosef counters, however, that the new legal source is really not sufficient to warrant the conclusion both he and Abayee are attempting to derive from it. Since Rav Naḥman explicitly disagrees with the position of Samuel regarding an *eruv teḥumin*, it is perhaps possible that he might disagree with Samuel's position in the new legal source as well. To this claim the *gemara* (or, perhaps, Abayee) responds that the original thesis allowing the resolution of the question of law on the basis of the new legal source is sufficient to warrant accepting it, since Rav Yosef's argument against accepting it is easily answered. The answer has two parts: (1) Had the new legal source included a disagreement between Samuel and someone else, then the source would not have been sufficient to resolve the question of law. Since Rav Naḥman is known in other cases to have exercised his judicial discretion against the position of Samuel, he might have done so in this case, too. (2) However, the new legal source records Samuel's view as undisputed, and this fact weakens Rav Yosef's argument enough to allow the conclusion that the new legal source is sufficient to resolve the original question of law in the second sense (as originally anticipated by both Rav Yosef and Abayee).[40]

In the final analysis, then, although this passage also accepts the new legal source as actually significant, it is the first we have seen that raises the possibility that the potential legal significance of the new source need *not* be actualized. The examples that follow will demonstrate that the potential legal significance of a new source is, indeed, often rejected. More important, they will offer some insights into the types of arguments and reasons that determine their rejection.

The Talmud records the following:[41]

---

40. See Tosafot Eruvin 80a, s.v. *amar*.
41. Niddah 25a.

They asked Rebbe, "What is the status of a woman who aborts a fetal sac full of flesh?"[42] He answered, "I have no tradition about this (*Lo shamati*)." Rabbi Ishma'el the son of Rabbi Yosé said to him, "Thus my father used to say, 'If the sac is full of blood, she is impure as a menstruant; if it is full of flesh, she is impure as one who has given birth.' " He said to him [i.e., Rebbe to Rabbi Ishma'el], "If you had reported an original decision in your father's name we would abide by it. But since the first part [of his statement] is in accordance with the nonmajority (*yeḥida'ah*) view of Sumkhus in the name of Rabbi Me'ir, perhaps he stated the latter part [of his statement] also in accordance with the view of Rabbi Joshua, and the law is not according to Rabbi Joshua. For we learned in a *baraita:* 'If a woman aborts a fetal sac with an unformed fetus, Rabbi Joshua says it is considered a birth, and the sages say it is not a birth.' "

Clarification of Rebbe's reference to the view of Sumkhus will help make the first half of the passage more comprehensible. The Talmud quotes a *baraita* in which Sumkhus says in the name of Rabbi Me'ir that if a woman aborts a lump-shaped embryo, and when it is cut open the presence of blood is revealed, she is considered as a menstruant with regard to ritual impurity.[43] The sages, on the other hand, require that the presence of blood in the aborted material be clear even without opening the embryo. If it is not, the woman is not considered impure. Rebbe equates the statement of Rabbi Yosé, "sac (*shefir*) full of blood," with the statement of Sumkhus, "a lump-shaped embryo (*ḥatikhah*) which, when cut open, reveals the presence of blood." In other words, *shefir* is taken to mean the same thing as *ḥatikhah*. On that basis, Rebbe asserts that the first statement of Rabbi Yosé reflects his exercise of judicial discretion in favor of the singular opinion of Sumkhus, against the majority position of the sages.

The second half of Rabbi Ishma'el's quotation is presented as a new legal source that answers the question of law in the second sense asked of Rebbe. Rebbe, however, rejects this legal source as insufficient to resolve the question of law. He says that since his father's first statement reflects the minority and nonprecedented position of Sumkhus, and is part of a *maḥaloket,* even though Rabbi Yosé's wording is not identical

---

42. I.e., is she to be considered ritually impure, as one who has given birth (*tumat leidah*), or is her ritual impurity that merely of a menstruant? See Leviticus 12:1–8 and 15:19–24, respectively. The contents of the sac were not formed into a recognizable fetal form.

43. Niddah 21b.

with Sumkhus' wording, it is plausible that his second statement could be similar. That is to say, since the sac "full of flesh" in the second half of Rabbi Yosé's statement seems to be the same as the "fetal sac with an unformed fetus" in the *baraita* that records the *mahaloket* between Rabbi Joshua and the sages, and since in the first half of his statement Rabbi Yosé is referring to an already existent legal source, although without using the same words as the original source, the second half of his statement might also be referring to an existent legal source, that is, the singular and nonprecedented view of Rabbi Joshua. And, if that be the case, the new legal source is demonstrably not "new" at all, and therefore is insufficient to warrant its being accepted as the resolution to the question of law in the second sense with which the passage began. In sum, the question remains unresolved.

What one can surely deduce from this passage is that one way of demonstrating that a new legal source is insufficient to warrant any legal action being based upon it is to demonstrate by defensible textual analysis that the new legal source is not "new" at all.

It is important to stress again that the conclusion of the passage we have been discussing leaves the original question of law unresolved. Although one might think that equating the second half of Rabbi Yosé's statement with the nonprecedented view of Rabbi Joshua would resolve the question in favor of the view of the sages, thus answering the question after all, that is not the case. Rebbe never claimed that the second statement of Rabbi Yosé was *indisputably* equivalent to the statement of Rabbi Joshua. Rather, he claimed that the fact that the first clause of Rabbi Yosé's statement could be equated with the view of Sumkhus, although differently worded, lent plausibility to the possible claim that the second clause could also be equated with the nonprecedented view of Rabbi Joshua. Rebbe's rejection of Rabbi Yosé's statement as the answer to the question was based, ultimately, on the fact that the equation of Rabbi Yosé's view with that of Rabbi Joshua was merely plausible but not certain. Similarly, resolution of the question in favor of the view of the sages who opposed Rabbi Joshua would also have been based on mere plausibility, not on certainty. In the absence of greater certainty, Rebbe rejected the statement of Rabbi Yosé as adequate to resolve the question before him, and the question remained unresolved.

Finally, it should be noted that the major premise of Rebbe's analysis of Rabbi Yosé's statement is the identification of the first half of Rabbi Yosé's statement with the view of Sumkhus. In theory, of course, another *posek* might demonstrate that Rebbe's major premise is untenable. He might, for example, reject the major premise on grounds of logic,[44] or, perhaps, on the basis of a new legal source unknown to Rebbe! If that were the case, this *posek* might reject Rebbe's rejection of Rabbi Yosé's statement as the resolution to the question of fact.

A second reason for rejecting the potential legal significance of a new source is reflected in the following passage.[45]

> *Mishnah:* In a case of partial repayment of a debt, Rabbi Yehudah says that he should make an exchange.[46] Rabbi Yosé says that he should write a receipt.[47] *Gemara:* Rav Huna said in the name of Rav, "The law follows neither the view of Rabbi Yehudah nor the view of Rabbi Yosé. Rather, the court destroys the original document, and writes another bill of indebtedness for the lender, dated as the original document." Rav Naḥman said to Rav Huna, ". . . If Rav had known that which we have learned in a *baraita*, 'The witnesses destroy the original document, and write another bill of indebtedness, dated as the original,' he would have retracted." He said to him, "He knew it, and he did not retract! Granted that the court has the power to expropriate monies (*Le-afko'ei mamona*), but can witnesses who have already fulfilled their original mission do it all over again?"

Clarification of the last sentence of the passage will enable us to understand the pertinence of the entire selection. As has already been noted, if a *shetar mukdam* (an antedated document) were considered legally valid, it would empower a lender to expropriate funds or goods

---

44. Cf. the question of the Tosafot Niddah 25a, s.v. *ke-Sumkhus*.

45. Bava Batra 170b.

46. I.e., that the borrower should write a new bill of indebtedness for the amount of the loan that remains to be paid. The date on the new document, however, should be the same as that on the original, even though this second bill of indebtedness is being written at a later date.

Under other circumstances, however, no document may be a *shetar mukdam* (an antedated document). The reason for this regulation is that the lender may exact payment of the loan even from goods that the borrower had either mortgaged or sold any time after the date that appears on the document. Since it was assumed that a loan made with a written bill of indebtedness would be known in the community (*milveh bi-shetar kala it lei*), purchasers from the borrower would be aware of the potential risk they were taking. If, though, a document written on December 1 were dated the previous October 1, purchasers from the borrower between October 1 and December 1 would have had no knowledge of his indebtednss and would find their purchases in potential jeopardy, without their having had any opportunity to take that fact into account before agreeing to purchase.

47. I.e., that the lender should provide the borrower with a signed receipt, while he himself retains the original bill of indebtedness. In that way, no *shetar mukdam* need be written, and the receipt affords the borrower protection against an attempt by the lender to collect the entire sum of the original loan.

from one who purchased them from the borrower in total ignorance of the possible risk.[48] No individual possesses that right. The court, however, by virtue of its authority to declare funds or goods ownerless on the basis of *Hefker beit din hefker,* can do legally that which would be illegal if done by some other party.[49] The witnesses, on the other hand, once having fulfilled their original function of witnessing the loan and writing and signing the original document, have no further legal standing vis-à-vis the case.[50] Who empowers them to destroy the original document and write another in its stead?[51]

In our passage Rav Naḥman asserts that a legal source unknown to Rav would have been deemed by Rav as sufficient to warrant the abrogation of the norm he had postulated, and Rav would have retracted. Rav Huna's response is that Rav had known the new source and had rejected it because he found it indefensible on legal grounds.[52] That is, a *posek* can reject the significance of a new source if he can demonstrate it to be illogical or legally erroneous. Theoretically, then, a later *posek* could demonstrate, either logically or on the basis of another new source,[53] that Rav's categorization of the new source as erroneous was itself in error, and then use it as grounds for the abrogation of the norm posited by Rav.

Yet a third reason for rejecting the actual significance of a new legal source is reflected in the following passage.[54]

> *Mishnah:* Meal offerings and libations that became impure before having been placed in the vessels of the Temple service can be redeemed.[55] *Gemara:* Samuel said, "They can be redeemed even if

---

48. See above, n. 46.

49. In the specific case in point, the second document would be a *shetar mukdam* in name only, for it replaces an original document carrying the same date which was not a *shetar mukdam* in either fact or name. For a discussion of the principle *Hefker beit din hefker,* see above, p. 193.

50. Except, of course, in appearing before the court to testify, if necessary.

51. Rashi, Bava Batra 171a, s.v. *ella edim.* But see Tosafot, ibid., s.v. *ella edim,* who finds the statement of the Gemara more problematic.

52. Even if Rav Huna had known that Rav did not know the source, he could have rejected it exactly as he does, claiming that had Rav known it he would have reacted to it just as he himself did.

53. Cf. the passage of the Gemara that follows immediately after the conclusion of the passage cited on p. 331.

54. Menaḥot 100b–101a.

55. The flour and the wine can be exchanged for money. This money, however, is holy and can be used only for the purchase of a new meal offering or libation, while the original flour or wine becomes appropriate for nonsacred use (*ḥulin*). Obviously, therefore, it is placement in the vessel used ritually for the meal offering or the libation that changes the status of the flour or wine from merely dedicated to actually sacred.

> they are pure. . ." Rav Papa said, "If Samuel had heard that which is taught in a *baraita*,[56] 'If one dedicates unblemished animals for Temple upkeep,[57] they can be redeemed only for sacrificial use;[58] for anything [that has been dedicated] that is fit for use on the altar can never suffer a change in that status '—even though its original sanctity was by virtue of its financial worth,[59] it cannot be redeemed since it is pure—he would have retracted."[60] But that is not the case! He [i.e., Samuel] had heard it, and had not retracted. Did you not say in that case[61] that since they are not frequently found [i.e., are difficult to acquire] they cannot be redeemed [i.e., desanctified]? Here, too, since there are so many and frequent blemishes that disqualify animals, for even minor eye cataracts disqualify them, therefore, animals, too, are not frequently found.

Again, the last part of the passage must be explained in order to comprehend its applicability to the theme under discussion. The *gemara* affirms that Samuel had indeed heard the source that Rav Papa asserted would have been sufficient to convince him to retract his view that even pure flour and wine not yet placed in Temple vessels could be redeemed. But, the *gemara* continues, Samuel had not only heard that *baraita*, he had rejected it as having no legal significance vis-à-vis his position. The *gemara* had already explained (in a part of the passage not quoted in our translation) that dedicated, but not yet sanctified, accouterments to sacrifices, such as wood and frankincense, could not be desanctified so long as they remained fit for sacrificial use. The grounds for that prohibition had nothing to do with the sanctified status of the

---

56. Tosefta Temurah 1:13 and Temurah 33b.

57. Which excludes sacrificial uses. This practice was discouraged. See Temurah 6a.

58. I.e., the redemption money will be used for the Temple upkeep, and the animal will be consecrated for use on the altar.

59. E.g., animals dedicated for the Temple upkeep, as opposed to those dedicated for sacrificial use (*la-mizbe'aḥ*); or flour and wine before their actual physical sanctification in the Temple vessels.

60. The thrust of Rav Papa's argument is as follows: The unblemished animals dedicated for the Temple upkeep are parallel to meal offerings or libations not yet placed in Temple vessels. Their similarity lies in the fact that in both cases they are not *physically* sanctified; rather, it is their financial worth that is sanctified. Since Rav Papa understands the *baraita* to mean that things sanctified only for their financial worth cannot be redeemed and desanctified so long as they remain fit for actual sanctification, he assumes that Samuel would have applied the principle of the *baraita* to flour and wine dedicated as meal offerings and libations, and would have forbidden their desanctification so long as they were fit for altar use (i.e., so long as they remained pure), if he had but known the *baraita*.

61. The reference is to a part of the talmudic selection we have not actually quoted. That section deals with the right to redeem either wood or frankincense that has been dedicated. The right is denied for the reason cited in the passage quoted.

accouterments. That prohibition had been motivated, rather, by a desire to ensure the availability of such necessary accouterments to sacrifice, which were generally hard to acquire. The *gemara* proceeds to assert that the case of unblemished animals is perfectly parallel to the case of the wood and frankincense: Since animals can be so easily and frequently disqualified from acceptability for the altar, unblemished animals are also difficult to acquire. Therefore, disallowing their desanctification ensures their availability when needed.

We must understand Samuel's rejection of the new source as follows: The prohibition makes no claim whatsoever about the theoretical question of whether it is permissible to desanctify dedicated objects in general. Since flour and wine are readily available, and not so easily disqualified for altar use, the reason for prohibiting the desanctification of wood, frankincense, and unblemished animals is inapplicable to them. In the final analysis, then, the new source about unblemished animals that Samuel had apparently failed to take into account had, indeed, been taken into account by him. He had considered it, had decided that it was inapplicable to the issue he was addressing, and, therefore, he had deemed it legally insignificant vis-à-vis that issue.

Clearly, then, a third reason for rejecting the legal significance of a new source for the abrogation of a norm is its apparent inapplicability to that norm. If the norm in question and the new source can be reasonably interpreted as reflections of ideas that are neither contradictory nor mutually exclusive, the new source may be deemed legally inapplicable to the norm in question. Should a later *posek* argue cogently against the reasonableness of the earlier *posek*'s interpretation of the ideas underlying the source and the norm, which he might do either on the basis of logical analysis or on the basis of another new legal source, as we have seen before, the later *posek* can dismiss the earlier *posek*'s rejection of the legal significance of the first new source.

The passages cited thus far in this chapter have all resulted either in the rejection or the acceptance of a new legal source as a basis for the abrogation of a norm or the resolution of a question of law. The following passage, though, indicates that total acceptance or rejection of a new legal source is not the only possible option.

The Talmud records the following interesting passage.

> Rabbi Yoḥanan said, "The putting on of shoes follows the pattern of the putting on of phylacteries. Just as phylacteries are put on the left arm, so the left shoe [is put on first]." An objection was raised from a *baraita:* "When one puts on his shoes he should first put on the right shoe and then the left shoe." Rav Yosef said, "Since the *baraita*

says one thing, and Rabbi Yoḥanan says another, one can do it either way." Abayee said to him, "Perhaps Rabbi Yoḥanan did not know this *baraita,* and if he had learned of it he would have retracted. Or maybe he did know it, yet held that the law was not in accordance with it." Rav Naḥman the son of Isaac said, "A God-fearing man does as both views. And who is it? Mar the son of Rabana. How does he act? He first puts on the right shoe without tying it, then puts on the left shoe and ties it, and finally he ties the right shoe."[62]

By paraphrasing each segment of this passage in the terms we have been using, the passage can be outlined as follows: Rabbi Yoḥanan expresses a norm. A contradictory norm, based on a *baraita,* is raised as an objection. Rav Yosef takes both sources at face value and declares that the two sources reflect a *maḥaloket.* Since, apparently, neither of the views has the clear weight of precedent behind it, he affirms the two as grounds for the legitimate exercise of judicial discretion. Abayee argues against Rav Yosef's explanation of the sources by raising two different theoretical possibilities. First, he says, it is possible that the *baraita* is a new legal source unknown to Rabbi Yoḥanan. Perhaps, had he known it, he would have deemed it of sufficient legal significance to warrant the abrogation of his own view. If this had been the case, normative behavior should follow the view of the *baraita,* and the matter should not be the subject of judicial discretion. The second theoretical possibility proposed by Abayee is that Rabbi Yoḥanan had indeed known the *baraita* and had rejected it as legally insignificant vis-à-vis his norm on the grounds that it was legally erroneous. If *this* was what happened, then normative behavior should follow the view of Rabbi Yoḥanan, and (still) should not be a matter of judicial discretion. Finally, Rav Naḥman the son of Isaac proposes a compromise position that incorporates the most important features of both views: Since the *baraita* gives clear precedence to the right shoe, it should be put on first. But since Rabbi Yoḥanan gives precedence to the left shoe, because he juxtaposes shoes and phylacteries, and since the distinguishing feature of phylacteries is that they are bound to the left arm, the left shoe should be tied first.

The claims of Abayee in this passage will be immediately recognized as reflecting the very options we have been discussing; the claims of Rav Yosef and Rav Naḥman the son of Isaac, however, introduce two elements that have not yet been mentioned. Rav Yosef introduces the idea that a new source can reveal the existence of a *maḥaloket* where none

62. Shabbat 61a.

was previously known. This possibility implies, ultimately, that the *posek* has the right to exercise his judicial discretion (subject, of course, to all the limitations and strictures of the rule of precedent). Rav Naḥman introduces the idea that a possible method of dealing with a new legal source is to attempt to effect some kind of compromise between the norm and the new source, a compromise that retains the important features of both, even though, as in this case, it might create a completely new pattern of behavior. In later sections of this chapter we shall see further examples of the options reflected in the statements of Abayee, Rav Yosef, and Rav Naḥman.

We have thus far demonstrated that although new legal sources are valid considerations in the decision-making process, they are only potentially significant legally, not necessarily so. The nature of the new legal sources cited thus far, however, has been such that recognition of them as new legal sources, and as potentially significant, was indisputable, because in each case the new source was independent of the norm upon which it was brought to bear. Not all new legal sources are of this nature, however. Anyone who has ever been exposed to rabbinic sources is aware that different versions of the same source abound. Sometimes the variant readings are discovered in the writings of the commentators, sometimes in manuscripts and manuscript fragments, sometimes in parallel rabbinic works. In many instances the existence of a variant reading is clearly demonstrable, while in other instances the existence of a variant is demonstrable only by deduction.

It is crucial that we analyze whether variant readings are admissible as new legal sources, because it is clear that the commentators, legalists, and codifiers of the past could not possibly have known of all the variants of a given passage that were (or are) actually in existence. Their comments and decisions were necessarily based only upon the limited number of variants available to them (each in his own time), either through the published works of their predecessors or through the manuscripts to which they had access. If we discover that variant readings do, in fact, qualify as new legal sources, students of rabbinics and *posekim* in modern times will have many more new legal sources available to them because of the fact that they now have access to so much more of the writings of earlier generations. Because of the discovery of previously unknown works written in all parts of the world, and of the publication of early works whose existence had been widely known but of which copies had been very limited, and of works whose existence had been known but of which there had been no copies at all, there is today a wide proliferation of critical editions of primary and secondary rabbinic texts that include, at a minimum, a listing of all the variant readings of all the sources now available in libraries and private collections throughout the world. Moreover, modern photocopying techniques allow relatively easy access to reproductions of rare books and manuscripts, significantly decreasing the chance of errors due to inaccurate copying. *Posekim* today, more than ever, must determine what the legal status of variant readings is, for the quantity of raw data grows constantly.

It is our position, based primarily on talmudic and medieval sources, that a variant version of a legal source has always been accorded the status of an entirely new legal source by the halakhic system. Moreover, consistent with the thesis advanced in this book, that modern *posekim*, are not only entitled, but duty-bound, to employ and utilize the methods employed and utilized in the halakhic process until now, if they themselves are not to be guilty of the vitiation of that process, we believe that it is legitimate for modern *posekim* to use variant readings as legal sources of potential significance in no less measure than did their illustrious predecessors, and that this legitimacy holds even with regard to the use of variants unknown to their predecessors but now known to them.

Regrettably, this position makes it necessary to reject some of the views of some of the most universally recognized *posekim* of modern times. Representative of the views we feel compelled to deny is that of Rabbi Avraham Yeshayahu Karelitz (Ḥazon Ish, 1878–1953) regarding use of the Munich manuscript of the Talmud.[63]

> He sought to explain a talmudic section . . . and to emend the text of the Gemara on the basis of the Munich manuscript.[64] . . . How can we know that the Munich manuscript was not one of those manuscripts which, in its own time, contained readings at variance with the majority of manuscripts (*nitbattel be-rov bi-zemanno*)? And how can we know that it was not known as an unreliable manuscript (*bilti medukdak*)? In any case, it is as null and void as a broken sherd against the recognized version (*ha-girsa ha-mekubbelet*). . . . I see almost no hope of reaching a true understanding through the variants that are being discovered from *genizot*.[65] The function (*to'elet*) of all of them is to pervert justice (*le-avvet mishpat*) and

63. S. Greiniman, ed., *Kovez̧ Iggerot Me'et Ḥazon Ish* (Jerusalem, 1954), pt. I, pp. 59 f.

64. A frequently quoted talmudic manuscript. Written in the mid-fourteenth century, it is the only complete manuscript of the entire Babylonian Talmud extant.

65. I.e., previously unknown versions culled from newly discovered sources, or versions that have been found in repositories for old books, manuscripts, and fragments. Such repositories are called *genizot*.

> distort the truth (*le-akkem et ha-emet*). They should be banned (*le-gonezam*), for the loss which results from them is greater than the profit.

Historians may well be able to explain the historical currents against which the Ḥazon Ish was railing so vehemently, and those explanations may mitigate the severity of his words, but, systemically, his words are indefensible. He is certainly correct in saying that some manuscripts are more accurate than others, but to condemn an entire manuscript on the basis that it might have had the reputation of inaccuracy is unprecedented, without basis in Jewish law. Moreover, even texts that may be generally unreliable might preserve some authentic variants of great significance. The worth of a variant can only be determined by means of the same degree of careful scrutiny and analysis of the text of which it is a part as is devoted to passages in the standard text of the Talmud or in other rabbinic sources. It is true that there is more than a modicum of subjectivity involved in concluding that a variant is or is not legally significant; but to issue a blanket invalidation of even the potential legal significance of all newly discovered variants is contrary to all the evidence which can be cited. It is to examples of such evidence that we now turn.

Rabbi Solomon ben Abraham Adret (Rashba, ca. 1235–1310) was asked the following question: Is one who performs a circumcision on either a convert or a slave obligated to recite a blessing both before and after the actual circumcision, or is one blessing before sufficient, with none needed after?[66] He answered:

> This is a very old controversy. Indeed, the disagreement among the *rishonim* is contingent upon the reading in the Gemara. Most copies (*be-rov ha-sefarim*) read in *Shabbat*, chapter "Rabbi Eli'ezer *de-Milah*": "He who circumcises converts recites '. . . who has sanctified us by His commandments and commanded us to circumcise converts and to draw from them the blood of the covenant, etc.' "[67] And this is the version found in the *Halakhot* of the Alfasi,[68] and with which most of the sages (*ha-gedolim*) agree. According to this reading a

66. *Responsa of Rashba,* pt. 1, no. 328.

67. Shabbat 137b. The reading quoted at this point by the Rashba is *not* the reading of the present standard version of the Gemara. Rather, our Gemara texts have the reading quoted by the Rashba in the name of the *Halakhot Gedolot*. See the E. Hildesheimer ed. (Jerusalem: *Mekiẓei Nirdamim*, 1971), pt. 1, p. 215.

68. As, indeed, it does appear in standard printed versions of the Alfasi (= the Rif), Shabbat 55b.

> blessing is recited prior to the actual circumcision, and no blessing at all is recited at the end. . . . But the *Halakhot Gedolot*[69] reads there: "He who circumcises converts recites '. . . concerning circumcision.'[70] And he who recites the blessing[71] says '. . . to circumcise converts.' " [This reading] implies that blessings are recited both before and after, as in circumcisions in general. But the view of the Alfasi, of blessed memory, and the Rambam, of blessed memory,[72] is not in accord with his [i.e., the author of *Halakhot Gedolot*] view, as I have already indicated. And though their view seems most plausible (*nirin divreihen*), I have seen some here who follow the view of the *Halakhot Gedolot*.

The Rashba is aware of two readings of the talmudic passage relevant to the question posed to him. This does not mean, of course, that either the Alfasi or the author of the *Halakhot Gedolot* was aware of two versions; more probably, since neither of them mentions another version, each codified his position on the basis of the reading in the Talmud before him, unaware of any other reading. Given the existence of the reading of the *Halakhot Gedolot*, however, the Rashba must decide whether or not it is to be deemed of sufficient legal significance to warrant abrogating the norm implied in the *Halakhot* of the Alfasi. It is important to note that the Rashba offers no evidence, either logical or in the form of other legal sources, that would allow him to judge either one of the readings as erroneous; he rejects neither reading outright. Furthermore, he makes no assertion that the reading he has before him is preferable per se to the reading of the *Halakhot Gedolot*, even if the latter is not erroneous. The Rashba argues in favor of the reading he has before him on two different grounds. First, he argues that it is supported by the view of the Alfasi, of Maimonides, and, according to the Rashba, of "most copies" of the Talmud. Implied in this argument is the claim that the reading of the *Halakhot Gedolot* is unsupported by other textual evidence. Second, he argues in favor of his reading because the behavior it enjoins has the weight of precedent behind it, as reflected in the statement "with which most of the sages agree." Thus, the Rashba offers

---

69. An early legal code, attributed by different scholars to various authors of the geonic period, primarily Shimon Kayyara and Yehudai Ga'on, eighth or ninth century. The *Halakhot Gedolot* should not be confused with the *Halakhot* of the Alfasi.

70. That is, he recites the same blessing that is recited at the *berit milah* (circumcision) of a Jewish infant *before* the actual circumcision.

71. This word is used to indicate the one who recites the benediction *following* the circumcision of a Jewish infant.

72. *Mishneh Torah*, Hilkhot Milah 3:4, which records but one blessing, as does the Alfasi in his *Halakhot*.

us two possible grounds for establishing which of two *equally valid* readings is *more* legally significant. The first is widespread textual support for one reading above the other, based on commentators and codifiers who quote the source in question,[73] and the second is the weight of precedent.

The Rashba decided in favor of the reading he had because of textual support and the fact that it was the precedented position. He apparently found no compelling reason to exercise his judicial discretion in favor of the nonprecedented view of the *Halakhot Gedolot*. Given his support of his own reading, it may seem puzzling that the last sentence of the passage attests, without evaluative comment, to the fact that some had opted for the view of the *Halakhot Gedolot*. Two possible theoretical explanations for the puzzle come to mind. Those who adopted the view of the *Halakhot Gedolot* may have done so because they were unaware of the second reading. This answer would be more plausible in a period earlier than the period of the Rashba; given the fact, though, that at least the Alfasi and Maimonides were widely known and studied in the Rashba's time, this answer is not plausible in this situation. Rather, it is likely that some *posekim*, viewing the existence of two equal readings as grounds for the free exercise of judicial discretion, exercised that discretion in favor of the nonprecedented position rather than the precedented position. (It must again be stressed that exercising judicial discretion is not to be equated with proving that one view is erroneous.)

Although the Rashba, regrettably, does not give any indication of the reasoning that may have prompted those who adopted the nonprecedented position, it is possible that the grounds might have been identical or similar to those expressed by Rabbi Asher ben Yehi'el (Rosh, ca. 1250–1327), who wrote:

> [A blessing both before and after the actual circumcision is required] even according to those versions (*sefarim*) that do not have "He who circumcises . . . concerning circumcision." [For its omission can be accounted for on the grounds] that it was not necessary to state explicitly the blessing "concerning circumcision," since there is no difference [between the circumcision of a convert and the circumcision of an infant Jew] except in the blessing that stands [in the case

73. This is not as simple a statistical matter as it might seem. Two commentators who quote the passage identically may not constitute two supporting texts if, for example, one was the student of the other, or if both of them were students of the same third party, or if one lived enough after the other that he might be quoting or copying from him without attribution.

of a convert] in lieu of the blessing recited by the father of the infant son.[74]

We must understand the thrust of the Rosh's comment as follows: The Gemara contains a lengthy passage dealing with the different blessings that accompany circumcision in different cases. The first case discussed is the one that occurs most frequently, namely, the circumcision of an infant Jew. In that case the blessings required by the Gemara include one to be recited by the man who performs the circumcision and one to be recited by the father of the child. For the circumcision of a convert, however, only one blessing is listed in these versions. But, claims the Rosh, this should not be taken to indicate that only one blessing is to be recited, even according to these versions. Rather, it is equally plausible that the Gemara lists only the one blessing for a convert because that blessing is, necessarily, different from the one a Jewish father recites for his own son. However, since the blessing "concerning circumcision" is applicable and pertinent to both the circumcision of an infant Jew and the circumcision of a convert, there was no need for the Gemara to repeat the fact of its requirement. The reader would be expected to understand that the latter part of the passage in the Gemara lists only those blessings that would not be otherwise known. Since the blessing "concerning circumcision" would be known on the basis of the first part of the passage, its omission from the latter part of the passage in no way proves that it should not be recited.

Assuming that a reason such as this motivated those *posekim* who opted for the view the Rashba rejected as nonprecedented, it follows that *posekim* can freely exercise their judicial discretion in favor of what appears to others as the nonprecedented position if they are able to interpret that position in a way that is not contradicted by the precedented view, even though other *posekim* interpret the versions as contradictory.[75]

In the preceding example, both variants were considered to be equally viable. The following examples will present instances in which one or the other of the variants is rejected as being unreliable. We will explore the grounds for and the possible ramifications of such rejection.

---

74. *Piskei Rosh* to Shabbat 19:11.

75. It is interesting to note, parenthetically, that although Tosafot Shabbat 137b, s.v. *avi*, deals with a totally different issue, it is one that is also contingent upon variant readings of the text we have been discussing. There, however, the variants refer to possible differences in the order of the blessings recited at the circumcision ceremony of an infant Jew. Variants reflecting order rather than word changes also have potential legal significance.

Maimonides codifies and explains his decision in a certain monetary matter as follows:[76]

> One who lends money in the presence of witnesses and says [to the borrower], "Do not repay me except in the presence of witnesses" . . . must be repaid by the borrower in the presence of witnesses, because of the condition imposed. If the borrower asserts, "I did so. I paid you in the presence of Mr. X and Mr. Y, who have since either left town or died," he is to be believed. . . . There are versions of the Gemara in which it is written: ". . . he is not to be believed."[77] But that is an erroneous version (*ta'ut sefarim hu*). Therefore, those who rendered their decisions on the basis of that reading have erred.[78] For I have thoroughly investigated (*ḥakarti*) the old versions and found "He is to be believed" in them. And I had access in Egypt to an old Gemara fragment, written on rolled parchment (*gevilin*) as they used to write them about five hundred years ago. And I found two versions of this law in the fragment, and in both of them was written," . . . He is to be believed."

The Rambam asserts that any decision of any *posek* that is predicated on the reading "He is not to be believed" is in error and should be overturned. His contention is not based on any logical evidence proving that view to be incorrect or his view to be correct; his claim is based solely on the assertion that one version is more textually reliable than the other. Underlying this claim is the assumption that, other things being equal, older texts tend to be more reliable renditions of the original statement than newer texts. The grounds for this assumption, though not actually spelled out by Maimonides, are that older texts, by virtue of their age alone, have been less susceptible to copyists' errors and conscious corrections. But the Rambam is careful to imply that one such version would probably be inadequate to warrant this conclusion.[79] He gives three reasons for preferring the reading he accepts: First, only *some* of the "newer" Gemara texts have the other reading; second, older versions are unanimously in favor of the reading he prefers; and third, the oldest versions, dating from manuscripts identifiable as coming from

76. *Mishneh Torah,* Hilkhot Malveh ve-loveh 15:1–2. Quoted by Elon in *Jewish Law,* 3:983.
77. Shevu'ot 41b.
78. See, for example, Rabbenu Ḥananel (on the printed page of standard editions of the Gemara) and the Alfasi *ad loc.*
79. Though this might not be true if that one version possessed some inherent or logical superiority over the other versions. In this specific case, however, neither version is inherently better than the other.

the seventh or eighth century, also support that reading. The reasons are clearly listed in ascending order of importance, the oldest versions constituting the greatest support. On the basis of such overwhelming evidence, Maimonides accepts the supported version as original and authentic and rejects the alternative, even though that rejection results in the abrogation of a norm codified by *posekim* such as the Alfasi. Finally, it should be noted that the abrogation results in the establishment of a more lenient position than that of the rejected version.

One further example from the Talmud itself will present another instance in which one or the other of the existing variants is rejected as being unreliable. The Talmud records the following:[80]

> *Mishnah:* An amputee may go out (*ha-kite'a yoẓe*) [on the Sabbath] with his artificial leg,[81] according to Rabbi Me'ir. But Rabbi Yosé forbids.[82] *Gemara:* Rava asked Rav Naḥman, "What is the correct reading in the *mishnah?*"[83] He answered, "I don't know." "What is the law?" He answered, "I don't know."
>
> It has been said, "Samuel said [that the reading should be] *ein ha-kite'a* [an amputee may not (go out)], and so did Rav Huna say [that the reading should be] *ein ha-kite'a.*" Rav Yosef said, "Since Samuel said *ein ha-kite'a* and Rav Huna said *ein ha-kite'a,* we, too, will adopt *ein ha-kite'a* as the reading in the *mishnah.*" Rava bar Shira objected, "They had not heard that Rav Ḥanan bar Rava was teaching Ḥiyya bar Rav in Rav's presence . . . [and quoted] 'An amputee may not (*ein ha-kite'a*) go out with his artificial leg, according to Rabbi Me'ir. But Rabbi Yosé permits,' and that Rav indicated to him to reverse the *mishnah.*" . . . And Samuel retracted . . . and Rav Huna, too, retracted.

It is probable that Rava's question was motivated by his concern to establish the correct reading of the *mishnah,* since there were two significantly different versions. Moreover, his teacher had no definitive

80. Shabbat 65b–66a.

81. On the grounds that it has the legal status of a shoe, and can be worn without violating any Sabbath prohibition.

82. On the grounds that it is neither a shoe nor an ornament, and, therefore, using it on Shabbat violates the prohibition against carrying.

83. Should it read "An amputee may go out *(ha-kite'a yoẓe)* with his artificial leg, according to Rabbi Me'ir," as the *mishnah* has it, or should it read "An amputee may not *(ein ha-kite'a)* go out with is artificial leg, according to Rabbi Me'ir. But Rabbi Yosé permits"? Depending on the reading, the views of the sages are different.

answer.[84] The Gemara reports that two sages affirm *ein ha-kite'a* as the correct reading. Rav Yosef is willing to accept that as the reading on the basis of their affirmation. Rava bar Shira objects to accepting their view on the basis of a claim which, by now, should be familiar, namely, that Rav Huna and Samuel were unaware of a new legal source. In this instance the "new" source was the clear indication by Rav that *ha-kite'a yoẓe* was the correct reading, not *ein ha-kite'a*. Apparently, both Samuel and Rav Huna somehow found out about Rav's rejection of *ein ha-kite'a* and reversed their own positions.[85]

No indication is given in the passage of the history of the original view held by Samuel and Rav Huna. In theory, that view could reflect the reading they knew in the *mishnah;* both of them being completely unaware at the time that a different reading existed. On the other hand, their position could be the result of their own grappling with the two readings, both of which were known to them. While a definitive answer to this question may be impossible, the thrust of the passage favors the first possibility. If their original assertion had been the end product of some reasoned choice between the two possible readings, we would anticipate some indication in the Gemara of the reasons for their retraction. But the passage records their retraction without any indication that any such reason had existed. It is, therefore, more probable to suppose that both they and Rav Yosef accepted Rav's version because they deemed it to be the more reliable.

Still, since no textual or logical evidence is presented to support Rav's view, it is reasonable to ask why his preference was accepted as the more reliable and authentic reading. It is likely that the summary nature of his reversal of the reading being taught to Ḥiyya bar Rav was taken as an indication of his certainty that he was correct; he would not have reversed the reading so summarily had he had any doubts. This certainty constituted sufficient evidence of reliability to convince Rav Yosef, and perhaps even Samuel and Rav Huna, to accept his position.[86]

---

84. Rava's second question may have been completely independent of the first. More likely, though, he may have felt that the correct reading could be ascertained by determining what the law was, since a systemic principle existed that dictated whose view was generally to be followed in a dispute between Rabbi Me'ir and Rabbi Yosé, viz., the view of Rabbi Yosé.

85. For each of them, the Gemara in this passage cites other sources that they could interpret as they do only if they had adopted the reading Rav affirmed.

86. The examples cited in which one version was adopted as more reliable than the other, have been instances in which both versions were potentially viable. The ultimate extension of the reliablity principle is found in instances where the potential viability of one of the versions is denied. Readings that lack such potential are generally referred to as *shibbushim* ("confused" or "corrupted"), although the word is often used more loosely. See below, p. 346, in Naḥmanides' comment.

Since, as we have just seen, variant readings *can* function as new legal sources of potential significance, it is logical to assume (once again) that instances exist in which a later *posek* claims that an earlier one would have retracted his decision had he been aware of the existence of another reading that is more reliable. Two examples, one from the Talmud and its early commentators and the other from a modern *posek*, will suffice to demonstrate that such claims are found regularly in halakhic literature.[87]

Rava distinguishes between the deed of which plotting witnesses[88] are guilty and the type of deed generally associated with other punishable crimes, by asserting that, in general, punishable crimes involve some kind of action, while the crime of plotting witnesses is dependent, according to the version of Rava's comment in the Gemara, only upon *re'iyah* ("seeing"). Although the entire passage in which Rava's comment appears is a difficult one, it is clear that the deed of plotting witnesses is being defined as one that lacks any real action. It is also clear that Rashi too had before him the reading *re'iyah*, for he explains that the crux of their culpability stems from the "seeing" (an actionless deed) that they purport to have seen, but which they have not actually seen. Rashi's explanation is very difficult, however, since, logically, the real crux of the culpability of plotting witnesses stems from their *testifying* about that which they purport to have seen, not from the fact that they are purporting to have seen something that they have not really seen. If, however, their culpability stems from their testifying, it follows that Rava is defining testifying as lacking real action, even though the Gemara has earlier defined the lip movements involved in speaking as an "action," a fact Rava could have been expected to know.

The Rif in his comments on Rava's statement lists three geonic variants for *re'iyah* that he claims are identical to each other. The variants for *re'iyah* that he lists, untranslated and untransliterated, are: איה אין, and אי. The Rif explains, in the name of the *ge'onim*, that these three words are not really words in the ordinary sense, but, rather, that they represent sounds, mainly vowel sounds, that can be spoken without any lip movements, much like the modern "uh-huh." Therefore, according to the ge'onic version of the Gemara as understood by the Rif, Rava's statement would mean that plotting witnesses are different from other categories of criminals, inasmuch as it is possible for them to testify (the crux of the deed that makes them legally culpable) by

87. The talmudic example is from Sanhedrin 65b, and the example from a modern *posek* begins below, p. 347.
88. *Edim zomemin*. See Deuteronomy 19:18–19.

saying one of these sounds without performing a real "action," since they can do so without movement of the lips.[89]

On balance, the explanation of the Rif seems to make more sense out of what Rava meant by defining the crime of plotting witnesses as actionless than Rashi's explanation, which, although clearly reflecting an actionless deed, misses the crux of their culpability. But it should not be overlooked that the variants the Rif lists never mean elsewhere what the Rif says they mean here. It is even difficult to know how they are to be pronounced in this context. So, while his explanation of Rava is more logical, it is not without its own difficulties, stemming from the very variants that he interprets in order to achieve the logic in the first place.

Commenting on the Rif, two commentators come to opposite conclusions about the version of Rava's statement that the Rif prefers. Rabbi Zeraḥiah ben Isaac ha-Levi Gerondi (Ba'al ha-Ma'or, late 12th cent.) writes: "The [correct] reading is, '. . . *re'iyah,*' as Rashi reads. It is not either איה , אין , or אי , as the Rif, of blessed memory, wrote." Although, regrettably, the Ba'al ha-Ma'or does not share the reasons for his decision with us, it is clear that he accepts Rashi's reading as the more reliable. It certainly does not seem unreasonable to posit that Rabbi Zeraḥiah ha-Levi favored Rashi's version about that of the Rif because of the difficulties described above.

On the other hand, in his comments on the Ba'al ha-Ma'or, Naḥmanides wrote:

> How could he [i.e., the Ba'al ha-Ma'or] disagree, with the readings of the [ancient] academies, and with Rav Hai Ga'on, of blessed memory, without reason? Indeed, had Rashi, of blessed memory, seen their version, he would surely have retracted. Only erroneous texts *(sefarim meshubbashim)* forced him to explain as he did.[90]

Naḥmanides implies that no greater attestation to the authenticity and reliability of any reading could be given than the clear and unambiguous testimony of so early a commentator as the Rif that his reading, and its meaning, is identical with the reading of the *ge'onim.* Surely the reading of the *ge'onim* must be judged more reliable than any other, particularly when it is so clear how the "perverted" reading probably came into being. Surely the simple and straightforward *re'iyah* is either a scribal

---

89. Precisely how they could do so is not so clear and is the subject of considerable discussion among commentators. For the purposes of the present discussion, however, the *realia* of the actual testimony are not relevant.

90. Naḥmanides, *Milḥamot ha-Shem* on the *Halakhot* of the Rif (Alfasi) to Sanhedrin 65b.

"correction" or an innocent copying error of the difficult איה .[91] Had Rashi but known of that reading, he would immediately have recognized its greater reliability and authenticity. Thus Naḥmanides makes the same claim vis-à-vis new legal sources that result from variant readings that we have already seen being made vis-à-vis new legal sources found elsewhere than in variant readings.

In addition, the statements of the Ba'al ha-Ma'or and Naḥmanides once again demonstrate the fact that subjective judgments are as much involved in determining the reliability of readings as in other areas of the decision-making process. What Naḥmanides rejects as an indisputable perversion is the authentic reading for the Ba'al ha-Ma'or. And the Ba'al ha-Ma'or rejects as inconclusive the very evidence Naḥmanides takes to be proof-positive of authenticity.

Although the primary point of the modern passage that follows remains the same, namely, that we can find instances in which a later *posek* claims that an earlier one would have retracted his decision had he been aware of the existence of another reading that is more reliable, it also constitutes one of many possible variations of this claim insofar as the "variant" in the example is not, actually, a variant reading of the same passage, but a different version of the same view of the same author, recorded in a different place.

A well-known *baraita* lists three categories of women about whom it claims that *meshammeshot be-mokh*, a phrase that can mean either "*may* use a *mokh* in sexual relations" or "*must* use a *mokh* . . ."[92] If it is interpreted to mean "may," it clearly implies that other women may not. If it is understood to mean "must," the *baraita* could be read to imply that other women may. This issue was a matter of dispute between Rashi and Rabbenu Tam.[93] Furthermore, since the word *meshammeshot* means "to engage in intercourse," the phrase seems clearly to indicate that the

91. The critical principle of *difficilior lectio* ("the more difficult reading") suggests that when two readings exist, one simple and straightforward and the other difficult, the latter is more likely than the former to be the original reading. The theory underlying the principle is that one is inclined to "correct" or emend a difficult reading in order to make it clear and meaningful. To do the opposite would be patently absurd. The principle, however, should be applied with discretion. Even a judgment about "difficulty" can have a subjective element. Is *re'iyah* more "difficult" because of its logical implausibility, or is איה more "difficult" because it is a *hapax legomenon* (the sole example of the use of the word in the entire corpus of this literature)? Furthermore, many *shibbushim* (confused or corrupted texts) are so "perverted" from the original that they would qualify as the *difficilior lectio* if we did not know, of course, that they are not the original readings.

92. Yevamot 12b and parallels.

93. See Tosafot *ad loc.*, s.v. *shalosh*, for example. The entire subject has received thorough treatment by Rabbi David M. Feldman in his book *Marital Relations, Birth Control and Abortion in Jewish Law* (New York: Schocken Books, 1974).

mokh may, or must, be present during the act of intercourse (in which case a *mokh* is a type of tampon inserted before intercourse).[94] But since this interpretation of the *baraita* would have it advocate the violation of the prohibition against *hashḥatat zera* (the wasteful emission of sperm), most have understood *meshammeshot be-mokh* to mean "may [or, must] use the *mokh after* intercourse" (in which case a *mokh* is an absorbent inserted after intercourse). Nonetheless, a few *posekim* did understand it to refer to a precoital tampon. The most explicit such statement comes from Rabbi Solomon ben Yeḥi'el Luria (Maharshal, 1510–1573).[95]

In commenting on the "may-must" controversy, and on the "tampon-absorbent" controversy, Rabbi Abraham Bornstein of Sochaczew (1839–1910) wrote:[96]

> It is clearly appropriate to render legal judgment according to the view of the Rosh [Rabbi Asher ben Yeḥi'el, ca. 1250–1327], whom we of the Ashkenazic communities follow, who decided (*she-hikhri'a*) in favor of the view of Rabbenu Tam.[97] Thus, too, did Luria decide in the first chapter of Yevamot.[98] But one ought not to rely on Luria concerning his addition, permitting even a precoital tampon even to women in general, for one of his proofs that the meaning of *meshammeshot be-mokh* is "before intercourse" is the implication of the language of the Rosh in his *Commentary*.[99] Yet the words of the *Tosfei ha-Rosh* state explicitly that even the three categories of women are forbidden to insert the *mokh* precoitally.[100] And it is probable (*ve- yesh lomar*) that had the Maharshal [i.e., Luria] known that the Rosh opposes him, he would not have allowed himself (*lo*

94. See Feldman, *Marital Relations*, chap. 9.

95. Luria, *Yam Shel Shelomo* to Yevamot 1:8.

96. *Responsa Avnei Nezer* (Piotrkow, 1912), *Even ha-Ezer* 81:10, p. 144, as quoted in Feldman, *Marital Relations*, p. 212.

97. I.e., that they "must" use a *mokh*.

98. See above, n. 95.

99. *Commentary* to Nedarim 35b (printed on the page of standard editions of the Talmud). There the Rosh writes: "The three categories of women must put the *mokh* in its appropriate place in order to catch *(liklot)* the sperm, so that she not become pregnant." Luria understood the word *liklot* to imply a precoital tampon, since it can be understood to refer to a postcoital absorbent only with greatest linguistic difficulty. Had the Rosh meant that, he would surely have used a word other than *liklot*.

100. *Tosfei ha-Rosh* (printed on the page of standard editions of the Talmud), Niddah 3b: "Even though the *baraita* states *meshammeshot be-mokh,* it does not mean that the *mokh* may be inserted precoitally, for that is surely forbidden because of *hashḥatat zera* even to the three categories of women who must use the *mokh* . . . Rather, she inserts it after intercourse in order *she-tishov* [to absorb, draw, sponge-up] the sperm, so that she not become pregnant." N.B., *Tosfei ha-Rosh* and his *Commentary* on Nedarim are different works by the same author.

haya makhnis aẓmo) to disagree with all of the *posekim*. But *Tosfei ha-Rosh* had not yet been published in the days of Rabbi Solomon Luria.

Bornstein's thesis can be rephrased as follows: It is clear that the two different clauses that appear in the two different works of the Rosh, "to 'catch' (*liklot*) the sperm, so that she not become pregnant," in his *Commentary on Nedarim*, and "in order to absorb (*she-tishov*) the sperm, so that she not become pregnant," in *Tosfei ha-Rosh* to *Niddah*, are functional equivalents of two variant readings (primarily *liklot* and *she-tishov.)* At face value, *liklot* implies "precoital," and *she-tishov* implies "postcoital." The roots of the Hebrew verbs themselves, however, are not so precise as to preclude the possibility that the former could mean "postcoital" or that the latter could mean "precoital." Were the context of one of the variants so clear as to leave no doubt what the Rosh meant by the particular verb he used there, it would be possible to elevate that version to the status of a new legal source sufficient to warrant abrogating the norm deduced from the other variant. This would be particularly true if one could demonstrate that the variant whose meaning is certain was unknown to the *posek* who rendered his decision on the basis of the other variant.

Beginning with the assumption that the Rosh is not contradicting himself in his two different statements, Bornstein claims that the language in *Tosfei ha-Rosh* to *Niddah* is so clear and unambiguous that it warrants abrogating any norm deduced from the language in the *Commentary on Nedarim*. The clarity of the *Tosfei ha-Rosh* to *Niddah* renders most probable the contention that *liklot* in the *Commentary on Nedarim* means "postcoital." Indeed, had Luria known the *Tosfei ha-Rosh* version, he, too, would have retracted his earlier view.[101]

In discussing an earlier passage, we noted the possibility of effecting a compromise between two conflicting legal sources.[102] Since variant readings function exactly as do new legal sources, we should also be able to find similar attempts in halakhic literature to effect a compromise

101. A modern *posek*, Rabbi Moses Feinstein, in *Iggerot Mosheh* (New York: Moriah Offset Co. 1974), *Even ha-Ezer*, no. 63, p. 161a, as quoted in Feldman, *Marital Relations*, p. 210, adopts a different approach. He utilizes the ultimate possible solution to a textual problem, namely, emending the problem text, or else attributing it to someone other than its purported author ("an erring student"). In Feinstein's subjective judgment, the preponderance of evidence from other sources dictates the conclusion that the Rosh's *Commentary* on Nedarim is erroneous. In theory, some *posek* could argue against his position by contesting the "conclusiveness" of the sources Feinstein finds so weighty.

102. Above, pp. 334–336.

between two conflicting variants. Before we discuss just such an example, however, it is important to note that conflicting legal souces can be, but need not be, entirely mutually exclusive. By "entirely mutually exclusive" we mean that in the compromise effected between the conflicting legal sources, no element of either conflicting source is retained as stipulated in the source. In the earlier passage about the shoes, for example, the legal sources were both conflicting and entirely mutually exclusive; that is, it is impossible to put both the right shoe and the left shoe on first. This fact dictated the type of compromise proposed. In the example that follows, however, the variants are conflicting but not entirely mutually exclusive, and that will be seen to affect the nature of the compromise.

The Talmud records several comments of some *amora'im* concerning imperfections in phylacteries.[103] (Since, however, there is considerable ambiguity in the terms they use, we find differing interpretations among the commentators.)[104] One assertion made by the Talmud is that both the number and the location of any broken stitches have a bearing on whether or not the phylacteries are disqualified for use. Further, in the final clause of the passage, according to the reading in our standard versions, the Talmud asserts that the disqualification of phylacteries having two consecutive broken stitches applies only to new ones, but that a similar imperfection in old phylacteries would not disqualify them.

In his *Tur,* Rabbi Jacob ben Asher (early 14th cent.), son of Rabbi Asher ben Yeḥi'el (Rosh), quotes Maimonides' codification of the norm exactly as we would anticipate given the reading in our Talmud, namely, that the disqualification applies to new *tefillin,* but not to old ones.[105] In reference to this statement Rabbi Joseph Caro writes:[106]

> Our Master [i.e., the Tur] wrote in his [i.e., Maimonides'] name that he disqualifies new phylacteries but permits old phylacteries. And that is according to the reading of the Rosh.[107] But it is not so.[108] Rather, he [i.e., Maimonides] permits in the case of new *tefillin* and

103. Menaḥot 35a.
104. The different interpretations of the commentators are irrelevant to the point for which this passage is being utilized here, although we will address the question of the legal significance of differing interpretations in the next section of this chapter.
105. *Tur, Oraḥ Ḥayyim* 33.
106. *Beit Yosef* to *Tur, ad loc.*
107. Whose reading is identical with the one in our Talmud.
108. I.e., Maimonides did not write that.

disqualifies in the case of old *tefillin*. And that is according to the version of the Rif.[109]

According to Caro, the *Tur* errs regarding the view of Maimonides. The *Tur* quotes Maimonides as though he had the same reading in the Talmud as the one found in our standard talmudic texts, when, in fact, Maimonides had the version of the Talmud that is reflected in the Rif, in which the words "new" and "old" are reversed.[110] In his own code, Caro stipulates the norm as follows: ". . . under what circumstances are they disqualified [i.e., when two consecutive stitches are broken]? When they are old. But they are permitted if they are new, so long as the base is intact."[111] In other words, Caro rejects the *Tur*'s reading of Maimonides as unreliable.

Rabbi Moses Isserles (Rema, ca. 1520–1572), though, adds a comment in both his commentary to the *Tur* and his glosses to Caro's *Shulḥan Arukh*.[112] In both he asserts that it is best to follow the stringencies of both positions, that is, that the imperfection under discussion should disqualify both old and new phylacteries. Since there is no logical reason that would support one of the versions indisputably above the other,[113] the Rema chooses to propose a compromise that retains the prohibition of each version, although admittedly, the compromise is actually at variance with both of the readings, insofar as in each case it disqualifies a type of phylacteries that the Talmud's statement does not disqualify. In the sense that the compromise cannot retain all elements of each version, the versions are mutually exclusive; yet they are not entirely mutually exclusive, since half of each version, the prohibitive half, can be retained in the final compromise effected between the two variant readings.

In the final analysis, then, the fact that the Rema adopts a compromise while Caro rejects one of the two versions indicates that the significance

---

109. *Halakhot of Alfasi*, Hilkhot Tefillin, p. 7b.

110. Standard printed versions of Maimonides are in agreement with Caro's contention that Maimonides disqualified in the case of old phylacteries. See *Mishneh Torah*, Hilkhot Tefillin 3:18.

111. Caro, *Shulḥan Arukh, Oraḥ Ḥayyim* 33:2.

112. Isserles, *Darkei Mosheh* to *Tur, Oraḥ Ḥayyim* 33, and his glosses to *Shulḥan Arukh, Oraḥ Ḥayyim* 33:2.

113. That is, one could give an acceptable reason to explain why new phylacteries should be disqualified with that imperfection, but not old phylacteries, e.g., that such an imperfection is degrading in new phylacteries, but a sign of regular use in old ones. And one could similarly give a cogent reason for the opposite claim, e.g., that the imperfection in old phylacteries indicates damage to them, while that is not the case with new ones.

of a new legal source based upon variant readings can be itself a matter of *maḥaloket* among *posekim,* and, consequently, grounds for the legitimate exercise of judicial discretion.[114]

We now turn our attention to another category of new legal sources of potential significance that consists neither of variant readings nor of new and independent legal sources, but which consists, rather, of different interpretations of the same passage.

Obviously, the same options that exist for a *posek* regarding new legal sources and variant readings should exist here, too. For example, it should be self-evident that a *posek* can reject for cause the view of another *posek* and adopt the view of a third *posek.* If the deciding *posek* finds one interpretation illogical or untenable, he will reject it. Or if he can offer new legal sources in favor of one position, he will reject the opposing one. If he finds both positions defensible, he may exercise his right of judicial discretion by opting for one position over the other on the grounds of precedent or on the grounds that one position is more logical than the other. Such logic may be contingent on factors internal to the text, as, for example, the claim of the *posek* that the passage being interpreted flows more smoothly according to one interpretation than according to the other. Similar reasoning could also result in a *posek*'s opting for a previously nonprecedented position. Also, the logic may be contingent upon extralegal factors of the nature discussed in Chapter 9.

Since it does not seem quite as self-evident that a *posek* might choose to effect some type of compromise between conflicting interpretations, one example of such an option is in order.

The Talmud records that both Rav Huna and Rabbah are concerned that if a man sends gifts to a woman (as an expression of a special relationship), it can cause speculation about whether the gifts have some significance pursuant to the possibility of a betrothal between them (*ḥosheshin le-sivlonot;* lit. "we worry about gifts").[115] Rashi explains the concern as follows: If a man has made preliminary arrangements to betroth a woman (*shiddekh*), but before transacting the actual betrothal he sends gifts to her, which she receives before witnesses, we are concerned that the function of the gifts may have been to effect the betrothal.[116] Thus, if she accepted an actual betrothal from a second man subsequent to receipt of the gifts from the first, she would require a bill of divorce from the first because of the suspicion that the gifts had been intended as the instruments of betrothal. Rabbenu Ḥananel, as quoted

114. Cf. above, p. 335.
115. Kiddushin 50b.
116. *Ad loc.*, s.v. *ḥosheshin.*

by the Rosh, however, explains the concern differently: After a man betroths a woman he is likely to send her postbetrothal gifts.[117] Thus, if a woman receives gifts from a man, even without witnesses, it may indicate that betrothal had preceded the sending of the gifts, even though we have no certain knowledge of that fact because the witnesses to the betrothal may have left the country.

According to Rashi, then, the gifts may be the instruments of betrothal, and according to Rabbenu Ḥananel they may indicate that a prior betrothal had taken place.[118]

In the course of the talmudic passage, Rabbah questions the validity of his own concern on the basis of the very *mishnah* the Talmud is discussing. The *mishnah* reads: "If one betroths a woman with less than a *perutah*,[119] she is not considered betrothed even if he sends gifts to her thereafter," which can be interpreted as negating the possibility that the gifts can be the instruments of betrothal. But if so, Rabbah asks, why should he be concerned that gifts might effect betrothal? The Talmud's resolution of Rabbah's concern is irrelevant to our discussion. The point is that the very fact that Rabbah considered the *mishnah* to invalidate his own concern proves that his concern must have centered on the possibility that the gifts might effect betrothal. Thus, this part of the talmudic passage supports the interpretation of Rashi.

Toward the end of the same passage, Rav Aḥa bar Rav Huna asks Rava what the status is of a woman for whom a marriage contract (*ketubbah*) had been seen in public, but concerning whom we do not know whether or not she had been betrothed.[120] That is, if the woman had accepted betrothal from a man subsequent to her marriage contract to another man having been seen in public, would the fact of the known existence of a marriage contract be taken as an indication that betrothal to the man who is listed in the contract as her husband had actually taken place or not? If it would be, then the betrothal to the second man would be null and void, since a woman cannot be betrothed to two men. The end of the passage parallels the beginning, and although the Talmud does not ask explicitly regarding the end of the passage, "Do we worry [about the implications for betrothal] because of the existence of the marriage contract," the question is clearly implied by the parallel to the beginning of the passage, where the question is, "Do we worry

117. *Piskei Rosh*, Kiddushin 2:20. Cf. Tosafot Kiddushin 50b, s.v. *hosheshin*.

118. The talmudic passage is quite complicated and includes variant readings reflected in the commentaries of Rashi and Rabbenu Ḥananel. Those complexities, however, are not germane to the present discussion.

119. A coin worth the minimum legal amount of money required to contract betrothal.

120. A marriage contract is not usually written until after the betrothal has taken place.

[about the implications for betrothal] because of the gifts the man sent?" And since nobody could possibly think that a marriage contract had been written to effect a betrothal, the implied question at the end of the passage is: Does the known existence of the marriage contract mean that a prior betrothal had taken place? Similarly, therefore, the parallel question at the beginning of the passage is: Does the sending of gifts by the man mean that a prior betrothal had taken place? Thus, this section of the talmudic passage supports the interpretation of Rabbenu Ḥananel, and not Rashi.

Rabbi Joseph Caro, after quoting the views of Rashi and Rabbenu Ḥananel and explaining how one part of the talmudic passage seems to support Rashi's explanation while another seems to support the explanation of Rabbenu Ḥananel, writes as follows:[121]

> And that is why our Master [i.e., the *Tur*] wrote: "It is desirable to be strict according to both explanations. And that is the conclusion of my father, the Rosh."[122] For since he [i.e., the Rosh] has indicated that each explanation has support within the Gemara, he must obviously feel that one ought to abide by both decisions.[123]

Thus, Joseph Caro in the name of the Rosh proposed that a compromise be effected between the two differing interpretations of the same source. Had it been the case that the entire talmudic passage exclusively supported either the position of Rashi or that of Rabbenu Ḥananel, Caro would probably have rejected the unsupported explanation in favor of the supported explanation.[124] But, since each interpretation gains credence from a different part of the passage, they have the status of two equally viable variant readings, or two equally viable legal sources, and Caro opts for the adoption of both interpretations as a compromise.

We have now discussed the potential legal significance of new legal sources, of variant readings, and of differing interpretations of the same text. Moreover, specific examples have clarified for us the options open

121. Caro, *Beit Yosef* to *Tur, Even ha-Ezer* 45.
122. See above, n. 117.
123. That is, one should adopt the stringency of each. Thus, if one sent gifts that were received before witnesses, we are concerned that he intended them to effect betrothal, even when we *know* there was no prior betrothal. This is the position of Rashi. And if one sent gifts that were not received before witnesses, and we do not know whether or not there was prior betrothal, we are concerned that the gifts indicate that a prior betrothal had actually taken place. This is the position of Rabbenu Ḥananel.
124. Though, admittedly, it would be difficult to fathom why either Rashi or Rabbenu Ḥananel would offer an explanation not only unsupported but even contraindicated by the passage they purport to be explaining.

to a *posek* in resolving the question of the potential legal significance of such sources. However, since each example was intended to demonstrate one option only, it is worthwhile to conclude this segment of the chapter with an example that will demonstrate how, in many cases, new legal sources, variants, varying interpretations, the acceptance of a new source as grounds for abrogation, the rejection of a new source as insignificant, and compromise are often intertwined in the halakhic decision-making process. Thus, all of the passages that follow will deal with a single subject, the status of women vis-à-vis the reading of *Megillat Esther,* and each will be analyzed in terms of the considerations introduced in this chapter.

The Talmud records a statement of Rabbi Yehoshu'a ben Levi:[125] "Women are obligated for the reading of the *megillah* on Purim,[126] for they, too, were involved in that miracle."[127] The first part of the statement is a legal norm; the second part is the historical justification of the norm. However, since the general rule is that women are exempt from positive commandments that must be observed at a specific time,[128] and since the reading of the *megillah* is just such a *mizvah,* even Rabbi Yehoshu'a ben Levi's justification of the norm leaves it at variance with the general rule.

The Gemara commonly understands the word "everyone" in a legal norm to intend the inclusion of a class that might otherwise have been logically thought to be excluded from the obligation to comply with the norm. The talmudic tractate Arakhin begins with a lengthy list of tannaitic norms that include the word "everyone," each of which is followed by a statement specifying the class intended by that word. Included in that section of Arakhin is the following statement:[129]

> Everyone is obligated for the reading of *(be-mikra)* the *megillah,*[130] and everyone is fit (*kesherin*) to read the *megillah.*[131] Who is meant to

---

125. Megillah 4a.

126. That is, they, just like men, must either recite the *megillah* or hear its recitation by someone else.

127. Their "involvement" has been explained to mean either that they, too, were included in the threat of annihilation and were saved by the miraculous delivery or that a woman, Esther, was primarily responsible for the miracle. See Tosafot Megillah 4a, s.v. *she-af*. Rabbi Yehoshu'a ben Levi also obligates women to kindle the Ḥanukkah lights (Shabbat 23a) and to drink the four cups of wine at the Passover *seder* (Pesaḥim 108a), on the grounds that "they, too, were involved in that miracle."

128. Mishnah Kiddushin 1:7.

129. Arakhin 2b.

130. Tosefta Megillah 2:7.

131. Mishnah Megillah 2:4, 19b.

> be included by the term "everyone"? It is meant to include women, in accordance with the view of Rabbi Yehoshu'a ben Levi, who said, "Women are obligated for the reading of the *megillah,* for they, too, were involved in that miracle."

The Gemara posits that the class of women is intended by the word "everyone" in the two norms concerning the obligations of Purim. The statement of Rabbi Yeshoshu'a ben Levi is quoted to demonstrate that the inclusion of women is the most plausible interpretation of the intention of the two norms.[132]

Since women have been specifically included in the two norms, it follows from what we have said above that there must have been some *prima facie* hypothesis that would have excluded them from each of them. We have already explained that the hypothesis that would have excluded them from the obligation for the reading of the *megillah* is their general exemption from positive commandments that must be observed at a specific time. Moreover, since unobligated women are rarely qualified to be the agents through whom others, specifically males, may fulfill their religious legal obligations,[133] it is likely that the intent of the second norm is to stipulate the legal implication of the first. As Rashi wrote: "They are obligated for the reading of the *megillah* and are fit to be the agents through whom males fulfill their legal obligation."[134] That is, it is his view that since women are obligated for the reading of the *megillah,* just as are men, the legal implication is that the right to serve as the agent through whom others fulfill their obligation vis-à-vis the *megillah* applies as much to women as to men. Although Rashi's statement is a commentary on the Gemara and not an actual *pesak,* the Gemara's statement *is* a legal statement. Therefore, if one assumes that the norms stated by the Gemara have the force of law, and if one assumes that Rashi's explanation of the Gemara is accurate, it would follow that Rashi would allow women to read the *megillah* publicly, *and* through that public reading to fulfill the obligation of the men present.

But there is another legal source that deals with the same subject. The Tosefta reads:[135]

---

132. It is possible that the statement of Rabbi Yehoshu'a ben Levi is not merely supportive of the Gemara's claim but, in fact, its impetus.

133. The reason is found in Mishnah Rosh ha-Shanah 3:8: "Whoever is not himself obligated cannot serve as the agent through whom others fulfill their obligation."

134. *Ad loc.,* s.v. *le-atoyei nashim.*

135. Tosefta Megillah 2:4.

> A *tumtum*[136] and a hermaphrodite[137] are obligated [for the reading of the *megillah*], but may not be the agents through whom the public *(ha-rabbim)* fulfills its obligation. A hermaphrodite may be the agent for other hermaphrodites, but not for nonhermaphrodites. A *tumtum* may not be the agent either for others of his own kind or for those not of his own kind. Women, slaves, and minors are exempt [from the reading of the *megillah*], and may not be the agents through whom the public fulfills its obligation.[138]

It is clear that this legal source contradicts both Rabbi Yehoshu'a ben Levi and Arakhin inasmuch as the latter two obligate women and the Tosefta exempts them. Still, given the view of the Tosefta exempting women from the reading of the *megillah,* its statements about the *tumtum* and the hermaphrodite are easily understood. Since the actual gender of every *tumtum* is in doubt, if a *tumtum* were able to be a public agent it could actually be the case that a female would be serving as the agent of males. Even in a group of *tumtumim,* some of whom must statistically be males and some females, the reader might, in fact, be a female attempting to be the agent for males. Thus, a *tumtum* cannot be the agent either for the general public or for its own kind.

Each and every hermaphrodite, on the other hand, is both male and female. While a hermaphrodite cannot be an agent for the general public, since the males in the general public would be fulfilling their obligation at least partially through the services of a female, in a group in which all were partially male and partially female, no complete male would be fulfilling his obligation through the agency of a partial female. Thus a hermaphrodite can serve as an agent for other hermaphrodites.

The *Halakhot Gedolot,* a third legal source, attempting to effect a compromise between Arakhin and the Tosefta, reads:[139]

> Women and slaves and minors are exempt from the reading of the *megillah* and (cannot serve as the agent through whom the general public fulfills its obligation).[140] But they are obligated to hear the

---

136. One whose sex cannot be determined, either because the sexual organs are so underdeveloped as to make identification impossible or because, by some aberration, the genitals are not visible, even if they are developed.

137. Each and every one of whom is *both* male and female.

138. The version of the Tosefta apparently quoted by the *Halakhot Gedolot* (below) ends with the words "exempt from the reading of the *megillah.*" See Tosafot Arakhin 3a, s.v. *leatoyei nashim,* and below, n. 140.

139. *Halakhot Gedolot,* E. Hildesheimer ed., Hilkhot Megillah, p. 406.

140. The statement in parentheses is found in Hildesheimer but is missing in standard printed versions of the *Halakhot Gedolot.* See above, n. 138.

> *megillah* (*ḥayyavin be-mishma*). Why? Since all were under the threat of total annihilation, all are obligated to hear.

The first statement of the *Halakhot Gedolot* is obviously the same as the norm of the Tosefta, while the last statement is obviously a paraphrase of the historical justification offered by Rabbi Yehoshu'a ben Levi. We have already asserted that the Tosefta and the norm of Rabbi Yehoshu'a ben Levi are contradictory, one obligating women and the other exempting them. This assertion, however, is predicated on the assumption that the words "obligated for the reading of the *megillah* (*ḥayyavot be-mikra megillah*)" in Rabbi Yehoshu'a's statement mean "must either recite the *megillah* or hear its recitation by someone else who serves as one's agent."[141] And, in fact, that is the general meaning of the words.

The *Halakhot Gedolot* effects its compromise between the conflicting norms by giving each of them a slightly different interpretation from the one a superficial reading might indicate. Thus, the language of the Tosefta, "exempt (*peturin*)," is interpreted to mean "exempt from the obligation to recite the *megillah*," but not exempt from the obligation to hear the reading of the *megillah*. The norm of Rabbi Yehoshu'a ben Levi is understood to mean "obligated to hear the reading of the *megillah*, but not entitled by virtue of that obligation actually to recite it." In essence, the compromise maintains that the sources do not contradict each other at all, the exemption of the Tosefta applying solely to the actual reading of the *megillah*, and the obligation of Rabbi Yehoshu'a applying only to the hearing of the *megillah*. The distinction is not as difficult as it seems. After all, the Tosefta obligates a *tumtum*, but denies to him the right to recite the *megillah* publicly. His obligation is restricted to hearing it.

A fourth source, the Tosafot, add another dimension to the discussion.[142] They wrote:[143]

> From here [i.e., the comment of Rabbi Yehoshu'a ben Levi] it appears that women can serve as the agents through whom others fulfill their obligation, since he did not say, "To hear the reading of the *megillah (lishmo'a mikra megillah)*."[144] And that, too, is the implica-

---

141. See above, n. 126.

142. Tosafot are distinct from the Tosefta. Tosefta is a collection of tannaitic statements roughly parallel to the Mishnah. Tosafot are commentaries to the Talmud and to Rashi's commentary to it, written by many medieval sages in many places. Both words mean "addition," the Tosefta being an "addition" to the Mishnah, and Tosafot being an "addition" to Rashi.

143. Megillah 4a, s.v. *nashim*.

144. That is, had Rabbi Yehoshu'a intended to restrict the obligation of women to the hearing of the *megillah*, he would have said "they are obligated to hear the reading of the

tion of Arakhin.[145] . . . But there is a problem, since the Tosefta teaches explicitly that a *tumtum* may not serve as the agent either for his own kind or for others, but a hermaphrodite may serve as an agent for its own kind, but not for others. And obviously, a woman is no better than a hermaphrodite. And thus has the *Halakhot Gedolot* decided: that a woman may serve as the agent for others of her own kind, but not for men.

The Tosafot emphasize a logical inconsistency between the implication of Rabbi Yehoshu'a and Arakhin, on the one hand, and the Tosefta on the other. Although, they say, the implication of Rabbi Yehoshu'a and Arakhin is that women may serve as agents for all others, the hermaphrodite clause of the Tosefta belies that implication. The only logic that can justify forbidding a hermaphrodite to serve as an agent for the general public is that the female part of the hermaphrodite would also be serving as the agent, and it is the services of this female part that would prevent whole males from fulfilling their obligation. If a being who is part male cannot be the agent for whole males because he is also part female, surely a being who is wholely female cannot be the agent for males. Therefore, following the logic of the *Halakhot Gedolot* (indeed, clearly attributing the logic to the *Halakhot Gedolot*), the Tosafot claim that a woman may serve as an agent only for other women. Nor, according to this logic, are the wording of Rabbi Yehoshu'a ben Levi's dictum and the norms of Arakhin as problematic as they would seem. Basically, women *are* obligated to hear the reading of the *megillah*, and, in addition, they may also serve as the agent for other women. Thus, the phrase "obligated for the reading of the *megillah*" retains most of its general meaning, merely restricting the class for whom a woman can serve as an agent, to other women; and the logic of such a restriction is supported by the Tosefta, which obligates hermaphrodites for the reading of the *megillah* while restricting the class for whom a hermaphrodite can serve as an agent to other hermaphrodites. In sum, then, the Tosafot accept the basic compromise of the *Halakhot Gedolot*, extending it only to include the right of women to serve as the agents for other women.[146]

Thus far, both the *Halakhot Gedolot* and the Tosafot have accorded the

---

megillah (ḥayyavot lishmo'a mikra megillah)," rather than "they are obligated for the reading of the *megillah (ḥayyavot be-mikra megillah).*" The fact that he uses the common idiom lends support to the contention that he also intended its common meaning, which includes the right to recite the *megillah* as the agent of others.

145. Above, p. 355. Cf. the statement of Rashi quoted there, as well.

146. They could not, however, serve as agents for hermaphrodites. For in that case, a whole female would be serving as the agent for someone who is at least partially male.

passage from the Tosefta the status of a legal source as viable and as potentially significant legally as Rabbi Yehoshu'a's dictum and the passage from Arakhin and have effected a compromise position by adopting the salient features of the conflicting sources.

Rabbi Yom Tov ben Abraham Ishbili (Ritba, ca. 1250–1330), however, takes a different approach. He writes:[147]

> That which is taught in the Tosefta, that women and slaves and minors are exempt from the reading of the *megillah,* reflects an inaccurate text *(meshabbeshta hi)* and denies the affirmation that "they, too, were involved in the miracle." For the [Tosefta] exempts them entirely, as the language itself implies,[148] and as the internal consistency of the passage dictates. [For it says that] a *tumtum* and a hermaphrodite are obligated, but cannot serve as the agents of others. Therefore, women are exempt altogether.

Since the Book of Esther makes abundantly clear that women were involved in the miracle, and since their involvement is incontrovertible evidence of their obligation, any source that either denies or ignores the legal ramifications of that involvement must be considered unreliable and erroneous. Since the statement about women appears in the Tosefta in connection with the statements about the *tumtum* and the hermaphrodite, the meaning of the statement about women cannot be explained except in relation to the other two statements. The *tumtum* and hermaphrodite are obligated, according to the Tosefta, even though they cannot serve as the agents for the general public. But if this is so, then what is the nature of their obligation? They are obligated to hear the reading of the *megillah.* That obligation is described by the words "obligated for the reading of the *megillah.*" Now, the statement about women has also been interpreted, as a result of the compromise effected by the *Halakhot Gedolot* and the Tosafot, to mean "obligated to hear the reading of the *megillah.*" That is, women are seen to have exactly the same obligation as the *tumtum* and the hermaphrodite. Why, then, in the selfsame passage of the Tosefta, would the obligation of the *tumtum* and the hermaphrodite be worded "obligated for the reading of the *megillah,*" and the same obligation for women be worded "exempt"? That is so illogical as to be completely untenable. Therefore, the Tosefta must be exempting women even from the degree of obligation that applies to the *tumtum* and the hermaphrodite. That is, women are

---

147. *Ḥiddushei Megillah* 4a, s.v. *ve-amar Rabbi Yehoshu'a ben Levi.*
148. I.e., *peturin* always means "completely exempt."

exempt not only from the actual reading of the *megillah*, but also from the obligation to hear it read! This, however, contradicts the incontrovertible evidence of legal obligation implied by "they, too, were involved in the miracle." Since that claim is incontrovertible, it must follow that the Tosefta passage vis-à-vis women is unreliable, because it is in error. If it is in error, the potential legal significance of the Tosefta source does not become actual, compromise is unnecessary, and the norm of Rabbi Yehoshu'a ben Levi must be understood to mean that women are obligated for the reading of the *megillah* and may also serve as the agents through whom the general public may fulfill its obligation.

Rabbi Nissim ben Re'uven Gerondi (Ran, ca. 1310–1375) wrote as follows on the same subject:

> There are some who claim that since they [i.e., women] are obligated, they may serve as the agents through whom men fulfill their obligation . . . and that is the view of Rashi, of blessed memory. . . . But others have written in the name of the *Halakhot Gedolot* that they are obligated to hear the reading of the *megillah,* but have no obligation to read it. Therefore, they may not serve as the agents of the general public. And he [i.e., the author of *Halakhot Gedolot*] brought proof from what is taught in the Tosefta . . . but it is not convincing. Nonetheless, it is desirable to take his view into account by being strict (*ra'ui laḥush li-devarav le-ḥumera*) [149]

The view of the Ran is not as definitive as that of the Ritba. The Ran, too, finds the view of the *Halakhot Gedolot* wanting, although he does not reject the proof of the *Halakhot Gedolot* as *totally* untenable, probably for the reasons we have discussed above.[150] And since, for the Ran, the position that the *Halakhot Gedolot* bases upon the Tosefta cannot be absolutely rejected as erroneous, he recommends accepting it as normative. It is most plausible that he so recommends in order to eliminate even the least suspicion of possible nonfulfillment of the obligation for the reading of the *megillah,* since even those who permit a woman to serve as an agent for all others never have made the claim that a woman *must* serve as an agent. In the final analysis, then, the Ran advocates acceptance of the view of the *Halakhot Gedolot*, even though it entails compliance with a norm based, at best, on an uncertain reading of a text.

The final passage to be cited in this extended analysis comes from the

---

149. Ran, *Commentary to the Rif* to Megillah 4a, s.v. *nashim*.

150. See above, pp. 358–359.

Or Zaru'a of Rabbi Isaac ben Moses of Vienna (ca. 1200–1270), who wrote:[151]

> Rabbi Yehoshu'a ben Levi said, "Women are obligated for the reading of the *megillah*, for they, too, were involved in that miracle." And we also say at the beginning of Arakhin[152] . . . And Rashi explained . . . that they are eligible to read it and serve as the agents through whom men fulfill their obligation. But the *Halakhot Gedolot* decided that women are obligated only to hear the *megillah*, but that their reading could not fulfill the obligation of males. . . . And he [i.e., the author of *Halakhot Gedolot*] brought his proof from what was taught in the Tosefta. . . . And according to the Tosefta, the passage in Arakhin should be explained to mean that women are eligible to serve as the agents for other women, but not for men,[153] on the grounds that we might otherwise have thought that since they cannot serve as agents for men, they should also not be allowed to serve as agents for other women. But that bothers me! For what kind of hypothesis is it to assert that I might have erroneously thought that since they cannot serve as agents for men, they could also not serve as agents for women? There is, after all, the case of *zimmun*,[154] which women can perform for themselves[155] but not with men.[156]
>
> And why does the Gemara not argue against Rabbi Yehoshu'a ben Levi from the Tosefta which exempts women? It should have argued against him and resolved the problem by introducing the distinction between "reading" and "hearing," just as the *Halakhot Gedolot* does! So it seems to me that since the *baraita* from the Tosefta is not mentioned in our Talmud, we do not rely upon it. Basically it seems to me correct as explained by Rashi, [that the word "everyone"] includes women, who are obligated for the reading of the *megillah*, and are eligible to serve as the agents for men.

It will be recalled that every time the word "everyone" is used in a legal dictum it is understood to intend the inclusion of a class that might

151. *Or Zaru'a* (Zhitomir, 1862), pt. 2, no. 368, p. 77d.
152. See above, p. 355, for the quotation from Arakhin.
153. Cf. above, p. 358, passage from the Tosafot.
154. The invitation to recite the Grace after Meals. The invitation is obligatory when three or more have eaten together.
155. Berakhot 45b.
156. Mishnah Berakhot 7:2, 45a.

otherwise have been thought to have been excluded.[157] Of all the passages cited, only this one returns to the Arakhin passage in any significant way. That passage quoted two norms pertaining to the reading of the *megillah,* and affirmed that in each it was the class of women that was meant to be included. Although we explained the Arakhin passage according to Rashi, it should be remembered that Rashi did not deal with the passage from the Tosefta. Given the Tosefta passage, however, how should the inclusive "everyone" dicta of Arakhin be understood? Even according to the Tosefta, the first norm can be understood to include women among those obligated to hear the reading of the *megillah.* Since, however, Rashi's interpretation of the second norm cannot coexist with the Tosefta, the author of the *Or Zaru'a* concludes that the second norm in Arakhin must be understood to assert that women are eligible to serve as the agents for other women. But, he asks, on what basis might we have thought that women should be excluded from that right, such that the second "everyone" norm informs us that they are not so excluded? He answers that since women were deemed ineligible to serve as agents for men, it might have been possible to think that they were ineligible to serve as agents of other women also. Thus, the second "everyone" norm teaches that they may, indeed, serve as agents for other women. But the author of *Or Zaru'a* immediately rejects his own argument on the basis of yet another legal source that demonstrates that this argument is really untenable. The new legal source deals with *zimmun* (invitation to Grace after Meals), in which the same distinction between women-women and women-men relationships exists, and in which the possibility that women might not perform *zimmun* with other women because they cannot do so with men had already been rejected.[158] Given that, there is no longer any reasonable hypothesis that would explain why women might have been excluded from serving as agents for other women in reading the *megil-*

157. See above, p. 355 f.

158. There are two possible grounds upon which the *Or Zaru'a* might be making this claim. One is that he is unaware that the same passage in Arakhin (3a) does, indeed, list an "everyone" dictum proving that women can perform *zimmun* with other women. If he is unaware of this part of the Arakhin passage, his proof of the untenability of excluding women from serving as the agents of other women for *megillah* reading would be based on the fact that no one ever raises the same question about *zimmun.* More plausibly, his argument is that the same issue is involved in *zimmun* and *megillah* reading regarding the exclusion of women as agents for each other. Since that principle has already been addressed in the *zimmun* section of Arakhin, it is no longer tenable to argue that women may not serve as agents for other women for *megillah* reading, even without an "everyone" dictum about *megillah.*

lah. And if that is the case, then the Tosefta passage and the Arakhin passage contradict each other irreconcilably.

Furthermore, argues the author of *Or Zaru'a*, given the wording of the Tosefta (i.e., "exempt"), would it not have been most logical for the Talmud to have questioned Rabbi Yehoshu'a ben Levi on the basis of that source, which apparently contradicts him and itself offer the distinction between "hearing" and "reading" which the *Halakhot Gedolot* forces upon both the Tosefta and Rabbi Yehoshu'a? The silence of the Talmud must more logically be understood to imply that the Tosefta passage is being purposely ignored, because the norm it states is not the law.

The *Or Zaru'a* argues on logical grounds against choosing the position of the *Halakhot Gedolot*. First, the view of the *Halakhot Gedolot* is contraindicated by Arakhin. Second, given the primacy of the Babylonian Talmud in *halakhah*, its omission of the Tosefta should not be ignored. Rabbi Isaac of Vienna has not demonstrated any inherent lack of logic in the Tosefta, nor has he rejected the text of the Tosefta as unreliable *qua* text. Rather, he has offered the reasoning that has prompted him to exercise his judicial discretion in favor of the view of Rashi.

Until now the sources cited in this chapter have been used to demonstrate that new legal sources, variant readings, and varying textual interpretations have always been considered to be valid data in the halakhic decision-making process. The sources were used, in addition, to illustrate the options available to *posekim* in dealing with the new material and the methods used by them in evaluating its actual legal significance. The idea that such data are valid considerations and the idea that *posekim* have both different options and different methods for evaluating them are, in fact, incorporated in systemic principles, because they govern the way the system functions *qua* system.

As we stated earlier, the systemic principles that analysis of these passages has yielded have been for the most part, implicit systemic principles.[159] One of these principles, a systemic principle that deals with the acceptability of new legal sources, was, however, stated explicitly in the middle of the fifteenth century by Rabbi Joseph Colon (Maharik, ca. 1420–1480) and has been reaffirmed explicitly in every succeeding generation. The principle deals with a conflict between two other principles: the principle of *Hilkheta ke-vatra'ei* ("the law follows the decision of the latest authorities")[160] and the principle that asserts the

159. See above, p. 318.
160. See above, chap. 4, pp. 102–105.

acceptability of new legal sources even if those sources are, in fact, very old.

In the course of his discussion, Colon focuses on two sources, the first of which is found in the Talmud.[161] It reads:

> Rav included a question to Rebbe between the lines of a letter of greeting:[162] "What is the legal status of goods mortgaged by the co-heirs of an estate?" . . . Rebbe answered, "Whether they sold the goods or they deposited them as surety, the goods can be expropriated in order to provide a dowry,[163] but not to provide food." . . . Rabbi Yoḥanan said that the goods cannot be expropriated for either reason. A question was raised: Had Rabbi Yoḥanan not heard the statement of Rebbe, but if he had heard it he would have accepted it, or perhaps he had heard it and did not accept it?

Given the examples that have already been analyzed in this chapter, the tenor of the Gemara's question can be recognized as far from unique.

The second source Colon uses is from the Rif, who wrote:[164]

> The law is according to Rabbah,[165] who says that the prohibition against noise-making *(hashma'at kol)* on Shabbat applies only to the production of musical-sounding noises.[166] . . . But we notice that some sages affirm the position of Ulla[167] and draw their support from the Palestinian Talmud, where we read in tractate Yom Tov: "Rabbi Elazar [whose view is the same as Ulla's] said, 'All types of noise-making are forbidden on Shabbat.' "[168] . . . But we do not affirm that view. For, since our Gemara is permissive in that regard, the prohibition of the Palestinian Talmud is of no concern to us. For we rely on our Gemara, which is later, and they [i.e., the sages of our (the Babylonian) Talmud] were greater experts than we in the Palestinian Talmud. Thus, had they not known that that passage of

---

161. Ketubbot 69a.

162. Cf. Rashi and Tosafot *ad loc.*, for two different explanations of the facts of the situation.

163. For their sister, who is entitled to be dowered from her father's estate.

164. Rif on Eruvin, p. 35b.

165. Eruvin 104a.

166. As opposed, for example, to knocking on a door. Thus, rhythmic clapping of a spoon on a glass would be *hashma'at kol*.

167. Eruvin 104a, who prohibits any type of *hashma'at kol*. The specific example there is of knocking on the door.

168. Yerushalmi Beiẓa 5:2, 63a.,

the Palestinian Talmud was not authoritative, they would not have permitted the behavior.

The Rif obviously alludes to the well-known systemic principle that *Hilkheta ke-vatra'ei.* He applies that principle to the relationship between the Babylonian and Palestinian Talmuds, the Babylonian being later than the Palestinian. Thus, according to the principle that *Hilkheta ke-vatra'ei,* it is clear that the law follows the view of Rabbah, and not that of Ulla. Yet it has surely been noted that our synopsis of the Rif's position has omitted mention of an apparently important dimension expressed by him, namely, the assumed expertise of the Babylonians in the Palestinian Talmud. It is precisely this assumption that Colon thinks requires some comment and to which he addresses himself in the following responsum.[169]

> It is surely true, when later *posekim* decide in opposition to the words of early scholars (*ha-ge'onim ha-kedumim*) which are written in well-known and famous books, that I would admit that one should follow the decision of the later *posekim*. For it is obvious that they, too, knew the words of the former sages and even so did not accept their view. In such an instance it must surely be the case that they [i.e., the later sages] found some reason for disagreeing with the former ones. And we, in our inferiority (*ba-aniyyuteinu*), should not decide in favor of the early ones, but rather should abide by the decision of the later ones, for they knew the words of the early ones better than we, and could not find their view acceptable.
>
> And thus did the Alfasi [i.e., the Rif] write at the end of tractate Eruvin.[170] . . . Note that that sage made his claim that the law follows the later view contingent upon the claim that had they not known that the view of the early ones was not authoritative, they would not have disagreed. So it seems to me that the claim [of *Hilkheta ke-vatra'ei*] is made only when the words of the early ones are written in a well-known and famous work. But if one finds a later *posek* deciding in opposition to the view of an earlier one whose view is written in some responsum which is unmentioned in any well-known book, one might claim that the later *posek* had not heard

---

169. *Responsa of Maharik, shoresh* 94, printed in complete form at the end of the volume, though not in its appropriate place. Cf. above, pp. 102 ff.

170. The passage omitted here is the quotation from the Rif cited above.

> that decision [i.e., of the early sage], and had he heard it, he would have retracted.
>
> And proof can be adduced for this claim from what we read in Ketubbot, chapter six.[171] . . . For in that passage one would surely have claimed that Rabbi Yoḥanan had heard and rejected the statement of Rebbe, had it been transmitted in a *baraita* in Rebbe's name, or been transmitted in his name by one of his students. In that case we would surely have decided in favor of Rabbi Yoḥanan's position, for they were expert in all the *baraitot* and the traditions passed on from teacher to student.[172] . . . But a doubt could arise whether a later *posek* had heard the words of the earlier one if the latter are found in some responsum, like the case of the question addressed to Rebbe between the lines of a letter of greeting.

At first blush, the systemic principle *Hilkheta ke-vatra'ei* seems to contradict the idea that later generations are inferior to earlier generations. However, since the first assumption of the principle is that later authorities make their decisions after having taken into consideration all the decisions of the earlier authorities as well as the raw data on which the decisions were based, the decisions of the later authorities can be accepted as authoritative, because if they reject the opinion of an earlier authority, the second assumption is that they do so for cause.[173]

This reasoning is valid, of course, only insofar as the "new" sources are such that they cannot have been known to the earlier authorities. In that case, the later authority can take account of the new data without putting himself in conflict with the principle *Hilkheta ke-vatra'ei*. But, Colon implies, if the new legal data are, in fact, "older" than the *posekim* they contradict, that is, if the new sources emanate from the writings of authorities earlier than those whose views they contradict, taking them into account puts the latest *posek* in direct conflict with the principle *Hilkheta ke-vatra'ei*. How could he possibly decide in favor of the "new" but "older" legal source when that source has already been contradicted

---

171. Cited above, p. 365.

172. These being the talmudic equivalents to well-known and famous works.

173. Obviously, therefore, to affirm the principle of *Hilkheta ke-vatra'ei* is to affirm that later *posekim* can reject the views of earlier ones for cause. It would be worthwhile for some of the "latest" *posekim* to recall that they, too, are *batra'ei* vis-à-vis the *posekim* of the generations preceding them, and to take cognizance of the fact that they, too, would be systemically justified in rejecting the views of earlier *posekim* for cause, as implied by the very principle of *Hilkheta ke-vatra'ei*.

by a later *posek?* Colon, therefore, adds a limitation to the applicability of *Hilkheta ke-vatra'ei,* namely, that the principle applies only when its underlying assumption can be presumed to be accurate. That is, we follow the later *posekim* when it is probable that they knew all of the potentially relevant data at the time they rendered their decisions. If, however, a *posek* knows of early data to which a later *posek* could not have had access, even though such data are actually earlier than the later *posek,* he is not duty-bound to ignore the new data in compliance with the principle of *Hilkheta ke-vatra'ei,* for in that case it is possible that the later *posek* would himself have retracted his own view had he but had access to the same data.

This limitation on the principle *Hilkheta ke-vatra'ei* was operative implicitly even before Colon's time. We ourselves saw it employed by the Rosh.[174] Colon, however, elevated it to the level of an explicit principle. Furthermore, the criterion he posited for determining whether a later *posek* could be presumed to have known the earlier source, namely, its publication in a "well-known and famous" work, was widely accepted. In the late fifteenth or early sixteenth century it is reiterated by the Radbaz (1479–1573),[175] in the seventeenth century by Rabbi Ḥayyim ben Israel Beneveniste (author of *Keneset ha-Gedolah,* 1603–1673)[176] and Rabbi Shabbatai ben Me'ir ha-Cohen (author of the *Shakh,* 1621–1662),[177] in the eighteenth century by Rabbi Malachi ben Jacob ha-Cohen (author of *Yad Malachi,* d. 1785/90),[178] in the nineteenth century by Rabbi Ḥayyim Hezekiah Medini (author of *Sedei Ḥemed,* 1834–1904),[179] and in the twentieth century by Rabbi Isaac Halevi Herzog (1888–1959).[180]

As we have already noted, the amount of new data available to modern *posekim* increases dramatically year by year.[181] The publication of the works of *rishonim,* commentaries and responsa, heretofore unpublished provides a wealth of new legal sources unknown to the most authoritative *posekim* of preceding generations. But having stressed this

---

174. See above, p. 98 ff.

175. *Responsa of Radbaz,* pt. 4, no. 1369.

176. Benvenisti, *Keneset ha-Gedolah* (Jerusalem: Foundation for the Publication of the Works of the *Keneset ha-Gedolah,* 1961), *Hoshen Mishpat,* no. 55, and notes to *Beit Yosef,* no. 8.

177. In his "Summary of Ritual Decision Making [*Kizzur be-hanhagat hora'ot issur ve-hetter*]," following *Yoreh De'ah* 242, letter *het.*

178. Ha-Cohen, *Yad Malakhi, "Kelalei She'ar ha-Meḥabberim ve-ha-Mefareshim,* no. 6, p. 138.

179. Medini, *Sedei Ḥemed, "Kelalei ha-Posekim,"* vol. 9, no. 48, p. 201.

180. Herzog, *Heichal Yitzchak, Even ha-Ezer,* vol. 2, no. 16, par. 24. Quoted by Feldman in *Marital Relations,* p. 163.

181. See also, p. 336.

increase in the availability of new legal sources, it must also be stressed again that new legal sources of all kinds are only potentially significant, not necessarily so. In the final analysis, whether or not a new source is significant is determined by the subjective judgment of the *posek*.[182] This entire chapter has been devoted to a description and analysis of the many options open to a *posek* in dealing with new legal sources. First of all, he can deny the legal significance of the new source. If, on the other hand, he does find the new source to be legally significant, he can use it in the abrogation of the previously existing norm, or he can effect a compromise between the new source and the old norm. Ultimately, then, *Ein lo la-dayyan ella mah she-einav ro'ot* retains its place as the ultimate systemic principle.

We have already discussed the manner in which legal presumptions function in the halakhic system, and have established that it is possible to reopen the discussion of the factualness of those presumptions.[183] In our previous discussion, however, we were concerned only with presumptions that serve as the bases for legal norms. But, it should be noted, systemic principles (some of which can also be legal norms) can also be dependent upon presumptions. Thus, the presumption that underlies the principle of *Hilkheta ke-vatra'ei* is that later *posekim* are aware of all of the earlier legal sources and decisions. The Maharik, in the passage from his responsum cited a few pages ago, perceived, however, that this presumption could no longer be considered factual in all circumstances. And in the same way as we saw that reopening the question of the factualness of legal presumptions that underlie norms can lead to a reassessment of the applicability of the norm, so too the Maharik's reopening the question of the factualness of the presumption underlying this systemic principle might lead to a reassessment of the applicability of the principle itself. In essence, Colon restricted the applicability of the principle *Hilkheta ke-vatra'ei* to those cases in which the presumption underlying it continued to be an accurate reflection of reality, and denied that the principle applied in circumstances in which the presumption underlying it could no longer be assumed to be an accurate reflection of reality. He refused to allow the presumption to be redefined as a legal fiction, in which case it would be considered true even if demonstrably false.

There are many presumptions underlying the systemic principles of the halakhic process, and the factualness of some of them are, at least,

---

182. See above, pp. 98 f.
183. See above, pp. 54 f., 64 f., and 254, for example.

open to serious question (if they are not, indeed, demonstrably false). For instance, in the passage cited above from the Rif, the presumption that the Babylonian sages knew the Palestinian Talmud was used to justify a certain conclusion, and in the passage cited from Colon, it was assumed as factual that *amora'im* knew all the *baraitot* and all the legal statements made directly by every *tanna* or transmitted in a *tanna's* name by one of his students. Modern rabbinic scholarship has called the factualness of such presumptions into grave question. Consequently, a modern *posek* should limit the applicability of such presumptions—indeed, of all presumptions—to circumstances in which they continue to be factual, and modify them accordingly. Since there is no precedent in *halakhah* for applying the status of legal *fiction* to norms or principles that are based upon *presumptions,* and since there is ample precedent for reopening the discussion of the factualness of presumptions, it is the *posek* who refuses to do the latter and insists on doing the former who is guilty of adopting an unprecedented position.

Yet, lest the above contention be misunderstood, it must be stressed again and again that no havoc would be wrought within *halakhah* by taking the systemically justified step described above. The primacy of the Babylonian Talmud in *halakhah,* for example, would not be seriously affected by denying the presumption that the Babylonian scholars knew the Palestinian Talmud. Under most circumstances, the false presumption that might underlie a norm based on the Babylonian Talmud would only be a historical source of the law, and, as such, legally insignificant. Only when the circumstances exist that would create a nexus between the historical and the legal sources of a norm would it be possible to consider using a source in the Palestinian Talmud, heretofore unusable on the grounds of the presumption of the superiority of the Babylonian Talmud (now, in this case, denied). And even when the Palestinian source attains the status of a new legal source of potential legal significance, the options open to the *posek* do not dictate that he consider it actually significant. We have seen that of the options open to the *posek,* the use of the new legal source as grounds for abrogating or modifying a precedented norm is only one of several.

If differing interpretations of a talmudic passage have always been treated as having potential legal significance, there can be no logic that can demonstrate that a modern interpretation of the same passage loses that potential significance merely by virtue of its being modern. Similarly, if the modern exegete finds compelling reason to deny certain of the presumptions that underlie classical talmudic exegesis, the potential legal significance of his interpretation of a talmudic passage cannot be denied simply because it is predicated on his assertion that an underlying presumption is false.

Earlier in this chapter we quoted a passage from the Talmud that can serve as an example of an interpretation, based on modern exegesis, that denies a certain presumption of classical talmudic exegesis.[184] The passage, again, reads as follows:

> Our rabbis have taught, "Who is to be considered an imbecile? One who goes out alone at night and who spends the night in a cemetery and who rips his clothing." It has been said, "Rav Huna said [that he is not considered an imbecile] until he does all of them." . . . Rav Papa said, "Had Rav Huna known that which we have learned in a *baraita*, 'Who is to be considered an imbecile? One who destroys [or loses] whatever he is given,' he would have retracted."

The passage as it stands testifies to the existence of two *baraitot*, one listing three characteristics of an imbecile, and another listing but one characteristic. Further, the locus of Rav Huna's comment indicates that his remark was made in reference to the *baraita* that immediately precedes it in the text. But if a modern exegete could cogently demonstrate that the editing process of the Talmud was such that it cannot necessarily be claimed to be true that a statement appearing in the Talmud is necessarily made in reference to the statement immediately preceding it, and if he could either prove conclusively or, at least, plausibly that Rav Huna may have made his comment with reference to yet a third *baraita* that combined the three characteristics of our first *baraita* with the one characteristic of our second *baraita* (i.e., to a *baraita* that contained four characteristics),[185] the modern exegete would have grounds to deny the assertion of Rav Papa in the Gemara. That is, he would bring to bear on Rav Papa's statement a new legal source (the third *baraita*) that would indicate that Rav Huna would have not retracted. If all this were to be the case, the modern exegete's reconstruction of the talmudic passage would then function itself as a new legal source of potential legal significance for a *posek*.[186]

---

184. Above, p. 323.

185. As, indeed, Rav Huna apparently does in Yerushalmi Terumot 1:1, 40b.

186. The entire reconstruction of the passage is purely hypothetical, although very similar to the type of reconstruction one might find in the writings of some critical scholars. For an actual critical analysis of this specific passage, see David Halivni, *Mekorot u-Mesorot* (Tel Aviv: Devir Publishing House, 1968), *Nashim*, p. 87.

Thus, if the precedented position followed the view of Rav Huna (requiring three characteristics), as stated in the Talmud, and if there were no compelling reason to seek to overturn the precedent, the reconstruction would be deemed legally insignificant, on the grounds that it was only a historical rather than a legal source. If, however, there were some compelling reason to add the fourth characteristic to Rav Huna's norm, the reconstruction could be deemed legally significant and would warrant modifying the norm to include the fourth characteristic.

Similarly, if the precedented position followed the view of Rav Papa (requiring only one characteristic), as understood by the Talmud, and there were no compelling reason to overturn the precedent, the precedent would stand even though the exegete had demonstrated that Rav Huna would not have retracted. The reconstruction would remain an interesting historical fact of no legal significance. If, however, there were some compelling reason to add to the number of characteristics required by Rav Papa, the reconstruction of the talmudic passage would allow the *posek* to reject Rav Papa's contention and adopt the nonprecedented, reconstructed view of Rav Huna's norm that raises the number of characteristics to four.

The possible grounds for legitimate *maḥaloket* among *posekim* as a result of this modern reconstruction would be numerous, but they would include, at least: (1) whether the exegete offered cogent proof that the editing process of the Talmud was not as has generally been presumed; (2) whether his proof that Rav Huna made his statement in reference to a third *baraita* was either conclusive or plausible; and (3) whether the nature of his reason for seeking a change in the precedented norm is compelling enough.

The question of the potential legal significance of a newly discovered or rediscovered *peshat* (to be defined presently) of a statement, however, involves us in new areas of concern because of the unique character of *peshat* as a source that can be both historical and legal at the same time. However, in order to deal with this question we must first define the term *peshat* and then consider what types of evidence and knowledge will allow us to discover (or rediscover) it. As we proceed, we shall see that the present discussion supplements our earlier references to *peshat*, which stressed the historical component of *peshat*.[187]

If one can say about the statement of another that one understands what the statement meant to the speaker when he said it, we call that

187. See above, pp. 116–117.

the *peshat* of the statement. On the surface, establishing the *peshat* of a statement would seem to be a relatively simply task; in reality, it can be quite difficult. In the passage cited above, for example, the *peshat* of Rav Huna's statement cannot be established until one knows to what *baraita* he was referring, since his statement would mean one thing if he were referring to the first *baraita* cited by the Gemara, and another if he were referring to some uncited *baraita* that lists four characteristics of imbecility.

If one can say about a comment made or a question raised that one knows to what the comment or question refers, what the comment or question meant to the one who offered it or raised it, and how the one who offered it or raised it must have understood the preceding statement in reference to which the comment or question was offered or raised, one can claim to understand the *peshat*. If certainty about any one of these factors is lacking, one's understanding is, in reality, only a hypothesis of what the *peshat* is; it may or may not be correct and is open to revision if and when new data become available.

The goal of the critical study of rabbinic texts is to discover the *peshat* of each statement, comment, and question in a passage, and then to establish the *peshat* of the entire passage. If the end product of such an analysis results in an interpretation different from the interpretation of the passage offered by the classical commentators or from that codified by the codifiers, its legal status is the same as that of another interpretation or a variant reading, and carries with it all the options that we have seen new interpretations and variant readings to provide to a *posek*. And, obviously, the greater the degree of certainty that the new interpretation is, in fact, the *peshat*, the less will be the hesitancy of the *posek* to employ his systemic rights.

But there is an additional factor involved in the determination of *peshat* that must be addressed as well. Since halakhic literature spans a period of twenty-five hundred years, and includes writings emanating from widely varying locations, it is not surprising that legalists from one time and place use words, idioms, and phrases the meanings of which were perfectly clear to them and to their contemporaries, but which were unclear, or were even completely unknown, to later legalists. On the other hand, a modern scholar, provided by modern scholarship with an understanding of ancient foreign languages and literatures unknown or unavailable to former generations, may well understand the *peshat* of an early legal statement better than any of his predecessors. The accumulation of knowledge in the fields of archaeology and history can be of inestimable help in understanding the *realia* that underlie a cryptic comment, *realia* that can run from fashions in hairstyles to the manufacture of clothing, and from idiomatic language to historical thought. To the extent that understanding the *peshat* of any statement assumes such knowledge, the possibility of understanding the *peshat* without that knowledge would be nonexistent. In claiming that he understands the *peshat* of a statement better than any of his predecessors, a modern scholar would be doing no more than those sages who have claimed that had some earlier sage had access to knowledge to which he, the later sage, has access, the earlier sage would have retracted his view. Sages in all ages have accepted reliable new data from any source if it permitted them to better understand the texts to which they devoted their lives.

The newly rediscovered *peshat* of a legal source derived from such evidence can be called a historical-legal source, possessing as it does some of the characteristics of historical sources, and some of the characteristics of legal sources. To the extent that the *peshat* is not reflected in precedented or codified norms, it is a historical source, that is, it lacks formal recognition by the law itself.[188] But it cannot be characterized completely as a historical source, because historical sources not only lack present recognition by the law, but have always lacked that recognition. This, of course, cannot be said of a newly rediscovered *peshat,* since it *was* recognized by the law at the time when its author uttered it, and was recognized as he intended it. In this sense, then, it is a legal source. Its loss of formal recognition took place over a period of time as its original meaning was forgotten and as the non-*peshat* interpretation of it gained legal recognition. It is a simple extension of a systemic principle—whose existence and validity we have seen demonstrated over and over again—to accord the newly rediscovered *peshat* the legal status of an interpretation of an early authority, forgotten for generations but available once more. Rabbi Joseph Colon clearly affirms that consideration of "new" data that are, in fact, "old" is permissible, and that such consideration in no way constitutes a violation of the halakhic process.

In many instances the newly discovered or rediscovered *peshat* of a legal statement will have no bearing on the legal implications of a given norm. Thus, for example, the Babylonian *amora'im* often understood the thrust of Greek words in tannaitic sources, even when they were unaware of their etymological *peshat.* But even in cases when the new *peshat* of a legal statement might influence the legal implications of a norm, the weight of precedent favors the classical interpretation when there is no compelling reason to seek a change. Demanding that a norm always be modified to fit the newly discovered or rediscovered *peshat* would be an instance of the genetic fallacy: It would be no more

188. See above, p. 5.

inherently reasonable than to demand that Passover revert to a rite of spring. Only when the new *peshat* actually influences the law, and when, at the same time, the abrogation or modification of the law, or a compromise position, is being sought, would it not be an instance of the genetic fallacy to consider the newly discovered or rediscovered *peshat* of potential legal significance. Only when a possible nexus between the historical and legal sources of a norm becomes actual, and the new *peshat* is different from the codified interpretation of it, can the new *peshat* function as a previously nonprecedented position, the adoption of which is one of the options of a *posek*.

There is one more area in which the potential relevance of the *peshat*, when it is not identical with the accepted classical interpretation, is problematic, and that is when the passage in question is to be found, not in the Talmud or in later rabbinic sources, but in the Torah, the *grundnorm* itself.

As with rabbinic sources, if one can say about a verse in the Bible that one understands what it meant to the speaker/Speaker when he/He said it, one can say that he understands the *peshat* of the verse. Bible scholars, utilizing many of the same tools and instruments of research as rabbinic scholars, are often able to shed light on the *peshat* of a verse in the Torah, an illumination that frequently results in an interpretation of the *peshat* of the verse that was unknown to any of the classical Bible commentators. Often the newly interpreted *peshat* of the verse is also at variance with the rabbinic interpretation of the verse that *purports* to be its *peshat*.[189]

---

189. A very important distinction must be drawn here between two types of rabbinic interpretation of biblical verses. The talmudic sages had a very keen sense of the Hebrew language and knew very well that many of their exegeses were not the *peshat* of the verses they were purporting to explain. See, as a classical example, Rabbi Ishma'el's exclamation to Rabbi Akiva: "Because you interpret a *vav* as you do, a priest's daughter should be burned?" (Sanhedrin 51b). Even the rabbinic school of thought that denied that "the Torah is written in the language of man *(dibberah Torah ki-leshon benei adam)*" recognized that it was only the Divine nature of the text that allowed the sages to "read-in" to biblical verses meanings clearly not intended by the *peshat* of the verse. Examples of such non-*peshat* meanings abound: taking a phrase like *ish ish,* which on the level of *peshat* means "everyone," and interpreting it to have legal implications beyond its *peshat;* or interpreting the meaningless definitive article *et* to have legal implications.

We contend that such exegesis does not even *purport* to be the *peshat* of the verse, and that this was recognized by the sages who offered this kind of exegesis. Thus, regarding any such exegesis, the *peshat* is a historical source in its most restricted sense, i.e., lacking all recognition by the law itself, and completely irrelevant legally.

There are, however, biblical verses which the sages interpreted according to what they actually thought was the *peshat*. Many of these interpretations are denied as *peshat* by biblical scholars. The sages who interpreted *onah* (Exodus 21:10) to mean "regular conjugal relations" undoubtedly understood that to be the *peshat* intended by the Speaker. It is to

The question is: Does the newly interpreted *peshat* of the biblical verse have potential legal significance, just as the newly discovered or rediscovered *peshat* of a rabbinic source does; or does the fact that it is an interpretation of the *grundnorm* that is at variance with the classical legal interpretation of the *grundnorm* preclude its having even potential legal significance?

If one is willing to concede the possibility that the *peshat* of a rabbinic statement could have been known, lost, and rediscovered over a span of no more than twenty-five hundred years, it seems no more logically difficult to posit the same possible history for the *peshat* of a biblical statement, considering that the span of its life can far exceed twenty-five hundred years! It is no more illogical to assert that had the talmudic sages had access to the literatures of the ancient Near East, and had they known the cognate ancient Semitic languages, they would have brought that knowledge to bear on their interpretations of the Torah than it is to assert that had an *amora* had a sufficient knowledge of Greek, he would have brought it to bear on his interpretation of a tannaitic statement. And just as the assertion of a modern scholar of rabbinics that he understands the *peshat* of a rabbinic passage as it has not been understood since it was spoken in no way denigrates the interpretation of his predecessors, so, too, a similar assertion about a verse from the Torah by a modern Bible scholar in no way denigrates the interpretations of his predecessors.

Nor do any of the above assertions regarding biblical verses impugn or violate the status of the Torah as the posited *grundnorm* of the halakhic system. Even if a *posek* were to advocate the abrogation of a norm based on a rabbinic interpretation of a scriptural verse, and even if he were to affirm the Naḥmanidean position regarding the *de-oraita* status of such norms,[190] his *pesak* would not violate the sacrosanct nature of the *grundnorm* itself. Rather, it would be an instance of *Hem ameru ve-hem ameru*. The establishment of the meaning of the *grundnorm* has always been entrusted to the sages. Thus, if the sages at one time said that the Torah meant X, and the sages of another time said that it meant Y, the legal status of X would be *de-oraita* until abrogated by later sages in favor

---

differences between this kind of rabbinic explanation and modern interpretations that the present discussion addresses itself.

Admittedly, there are many gray areas with regard to which the *posek* must be very wary. Did the sages understand their interpretation of *le-olam* (Exodus 21:6) as being the Jubilee year to be *peshat* or not? Is their interpretation of *le-ot al yadekha* (Deuteronomy 6:8) as being a hand phylactery *peshat* to the sages or not? It is most likely that a *posek* would refrain from exercising any of the rights we have been discussing if it is unclear whether the rabbinic interpretation of a biblical verse is meant to truly represent the *peshat* or not.

190. Discussed at length in chap. 2.

of Y, which would then assume *de-oraita* status. X may become null and void, but the status of the Torah as the *grundnorm* remains untouched.

As the precedented and codified interpretations of rabbinic sources remain normative except in the face of compelling reasons, so, too, the precedented and codified interpretations of the Torah itself would remain normative except in the face of compelling reasons to overturn the precedent. Indeed, much of this book has been devoted to analysis of the factors, conditions, and circumstances that warrant abrogating or modifying precedent. An entire chapter has been devoted to a discussion of rabbinic rights vis-à-vis matters *de-oraita*. If rabbinic rights extend to the point of active, outright, and long-term abrogation of norms of the Torah, rights exercised only under the careful aegis of God-fearing *posekim*, surely those same *posekim*, duly conscious of the complexities of the halakhic process and aware of the kind of circumstances that might warrant the adoption of a previously nonprecedented norm above a precedented norm, have the systemic right to utilize their status as the authoritative interpreters of *halakhah* even when the norm in question is found in the Torah itself.

Index of Sources

(an asterisk [*] indicates that the reference is in a note)

MISHNAH COMMENTATORS

OTHER BAVLI COMMENTATORS

SHULḤAN ARUKH COMMENTATORS

MINOR CODES

RESPONSA

SIFREI KELALIM

MISCELLANEOUS

Subject Index